Practicing Piety
in Medieval Ashkenaz

JEWISH CULTURE AND CONTEXTS

Published in association with
the Herbert D. Katz Center for Advanced Judaic Studies
of the University of Pennsylvania

David B. Ruderman, Series Editor

Advisory Board
Richard I. Cohen
Moshe Idel
Alan Mintz
Deborah Dash Moore
Ada Rapoport-Albert
Michael D. Swartz

PRACTICING PIETY IN MEDIEVAL ASHKENAZ

Men, Women, and Everyday
Religious Observance

Elisheva Baumgarten

PENN

UNIVERSITY OF PENNSYLVANIA PRESS

PHILADELPHIA

Publication of this volume was assisted by a grant from the Herbert D. Katz Publications Fund of the Center for Advanced Judaic Studies.

Copyright © 2014 University of Pennsylvania Press

All rights reserved. Except for brief quotations used for purposes of review or scholarly citation, none of this book may be reproduced in any form by any means without written permission from the publisher.

Published by
University of Pennsylvania Press
Philadelphia, Pennsylvania 19104-4112
www.upenn.edu/pennpress

Printed in the United States of America on acid-free paper
10 9 8 7 6 5 4 3 2 1

Library of Congress Cataloging-in-Publication Data
Baumgarten, Elisheva.
  Practicing piety in medieval Ashkenaz : men, women, and everyday religious observance / Elisheva Baumgarten. — First edition.
    pages cm. — (Jewish culture and contexts)
  ISBN 978-0-8122-4640-7 (hardcover : alk. paper)
  1. Judaism—Europe—History—To 1500. 2. Jewish way of life—History—To 1500. 3. Ashkenazim—History—To 1500. 4. Hasidism, Medieval. 5. Jews—Europe—Social life and customs—To 1500. 6. Jews—France—Social life and customs—History—To 1500. 7. Jews—Germany—Social life and customs—History—To 1500. 8. Judaism—Relations—Christianity—History—To 1500. 9. Christianity and other religions—Judaism—History—To 1500. I. Title.
BM290.B38 2014
296.7094'0902—dc23

2014006034

Dedicated to the memory of our grandmothers:
Frances Feder Karp (1906–1970)
Ella Fischer Deutsch Williams (1909–1994)
Sabina Baumgarten Berkowitz (1909–2004)
Margot Darmstädter Seeligmann (1916–2010)

CONTENTS

Introduction   1

Chapter 1. Standing Before God: Purity and Impurity in the Synagogue   21

Chapter 2. Jewish Fasting and Atonement in a Christian Context   51

Chapter 3. Communal Charity: Evidence from Medieval Nürnberg   103

Chapter 4. Positive Time-Bound Commandments: Class, Gender,
and Transformation   138

Chapter 5. Conspicuous in the City: Medieval Jews in Urban Centers   172

Chapter 6. Feigning Piety: Tracing Two Tales of Pious Pretenders   195

Chapter 7. Practicing Piety: Social and Comparative Perspectives   212

Abbreviations   225

Notes   227

Bibliography   287

Index   323

Acknowledgments   331

Figure 1. A stork in her nest. From *North French Miscellany*. © The British Library Board. Ms Add. 11639, fol. 325v, detail. Northern France, late thirteenth century.

Introduction

> R. Judah said: The hasidah is a white stork. And why is she called hasidah? Because she shows kindness (*hasidut*) to her companions.
> —BT Hullin 63a

> This is a white bird, *cygonia*,[1] and why is she called hasidah? Because she acts with kindness (*hasidut*) unto her friends with food.
> —Rashi, Leviticus 11:19, s.v. "hasidah"

The talmudic passage above offers an etymological explanation of the Hebrew term for stork (hasidah) by connecting the stork's behavior to the word *hesed* (kindness) and its derivative, *hasidut* (piety).[2] During the Middle Ages, the famous French commentator Rashi (Solomon b. Isaac of Troyes, d. 1105) understood the stork's kindness through her custom of voluntarily distributing food to her friends, an act of sharing that was in no way obligatory (see Figure 1). Other commentators provided alternate interpretations for her gentle behaviors, such as allowing others to tread on her and showing mercy to her friends.[3] Moving from animals to humans, the adjective *hasid* (pious) and the noun *hasidut* are used in Jewish texts since late antiquity to describe forms of religious behavior and fervor, as well as individuals known for their devotion to God.[4]

This book presents a social history of pious practice, focusing specifically on the Jewish communities of northern France and Germany during the High Middle Ages. In *Practicing Piety*, I wish to revive the sense of piety implicit in Rashi's comment and to examine pious observances in their social settings, among medieval Ashkenazic Jews and the cultural currents in which they were immersed. For the purpose of this study, I have defined the term "pious" broadly, ranging from acts that were seen as unusually devout to practices that can be seen as a dedicated fulfillment of one's religious obligation. By focusing on social practices and the ideas they expressed, I have aimed to capture the religiosity of Jews whose modes of observance are far more accessible to us than their convictions. Throughout the book, I contend that these acts were no less critical to the development and coalescence of religious identity than intellectual engagement with theological concepts.

Piety is often associated with the Jews of northern Europe, much as medieval Christian society is well known for its fascination with piety, which was sometimes expressed by extreme asceticism. The spirit of holiness and sanctity in European life was not the exclusive purview of Christian clergy and the aristocracy. Rather, this aspiration was prominent in the lives of the laity whose efforts to integrate piety into their religious practice is often known as "lay piety" or "popular piety."[5] As a result, piety was an intrinsic feature of both medieval Jewish and Christian life as well as a means for each community to manifest its expression to members of the other faith, making explicit the social tensions and divisions between these competing religions.[6]

Practicing Piety focuses on observance rather than intellectual legacies and, by extension, on the widest sweep of Jewish community members possible, rather than the few who authored medieval compositions.[7] The medieval Hebrew sources that have reached us are all products of a select circle of scholars, a fact that presents significant barriers to the consideration of other segments of the community. My primary tool for pursuing a wider representation is a constant comparison between the actions of both men and women,[8] in every aspect of medieval Jewish society.[9] Such gendered reading also facilitates a gauge of how deeds and practices were perceived when performed by the non-elite.[10] Following feminist theorists, I have used gender as a principal measure for signifying the exercise of power and struggles over authority,[11] since scholars have demonstrated that gender is often a lightning rod for societal tensions and shifts. Conflicts regarding identity and institutional control are often imposed on and reflected by women. In terms of this study, women practiced piety and piety was practiced on them.[12] Therefore, a comparison of Jewish women's and men's observance is central to this volume.

Throughout this study I suggest that piety was determined by its social context: the pious were identified among their contemporaries by their actions, while their distinctive conduct set a standard for the religious values in their cultural milieu. Just as the kindness of the hasidah was conveyed by her deeds, so, too, Jews in medieval Ashkenaz would merit a reputation for piety based on actions that reflected on their co-religionists as well as on themselves.[13]

The second emphasis of this study locates the Jewish community, its practices and beliefs, in the context of medieval Christianity.[14] Situating Jewish communities within Christian society while also investigating the role of gender in both groups allows for a dual comparison, assessing certain practices among Jews and Christians and between men and women of each religion. I approach the medieval Christian world as a vibrant and multi-faceted environment where Jews of Germany and northern France encountered deep hostility as well as a home where the Jewish community (co-)existed.[15] This complexity, on the spectrum from hostility to acceptance, was a constant component of the daily rhythm of medieval Ashkenazic life.

In the pages that follow, I set the stage for this volume by surveying the medieval Ashkenazic communal frameworks and sources I have examined. I then address the parameters of religious comparison with an overview of the wider social framework in which Jews and Christians lived side by side and an outline of how social historians have addressed Christian and Jewish piety, including the Ashkenazic phenomenon known as *Hasidei Ashkenaz* or German Pietism. Finally, I consider how Jewish and Christian societies, separately and jointly, treated their male and female members.

The Medieval Jewish Communities of Germany and Northern France

The Jewish communities that dwelled in the areas known today as Germany, northern France, and their environs during the twelfth to the mid-fourteenth century occupy the heart of this study. This region is generally referred to as "Ashkenaz" in historical writing about medieval Jewry. My decision to jointly examine areas that are part of contemporary Germany and northern France stems from the close contact that existed between their communities and relies on medieval territories that roughly correspond with modern entities rather than on actual borders.[16]

Whereas a number of French Jewish communities date back to the early Middle Ages, little documentation from the ninth and tenth centuries is extant. Nonetheless, scholars recognize that the Jews of northern France played a vital role in the urbanization of Europe during the Carolingian era, a culture of trade fairs and active commerce.[17] By the High Middle Ages, substantial communities—numbering several hundred families—lived in the large cities of France (Paris, in particular), while many smaller Jewish communities—sometimes just a few families—had been established along trade routes.[18]

During the ninth and tenth centuries, Jews also settled along the banks of the Rhine River in cities that, over time, became prestigious Jewish establishments. Among these, the "Shum" communities— Speyer, Worms, and Mainz, together with Cologne, Frankfurt, Würzburg, Nürnberg, Regensburg, and other urban centers—became home to notable rabbinical figures and leading merchants. Additional communities on trade routes in central Europe also grew and thrived during the Middle Ages.

Frequent travel between centers of learning along major rivers in northern Europe led to a permeating familiarity among the Jews of these communities. While some prevailing patterns changed over time—in the tenth and eleventh centuries, students often traveled from France to Germany, whereas in the twelfth and thirteenth centuries, that tide was reversed—there was significant movement within this area, not only by individual merchants but by their families.

The Jews of northern France and Germany maintained close contact with each other and with Jews who shared their customs in other locales, specifically Bohemia, Austria, and Italy (where many Ashkenazic Jews originated and later emigrated).[19] Selected texts from these regions are examined here as well.[20] I have not included the Jews of England as a distinct group in this discussion, since sources from that community are not plentiful enough to provide an adequate picture of daily pious practice.[21] However, following scholars who have suggested that English customs most closely resembled the practices of Jews in northern France, I refer to evidence from England at various points in this book. As such, the corpus that forms the basis for this study was shared by Germany, northern France, and neighboring areas. However, since some texts from which I have drawn demonstrate that medieval Jews were well aware of local differences, I have sought to balance the evidence suggesting that many customs were common to Jews living throughout Ashkenaz and textual references that indicate distinct practices.

This geographic breadth is also necessary because extant sources cannot adequately describe the practice in any one location for most of the topics examined here.[22] Therefore, as in my previous work,[23] I set out to reconstruct medieval practices and ideas by aggregating sources from various places and contexts, forming a sort of bricolage. Another limitation that characterizes medieval sources is the relative homogeneity of available texts, despite their varied genres. This phenomenon is especially evident among the Hebrew material.

The main body of sources examined in this volume was written between the First Crusade (1096) and the Black Death (1349). My analysis of select writings dated after the Black Death highlights some of the shifts in observance that resulted from these cataclysmic events and explores the extent to which observances continued without change, were accentuated, or became transformed after the mid-fourteenth century. Despite the fact that the ninth and tenth centuries were formative for Jewish communities, their Christian neighbors, and their respective institutions, relatively sparse Latin texts and even fewer Hebrew sources have come to us from this period. By comparison, the relative abundance of Hebrew sources from the late eleventh century onward allows for a fuller and more nuanced understanding of the lives of Jews in medieval Europe. This pattern of source transmission is paralleled in the Christian world, where we find a wealth of sources from the twelfth century forward,[24] as many scholars of social history—especially of piety—have noted.

For this study, I rely on the classic rabbinic texts composed by medieval Jewish men: commentaries on the Bible and Talmud, compendia of halakhic discussions, and formal responses to questions from community members. I have also mined collections of stories, exempla from *Sefer Hasidim* and elsewhere, custom books, communal records, and manuscript illuminations. In some cases, I have included sources that are found only in manuscripts, thus incorporating content that was overlooked or censored by later copyists, especially as practices changed over time. I also consulted parallel Christian materials: penitential and preaching manuals and biblical interpretations along with statutes and collections of exempla. In addition, I have delved into the abundant scholarly work on Christian society that, beyond its obvious informing role, has further sensitized me to nuances within the Jewish evidence that I otherwise might not have recognized.

Toward a Social and Comparative History of Jewish and Christian Medieval Piety

Research on medieval Jewish piety has primarily focused on reactions in Ashkenaz to the First Crusade (in 1096) and later persecutions, from the Rintfleisch attacks of 1298 in many German communities, repeated expulsions from parts of northern France in the early fourteenth century, to the Black Death in the mid-fourteenth century.[25] The deaths of many Jews at their own hands or by attackers during assaults on their communities transformed those who died into martyrs (*kedoshim*) in a way that has been interpreted by subsequent generations, including modern historians, as the ultimate and uniquely Jewish expression of pious devotion to God.[26]

A second historical phenomenon that reinforced the association of Jews in medieval northern Europe with piety relates to the rich and varied writings that were produced by the intellectual elite of Jewish communities in medieval Germany and northern France.[27] These medieval authors were instrumental in portraying the Jews of this period as pious through their religious guidance for fellow Jews and their overarching approach to Jewish observance. Furthermore, these are the medieval Jewish personages that have been most rigorously studied since the late nineteenth century.[28]

Whether explicitly or by implication, scholarly narratives have positioned the Jewish community and its piety at odds with their Christian counterparts. After all, when medieval Jews opted for death (*kiddush hashem*; lit., sanctifying the Divine Name), either actively or passively, that decision was the direct consequence of their refusal to embrace Christianity. Similarly, Jewish intellectual culture was often seen as a significant internal achievement amid, and at times despite, perilous circumstances.[29] This approach focuses on points of crisis and confrontation at the expense of considering everyday life, thereby highlighting interreligious tensions in medieval society over harmonious aspects of coexistence, effectively obscuring the interplay of tension and coherence that fostered a sustainable social environment.

A more inclusive approach for evaluating Jewish life in medieval Germany and northern France was suggested during the late nineteenth and early twentieth centuries, and has reemerged periodically, recently regaining currency by pointing to the affinities between Jewish and Christian cultures alongside the separate identities that medieval Jews and Christians were actively producing and propagating.[30] Present-day scholars have suggested that, despite the clear distinctions between Jews and Christians, in theory and in practice, adherents of these two religions shared far more than previous studies have assumed.[31]

During this period, the Christian communities among whom Jews resided were undergoing significant social and religious changes and doctrinal revisions. Beyond the Crusade movement, which marked much of the period in question, new doctrines were being instituted and more firmly established, such as celibacy of the clergy, which was transformed in the eleventh century; the growth and expansion of monastic orders throughout the twelfth and thirteenth centuries; and, most notably, the Fourth Lateran Council (1215), which redefined the role of laity in medieval Christian society and reassessed central doctrines, including transubstantiation and the sacraments of baptism, marriage, confession, and the Eucharist.[32] Not only were Jews cognizant of many of these changes, but recent studies have demonstrated that they had bearing on their lives as well. Living side by side, Jews and Christians alike were participants in the growing urban life of the High Middle Ages.[33]

Perhaps most dramatically, the Black Death had significance for Jewish as well as Christian societies while also serving as a catalyst for change in Europe's Jewish communities and in European attitudes toward Jews; thus, the mid-fourteenth century serves as a suitable closing frame for this inquiry. At that time, the expulsion of Jews, which had begun in England in the late thirteenth century and took place in France during the early fourteenth century, spread to many cities in Germany.[34] In response, many French and German Jews moved south to Spain or eastward to Poland.[35] One result of these forced and voluntary migrations was the creation of a new Jewish geography as well as a new chapter in Jewish-Christian relations.[36]

Following this view of medieval Jewish-Christian coexistence, the High Middle Ages can be defined by a shared environment of burgeoning urban centers, with concomitant economic and social expansion. Despite the ideological and theological tensions that existed between Jews and Christians during this period, Jews lived comfortably in medieval urban centers where Jewish scholarship flourished.[37] In fact, many religious tensions and polemics of that period were founded on mutually held ideas and common values, and the violence of that era often drew its meaning from the dissonance of coexistence rather than a desire for separation.[38]

Scholars have also discussed how Jews as a minority culture adopted ideas and practices from their Christian neighbors, even if they may have appropriated them subconsciously.[39] Leaders of both religious communities strove to underscore the differences between their religions in an effort to bolster distinct identities in a milieu where Jews and Christians dwelled in close proximity and had similar daily routines. Although Jews often resided in specific city districts during the centuries studied here, they rarely lived in the segregation that typified later periods.[40] From a historiographical perspective, modern concerns regarding the process of identity development have informed recent attempts to examine degrees of engagement versus separation of Jews and their neighbors in earlier periods.[41]

While some scholars view these reassessments as simplistic attempts to formulate "either-or" statements—to categorize Jews as being either so intimately connected to non-Jewish society as to practically belong to "their" world, or so thoroughly set apart that contact was meager at best. In contrast to these approaches, and following other recent studies,[42] I have pursued a middle ground by assuming the distinctiveness of the Jewish communities while associating them with their cultural surroundings. With regard to religiosity, there were no intermediate categories of religious belonging: one was either Jewish or Christian.[43] The clear designation of membership in the Jewish minority[44] (or not) may have allowed Jews and Christians greater latitude for nurturing their beliefs and practices: namely, the pious aspirations that characterized both societies. Devotion to God was not merely a common feature of medieval Jewish and Christian life; it was also a source, if not the driving factor, in the need for distinction and a trigger for the production of marked differences and separate religious identities, a "narcissism of small differences."[45] As I suggest throughout this study, within the medieval atmosphere, a competitive piety[46] developed that simultaneously emphasized mutually held ideas about religious expression and heightened divisions between Jews and Christians. These religious connections are herein examined from multiple vantage points—moving along a continuum from seeing Jewish and Christian societies as two separate faith communities to viewing them as a shared unit—but at all times as entangled with each other, bound by what has recently been termed "*histoire croisée*" or "connected histories."[47] Throughout this book, I reflect on how medieval Jews and Christians might have been aware of one another's customs, practices, and beliefs.[48]

The assumption that Jews and Christians were in continuous contact and shared local circumstances as well as many values and understandings is the product of social and cultural perspectives that have become integral elements of historical inquiry, particularly in medieval studies, over the past decades. Historians have increasingly focused not only on the intellectual pursuits of the literary elite but also on how the general population lived in relation to and in contrast with the authors whose texts have reached us.[49] Researchers have also sought out the connections between daily life and the cultural mindsets of those who were unlikely to express themselves in writing.[50] In studies of medieval Christian Europe, this heightened interest in social and cultural history has translated into the laity—women, children, and uneducated men—as well as the poor, the sick, and outcasts[51] receiving more attention in historical writing and inquiry, whereas the clergy had been the dominant subject of prior scholarship.

While scholars of medieval Jews have participated in this trend, as exemplified by the work of Shlomo Dov Goitein on the Cairo Genizah,[52] the articulation of a Jewish social history, especially in medieval Ashkenaz, has been far from straightforward. How do we embark on such an endeavor when the sources at our disposal were composed by the ruling elite (almost without exception) and represent their values? Furthermore, these writings, predominantly religious commentaries and compilations, lend themselves most naturally to intellectual analysis rather than social history.

Previous scholarship includes a number of remarkable works on the lives of Jews in medieval Ashkenaz, such as writings of Adolf (Abraham) Berliner, Moritz Güdemann, and Israel Abrahams in late nineteenth-century Germany, Austria, and England, respectively.[53] Without a doubt, Salo Baron's multivolume *Social and Religious History of the Jews*[54] attempted to veer away from legal and intellectual history by describing how Jews actually lived. Baron notes that the contrast between "Jews" and "Judaism" is theoretical rather than real, and his work endeavors to strike a balance between the experiences of the community as a whole and the individuals within it.[55]

Jacob Katz, another pioneer in social history, aimed first and foremost to map the models of Jewish society by examining their breakdown with the advent of modernity.[56] Of particular interest for this study, Katz also devoted attention to the field of Jewish-Christian relations, noting that the distinctions between Jews and their neighbors were not always as robust as historians were wont to believe.[57] Katz's work, which remains paradigmatic, concentrates on what the anthropologist Pierre Bourdieu refers to as the *habitus*, a set of dispositions that generate practices and perceptions, rather than the lives of actual persons.[58] An element that Katz's work shares with Baron's is a near exclusive focus on adult males as societal representatives.[59]

Following Katz, a generation of scholars, especially in Israel and North America, has sought to delineate the social and cultural lives of medieval Jews. Robert Bonfil's work on medieval and Renaissance Italy outlines structures rather than everyday practice. Bonfil and Ivan Marcus have introduced anthropological theory into medieval Jewish historiography and numerous scholars have followed their lead.[60] Studies of defined groups, such as children and women, have become more common.[61]

Popular Piety

Despite these studies, most research on Jewish communities in medieval Ashkenaz has investigated halakhah and its development; that is to say, most scholars have assumed that halakhah shaped Jewish life without reflecting at length on how the realities of Jewish life shaped halakhah.[62] This is especially evident in discussions of piety and religious practice, which are most typically examined in the context of legal requirements and rulings, rather than as components of daily practice that might not necessarily conform to prescriptive rules or that were the product of imitation and not the product of book learning.[63]

Medieval piety has generally been presented within the history of halakhah, the domain of the learned male elite, reasoning that, if piety is defined as devotion to God that exceeds the letter of the law, then a requisite level of halakhic familiarity is necessary preparation for pious action. Indeed, knowledge of Torah and Jewish law has been seen as a sign of piety, in and of itself. One of the most important recent studies on this topic is Ephraim Kanarfogel's *Peering through the Lattices*, where the author applies a broad definition of piety—"self-denial and humility"—and examines the use of *notarikon* and *gematriyah* in his investigation of intellectual trends and evidence of pious and, especially, mystical ideas. As a result, his study combines and often fuses piety with mysticism and magic.[64] Kanarfogel's book is highly relevant to the present study because he convincingly demonstrates how widespread such pious practices were, albeit among elite males. However, in his search for the internal stimuli of piety, Kanarfogel emphasizes the intellectual motivations for select practices rather than their practical aspects.[65]

As noted above, the definition of piety that I propose steers away from privileging elite circles of learned men by examining the field that scholars of other religions refer to as "lay piety" or "popular religion."[66] Moreover, I prioritize praxis, and only then do I turn to beliefs and ideas. These interrelated choices are informed by the methodology presented in studies of lay piety in Christianity and Islam. In the context of medieval Christianity, for example, André Vauchez presents three definitions of Christian lay piety: folkloric customs, which have been treated as the lot of the uneducated; extreme piety (such as flagellants and Crusaders); and pious acts related to everyday religious beliefs and performed throughout society, irrespective of the practitioner's status. This third category forms the core of this study.[67] Although lay piety has often been seen as a grab bag of superstitions and magic, per Vauchez's category of "folkloric customs,"[68] this area has recently been recognized as a useful lens for understanding past societies. I follow scholars who have narrowed the distance between "high culture" and "popular culture," by arguing that, in terms of religious customs, fewer differences divided the elite from the less educated than has often been posited. Furthermore, for a member of the elite to be acknowledged as pious, wide social recognition was needed. As a result, even acknowledgment of the piety of distinguished individuals was dependent on their social context. Thus, although I do not claim that elite practices represented society as a whole, when sources refer to the pious acts of community members in general, I presume that they were often performed by the privileged as well.[69] This societal trend seems logical, especially given that this study is based on textual sources written by the educated elite.[70]

With this definition of piety as my guide for focusing on practice, I have tried to uncover the religious lives of Jews who were not part of the intellectual echelon by examining how their behaviors were reflected and molded by those who wrote authoritative texts. One approach to searching for popular piety that I ultimately rejected was to seek out deviance as an opposition point that could assist in the identification of pious practice. Numerous studies use deviance (or heresy) as a guide for locating the norm.[71] While this approach lends itself to the demarcation of boundaries between who belongs and who does not, whether socially, religiously, ideologically, or otherwise, it serves to identify perceived outsiders rather than insiders who might hold any of a range of conventions. As a result, the use of deviance in this search would not have strengthened my ability to access piety; and, in some cases, it would have hindered my effort, since deviance may help to uncover accepted standards, but it is not the inverse of piety. While both deviant and pious observances depart from the norm, they do not necessarily occupy the same axis or receive the same treatment.[72]

Furthermore, defining a practice as deviant if it diverged from common conduct presumes that rituals were regularly performed as prescribed within medieval books and manuals, and that anyone who acted otherwise was considered a sinner. In this study, I try to discern how medieval Jews observed the law while going beyond their perceived call of duty; I have not attempted to write a history of how the learned elite believed religious customs should have been carried out. As we shall see, those considered pious were at times ridiculed for practices that exceeded halakhic mandates.

Despite these drawbacks, scholarship on deviance has provided a perspective that I find useful in the search for piety. Scholars of deviance have asked questions that inform my research, such as the following: Who holds the social power to label a practice as deviant? Why are certain labels used? What are the criteria for a given definition? And, how did this categorization function socially? Stated differently, labeling and classification come from the collective audience rather than the individual, regardless of whether one is being defined within or beyond a specific category.[73]

Following these insights, the relationship between the collective and the individual is central in this study. On the whole, the practices examined in this book were publicly performed, although the definition of the public sphere varies slightly for each ritual.[74] Many of these practices could have been easily discerned, and could have been learned on the street or in the synagogue without elaborate explanation. I have tried to straddle the individual and the communal realms by focusing on rituals that were performed by individuals yet were also seen as reflections of corporate religious identity.[75]

German Pietism

One subject that exemplifies some of the definitions and distinctions that I have outlined and that is worthy of particular attention is the Ashkenazic pietist group from the Rhineland known as Hasidei Ashkenaz, or German Pietists.[76] This appellation has been used to describe Samuel b. Judah (twelfth century) and two of his disciples, his son Judah (known as Judah the Pious, d. 1217) and Judah's student, Eleazar b. Judah of Worms (d. before 1232), along with their assumed followers.[77] These rabbis composed influential works— *Sefer Hasidim* and *Sefer haRokeah* among them—in which they present their ideas for conducting pious lives, in constant fear and awe of God.[78] Some scholars have described their philosophy and outlook on life as "sect-like" and too radical to be widely influential, others as consonant with the Christian practices of their time, and still others as theoretical rather than practical.[79] Many scholars have studied these texts for the mystical worldviews and the theological principles set forth in them. Without distracting from their importance for the history of mysticism, my reading of them concentrates on the evidence of practice reflected in them.[80] These guidebooks outline behavior for their contemporaries who wished to raise the level of piety in their lives; therefore, they serve as important sources for this study. One of the questions I ask when examining materials that originate with Hasidei Ashkenaz (whose leaders first lived in Speyer and Worms, then in Regensburg) is to what extent the pious practices that they recommended were already widely known; or, in other words, how innovative were these teachings in their immediate vicinity and in northern France?[81] That is, were these zealous versions of the practices that other Jews performed less stringently?

These questions are related to a key issue that has been raised in research on Hasidei Ashkenaz: should they be called "Pietists" as a defined group rather than "pious," without any specifics to indicate their unique position in medieval Jewish society?[82] The claim that Hasidei Ashkenaz should be denoted as "Pietists" has been promoted by Ivan Marcus, Haym Soloveitchik, and others, in studies that have been instrumental for those seeking to delineate the intellectual and doctrinal contours of pietistic thought over and above its social framework. Haym Soloveitchik has studied a number of pietisms, German and otherwise, in an effort to articulate the distinctions between them.[83] In contrast to Soloveitchik and Marcus, I am not seeking to distinguish between the pious and the Pietists. Rather, I am investigating the rituals that were performed by Jews who wished to fulfill their religious obligations; thus, I use the term "pietistic" to characterize the attitudes of leaders such as Judah and Samuel, who occupy the far end of the religious spectrum. In some cases, these "pietists" are presented as virtuosi, stellar examples of ardent belief and ascetic practice. However, my main interest lies in how pious practice was promoted, diffused, and explained within the medieval world, not the intellectual biographies or thought processes of the rabbis and individuals whose praxis characterize them as extreme rather than representative.[84] Much as the word hasid (pious) conveyed different meanings and inflections in medieval texts, so it is in this study, where it can carry prescriptive and descriptive senses that allow a more nuanced understanding of Jewish society in medieval Ashkenaz.[85]

Piety and Gender

Gender serves as a critical prism for examining piety in this study, which is motivated by the desire to include community members who are rendered nearly invisible in medieval accounts but who surely composed a considerable segment of the medieval Jewish population. Adult men who were not especially learned represent one such category, since most male members of medieval Jewish communities were neither halakhic authorities nor learned scholars, yet information on them is especially sparse. Another significant group within the community's fabric were women. Children, too, constituted a meaningful cohort of the community to whom I refer throughout this book.

The piety of medieval Ashkenazic women, like that of the entire community, has most prominently been noted in descriptions of their deaths, by the Crusaders or by their own hands.[86] Women's piety has further been remarked upon in the context of religious rituals, especially those defined as "positive time-bound commandments," such as precepts related to the holidays and the obligations of tefillin and tzitzit.[87] As feminism and gender theory have increasingly influenced Jewish studies in the past two decades, research on medieval Jewish women has flourished. Of special note is the work of Judith Baskin, who was one of the first scholars to address these issues in the

Ashkenazi context.[88] Avraham Grossman has provided the most comprehensive overview of medieval Jewish women thus far in his comparison of Jewish life in Europe and Islamic lands, which includes the status of Jewish women in their environs. Grossman's work dedicates one full chapter plus occasional references to aspects of daily religious practice among medieval Jewish women.[89] Most recently, Bitha Har-Shefi wrote her dissertation on select halakhic developments pertaining to women in Ashkenaz during the Middle Ages.[90] While I concentrate throughout this volume on the comparison between Jewish and Christian piety in northern Europe, I occasionally reference examples from Jewish life in Christian Spain and Muslim lands.

Practicing Piety seeks to move scholarly discourse on medieval Jewish women a step further by studying the pious practices of Jewish women and men, separately and together. In some instances, women serve as representative examples of the less educated members of the community, leading to comparisons of men's and women's observance. At other times, I examine how women's piety was defined in contrast to men's practices, generally and from specific angles,[91] by asking how gender produced, preserved, and challenged social hierarchies as a means of privileging the deeds of one group over another in discrete contexts.[92] Thus, gender serves as a tool for examining broader patterns of piety and offers a fuller view of community members. Although they did not compose our transmitted texts, this more diverse Jewish population is present in the writings that we have, for they are featured in them and their lives shaped these texts even as they were reciprocally guided by them. Prioritizing practice when examining the past is hardly new, particularly when studying the religious lives of women. This approach is especially pertinent in medieval Jewish history, given the absence of texts produced by women and the scant writings intended for them as a readership.[93]

Gender serves not only as a category of differentiation but also as one of comparison in the Jewish-Christian context. Despite the deep divergence in their religious beliefs presented above, Jews and Christians shared a patriarchal outlook that enforced and perpetuated hierarchal gender relationships, where women were considered subservient to men. Although one can point to contrasts between Jewish and Christian societies that were crucial in determining the life paths of their members, such as the centrality of celibacy in Christianity and of marriage among Jews,[94] I would argue that these distinctions did not eradicate gendered conventions. As such, gender can reveal divisions and commonalities, while it also exposes power struggles and ideological shifts, since women and their bodies frequently personified cultural borders and barriers.[95] From a historiographic perspective, it is noteworthy that while scholars have labored to distinguish Jewish men from their Christian peers, these same researchers have been far less hesitant to categorize Jewish and Christian women as a homogeneous group. My attention to gender gives voice to both perspectives, assessing medieval women by religion and as one cohort.

My research relies on testaments to the involvement of medieval Jewish and Christian women in religious life and their ongoing quest for piety. Indeed, medieval Jewish and Christian authors alike have remarked that women led active religious lives. As Berthold of Regensburg (1220–1272) states: "You women, you go more readily to church than men do, speak your prayers more readily than men do, go to sermons more readily than men do."[96] Some Hebrew sources convey this same message.[97] Scholars have argued that a major shift in the perception of women, their roles in society, and the overall conceptualization of gender relations took place during the High Middle Ages, with a general trend toward excluding women's ritual and religious practice from the thirteenth century onward, after a period when women enjoyed relative freedom.[98] Many other variables of medieval life were also in flux during the thirteenth century, as manifested by both internal Christian turmoil and transitions in key elements in Jewish-Christian relations. I have explored the intersection of gendered conventions and concepts with the fervor for piety to detail some of these changes.[99]

An added benefit of comparing medieval Jewish and Christian societies for the purpose of this study is the information contributed by the substantial literature on piety—especially lay piety and gender—in the Christian world, which has further elucidated the settings in which medieval Jews practiced piety. One significant finding from recent work on gender and piety among medieval Christians in northern Europe is the remarkable encouragement of lay piety by Church authorities that increased during the Middle Ages.[100] The centrality of confession, a hallmark of medieval Christianity, affirms this interest in the pursuit of piety by clergy and parishioners alike. Recent studies have also focused on the composition of popular guidebooks for lay practice during the thirteenth century.[101] This work has led me to ask new questions of contemporaneous Jewish sources, by way of contrast and comparison.

Admittedly, the routes available to Christians who wished to pursue religious life were more numerous and far broader than the options that existed among Jews. Beyond lay piety, additional alternatives were open to medieval Christian men and women, including formally joining established orders (that lived among the laity or within cloistered communities) and privately exercising chastity at home. These paths often entailed taking vows of celibacy and adopting an ascetic life. Jewish society, with family life as the expected norm, had no equivalent structures. However, on average, medieval Jews may have had higher levels of participation in communal rituals and prayers than Christian laity; and the modest size of Jewish communities may have, at times, softened the disparity between leaders and members.

Jews and Christians differed not only in the available choices in spiritual life, but in their performance of analogous deeds. Each religious group had its own vocabulary, reasoning, and concepts associated with their actions. The differences in language go beyond translation, for "piety" and "pious" emerge from the Christian context, but they are not synonymous with the Hebrew terms "hasidut" and "hasid" or "hasidah" of Jewish parlance. Likewise, *tzedakah* (charity) is not identical to alms (*elemosyna*) or *caritas*, and each religion had its own definition of ritual purity. Furthermore, the artifacts for expressing devotion to God differ between the two religions, such as tefillin (phylacteries) and Torah scrolls among Jews in contrast to Christian relics and rosaries, despite the resemblance found among rituals related to some of these objects.[102] I enlist these distinctions to illustrate how Jews nurtured and accentuated their separate religious identity. That is to say, similarity does not imply sameness, nor does comparison serve to equate or simplify distinctions between the two religions; rather, these nuances contribute to the clarification of these intricate relationships.

On a certain level, the dual focus on piety as seen and defined within the Jewish community and as understood in cross-religious dialogue results in some slippage between the notions of piousness and Jewishness in this book. While this may at first seem incongruous, I would argue that this ambiguity reflects the complexity of medieval Jewish life, since members of Jewish communities were constantly involved in reinforcing their stance in the eyes of fellow Jews and in their Christian environment.

Practicing Piety

The practices herein include classic deeds that express devotion to God with an emphasis on how they were practiced in medieval Jewish communities and how their performance changed during the Middle Ages. Anthropologists have discussed the challenge of finding a consistent meaning in any given practice or ritual behavior over time. Indeed, I am interested in the ritualization of daily activities rather than the absolute coherence of symbols.[103] The acts of piety that were performed on a regular basis are myriad, and they took place in a range of settings. This study includes home-based and public practices, including the synagogue, at home, and on the street.[104] These activities offered avenues for the expression and production of religious identities for all community members, be they learned or not.[105]

Medieval Jewish men and women could have practiced one or many of the customs discussed in the chapters that follow. They could have been exceedingly devout or hoping to conform to the conduct that their society considered appropriate. From that perspective, even without earning the label pious, one could still perform pious observances that were considered not only good but virtuous, fulfilling one of many religious obligations. Moreover, piety meant different things in different settings. Yet as meaningful as these actions could be for an individual, being classified as pious reflected on the community at large and its members' shared values.

Medieval epitaphs reflect varied degrees of piety. Some of the deceased were called pious (*hasid/ah*), whereas others were termed righteous (*tzaddik/ah*). Yet others were said to be upstanding (*hagun/ah*) and important (*hashuv/ah*).[106] While the first two adjectives suggest devoutness and the latter two status, they often combined with one another, implying that these traits were seen as more intertwined than discrete. In my eyes this entanglement is suggestive of the range of pious practices and beliefs that were expressed within the medieval community, a spectrum rather than a predetermined set of practices.

Each chapter in this book concentrates on a core topic through which piety was expressed, presented from a specific angle that highlights the key issues of this study. Three central attributes that have characterized many religions since ancient times—prayer, fasting, and charity—are conveyed in the first three chapters. In the Jewish tradition, these observances are explicitly linked to atonement on Yom Kippur: *tefillah, teshuvah* [lit., repentance], and *tzedakah* in the corresponding Hebrew terminology.[107]

In the case of prayer, the subject of Chapter 1, I concentrate on how synagogue attendance and avoidance correspond to corporeal purity as a prerequisite and impurity as an impediment to participation in communal prayer. By comparing the roles of men and women alongside Jewish and Christian concepts of purity and impurity, I track changes in synagogue practice during the medieval period.

Chapter 2 concentrates on fasting as a form of repentance, describing the development of Jewish fasting from late antiquity to medieval Europe with particular attention to its medieval features, and contextualizing Jewish fasting practices in their medieval Christian context. The comparison of these Jewish rituals with Christian observance focuses on patterns of daily life by detailing the distinctions and similarities between Jewish and Christian activities.

Charitable giving is the focus of Chapter 3, using data from the Nürnberg Memorbuch to present a case study of donations that were contributed as gifts for the soul (*pro anima*) in the Nürnberg Jewish community during the late thirteenth and early fourteenth centuries. Here I explore gender distinctions by examining tensions between the control of resources and the desire to make contributions as evidenced in this extraordinary record.

Chapter 4 studies the well-known practice of Ashkenazi women performing positive time-bound commandments that are typically considered in the realm of exclusive male praxis. This discussion reflects on the scholarly attention that this topic has received in earlier studies of women's history and piety in two ways: first, by locating the evidence of women's deeds within the context of conventionally male observances; and, second, by demonstrating how these practices developed and were transformed during the medieval period. I argue that class rather than gender played a role in the initial practices adapted by women, and I document the cultural trends in the thirteenth century pertaining to male practice that led to further changes in women's practice.

In Chapter 5, I consider piety as displayed via hair, dress, and appearance and ask how Jews established themselves within and in contradistinction to the majority culture. Here I underline the importance of what medieval Jews and Christians noticed on the streets of their cities, a topic that has largely been ignored to date.

In Chapter 6, rather than investigating piety per se, I present textual evidence of pretenders: Jews who feigned piety and whose deceptions were discovered. Unlike religious deviants, these individuals mimicked communally recognizable pious behavior, were later revealed as frauds, and then were called to account by community leaders. These stories provide another context for reflecting on male and female piety and impropriety. Chapter 7 draws together many of the recurring social and comparative themes of the entire study.

This introduction would not be complete if I did not reiterate that most topics covered in the volume pertain to many religious cultures, certainly medieval Christianity and Islam. For example, fasting and charity were common methods for expressing piety in all three religions.[108] So, too, corporeal impurity during prayer was a concern among Jews, Christians, and Muslims. Despite the pervasive nature of these themes, their associated rituals were adapted over time and space.¹⁰⁹ The chapters in this study address how Jewish men and women displayed piety within their Jewish communities and in the context of the northern European Christian urban spaces where they lived, making vivid their roles as active participants in this culture. Their performance of religious deeds made explicit their views on proper religious conduct, their relationships with God, and especially links with one another.¹¹⁰ Much as Rashi defined the piety of the stork as intrinsically tied to the friends with whom she shared her food, this study endeavors to describe how Jewish piety was defined within the social context of the medieval urban centers of northern France and Germany.

CHAPTER I

Standing Before God: Purity and Impurity in the Synagogue

> Blessed are you . . . who has sanctified us with his commandments . . . separating us from impurity and cautioning us to beware of menstruants and (their) discharges.
> —Eleazar b. Judah, *Sefer Rokeah*, #317, p. 195

Rashi and his students produced a number of books that detail the customs observed in their communities.[1] In several such works, there is a recurring passage that describes a practice attributed to select women of their time:

> There are women who refrain from entering the synagogue when they are menstrually impure although they do not need to do so. So why do they do this? If they believe that the synagogue is like the Temple, then why do they enter even after having immersed?[2] . . . In that case, one should avoid entering the sanctuary forever, [that is] until a sacrifice is brought in the future (after the arrival of the Messiah). But if the synagogue differs from the Temple, they should surely enter. After all, we [men] are all impure due to nocturnal emissions and [exposure to] death and insects, yet we [still] enter the synagogue. Thus we deduce that [a synagogue] is not like the Temple, and women may [also] enter. But in any event, it is a place of purity and [these women] are acting admirably (*yafeh hen osot*).[3]

According to this text, some medieval Jewish women avoided the synagogue when they were menstruating, even though this practice was not required by halakhah, and their decision was considered praiseworthy. As in most religious cultures, medieval Judaism valued engagement in communal prayer in a specially designated venue as a preferred manner of communicating with God. In the medieval Jewish context, prayer services were primarily conducted in the synagogue[4] and necessitated the presence of a male quorum.[5] In this citation attributed to Rashi, certain women who were accustomed to attending prayers with their congregation chose to express their devotion to God and respect toward their community by refraining from entering the synagogue during their menstrual cycles.[6] Their decision can be read as paradoxical, since presence rather than absence often defines piety.

As noted in the introduction, the search for popular piety straddles the boundaries between the individual and communal spheres. Each Jew who engaged in religious practices, both "pious" and conventional, did so in anticipation of ultimately being personally judged by God. However, their actions were also expected to have bearing on the standing of the congregation as a whole. As such, concerns about corporeal purity were understood to have ramifications for individuals and for the entire community.

This chapter discusses the heightened sensitivities to physical purity and impurity that led to pious practices which influenced participation in synagogue prayer.[7] By tracing the development of observances that relate to corporeal purity in medieval Ashkenaz, this chapter investigates how presence (and absence) in the synagogue came to signify piety and the extent to which concerns about bodily purity became correlated with gender.[8] After examining the evidence for these practices and their developments among Ashkenazic Jewry during the High Middle Ages, I then situate this data within the framework of Christian customs that were associated with female and male bodily purity and access to sacred spaces, especially entering the church to celebrate Mass. This contextualized investigation leads to the conclusion that the medieval Christian environment provides essential data for understanding the development of Jewish customs and ideas on the relationship between personal purity and communal participation in sacred spaces.

Absence and Presence in the Medieval Synagogue

It would not be an exaggeration to claim that the synagogue was the institution par excellence of medieval Jewish life, as the setting where the community prayed, shared meals, conducted legal discussions, celebrated and commemorated life-cycle rituals, and gathered in times of joy and crisis alike.[9] The synagogue symbolized Jewish distinctiveness for adherents of other religions while it constituted a common space for Jews themselves.[10] "Interrupting prayers" (a juridical procedure that involved imposing a break during prayer services so an individual's complaint could be voiced and addressed) and *herem* (excommunication—the ultimate punishment, regularly exercised in medieval Europe) were effective precisely because of the close-knit nature of the Jewish community and the constant interdependence that bound the average Jew to the synagogue and related communal institutions.[11]

Prayer services were typically held in synagogue: twice a day on weekdays[12] and with more elaborate formats and schedules on the Sabbath, festivals, and fast days. Almost all medieval communities, except for the very smallest, had at least one synagogue,[13] which would be located in buildings designated for communal purposes or in dedicated rooms within private homes.[14]

Despite serving as the venue for a full range of Jewish communal gatherings,[15] few studies have examined the synagogue as a center for social interaction, a forum for communal policies and religious politics, and a locus where piety was constantly expressed, monitored, and assessed. Among the scholars that have noted the social significance of the synagogue, Israel Abrahams opens *Jewish Life in the Middle Ages* by describing the synagogue as the "centre of social life" and illustrates this idea with several examples. The vast geographic and temporal sweep of his focus, however, on medieval Europe from north to south and on sources from the tenth to eighteenth centuries, precludes a comprehensive discussion of his claims.[16] In his study of the function of the synagogue in the late Middle Ages, Jacob Katz primarily treats the synagogue as a religious setting, with minimal attention to its other roles.[17] In more recent contributions to this line of inquiry, Robert Bonfil has discussed the synagogue in comparison to the medieval church and as a focal point of Jewish social life. He emphasizes the synagogue as a general meeting place where Jews from all strata of society would encounter each other and where the sacred and the profane would meet, emblematic of Jewish time and space.[18] Alick Isaacs depicts the synagogue as a social center by focusing on the Torah, through public readings and other rituals related to it.[19] Simha Goldin has explored the role of the synagogue in social mediation and community gatherings, especially as a setting for the socialization of children.[20]

In contrast to these studies, most research to date has traced the history of specific synagogue-based prayers or religious practices, subjects that pertained most directly to learned male members of the community, particularly religious leaders who determined the order of services and, in some cases, wrote liturgical compositions or introduced prayers to their congregations.[21] These studies presuppose synagogues that were populated by Jews who shared a high degree of liturgical competence. However, as Ephraim Kanarfogel has recently suggested, it is unlikely that this standard characterized Jewish men in medieval Ashkenaz, much less their female counterparts.[22]

Irrespective of their literacy levels, medieval Jews seem to have attended prayer services regularly. Nevertheless, a range of factors prevented full participation in the synagogue. Simply stated, laxity may well have been the primary deterrent, a quality that is rarely mentioned in medieval sources but was probably manifest in varied if inconsistent ways.[23] In stark contrast to this passive causality, excommunication constituted another cause for keeping a distance; however, permanent banishment from the community cannot be placed on a spectrum with piety except perhaps as its opposite.

Numerous explanations underlie intentional decisions to refrain from attending synagogue, among them a pious stance to avoid participation if one deemed that the rituals were not being conducted properly.[24] In a unique case from the late thirteenth century, Meir b. Barukh of Rothenburg (d. 1293), in a ruling that stands out for its passion and intensity, instructs men to leave the synagogue rather than participate in circumcisions where women serve as *ba'alot brit* (formal participants in the circumcision ritual), bringing the infants into the sanctuary and holding them on their laps during the ceremony. Meir of Rothenburg himself enlists the language of piety in his reasoning: "Any man who fears the Lord should leave the synagogue."[25]

The extreme directive conveyed in this instruction especially stands out given the absence of comparable instructions in medieval sources. For example, *Sefer Hasidim* mentions the possibility that a pious man might prefer to pray alone rather than in a synagogue where prayers were not being led according to his standards. In that case, Judah suggests that this pious man should pray at home before going to synagogue, but under no circumstance should he avoid participation in communal services.[26] Overall, medieval Jews followed the talmudic teaching that prayers are most efficacious when recited with the community in synagogue.[27]

Purity and Impurity: Changing Observance

Another reason to distance oneself from the synagogue, and the main subject of this chapter, is impurity. Like all synagogues after the destruction of the Temple, the medieval synagogue was considered a *mikdash me'at* (a little

Figure 2. A Jew praying. © Universitäts- und Landesbibliothek Darmstadt. Cod. Or. 13, fol. 38v. Mahzor, Germany, 1348.

sanctuary), less holy than the Temple but treated similarly.[28] Ashkenazic ideas about the physical impurities that could render men and women temporarily disqualified from attending synagogue, and, as a result, diminish their ability to communicate with God in communal rituals, provide a window not only onto the everyday practices of medieval Jews, but also on some of their understandings of sanctity and the development of these notions over the course of the Middle Ages, especially in gendered terms.

Medieval conceptions of purity and impurity are rooted in precedents from the Bible and the Temple period, as first outlined in Leviticus. When the Temple was standing in Jerusalem, any man who experienced a seminal emission was prohibited from entering until he had washed.[29] Similarly, any woman who was either menstruating or who held post-partum status and had not yet undergone ritual immersion was barred from bringing a sacrifice to the Temple. This requirement to perform ritual immersion before approaching the Temple applied to other individuals, due to a physical condition or recent action (e.g., lepers or anyone who had been exposed to a corpse).[30] These biblical traditions and their implications are debated in rabbinic discourse; thus, ongoing engagement in these topics constitutes part of the medieval Jewish cultural and textual inheritance.

Despite their transmission in rabbinic literature, the applications of Levitical standards of purity received less attention in the medieval world than they did in antiquity. This reduced emphasis is exemplified in discussions about *Takanot Ezra*, a collection of statutes on central aspects of ritual life that have been attributed to Ezra the Scribe.[31] The most relevant instruction for our context declares that any man who is impure due to a seminal emission should neither study Torah nor pray before having washed.[32] This statute was suspended by the classical rabbis (prior to the medieval period), who reasoned that, after the Temple's destruction, impurity had become ubiquitous since sacrifice was no longer available as a means for nullifying the effect of contact with the dead or atoning for sins; thus, this restriction had been rendered inapplicable.[33] Nonetheless, from the second half of the first millennium through the Middle Ages, the question of whether men who were ritually impure must wash before entering the synagogue continued, albeit tangentially.[34] However, male impurity was no longer defined by sexual relations but rather by incidental nocturnal emissions of semen (*keri laylah*), which could affect any man.

Most medieval halakhic authorities note that such stringencies were no longer practiced and that men who remained concerned need not worry.[35] Even Judah the Pious, who frequently addresses matters of purity, devotes far more attention to instructions for avoiding nocturnal emissions than to guidance on restoring purity after they occur. For example:

> Once there was a pious man (or a pietist) who would not lie in his bed on the nights when his wife was *niddah* [menstrually impure]; rather he would sleep sitting or reclining [in a chair], for he said, "If I lie comfortably in my bed, I would sleep too well and perhaps I might have a nocturnal emission. Rather I should sleep uncomfortably, without a pillow, so I will not see an emission." [Sometimes] he would stand all night studying Torah.[36]

In this teaching from *Sefer Hasidim*, a man who is barred from sexual contact with his wife due to her menstrual impurity fears that he too will become ritually compromised by nocturnal emission; he thereby draws a connection between male and female states of physical impurity.[37]

This association reflects an imbalance that came to characterize female ritual purity, where menstrual and post-partum blood represented the exception rather than the rule in Jewish praxis. In contrast to all other causes of ritual impurity that had been observed when the Temple existed and were then suspended after its destruction,[38] not only did the effect of menstruation continue to have currency, but over time this category of ritual purity became a hallmark of Jewish female identity.[39] The laws of menstrual purity cover a category of practices that mainly relate to intimate relations between married couples.[40] Despite its personal nature, there is evidence that medieval neighbors and fellow community members were aware of each woman's *niddah* status according to her apparel since all women wore *bigdei niddut*, special clothes for menstruation,[41] which differed from their regular attire.[42] This practice is echoed in a teaching in *Sefer Hasidim* that, when relevant, men should emphasize their own state of purity by wearing white, following the verse "At all times your clothes should be white" (Eccles. 9:7). However, his comments suggest that this custom was limited to especially pious men.[43] Later sources also discuss men wearing white as a demonstration of purity, but those instructions are often in the context of Yom Kippur, when everyone would wear white.[44]

Observance of the laws of menstruation had numerous public implications beyond the realm of attire, including questions regarding women's synagogue attendance, as the quotation ascribed to Rashi above suggests. According to this source, some women absented themselves from the synagogue during their menstrual cycles because they understood that, as with the Temple, they were excluded from it during times of ritual impurity.[45] In their analyses of this passage, a number of scholars have attributed this custom to an esoteric text, known as *Baraita deNiddah*, which was written during the early centuries of the first millennium and contains many strict regulations concerning menstruants and their impurity,[46] such as "And she shall not come to the Temple" (Lev. 12:4). She is not permitted to enter places of learning or synagogues."[47] This teaching is not widely quoted. For example, sources from early medieval Babylonia discuss the applicability of this verse in the absence of the Temple, and draw the opposite conclusion of *Baraita deNiddah*, declaring women's avoidance of settings for prayer and study to be excessive.[48]

Whether Rashi and his students were familiar with *Baraita deNiddah* remains a question of scholarly debate; however, it is likely they did not. None of the writings from Rashi or his school refer to *Baraita deNiddah* and it is notably absent from the passage cited above.[49] Moreover, our citation from Rashi indicates that the custom of distancing oneself from the synagogue was not widespread among menstruants in the late eleventh and early twelfth centuries and was an exception rather than the rule.[50]

This practice is mentioned again in several texts from the twelfth and thirteenth centuries. Its next appearance, about a century after Rashi, is in *Sefer Ra'aviah* by Eliezer b. Joel haLevi (1160–1235, known as Ra'aviah). In a discussion concerning men who were impure as a result of seminal emissions, Ra'aviah reports:

> Women exercise stringency and piety (*nahagu silsul be'atzman u'perishut*) when they are impure (*niddah*) by not entering the synagogue. Moreover, when praying, they do not stand behind women who are impure. I have also seen this written in the words of our Ge'onim, in the language of a *baraita* that is not found in our *tosefta*. This custom is indeed valid, just as I have heard of men who behave more and less stringently when they are impure due to nocturnal emissions: those who are more stringent live longer days and years.[51]

This passage demonstrates that Ra'aviah was familiar with *Baraita deNiddah* via a ge'onic source, albeit an unnamed one.[52] One outstanding aspect of this text, as with the selection from Rashi,[53] is Ra'aviah's statement that women initiated this practice, unprompted by rabbinic authorities, even if this custom received formal approval post-factum. Ra'aviah discusses two restrictions that women took upon themselves: the first reflects the observance noted by Rashi, linking ritual purity to entering the synagogue; the second relates to how women positioned themselves during public prayers. This further constraint regarding location in services does not appear in the versions of *Baraita deNiddah* that have reached us, but similar limitations appear in thirteenth-century sources (as discussed below).

Both of these texts raise a theme that has received negligible attention to date:[54] Rashi and Ra'aviah compare the actions of these women to the practices of men who were ritually impure.[55] Although the text attributed to Rashi does not report any special customs related to men, it comments on male and female impurity, noting that men, who were also impure by definition, attended synagogue seemingly without reservation.[56] In contrast, Ra'aviah remarks that particularly pious men took care to wash before entering the synagogue after experiencing nocturnal emissions. This male observance is repeated in other twelfth- and thirteenth-century medieval texts as well, usually in connection to preparations for Yom Kippur, when many men immersed[57] Although most sources state unequivocally that men participated in prayers in all states of purity and impurity, texts such as Ra'aviah's acknowledge the existence of stricter approaches. More exacting standards are also articulated in *Sefer Hasidim*, where men are instructed to wash[58] after sexual relations before praying.[59]

In sum, irrespective of their status with regard to purity, men participated fully in communal prayers throughout the medieval period, as textual evidence from northern France and Germany demonstrates with a few suggestions of singular exceptions. In the case of women, the sources attributed to Rashi and Ra'aviah indicate that a segment of especially pious women placed a self-imposed exclusion on synagogue participation during their menstrual cycles, and that this stringency could extend to physically distancing themselves during public prayers from their peers who were menstrually impure.

This idea is further developed by Eleazar b. Judah of Worms (d. 1230), who notes: "[A menstruant] is not permitted to enter the synagogue until she immerses in water because [even] her saliva [has the power to] contaminate."[60] This statement represents a major shift: Eleazar is not referring to a cohort of pious women who chose this custom; rather, he describes a prohibition that could keep all menstruants from entering the synagogue. Eleazar attributes this exclusion to *Ma'aseh haGe'onim*, an early Ashkenazic composition, but no such ruling appears in that book as we know it today.[61]

Sefer Likutei haPardes (attributed to the Rashi school, dated to thirteenth-century Italy) reports an intensification of this restriction that mirrors the language of *Sefer Ra'aviah*: "And there are women who abstain from entering the synagogue when they are menstruants and from seeing the Torah, and from touching the book (the Torah scroll). This is an unnecessary stringency . . . but it is a holy place and they are acting appropriately. May they be blessed in this world and in the World to Come."[62]

Isaac b. Moses (d. ca. 1250), the author of *Sefer Or Zaru'a* and a student of Ra'aviah and Eleazar of Worms, also writes about this practice. He paraphrases Ra'aviah almost verbatim.[63] His son, Haim b. Isaac, wrote: "She should not say the name of God when she is menstrually impure; furthermore, she is forbidden from entering the synagogue on any day when she sees [blood] until she is white [not bleeding]."[64] Haim altered some of the details: rather than depicting pious women praying at a distance from impure peers, he suggested that menstruating women should stay away from the synagogue entirely. Moreover, his tone varies substantially from that of his father. Haim does not differentiate between pious women who choose to keep a distance from the synagogue and other women. Rather, following Eleazar of Worms, he recommends that all menstruants be proscribed from entering the synagogue.

By the late thirteenth century, this prohibition seems to have become an accepted standard as indicated by Isaac b. Meir haLevi of Düren (a student of Meir b. Barukh from the second half of the thirteenth century), who wrote what can be considered the earliest manual pertaining to the laws of menstruation, *Sha'arei Dura*. His instructions echo the words of Isaac b. Moses (who, as we have seen, cited and built on teachings from Ra'aviah):

> A woman who is menstruating should not wear fine clothing or adorn herself, comb her hair or cut her nails. Neither should she say the name of God on the days when she menstruates nor should she enter the synagogue on any day when she sees [blood] until she is white. For it says: "And she shall not touch the holy and she shall not come to the Temple" (Lev. 12: 4). That [is to say,] she should not bring a sacrifice until seven clean days [have been completed]. This is what it says in *Sefer haMiktzo'ot*, but Rashi permitted her to come to synagogue.[65]

Isaac b. Meir does not specify that this course of action is that of pious women. Rather he suggests that this is the custom at large.

Over a century later, in his *Sefer haAgur*, Jacob b. Judah Landau (fifteenth century) mentions only a prohibition against menstruants seeing the Torah,[66] whereas Isaac b. Meir of Düren noted a dual warning against both entering the synagogue and saying God's name during menstruation. Landau's account also introduces a new prooftext from *Sefer haMiktzo'ot*, a mid-eleventh-century source that transmits many rulings from Babylonian Ge'onim and is often quoted in late medieval Ashkenazic writings.[67] Simcha Emanuel has recently proposed that, in this particular case, thirteenth- and fourteenth-century rabbis were constructing a source rather than citing directly from the corpus available to them.[68] He proposes that this "construction" was correlated to innovative practices that were introduced at that time and the consequent search for precedents to validate them.[69]

Thus not only had the motivations for these customs changed, but the norms were in flux. The instructions provided in the sources cited above are ambiguous with respect to intended duration of these restrictions, for Jewish women's menstrual impurity consisted of two distinct parts. The first encompassed the days when blood was seen. After bleeding ceased, women counted seven days, known as the "clean" or "white" days (because of the white clothing worn on those days);[70] not until that second set of days was complete would women immerse in the mikveh (the ritual bath) and resume sexual relations with their husbands.[71] Did women refrain from going to synagogue and saying God's name throughout their entire time of ritual impurity, or only when they were bleeding? Both Haim b. Isaac and Isaac b. Meir specify that these restrictions were in effect only while a woman was bleeding, "until she is white" (*ad shetitlaben*).[72] Only Eleazar of Worms instructed that a woman must absent herself from synagogue "until she immerses in water."[73]

Northern French sources do not discuss women's presence in the synagogue with relation to menstruation, despite the initial appearance of this theme in texts attributed to Rashi. For example, thirteenth-century compendia that discuss the laws of menstruation, such as *Semag* (*Sefer Mitzvot Gadol*) by Moses of Coucy and *Semak* (*Sefer Mitzvot Katan*) by Isaac of Corbeil (d. 1280), mention no such restrictions.[74]

Thus, evidence for these restrictions is predominantly German in origin. These sources indicate that the practice of menstruants refraining from synagogue attendance continued well into the early modern period among Ashkenazic Jews. For example, in *Sefer Terumat haDeshen*, Israel Isserlein (1390–1460) discussed this custom as it was practiced in his lifetime:

> With regard to women who are impure, it is true that I have allowed them on the High Holidays and other days when many of them gather at the synagogue to hear the prayers and the [Torah] readings. And I have based my position on Rashi, who allowed women in [his writings on] the Laws of Niddah on account of spiritual pleasure (*nahat ruah*),[75] since [the prevailing custom] saddened their spirits and led to heartbreak[76] while the rest of the community was gathering and they were left standing outside. ... Look in the Laws of Niddah written by my esteemed uncle, Aaron,[77] and you will see that he copied from *Sefer Or Zaru'a* in the name of the Ge'onim, where it seems to be absolutely forbidden [for menstruating women to enter the synagogue], but he also noted that in *Sefer Or Zaru'a*[78] certain women refrain [from entering the synagogue] and act admirably. From this [opinion] one can understand that this [practice is prompted by] enthusiasm (*zerizut*) and piety alone [and is therefore not required].[79]

Isserlein's discussion underlines not only the popularity of this custom but also suggests that women may have stood outside rather than enter the synagogue, a possibility that is also raised by the pair of verbs used by the compiler in *Sefer Likutei haPardes*.[80] Isserlein highlights the individual and communal significance of synagogue attendance by noting the sorrow caused to women who were excluded from synagogue rituals, especially on holidays. Later sources, such as the commentary on the *Shulhan Arukh* by Remah (Moses Isserles, 1525–1572), include a summary of Isserlein's opinion but then counter his prohibition by explicitly charging women to enter the synagogue:

> Some have written that during the days of her discharge a menstruant may not enter a synagogue, pray, mention God's name or touch a Hebrew book, but others say that she is permitted [to perform] all these [acts], and this [latter] view is correct. However, the practice in these countries [meaning Ashkenazic lands] follows the first opinion, although during white days their custom is to allow [her to perform all these acts]. Even where the stringent practice is upheld, on the Days of Awe and other such occasions when many gather in synagogue, [menstruating women] are permitted to enter the synagogue like other women on account of their great sadness if everyone gathers [in synagogue] but they remain outside.[81]

These restrictions that pertain to menstrual impurity and the synagogue belong to a broader class of practices relating to menstruation that were enforced during the High Middle Ages. Northern French and German sources instruct men to curtail physical contact with their wives throughout both phases of *niddah*. Not only was direct touch restricted, but handling common objects was also regulated (e.g., couples were not to eat from the same bowls or to pass objects directly to one another).[82] In contrast to synagogue attendance, these domestic constraints were applied from the onset of bleeding until the woman had immersed. Indeed, some thirteenth- and fourteenth-century sources indicate that the rabbis were aware that they were demanding a degree of strictness that differed from previous generations.[83] Moreover, regulations regarding purity after childbirth also became much more rigorous during the thirteenth and fourteenth centuries, requiring couples to extend their period of abstinence from sexual activity from one week to at least six weeks.[84] As such, restricting menstruants from synagogue participation is consistent with stricter observances of that era. Not until the sixteenth century—when rabbinic authorities recognized that blocking menstruant women from synagogue attendance caused extreme distress and isolation—was this custom suspended.[85]

If we review the customs regarding the physical presence of ritually impure women in the synagogue in medieval Ashkenaz, we see that during the late eleventh and twelfth centuries some highly observant women stopped entering the synagogue while they were menstruating as an expression of reverence and piety. In Germany (at least), this behavior became increasingly normative for all women by the late thirteenth or early fourteenth centuries. Interestingly, this practice was only applied during the first phase of menstruation, whereas women returned to the synagogue when their "white days" had begun, without waiting until immersion.[86]

Although the customs associated with menstruants have parallels with respect to other causes of female impurity, such as immediate post-partum status, no evidence of ritually impure men remaining outside the synagogue has been recorded—neither at their own initiative nor by rabbinic instruction—despite the endorsement of such restrictions by Ra'aviah, Judah the Pious, and other authorities. This disparity comes without surprise since, as Sharon Koren has noted, it follows the asymmetrical biblical attitudes that show greater leniency toward male impurity than its female parallels. Furthermore, this approach to male impurity is congruent with communal reliance on a quorum of men to hold prayer services; had men been instructed to avoid synagogue during their states of impurity, the established rhythm of public prayer might have been endangered!

Consequently, even the most pious men went to synagogue regularly, without taking their purity status into account; while these individuals were more meticulous about washing after nocturnal emissions, under no circumstances were they dissuaded (much less prohibited) from entering the synagogue. Rather, men were encouraged to temper the conscious and unconscious sexual thoughts that caused their impurity. Furthermore, impurity was never raised as a factor that might interfere with men's participation in prayers services or their recitation of blessings. This, of course, differs significantly from the religious imperatives linked to menstruation, the manifestation of an involuntary bodily function.

As we have seen, among women, the inception of "white days" (and in some cases, immersion) marked their return to regular synagogue attendance, and ritual immersion punctuated their cycle of sexual relations. Even though men's immersion did not typically determine their cycles of religious activity in the same way, male immersion emerged as a custom on the eve of the Day of Atonement. Medieval sources identify this as a practice that was intended to substitute for all immersions that should technically have been performed during the remainder of the year in addition to its more obvious assurance of male purity on the holiest of days.[87] Let us now turn to this annual custom to explore how it might shed light on rituals that were performed by women throughout the year.

Men, Women, and Angels

The idea that the Day of Atonement requires a heightened level of purity is not a medieval innovation. In the Bible, it is already described as a day of utmost significance, when purity was crucial. This principle was operative when the Temple stood and following its destruction. The Day of Atonement's unique status is evident from rabbinic texts that describe priestly rites in the Temple and in medieval discussions of Yom Kippur, which are especially relevant to our study given their attention to the fear of a nocturnal emission on this holy day. Such an occurrence was understood as a signal that the affected man must immediately repent lest he die in the coming year.[88] In many ways, this concern represented a commitment to piety for the entire community since all men were elevated to the status of the high priest in the Temple on Yom Kippur. As such, efforts to achieve a state of purity were intrinsic to preparing for the holiest day in the Jewish calendar.[89]

Rabbinic and medieval sources provide various explanations of the need for purity and thus for immersion prior to Yom Kippur.[90] The midrashic image of all Israel—men, women, and children—poised like angels before God on Yom Kippur had enduring popularity: originating in Midrash Leviticus Rabbah, it was often repeated by later generations,[91] as in *Mahzor Vitry*: "Yom Kippur arrives and all Israel fasts. Men, women, and children wear white, like the angels who serve God (*malakhei sharet*). They stand barefoot, like the dead. [In response,] God is filled with mercy and grants atonement for all their sins."[92]

While repentance (*teshuvah*) is the obvious reason for fasting, numerous medieval sources make explicit the connection between this midrash and purification from nocturnal emissions.[93] The most marked among them is a fifteenth-century reference to Judel, son of Shalom of Neustadt:[94] "Judel, the son of our teacher Shalom, states that it seems to him that women should not immerse in preparation for Yom Kippur eve because they cannot be like angels."[95] The halakhic topic at issue here is whether immersion in the mikveh on the eve of Yom Kippur was a component of repentance that every Jewish adult performed before Judgment Day,[96] or whether this ritual was carried out to release men from impurities related to nocturnal emissions. The latter process could not apply to women since, by definition, the sin of nocturnal emission does not pertain to them.

Judel assumes that immersion prior to Yom Kippur counteracts the impurity caused by nocturnal emissions and, since this matter is uniquely related to male anatomy, women need not perform this ritual. However, this physiological distinction bears no relationship to his rationale: Judel reasons that women need not immerse because, in contrast to men, they cannot be like angels. His words reflect a gendered hierarchy that depicts a world where God reigns, followed by angels, men, and, lastly, women.

Judel's teaching provides fertile ground for further examination of the main issues that we have seen so far. Male impurity did not present an impediment to entering the sanctuary or participating in prayer; even the men who were most cautious about ritual impurity would wash, then attend synagogue, without immersion in the mikveh. On Yom Kippur, an additional level of stringency was prescribed and, therefore, many men immersed in preparation for that most holy day.[97] In the early thirteenth century, Eleazar of Worms suggested that exceptionally pious men (*perushim*) immersed before Yom Kippur, whereas by the fifteenth century, as we have seen, this practice had become customary for all men.[98]

As we have already seen, women immersed regularly as a component of maintaining menstrual purity.[99] The passage by Judel implies that some women also immersed on the eve of Yom Kippur, and his objection focuses on that practice.[100] Although the Yom Kippur eve immersion is mentioned frequently in sources from the thirteenth to fifteenth centuries,[101] only Jacob Moellin (known as the Maharil, 1360–1427) explicitly describes it as an observance for both men and women:[102]

> Mahari Segal (an acronym for Maharil's name) says that one can argue that [immersion] is for the sake of repentance since it is customary for men and women, youth and virgins who have reached bar and bat mitzvah [age] to immerse [on Yom Kippur eve]. Clearly men immerse because of seminal impurity or because they touched some impurity, but why do the women immerse, given that they don't emit semen? The same reasoning applies to elderly (menopausal) women, and to youth and virgins whose bodies are clean from any impurity. Rather [this immersion] is certainly on account of repentance.[103]

In contrast to Judel, Maharil unambiguously separates this immersion from purity. Although Maharil's opinion was widely accepted, Judel's comment allows for further reflection on medieval Jewish notions of corporeal purity.

Judel's comments cast a doubt on women's potential to be like angels. This comparison between Jews and angels originated in late antiquity. Texts from that era discuss how men and women could resemble angels, although some late antique sources claim that men are more capable of reaching the level of angels (beings who were considered asexual by their very nature).[104] Medieval sources continue to compare both men and women to angels, as, for example, in the thirteenth-century composition *Semag*:[105]

> When God created the world, he created heaven and earth on the first day and the angels on the second day. [The angels] had no evil inclination but know how to worship and serve their Creator, whereas animals possess evil desires but know not how to serve their Creator. On the sixth day, he created man, who resembles both angels and animals. For that reason, when a human eats, drinks or goes to sleep, it should not be for the sake of pleasure, like an animal. Rather he should eat with the intention of gaining the strength needed to worship God as angels do.[106]

This passage features humanity—without distinguishing between men and women—as an intermediary category of beings that share certain characteristics with angels and others with animals, respectively.[107]

However, a close reading of other passages from thirteenth-century Germany reveals that women were often viewed as an impediment to men becoming like angels. For example, Judah the Pious writes: "He who stops himself [108] from looking at women and avoids idle talk with them will surpass the angels who serve God."[109] This passage continues by drawing a contrast between angels, humans who are unable to restrain their tempers, and menstruant women:

> And also, a man should avoid looking at an angry individual because (in that moment of anger) a bad angel is present [and encourages the angry one] to take swift revenge and [also at that instant, the bad angel] causes him (the one who gazed upon the other's angry state) to forget all that he has learned. The same is true for one who looks at a woman who is menstruating whose blood is in her.[110]

Although this selection from *Sefer Hasidim* does not deny that women could be like angels, it presents women as an obstacle to the fulfillment of male spirituality. The idea presented by Judel in the fifteenth century takes this understanding a step further by portraying women as categorically incapable of resembling angels.

If this trajectory is examined alongside the changing expectations of menstruants in the synagogue during the High Middle Ages that we mapped out above, the contours of a transition become quite evident. Purity regulations for all women became more stringent while men entered the synagogue without restriction. How can these shifting concepts and practices be elucidated? Prior research has generated two lines of reasoning to explain why women stopped attending synagogue during menstruation. Some scholars have termed the emergence of women's self-imposed constraints in earlier sources and the widespread adoption of those strict beliefs and practices in later sources as "a natural response." This position has most recently been articulated by Bitha Har-Shefi, who contends that women were preserving a custom inherited from earlier generations of women that concretizes inherent fears and anxieties related to blood.[111] However, as feminist scholarship and cultural studies demonstrate, it is hard to define natural responses,

Figure 3. Entrance to the Garden of Eden. From *Birds' Head Haggadah*. Note that only men are portrayed here. © Israel Museum, Jerusalem. B46.04.0912; 180/057 fol. 33r, detail. Southern Germany, ca. 1300.

since all rituals are products of the cultural milieu where they develop and are performed. Moreover, characterizing a certain behavior as "natural" cannot explain adaptations over time, since stability rather than dynamism would be expected in such a paradigm.[112] Thus our search for catalysts behind the transformations that occurred in medieval Ashkenaz between the generations of Rashi and Judel continues.

A more common explanation has linked these changing practices—with respect to menstruation and male impurity—to increasing familiarity with traditions that originated in late antique Palestine and that spread among Ashkenazic scholars from the twelfth century onward.[113] This hypothesis concentrates on the elite strata of halakhic authorities as catalysts for new practices and rulings. While this approach may provide convincing background for restrictions concerning the seven "white days" recommended by leading rabbis, in my opinion it does not clarify the dynamic process that we have documented concerning women's physical presence in the synagogue.[114]

I opened this chapter with a passage from Rashi's circle that attempts to explain a custom whose genesis stems from the agency of women. While it may be argued that the belief that menstruating women should not enter a synagogue was based on esoteric sources that gained currency over time, such as *Baraita deNiddah*, if those texts were unknown to men in the eleventh and twelfth centuries, they were surely inaccessible to the women who chose to express their piety by remaining outside the synagogue during Rashi's lifetime (or perhaps earlier). It is plausible that the strict behavior initiated by these women was more readily accepted and adapted over time due to a growing conversance with *Baraita deNiddah* and other ge'onic works. Nevertheless, that influence does not alter the sequence of events that emerges from the sources, relating to a custom that was begun by a self-selected group of women that became commonplace as a result of rabbinic directives.[115] At this point, let us turn to the Christian setting in which Ashkenazic Jews lived to contextualize these developments in custom and belief.

Impurity, Accessing the Sacred, and Approximating Angels: A Christian Comparison

Examinations of medieval northern European Christian communities in recent works by Rob Meens, Charles de Miramon, and other scholars reveal significant parallels to Jewish trends with regard to longstanding attitudes toward menstrual blood and male impurity. The question of whether it is appropriate for impure men and menstruating women to enter a church and participate in religious rituals—and particularly to approach the altar during Mass—has been debated by Christian theologians since late antiquity.[116] In Christian writings as in Jewish sources, male and female impurity are often treated as two aspects of a single topic. The opinion attributed to Gregory the Great (540–604) that pronounced sexual relations and church attendance to be permissible during times of impurity reached northern Europe through eighth-century compositions by the Venerable Bede (673–735):

> Apart from childbirth, women are forbidden from intercourse with their husbands during their ordinary periods. . . . Nevertheless a woman must not be prohibited from entering a church during her usual periods, for this natural overflowing cannot be reckoned a crime: and so it is not fair that she should be deprived from entering the church for that which she suffers unwillingly. . . . A woman ought not to be forbidden to receive the mystery of the Holy Communion at these times. If out of deep reverence she does not venture to receive it *that is praiseworthy. Let women make up their own minds*[117] and if they do not venture to approach the sacrament of the body and the blood of the Lord when in their periods, they are to be praised for their right thinking: but when as the results of the habits of a religious life, they are carried away by the love of the same mystery, they are not to be prevented, as we said before. . . . A man who had intercourse with his wife ought not enter the church unless he has washed himself, and even when washed he ought not to enter immediately. . . . A man then who, after intercourse with his wife has washed, is able to receive the mystery of the Holy Communion, since it is lawful for him, according to what has been said, to enter the church.[118]

The similarity between these teachings attributed to Gregory and Rashi's instructions, despite the centuries that divided them, is unmistakable. Both state that while pious menstruants were not required to refrain from public religious observances, their strict behavior was laudable. Moreover, the practice recommended for impure men—washing before entering the church—is based on a shared biblical foundation.[119] Despite Gregory's rejection of women remaining outside the church during their menstrual cycles, Christian communities maintained this practice for centuries. As Pierre Payer has remarked: "This is another example of Gregory's response to Augustine having little effect on the subsequent tradition in the medieval Church."[120] Gregory the Great's opinion was eventually accepted, but not until the thirteenth and fourteenth centuries.[121]

During the High Middle Ages, Christian authorities and leaders in northern European dissuaded menstruants from approaching the altar.[122]

For example, in his manual *De institutione laicali*, Jonah of Orléans (d. 844) praised women who refrained from going to church during their menstrual cycles, declaring a clean body and pure thoughts as prerequisites for entering church and participating in Mass. Jonah's discussion reveals that adherence to this custom depended on the women themselves and local norms. Burchard of Worms (d. 1025), in his manual *The Corrector*, prohibited post-partum women from entering church,[123] whereas he permitted menstruants to enter church but forbade their participation in Mass. With respect to impure men, these same authorities recommended that they wash prior to entering church and attending Mass.

C. Colt Anderson has recently outlined the centrality that themes of impurity and fear of pollution hold in instructions for medieval clergy and laity.[124] It is noteworthy that these discussions took place in the same regions where we have seen Jews debating them. Although Christian authorities arrived at conclusions that differed from those reached by their Jewish counterparts, the resonance between the discourses conducted by these two sets of religious leaders is significant.

Gratian (mid-twelfth century) was instrumental in promoting change when he adopted Gregory the Great's opinion and declared that women could attend church and participate fully in Mass during menstruation.[125] However, some thirteenth-century texts still caution that menstruants should not approach the altar.[126] Miramon has argued that during the thirteenth century it became more commonplace for menstruating women to receive communion, whereas limitations on access was transferred to post-partum purity. After childbirth, women were still required to wait several weeks before they could enter the church and undergo a purification ritual that marked their return to the community.[127] This focus on impurity in relation to childbirth allowed women who would not have children, namely members of female religious orders, to participate in Mass without interruptions caused by their menstrual cycles.

In the case of Christian men, especially religious leadership, Dyan Elliott's *Fallen Bodies* and other recent studies have outlined the heightened fear of male impurity among medieval priests and other religious authorities.[128] During the twelfth and thirteenth centuries, after the sanctification of male celibacy during the Gregorian Reform, the subject of nocturnal emissions was elevated in importance as theologians deliberated on matters of clerical purity.[129] Analogous to the Jewish sources examined earlier, although these issues had been discussed among Church leaders since late antiquity, the medieval preoccupation with impurity prompted a remarkable shift in discourse.[130] As Elliott has shown, the greatest attention was directed toward those who had taken vows of celibacy. The perils of impurity at Mass and among the clergy were of paramount concern.[131] Concerns for male impurity dominated this literature, which is hardly surprising since the authors were members of a celibate clerical elite that viewed sexuality with great anxiety.[132]

The attempts to remedy this danger took two principal forms. The first was a concerted effort to divert responsibility for nocturnal emissions from the clerics themselves. Demons, often disguised as women, were blamed for such occurrences. Elliott has argued that, as a result, women, femininity, and especially menstruants were depicted in negative terms, as menaces lurking in the shadows, ready to sully unsuspecting men. A second strategy for contending with the mounting fear of impurity advocated confession at the earliest opportunity after an incident occurred. The sin of a cleric who repented for his nocturnal emission was easily forgiven.[133]

Not only did impurity and access to the sacred represent core themes in Christian thought during the High Middle Ages; so, too, did ideas about purity and angels. As R. N. Swanson has noted, the desire to distance the clergy from physical impurity was rooted in the belief that priests should be "angels incarnate" or as close to angels as was humanly attainable. This underscored the impetus for priests to strive to resemble angels, in juxtaposition to women who were merely human.[134] As Jacqueline Murray has argued, the belief that men could more readily attain a sexless soul dominated twelfth- and thirteenth-century thinking. As in Judaism, angels in Christianity were believed to be asexual; therefore men were better positioned to approximate them.[135]

Jews, Christians, and Bodily Purity

The different threads presented in this chapter weave a medieval tapestry in which purity and impurity, in general and especially in sacred venues, are depicted as key concerns for Jewish and Christian societies. Each religious community discussed these subjects in light of earlier debates within their respective traditions. These communities articulated commonly held understandings of impurities using shared language, albeit from distinct perspectives. Although these commonalities were specific to Christian Europe in the Middle Ages, they were grounded in antique Judaism. While Jews and

Christians continued to debate and discuss menstrual impurity and seminal emissions, contrasting approaches and developments emerged: within medieval Jewish culture, menstruation and its correlated impurity became ever more central, whereas male impurity as well as the relationship between men and angels became a focus of Christian discussions.

It is noteworthy that the geographic scope of the trends and practices analyzed here can only partially be pieced together. While this chapter opens with a source that originated in northern France, the overwhelming majority of the evidence for Jewish practice comes from Germany. Despite this relatively sparse textual evidence, pronouncements concerning the importance of menstrual purity have been attested in contemporaneous writings by French Jews.[136]

An illustration of the Jewish emphasis on menstrual purity can be seen in *Sefer Rokeah*. Its author, Eleazar of Worms, introduced the section on *niddah* with a benediction: "Blessed are you, God of Israel, from this world to the next world, who has sanctified us with his commandments, separating us from impurity and cautioning us to beware of menstruants and (their) discharge."[137] This blessing was not recited liturgically or in relation to any practice. Rather, Eleazar of Worms used it as a rhetorical device in his writing to underscore the gravity of the topics being presented.[138] His decision to highlight the significance of menstrual purity in Jewish tradition and in his community, while simultaneously dividing those who adhered to these observances from those who didn't, mirrored popular sentiment among medieval Jews.

As noted, research by contemporary scholars—including Shaye Cohen, Alexandra Cuffel, Judith Baskin, and David Biale—have demonstrated the bond that tied observance of the laws of menstrual purity to Jewish identity in medieval Europe.[139] During the High Middle Ages, scrupulous adherence to menstrual purity came to be understood as a major tenet of the Jewish covenant with God. This principle is reflected in the medieval Jewish response to the classic question: If circumcision, an exclusively male ritual, is the defining sign of the covenant in Judaism, how do Jewish females qualify as members of the covenant? Medieval Jewish scholars departed from the traditional answer—that Jewish women belong to the covenant by association with the men in their families—by providing this novel response: "Since God commanded males (to be circumcised) but not females, we may deduce that God commanded that the covenant be sealed at the locus of masculinity, and the blood of menstruation that women observe so they can inform their husbands of the onset of their menstrual cycles is the equivalent of the blood of circumcision."[140]

This idea is stated in similar terms in *Sefer Nizzahon Vetus*, whose author explains that although Jewish women are not circumcised, they "are accepted [in the covenant] because they watch themselves and carefully observe the prohibitions connected with menstrual blood."[141] These sources suggest that the observance of menstrual purity was vital for Jewish communal identity.

In this vein, many modern scholars have presented medieval Jewish menstrual observances as so unique to Jewish religious culture that it precludes contextualization in a broad European cultural framework except as a symbol of Jewish-Christian difference. To the contrary, this chapter situates Jewish approaches to impurity—menstrual and otherwise—within the surrounding Christian society. From that perspective, the medieval Jewish focus on menstrual impurity may have emerged as a counterweight to the medieval Christian concerns about male impurity.[142]

I am neither positing that Christian discussions of these issues represent the sole impetus for Jewish preoccupation with them nor that Jewish concerns were primary motivating factors in Christian deliberations. Prior to this encounter in Ashkenaz, both Judaism and Christianity had well-established traditions regarding impurity in the *sancta* that originated in Leviticus and developed according to their respective trajectories over the centuries. I am suggesting, however, that medieval Jewish ideas and practices were reinforced by contact with Christians and knowledge of their customs. Jews and Christians lived in close proximity and Jewish households often employed Christian domestic workers.[143] It is likely that Jews knew when their neighbors and employees changed their patterns of church attendance since they saw them regularly enough to be familiar with their daily schedules. Given that Jewish and Christian women exchanged medical and especially gynecological knowledge, Jewish women could have easily heard about their peers' menstrual practices. Evidence indicates that Christian women also wore specific clothing while menstruating, although, unlike the Jewish women, they did not wear white when bleeding ceased.[144] One could say that a common "ritual instinct"[145] was at work in both societies, founded on common traditions that originated in the Bible and on shared cultural conceptions of blood and impurity.[146]

I propose that this comparative analysis can help explain the assertions in twelfth-century Jewish literature that liken the blood of menstruation to the blood of circumcision and describe it as a symbol of the covenant between God and the Jews. As a minority, Jews were distancing themselves from and defining themselves in contrast to Christian society. On some level, one may also see medieval Christian scholars as continuing on the paths of their spiritual ancestors by defining Christianity according to its divergence from the menstrual practices identified with Jewish tradition.[147]

Christians were aware of Jewish menstrual practices, which they regarded with ambivalence. For example, Christian theologians noted this aspect of Jewish purity when warning their congregants against having sexual relations during their wives' menstrual cycles. As Peter of Poitiers (ca. 1130–1215) wrote: "The Jews are rarely defiled by the stain of leprosy because they do not approach menstruating women."[148] Thus, Christians acknowledged this Jewish observance and held shared medical and religious beliefs concerning its merits. At the same time, contemporaneous Christian scholars were actively diverting discussions of women's impurity from menstruation to birth.

Jews were aware that Christians had fewer and less exacting rituals associated with menstruation, as evidenced by their pejorative term for Christian men, *boʿalei niddot* (those who have sexual relations with impure women). Moreover, in his instructions to Jewish men against having sexual contact with their menstruant wives, Eleazar of Worms not only warned his readers that any child born from such relations would contract leprosy,[149] but he also threatened that failure to observe the laws of niddah would lower their status to the level of their Christian neighbors: "For non-Jews have sexual relations with their wives while they are menstruating, as insects do, and that is why they are sent to hell." He concluded by stating that any man who had intercourse with his wife while she was menstruating should fast for two hundred and seventy days, be flogged on each of those days, and also give extra charity.[150]

In a cultural environment where managing impurity was a major concern and the anxiety associated with pollution was mounting,[151] Jews and Christians alike sought ways to sustain their purity while distinguishing themselves from one other. This competitive piety was manifest in the deeds of Jewish women and Christian men. It was also communicated in each group's accusations against the other: Jews claimed that Christians were harming themselves by neglecting the laws of niddah and Christians ridiculed Jewish men by depicting them as menstruants.[152]

Yet, despite their myriad differences, rabbis and priests shared a foundation that was based not only on a common biblical heritage but also on the beliefs and practices that permeated medieval northern Europe. Among their mutual values was an emerging desire among the male elite in each society to resemble angels, as attested in late medieval writings. This aspiration was part of a self-reinforcing hierarchical ethos: the male leadership in both religions agreed on women's roles and their inferiority to men.

While holding certain shared beliefs and practices, Jews and Christians also defined themselves vis-à-vis each other. We have seen the centrality of bodily purity in settings for communal prayer, the church and the synagogue. In the Jewish context, we have traced the avoidance of synagogue prayer during menstruation from its inception as a practice that was initiated by pious women to its adoption by religious leaders and its establishment as a standard practice in Jewish society. Customs related to male impurity never became widespread among Jews. Among Christians, we have examined the development of inverse priorities: male impurity became the prime focus whereas concern for menstrual purity was dismissed as a Jewish matter. While it is impossible to study the full range of connections between learned and lay practice and the interactions between Jewish and Christian thought and custom, this discussion confirms gender as a fulcrum point for both dialogue and displaying difference.[153]

Visible Piety, Visible Practice

By way of returning our attention to how medieval Jews practiced piety over and above their thinking about purity and impurity as abstract concepts, let us revisit the men and women whose concerns about purity led them to contend with their physicality and their beliefs. Ultimately, menstrual blood and seminal discharges are inseparable from the reality of each individual body. In contemporary societies, such matters belong to the private sphere without necessarily impinging on public knowledge. In the medieval world, at least for those who adhered to the instructions of religious authorities, these issues were far from personal. In the Christian world, men and women were supposed to admit impurity to their confessors. Where it was customary for men and women who were ritually impure to avoid coming to church or approaching the altar during Mass, presumably clerics and laity could readily surmise why women would cyclically distance themselves from attending Mass and taking the Eucharist.[154] In another sign of constant vigilance toward impurity, church seating was separated by gender to quell lust.[155]

As we have seen, menstrual status was also readily visible within Jewish culture. Furthermore, since it was not customary for women to go to the mikveh alone, at least some peers would witness a woman's visit and know whether she was ritually pure or impure.[156] During the High Middle Ages, limitations on a menstruant's activities were augmented in both the domestic and public realms. In addition to refraining from synagogue attendance and from physical contact with their husbands—from the mundane sharing of utensils to the intimacy of sexual intercourse—women would cease to cook and bake at this time as well.[157] We have also seen that women donned white clothes on "white days," and some of their peers would adjust their seating in synagogue to avoid praying behind menstruants. These actions would all have provided communal knowledge of each woman's level of purity.[158] Such tangible evidence explains how medieval scholars could warn their followers about the dangers inherent to gazing at menstruants.[159] In short, menstrual purity was as much a communal affair as a personal and marital responsibility, since the purity of the entire community depended on women's painstaking observance of these rules. From one angle, it could be claimed that women performed purity rituals for their husbands' sakes[160] so that piety insofar as it was linked to menstruation was bound to both women and men. And, returning to our opening theme, the synagogue was a primary location where information regarding purity was conveyed.

Considering this examination of the commonalities and differences expressed among Jews and Christians, one can understand how personal purity came to reflect the holiness of the Jewish community to such an extent that medieval rabbis identified niddah as the defining symbol of the Jewish people and Jewish women's covenant with God, and how women's observance of ritual purity came to represent Jewish distinctiveness.[161] The (male) leaders of Jewish communities were using menstrual purity, which they viewed as inherently Jewish, to emphasize the singularity of Jewish practice and, to a certain extent, as a counterpoint to celibacy, a salient element of Christian identity. As a result, in a world where impurity was often associated with sexual relations and corporeality, menstrual purity was a defining factor for Jewish society as a whole. Thus pious Jewish women were commended for immersing in the mikveh at the earliest permissible time even if their husbands were out of town and, consequently, sexual relations would necessarily be delayed. This scenario is illustrated in the writings of Peretz b. Elijah, who recorded that the daughter of Isaac of Evreux (who was also known for his piety) was so strict in her observance that she immersed in the mikveh at her first opportunity, even when her husband was traveling.[162]

By framing menstruation as a covenantal sign, medieval rabbis intensified and perpetuated the position of women's purity relative to their husbands and to Jewish society. This served to diminish the already marginal role that women held in communal prayer.[163] Gender roles, domestic responsibilities, and the laws of menstruation converge in relation to the topic of whether men should instruct and supervise their female relatives on purity practices, an issue that arises with fair regularity in this geographic region. It is hardly surprising that Judah the Pious and other medieval rabbis suggested that fathers teach their daughters the laws of niddah rather than entrust their wives with this sacred obligation.[164]

Ironically, a logistical question embedded in this study remains virtually untouched: Throughout these discussions of women remaining outside the synagogue, precisely which architectural structure were they avoiding? The lack of data on this seemingly basic question characterizes the sources available from the Jewish community in this region and time period. Excavations from medieval cities (e.g., Cologne, Worms, Speyer, and others) have pointed to an archaeological feature that appears to have been innovated during the High Middle Ages, a *frauenschul* (a women's synagogue) in the form of a separate prayer space adjacent to the main sanctuary.[165] Evidence from other communities, such as Prague, also points to synagogues with galleries for women's prayers that were adjacent to the main sanctuary, while other locations, such as Regensburg and Erfurt, had no such area. Are such women's synagogues the physical setting for textual descriptions of limitations on entering synagogues? Furthermore, did these constraints apply to all menstruants in the Jewish community? Were women without husbands, namely widows and divorced women, expected to perform the public aspects of the laws of niddah? Or did these practices only apply to married women? These more nuanced questions are not addressed in medieval rabbinic sources. Archaeological excavations from urban sites in Germany reveal that ritual baths (mikvaot) were first built in many communities from the late twelfth to the late thirteenth century, almost always beside the synagogue.[166] These findings contribute to our understanding of pious practice in Ashkenaz during this era, since such structural remains offer yet another indication of a growing communal concern with purity.

Thus, we see that during the twelfth and thirteenth centuries, a process that began with rigorous ritual observance by a few women led to the absence of menstruants from the synagogue. As women's practice of menstrual restrictions became defining aspects of female Jewish identity and Jewish communal purity, women were increasingly distanced from the institutional and geographic center of their community. What began as a personal expression of piety became a justification for the marginalization of women in the synagogue.

However, the intensification of these restrictions did not necessarily preclude menstruants from approaching the synagogue vicinity or block their knowledge of communal life within its walls. On the contrary, the imposition of physical distance may have elevated women's awareness of synagogue activities and their longing to return. The exclusion of women from the synagogue during their times of impurity may have accentuated the centrality of the synagogue in medieval Jewish life.

A number of medieval sources refer to women attending synagogue services during the week, on the Sabbath, and on holidays. In one responsum, Rashi tells of a woman whose servant came to synagogue, beckoning her Jewish employer to leave services so they could discuss an urgent matter.[167] So, too, Isaac b. Abraham (Ritzba, twelfth century) tells of a woman who initiated the procedure of "interrupting of services" to present a claim against her purportedly impotent husband, which the community could then address.[168]

The sources suggest that women, like men, attended daily and festival synagogue services, although such descriptions are always in the context of specific events rather than as a normative or expected practice. Fusing synagogue etiquette and piety, *Sefer Hasidim* reprimands men and women who arrive late for services or leave early, and praises those who are present throughout by promising that such devotion will ensure them respectable places in heaven.[169] Comparing the instructions for men at prayer in *Sefer Hasidim* with the eulogy that Eleazar of Worms composed about his wife, Dulcia, we see that she is described as having fulfilled many of those observances.[170] Dulcia attended prayers (coming early and staying late) and recited additional psalms and petitions, including some that were particular to Hasidei Ashkenaz. Dulcia also led women in prayer and taught liturgical prayers to her female peers. Her presence in the synagogue was an expression of her personal devotion, which went beyond her participation in daily and holiday practice to include preparing wicks for synagogue candles and standing throughout all prayers on Yom Kippur.[171]

One could discount the abundant pious practices attributed to Dulcia as unrepresentative if such descriptions did not also appear on numerous epitaphs from the Middle Ages and the early modern period. Tombstones memorialize women with descriptions of their piety (e.g., praying with great devotion, arriving early for synagogue services, and praying with a positive and pious attitude).[172] Yemima Hovav has shown that remarks on piety in connection to prayers were distributed quite evenly among epitaphs for men and women during the early modern period.[173]

Given the textual evidence that attests to women's participation in synagogue life, the rabbinic instruction that women absent themselves from this vital institution during menstruation underscores the prioritization of female purity over other expressions of piety. In contrast, Jewish men's concerns about their own purity did not diminish rabbinic advocacy of their synagogue attendance. Rather, medieval writers emphasized that men should pray in private and attend synagogue prayers without interruption despite their state of impurity. By comparison, irrespective of their high level of participation in synagogue prayer, women's access to the sacred was ever more constricted by their status with respect to impurity during the High Middle Ages.

CHAPTER 2

Jewish Fasting and Atonement in a Christian Context

> I knew that Jews and Christians did not observe the same rules of fasting.
> —Herman-Judah, *A Short Account*, 92, ll. 1128–29

As the previous chapter demonstrated, pious practices were often linked to precise times and places. This chapter further examines pious practices as they related to eating and abstaining from food, with a specific focus on fasting. Just as culinary norms—what is eaten; when, where, and with whom; and, of course, how food is prepared—constitute individual and communal understandings of belonging, belief, and status, so too fasting serves to signify social and religious identity in all cultures.[1]

During the past century, anthropologists have assessed the many roles that food plays in communal and self-definition,[2] and they have also demonstrated the dynamic nature of these symbols.[3] The phenomena that have been elucidated by this research are hardly limited to modernity; they were manifested in pre-modern life and religion as well. Jewish dietary laws offer a prime example of practices whose constant elements and changing factors have been studied in great detail. These precepts were initially set forth in the Bible and continued to develop through late antiquity and the Middle Ages according to each era and location, ever integrating local realities while preserving ancient traditions. Within the Jewish community, dietary practices cultivated a preoccupation with food and bound the acts of preparing and eating meals within the group.[4] In each generation and setting, these instructions effectively separated Jews from their non-Jewish neighbors.

The significance of fasting for medieval Jews was not dissimilar to the meanings imbued in culinary practices, and in many ways refraining from food and drink complemented dietary regulations. The roles of food and fasting in daily rituals and in rhythms of commemoration and celebration are among the primary building blocks of any religious community, fostering a shared sense of purpose and belonging.[5] These patterns affected relations between medieval Jews and Christians, who observed individual and communal fasts at different times of year.[6]

The practice of fasting connected the body and its physical needs with less tangible values, such as self-denial and repentance.[7] Rituals performed by individual bodies are often attributed to the social body as well, thus reflecting the community as a whole.[8] By definition, fasting was conducted on a personal level by each individual who practiced this ritual; in the case of collective fasts, hunger and self-denial were simultaneously individual and communal experiences. Since communal fasts were accompanied by public rituals (e.g., prayer services with related liturgical content), these experiences were internally and externally based for a community and its members. Fasting can thus provide a window onto individual and collective practice.[9]

This chapter seeks to outline Jewish fasting practices in medieval Ashkenaz in terms of communal and personal piety alongside notions of repentance and atonement (*teshuvah*) that developed during the High Middle Ages. In this analysis of sources on fasting, close attention is given to the particularities of the practice itself, including the treatment of both men and women, as well as to gender as a determining factor in the significance ascribed to fasting.[10] In light of the abundant scholarship on fasting and penance in medieval Christian Europe,[11] this study assesses Jewish fasting practices in the context of fasting among medieval Christians.[12]

My discussion of medieval Jewish fasting within Christian contexts is founded on three assumptions. First, although fasting has held a central role in nearly all religions and confidence in its efficacy has remained cogent over time, the precise modes of fasting are particular to each religion and vary relative to the others. In fact, religious communities distinguished themselves from one another in many ways, most notably here via their distinct ritual calendars and their interpretations of fasting as reflected by their own ideals and beliefs. These differences honed the identities of those who fasted even when they participated in a general practice that transcended the particularities of their own community (e.g., by fasting during a drought).

Secondly, no special designation or officially conferred status serves as a prerequisite for pious fasting. This point has far-reaching implications for the accessibility of this pious practice in its medieval context: fasting did not

Figure 4. A community fasting. © Staats- und Universitätsbibliothek Hamburg. Cod. Heb. 37, fol. 153r, detail. Siddur, fifteenth century.

require specialized knowledge or publicly recognized stature, nor was it hierarchically controlled or determined, although rabbis and Christian clergy had a role in instructing when and even how fasts should be conducted. Each individual, whether learned or uneducated, could fast as an act of devotion. Neither was this custom geographically or logistically restrictive: one could fast at home, in the church, or on the road. These qualities render fasting a readily accessible expression of piety.

Finally, a comment on the broader medieval cultural landscape is in order. As is well known, Islam advocated fasting in a manner that resembles Judaism and Christianity. Goitein and others have compared Jewish fasts to parallel customs among Muslims and Christians.[13] A presentation of practical and conceptual comparisons between Jewish and Muslim fasting extends beyond the scope of this study which focuses on the Jewish and Christian praxes only.

Jewish Fasting in Late Antiquity

Since medieval Jewry cannot be fully understood without an awareness of earlier Jewish practices and norms, I lay the groundwork for our examination of medieval Ashkenazic fasting by surveying the practices among Jews in antiquity.[14] Starting with the Bible, ancient Jewish texts discuss fasting in various contexts, the most prominent being Yom Kippur (Lev. 16), the day designated for the atonement of sin.[15] The Bible emphasizes self-denial as a central component of the Day of Atonement, "made for you to cleanse you of all your sins" (Lev. 16:30), a day "when atonement (*kapparah*) takes place" (Lev. 23:28). The Bible also presents fasting as a primary means of expressing submission and devotion to God, preparing for contact with the Divine, and responding to critical situations.[16] Critiques of fasting are also included in the biblical text, as frequent fasting sometimes evoked disapproval from prophets who argued against outward displays of piety if they were not accompanied by comparable inner reverence.[17] It is noteworthy that these exhortations against fasting are rarely referenced in medieval Ashkenazic sources.[18]

Late antique sources, among them Tractate Ta'anit, discuss communal and individual fasts. Besides longstanding annual fasts like Yom Kippur and Tish'ah beAv (the day that commemorates the destruction of the Temples), communal fasts responded to crises—with drought being the classic example from antiquity. The Mishnah and the Talmud each delineate clear and graduated procedures at those times, beginning with fasts by community leaders and progressing in intensity and inclusiveness until the entire community participated.[19]

Individuals also fasted for a range of personal reasons during that period.[20] Two common motivations that led people to fast were the hope of neutralizing an omen envisioned in a threatening dream (*ta'anit halom*)[21] and the desire to honor a parent's memory on the anniversary of his or her death.[22] Some Jews fasted at critical times in the calendar cycle: specifically during Elul and Adar, the months that precede the High Holidays and Passover, respectively.[23] Further substantiation that fasting had become widespread appears in *Megillat Ta'anit*, which lists the days when fasting was not permitted.[24] Such instructions would not have been necessary if fasting were not practiced extensively.

Numerous talmudic discussions consider the reasons for fasting and its efficacy, as Eliezer Diamond discusses at length in his study of ascetic fasting in the Talmud.[25] In his presentation of the dilemmas associated with frequent fasting, Diamond demonstrates that some rabbis cast this practice in a positive light, as exemplified in a passage in Tractate Berakhot that records personal prayers that certain rabbis would add to their recitation of communal liturgy. On fast days, Sheshet was reputed to include these words:

> Sovereign of the Universe, You know full well that when the Temple was standing, when a man sinned, he would bring a sacrifice and even though only its fat and blood was given as an offering, atonement was granted to him. Now, having fasted, my own fat and blood are reduced. May it be Your will to reckon the diminishment of my fat and blood as if I had offered them on the altar before You, so You will favor me.[26]

The power of fasting is also emphasized by the third-century amora Eleazar b. Pedat: "Fasting is more efficacious than charity . . . for the former is performed with a man's money, but the latter with his body."[27] However, Eleazar is quick to clarify that prayer is the preferred way to reach God.

Amram Tropper has suggested that some Jews, particularly in the intellectual strata of society, adopted fasting as a form of self-discipline during the Second Temple period as one aspect of their embrace of Hellenic ideals and ideas.[28] Diamond also describes holy men in the talmudic period who fasted in an effort to fortify their reputation for piety.[29] While men are depicted in the majority of antique Jewish sources that mention individual fasts, this should not be taken to imply that women did not fast. Rather, this rhetorical pattern suggests that in a society where men represented the norm, women were aggregated into the general community so did not merit special mention.

The talmudic descriptions of women fasting can be divided into two categories. Most focus on mandatory communal fasts, such as Yom Kippur, discussing whether pregnant and nursing women are required to participate and clarifying their responsibilities.[30] In the remaining texts, women who fast are featured in anecdotal passages. This vignette from the Palestinian Talmud, which appears in numerous medieval texts, is a fair exemplar:[31] "Once a righteous man traveled to the netherworld, where he saw a woman named Miriam hanging by her ear from the hinge of hell's door[32] because 'she fasted and announced her fast publicly.'"[33]

This passage raises questions regarding the appropriate behaviors involved in fasting. According to the instructions outlined in the Talmud, abstaining from food was but one aspect of this practice. Fasting required intention and forethought.³⁴ In preparation, it was necessary to articulate one's commitment to taking on a fast during the afternoon prayer service that preceded the fast (which began, with the Jewish calendar day, at sunset).³⁵ That declaration seems to have been made silently, therefore privately, during communal prayers. Personal fasting was also accompanied by symbolic actions (e.g., wearing sackcloth) that were visible to the community.³⁶ Thus late antique sources indicate that even individual fasts incorporated public rituals, since abstaining from food was signaled by mode of dress, not only by absence from communal meals.³⁷

Scholarly discussions of biblical and late antique sources are characterized by debates on whether ideas of repentance and atonement are found in premedieval texts and by investigations of the social identity of Jews who fasted frequently. As we have seen, the Bible mentions self-denial (*inui nefesh*) and atonement.³⁸ While these texts affirm the early roots of these practices, they also invite questions: How was atonement defined in late antiquity? Had fasting been conceptualized as a form of repentance yet? Over thirty years ago, Moshe Beer published a short article that engages with that second query. Having examined evidence from a range of pseudo-epigraphic sources (from the final centuries BCE to the early centuries CE) on penitential practices of that time, Beer observes that these texts address remorse (*haratah*) rather than teshuvah per se. According to his analysis, prayer, charity, and extreme fasting were practiced by members of the general population but not by the elite, for when hints of these practices make their way into talmudic discussions, they are ridiculed or dismissed as often as not. Since his article first appeared, Beer's major conclusions have been supported by further research.³⁹

Let us return to Miriam who publicized her fasts, according to the Palestinian Talmud. Why was she criticized? We see that the talmudic discussant also wondered about this, for he provides further details: first informing us that she described her fast inaccurately, then explaining the implications of her misdeed. By exaggerating her actions, she gave the impression of being more pious than she actually was.⁴⁰ Thus, this Miriam was criticized for overstating her observance, not for fasting.

Other tales of fasting in the Talmud demonstrate that the practice and significance of intensive fasting occupied rabbinic scholars in late antiquity, without arriving at univocal conclusions. Some saw excessive fasting as harmful and undesirable, whereas others declared its practitioners as "holy."⁴¹ A consistent division in perspective emerges between sages in Babylon and Palestine: the Babylonians rabbis seem to have discouraged fasting, at least indirectly, in that many public fasts were not observed in their communities, whereas their Palestinian peers appear to have promoted and praised fasting.[42] These contrasting attitudes surface most notably in discussions of fasting on the Sabbath and holidays, especially fasting on Rosh haShanah, a custom that was rejected in Babylon but practiced quite widely in Palestine.[43] Despite the differences between these two centers, it can be concluded that many Jews in late antiquity fasted regularly and that this practice was generally interpreted as a sign of devotion and piety.

Christian Fasting in Late Antiquity and the Middle Ages

Fasting was also a central practice in late antique Christianity, having developed from the foundations it shared with Judaism. Theresa Shaw has detailed fasting practices in late antiquity by emphasizing the connection between fasting and asceticism,[44] with special attention to the link between fasting and virginity. In her textual analysis, Shaw presents individuals who sought to achieve the highest level of holiness possible and, as part of that pursuit, retreated from the everyday practices of most Christians and from urban society.[45]

Fasting was neither exclusive to individuals who adopted ascetic practices, nor was it necessarily taken to extreme forms of observance. For many Christians weekly fasting was part of their religious routine, reflecting the long-held belief that fasting was pleasing to God. Fasting was one of a trio of deeds that included prayer and charity that Church fathers saw as central to all religious practice. Indeed, late antique texts commonly assert that prayer is strengthened when accompanied by fasting and giving alms.[46] One of these practices was at times substituted for the other.

In medieval Europe, the role of fasting in Christianity gained significant meaning as a symbol of religious status. Caroline Bynum and André Vauchez each demonstrate the centrality of fasting for the most pious Christians, as exemplified by daily life in various religious orders.[47] Bynum's study of the fasts undertaken by radical ascetics in the High Middle Ages brought scholarly attention to gender as a distinguishing factor in fasting norms and habits and, more broadly, to the significance of food in medieval piety.[48] Vauchez's research on sainthood emphasizes that perfection was measured by the degree of austerity practiced with regard to food, such as the length of fasts and the intensity of privations that were grounded in the belief that fasting provided a mechanism for denying the physical world and dedicating oneself to God.

This view of fasting among candidates for sainthood and canonized saints pervades the observations of their deeds, as noted by witnesses and recorded by hagiographers.[49] Both Bynum and Vauchez and others who followed them have demonstrated that displays of abstinence represented a valuable form of social capital that religious leaders leveraged to assert their place in the societal hierarchy. Thus the vitas of bishops commonly detail their acts of fasting, prayer, and charity.[50]

Medieval Christian society was also home to individuals who took on public penance, whose observances were marked by wearing special shirts or robes and fasting more frequently than the general population. Many (but not all) of them committed themselves to celibacy[51] and joined religious orders. No less significantly, moderate fasting and refraining from select foods were so commonly practiced in medieval Europe that they can reasonably be described as routine for clergy and laity alike.[52] These practices stemmed from a culture of penance that endorsed self-denial as a path to salvation.

Medieval Christian worshipers fasted on communally recognized occasions, in accordance with the annual calendar cycle, and as individual and social circumstances prompted: for instance, three-day communal fasts were often undertaken in preparation for special religious celebrations, such as the authentication of a relic or the dedication of a cathedral;[53] the entire community would fast throughout Lent and at other designated times, such as Ember and Rogation days; and individuals took on volitional fasts in response to events in their lives, such as an illness or a death in the family, as well as at times of danger and warfare.[54] A recent study estimates that the average Christian abstained from selected foods or fasted 220–240 days per year,[55] attesting to the ubiquity of this practice during the medieval period.[56]

As this survey shows, fasting was a fundamental religious practice in the Christian society in which medieval European Jews lived. It seems noteworthy for the consideration of medieval Jewish fasting that medieval Christian sources present their practices at odds with Jewish ones. Let us consider a text that situates our investigation of Jewish practice in its medieval Christian environs. In June 1239, Pope Gregory IX (d. 1241) sent a letter containing thirty-five accusations against the Talmud—presented as the causes of Jews' blind refusal to embrace Christianity[57]—to the Bishop of Paris and many other Christian authorities throughout Europe. The content of that papal dispatch was based on Gregory's conversations with Nicholas Donin, a convert from Judaism, who was appointed to deliver the document to Church officials.

Donin subsequently served as the lead prosecutor in the 1240 disputation against the Talmud that resulted in its burning in 1244.[58]

One topic in that letter from 1239 stands out for its seeming lack of connection to the broader charges levied therein. According to accusation #33, the Talmud declares that anyone who fasts is a sinner:

> "And all who fast are considered sinners." This is read in Seder Mo'ed, in the first chapter of Tractate Ta'anit, where it is said: Samuel said: "Whosoever sits in fast is called a sinner, since we read this about the Nazarite: 'And make expiation on his behalf for the guilt that he incurred through the corpse.'" And we read that Eleazar haKappar said: "What does 'And make expiation' mean? Against which soul did he sin? It means that [he incurred guilt because] he denied himself by abstaining from wine. Certainly we can reason, inferring from a minor assertion to a major one, that if this man who only denied himself wine is called a sinner, how much the more so one who denies himself enjoyment of ever so many things.[59]

This allegation is an almost verbatim citation from Tractate Ta'anit 11a in the Babylonian Talmud. However, a close reading of this passage in its original context quickly reveals that the pope and his counsel, Nicholas, were quoting selectively. This talmudic discussion continues with Eleazar taking the opposite position by claiming that one who fasts is holy, which concurs with the stance that the pope ascribes to Christianity.[60]

Why was this talmudic quotation (albeit taken out of context) inserted in this papal communiqué? Chen Merchavia reads its inclusion as a protest against a perceived attack on Christian fasting customs, especially those practiced by monks, whose position was seen by Christians as analogous to the biblical Nazarites. The charge that the Talmud equates fasting with sin was meant to highlight the absurdity of Jewish practice as exemplified by the Jewish miscomprehension of this key Christian ritual. This claim also provided an opportunity, in the spirit of Jerome, to condemn Jews of being excessively materialistic and, as a result, unable to put their spiritual interests over their carnal needs.[61] In that cultural environment, the inclusion of an accusation against the alleged Jewish condemnation of fasting in a papal writ stresses the significance of fasting as a spiritual and tangible mode of devotion to God.

In order to contextualize this accusation, let us turn to the Jews of medieval Ashkenaz to examine the role of fasting in their religious practice.

Jewish Fasting in Medieval Europe

The influence of the late antique heritage of fasting in Jewish communities seems to have faded somewhat over the centuries that followed, for the Ge'onim did not emphasize the value or practice of fasting. While ge'onic writings indicate that major fasts were maintained, consistent with earlier generations of the Babylonian schools of thought, they prohibited fasting on the Sabbath and other holidays, especially prior to Rosh haShanah and on a second day of Yom Kippur. Fasting an additional day for Yom Kippur was a late antique custom that was often reproved but that persisted throught the medieval period. Judai Ga'on (d. 761) notes that this period is known as the "Ten Days of Repentance" (*aseret yemei teshuvah*), not the "Ten Days of Fasting." He questions what might have inspired a tendency to fast during these days. Similar views are attributed to Hai Ga'on (d. 1038).[62] Nevertheless, these opinions represent points on a spectrum that extended from endorsement of fasts to discouragement from this practice, and it is evident that some people did fast during these times.[63] As for fasting on the Sabbath following bad dreams, the Ge'onim condoned the practice only after truly menacing ones.[64]

These heterogeneous stances toward fasting in Babylonian sources may explain why the lists of fast days that have reached us from the ge'onic period are less elaborate than their medieval parallels.[65] These distinctions should not be mistaken for a claim that medieval Jews living in Islamic societies did not fast; however, Jewish fasting practices in Muslim lands deserve consideration within their cultural context as well as a detailed comparison to Muslim practice, a topic for future consideration.

As we shift our focus from Babylon to Europe, it is important to acknowledge that medieval Ashkenazic Jews were well aware of Babylonian halakhic trends and instructions.[66] In her recent book *Lama tzamnu?* (Wherefore have we fasted?),[67] Shulamit Elizur traces the history of *Megillat Ta'anit Batra*. This text first appeared in eighth-century Babylon under the title *Sefer Halakhot Gedolot*; it was copied widely then ultimately renamed and appended to *Megillat Ta'anit*. *Megillat Ta'anit Batra* enumerates fasts that were observed on dates that Jews have historically associated with biblical events (e.g., the deaths of Miriam, Aaron, Moses, and Joshua) and on post-biblical milestones, such as the day when the Greek translation of the Bible was completed. Elizur focuses on textual transmission rather than actual or presumed practices. Even though this list originated in early medieval Babylon, it is significant that it was copied and circulated most extensively in twelfth- and thirteenth-century Ashkenaz; indeed, custom books from medieval Ashkenaz attest that at least some of these fasts were observed.[68]

Although our earliest (eleventh century) sources from Ashkenaz bear no mention of widespread fasting, as other scholars have remarked, many prominent community leaders and scholars from that time in both Germany and northern France describe fasting as a regular component of their annual observances. Most notably, Rashi's teachers, Judah b. Barukh (eleventh century) and Isaac b. Eliezer haLevi (ca. 1000–1080) in Worms, fasted for two days in observance of Yom Kippur, a practice that the Ge'onim had discouraged.[69] Other leading German rabbis, such as the twelfth-century scholars Eliezer b. Joel haLevi (Ra'aviah) and his younger contemporary, Judah the Pious, also fasted for two days of Yom Kippur. Ra'aviah wrote about individuals who abstained from meat for the three-week period before the fast on the Ninth of Av, more than doubling the normative nine-day restriction.[70] We have additional evidence of leading twelfth-century rabbis in northern France who fasted regularly.[71] Isaac b. Samuel of Dampierre (known as R"I, ca. 1100–ca.1178) is known to have fasted almost every Sunday, Monday, and Thursday, as well as on personally selected days;[72] Isaac b. Joseph of Corbeil was also known for his asceticism. At critical times in the year, such as the Sabbath before Yom Kippur, some texts suggest that only prominent scholars were qualified to fast.[73]

These intensive fasting practices linked to the Jewish calendar—such as fasting on the Sabbath, on Rosh haShanah, on two days for Yom Kippur, throughout the Ten Days of Repentance, for the fast of the firstborn preceding Passover,[74] and during the months of Av and Elul[75]—all have late antique precedents. In medieval Ashkenaz, the fasting practices that Babylonian authorities sought to curtail seem to have emerged with renewed rigor.[76] For example, Eleazar of Worms explained that fasting on Rosh haShanah was commendable since it was inappropriate to feast when the Lord's table was empty. His comment suggests that fasts were food for God, recalling the sacrificial dimension of fasting we noted above.[77] In the late thirteenth century, Samson b. Tzadok

סליחות לשני וחמישי ושני · ולשאר תענית ציבור

אבינו מלכנו כי כרוב אויליתנו אין לנו שגינו מחול לנו מלכנו כי רבו
עונינו · אל ארך אפים אתה ובעל הרחמים
וגדולת תשובה הוריתה וגדולת רחמיך וחסדיך תזכור היום
ובכל יום לזרע ידידיך · תפן אלינו ברחמים כי אתה הוא
בעל הרחמים · בתחנונים ובתפילה לפניך נקדם כהורעת לענו
מקדם · מחרון אפך שוב כמו שכתוב בתורתך · ובצל כנפיך
נחסה ונתלונן כיום וירד יי בענן · תעביר על פשע ותמחה
אשם כיום ויתיצב עמו שם · תאזין שועתינו ותקשיב מנו
מאמר · כיום ויקרא בשם יי ושם נאמר ·

ויעבר יי על פניו ויקרא יי יי אל רחום וחנון ארך אפים
ורב חסד ואמת נוצר חסד לאלפים נושא עון ופשע וחטאה ונקה ·

וסלחת לעוננו ולחטאתנו ונחלתנו · סלח לנו
אבינו כי חטאנו מחול לנו מלכנו כי
פשענו · כי אתה יי טוב וסלח ורב חסד לכל קוראיך ·

Figure 5. Prayers for Monday and Thursday fasts. © The Bodleian Libraries, Oxford University. MS. Mich. 569 (1098), fol. 49a. Siddur, thirteenth century.

exclaimed wistfully: "If only all of Israel would fast on Rosh haShanah!"[78] Medieval Ashkenazic rabbis were supporting practices that were commonplace in late antique Palestinian texts, even though Babylonian sources were in greater circulation in Germany and northern France.[79]

The inventory of fasts related to the annual calendar provided a baseline to which individual and ritual fasts were added. Whereas Jews in late antiquity fasted Mondays and Thursdays[80] as part of their supplication for rain, medieval European Jews in northern France and Germany modified that practice to fasting on Mondays and Thursdays during Iyar and Heshvan, which reflects the lesser dependence on seasonal rains in their locales.[81] In addition, the medieval Ashkenazic pattern of fasting also included the whole month of Elul and the Ten Days of Repentance (forty consecutive days).[82] Moreover, fasting on Mondays and Thursdays during the *shovavim* (designated weeks in winter) became customary in medieval Ashkenaz.[83] This practice was ritualized by a blessing that was recited on the Sabbath prior to a Monday-Thursday-Monday fasting series: "May the One who blessed our ancestors, Abraham, Isaac and Jacob, bless this community that commits itself to fasting on Mondays, Thursdays and Mondays and to attending this synagogue every morning and evening. May God (*haMakom*) hear their prayers, accept their fasts, and save and redeem them from all hardship and adversity together with all of Israel. Amen."[84]

In medieval prayer books (*siddurim*), this prayer[85] sometimes appears with the word "individual" (*yahid*) as a gloss or inserted in the text, an indication that although these fasts were fixed in the calendar, they were exercised by individual choice rather than communal obligation.[86] If more than ten men fasted on a single day, the liturgy was augmented with a special Torah reading and liturgical poetry (*piyyutim*). The inclusion of collected liturgical poems in medieval prayer books signals that they were regularly recited.[87] Furthermore, fasting was often complemented by charitable contributions.[88]

Ominous events also prompted communal fasts. Numerous reports of responses to peril describe the entire community fasting at such times, including children and sometimes even toddlers. The following account of the Jews of Trier in 1096 serves as an example:

> And in those days, they fasted many times and abstained; they atoned and gave charity. They fasted for six weeks, day by day, from Passover until Shavuot, and every evening they scattered coins for the poor. They were taxed four times and for each libra

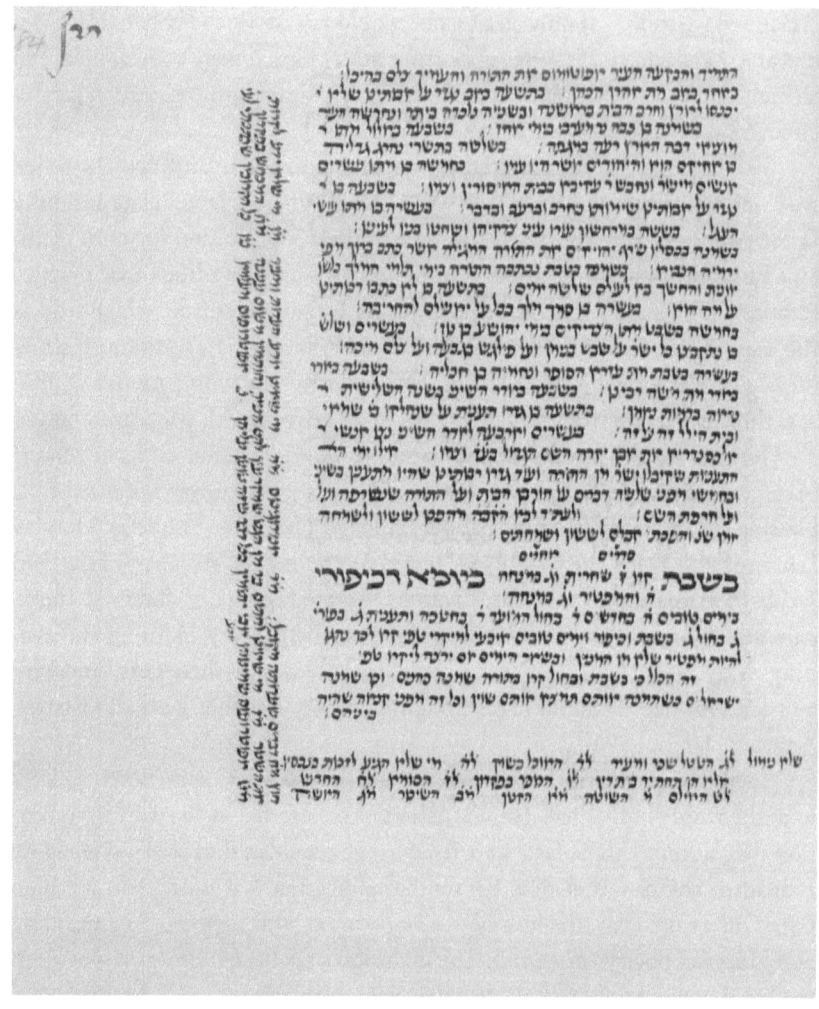

Figure 6. List of fasts. From *North French Miscellany*. © The British Library Board. Ms Add. 11639, fols. 683v, 684r. Northern France, late thirteenth century.

of tax payment, they gave a denarius for protection. When that was not sufficient (payment for protection), the bribes multiplied until they had given all of their property, even the shawls[89] on their shoulders.[90]

Other communities fasted when they were under attack and during various commemorations.[91] For example, a well-known description of the Blois Affair

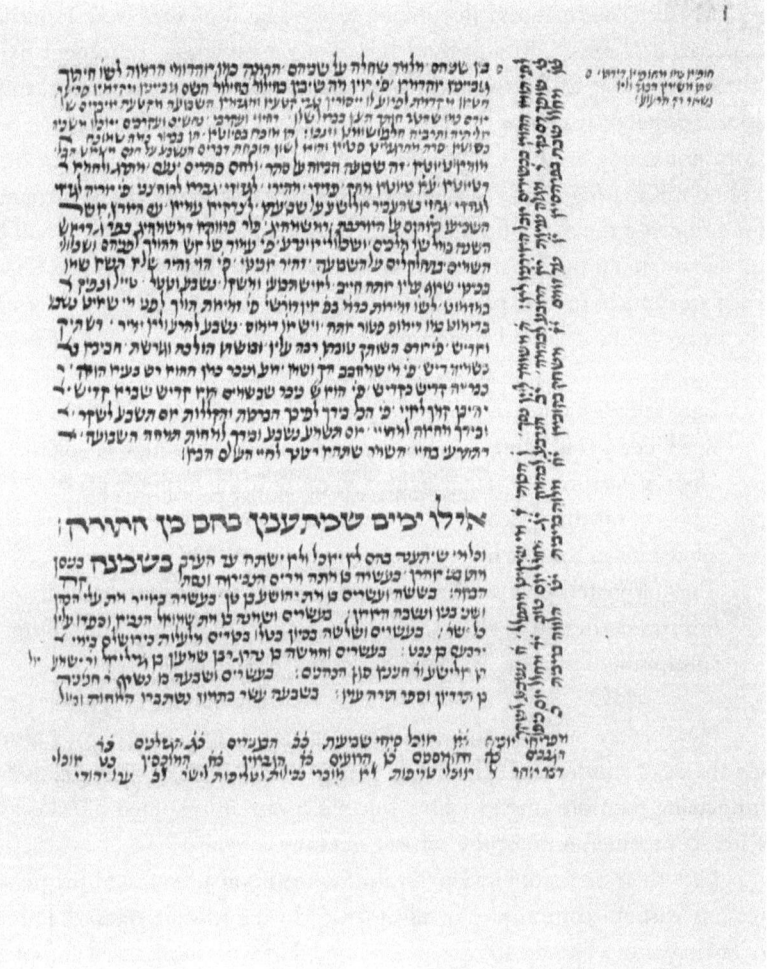

of 1171 concludes by stating that the Jewish communities of France and the Rhine all established that day as "a day of mourning and fasting, as a result of their own desire and the instructions of our rabbi, the Ga'on, Jacob b. Meir (Rabbenu Tam, ca. 1100–1171)—who wrote books informing them that it was fitting to designate this as a fast day for our entire people, a fast that will surpass the fast of Gedalyah b. Ahikam in importance because it is a Day of Atonement."[92] The institution of commemorative fasts continued throughout the Middle Ages, as when the Talmud was burned and during the Black Death.[93]

Medieval sources also document communal fasts that were induced by concerns and sensibilities beyond the calendar cycle and imminent danger. These fasts point to motivations from self-discipline and self-torment to penance. Textual instructions for fasting illustrate the many ways to observe a fast, from not eating at all to partaking of specific foods refraining from others. Ephraim Kanarfogel has analyzed a fascinating community fast as preparation for conjuring the soul of a dead man. In response to a father who had been unable to attend the funeral of his murdered son, Rabbenu Tam and Elijah of Paris are reputed to have permitted the use of the Tetragrammaton to resurrect the image of the deceased:

> Isaac said: It happened that twenty-year-old Elijah, son of Todros, was killed in his home city. His father was away when he was buried. Upon his return, the father refused to eat or drink until the great rabbis of his time, Jacob of Ramerupt and Elijah of Paris, would allow him to conjure his son's image by using the Divine Name. . . . They ultimately granted him permission to do so. He then bathed, immersed, dressed in white, and then, [along with Todros,] the entire community fasted on Thursday and went to synagogue.[94]

Here we see personal and communal fasting as preparation for summoning the dead youth's soul. The father prepares for this ritual most intensely, by immersing then dressing in white, but the community joined him in fasting and accompanied him for the actual ceremony.

Like their ancestors in late antiquity, medieval Jews fasted for personal reasons without community involvement.[95] In the Middle Ages, the practice of fasting after a bad dream was maintained, but with more ritual complexity: the fast was initiated by an announcement and chanting a set group of verses in the presence of three male witnesses, and while fasting the "dreamer" would refrain from grooming in the form of shaving or hairstyling.[96] This fast was thought to prevent the omens in that dream from reaching fruition.[97] Despite talmudic debates over their appropriateness and ge'onic restrictions on their applicability,[98] observance of these fasts on the Sabbath continued throughout the Middle Ages in Germany and northern France. Medieval Ashkenazic authorities tried to balance opinions that discouraged such Sabbath fasts with those that favored them: thus it became customary to nullify fearsome dreams that occurred before the Sabbath by fasting on the Sabbath and to make amends for that very fast by refraining from eating on Sunday.[99]

Fasts were also taken on to mark a wide array of personal decisions, physical transitions, and life-cycle junctures. As in late antiquity, brides and grooms fasted on the day of their wedding,[100] a gesture that resonated with the biblical description of Daniel's preparation for revelation. Medieval sources mention fasting as an expression of regret after insulting a fellow community member[101] and after drinking wine produced by non-Jews.[102] As we will see in greater depth later in this chapter, converts would fast as one component of their process of returning to Judaism.[103] In addition, a narrative in one thirteenth-century manuscript tells of a woman and her husband who fasted before a much-feared confrontation.[104] Thus fasts were undertaken for a wide variety of reasons.[105]

Not only adults but also children fasted. They are explicitly mentioned with women and men in certain contexts for fasting, particularly during community-wide fasts after traumatic communal events[106] and on annual fast days.[107] Rashi notes that children who had reached the "age of education" (*gil hinukh*) should fast, recommending nine or ten years as the appropriate starting point.[108] Rashi's grandson, Jacob b. Meir (Rabbenu Tam), also addressed this subject when queried on his opinion of especially pious people[109] who not only refused to feed their own young children (who were under the age of education) on Yom Kippur but who also claimed that parents who fed their young offspring on that day were transgressing the law. In his reply, Jacob b. Meir supports parents whose children ate and drank on Yom Kippur, refuting the arguments posed by the more stringent members of his community.[110] Thirteenth- and fourteenth-century sources acknowledge that some parents instructed their children, boys and girls, to fast from a very young age even though that practice exceeded halakhic guidelines.[111] Despite assertions that such fasting was not only unnecessary but potentially dangerous for young children, an undercurrent of approval for this approach to fasting persisted.[112]

While there is little need to detail men's practice as a specific category given that the sources above feature men as the primary population that fasts, it is significant to highlight the select texts where women's fasts are explicitly mentioned,[113] many of which are listed by Bitha Har-Shefi in her research.[114] Women, like men, fasted as individuals and with the community; for example, their fasts followed the annual calendar during the Ten Days of Repentance[115] and the Fasts of Gedalyah and Esther.[116] Admittedly, "one (*ehad*) [who]" is the protagonist in the stories that are regularly told of paradigmatic man.[117] Yet, as mentioned earlier, this use of the masculine singular form represents the rhetorical norm, whereas women are specifically mentioned in circumstances that pertain to them exclusively[118] or where a woman is the primary subject. This literary pattern is represented in the famous case of a businesswoman who asked Rashi if she were required to observe the Fast of Esther when it coincided with her work-related travel.[119]

Fasting among women is notably recorded when a mother and father fasted together as part of their shared concern for their sick child or when the family was separated due to travel,[120] as when

> someone departed from the city where his father and mother dwell, if his journey is considered dangerous—and his father and mother are worried about his welfare, whether or not they have elected to fast on his behalf—it is his duty to hire a messenger as soon as possible to send a letter notifying his father and mother that he is out of danger, having arrived safely to his destination, and that they should neither worry nor fast any longer.[121]

What motivated these parents to fast? They were clearly moved by a desire to petition for their child's welfare, yet they also were working from a belief that their own suffering would help secure his safe transit. Thus fasting could convey piety and supplication simultaneously. The parallel mention of the mother and father in this source signals its depiction of a standard practice.

In the rulings attributed to Peretz b. Elijah (Rabbenu Peretz, d. 1297), one source discusses whether it is permissible to commit oneself to a fast and then postpone it. This sage was asked: "About a woman who said, 'I will fast today.' Can she delay it to the morrow for her sister?"[122] He responded that although one may defer a fast, it was unwarranted in this situation. Notwithstanding the vagueness of this case—it is not clear whether the woman sought to postpone her fast because of her sister or if she was in fact fasting on her sister's behalf—this text offers no indication that a woman fasting was considered exceptional. The relationship between accepted practice and exceptional piety is imprecise in these cases, for these fasts were part of the established routine, yet I would suggest that frequency and intensity rather than the observance of fasting per se was what had social and religious significance.

The writings of Meir b. Barukh of Rothenburg are replete with references to fasting, including men and women who committed themselves to Monday and Thursday fasts and then wished to delay or cancel their vows.[123] Meir of Rothenburg tells of a woman who planned to fast on Mondays and Thursdays, but she was unsure of the procedures involved.[124] His response too was gender neutral.

Mordekhai b. Hillel (1250–1298) relates the case of a woman who was allowed to pause between two fast days rather than fast consecutively. She had fasted on the Sabbath on account of a bad dream. Typically she would have been expected to fast on the following day (Sunday) to atone for fasting on the Sabbath; however, she could not. Thus Asher recalled precedents from similar cases: "Samuel of Bamberg allowed a woman to fast on the Sabbath on account of a dream. But she was not able to fast for two days in a row, so he allowed her to fast on two separate days of the week, neither being the Sabbath. And Eliezer of Metz also ruled the same way."[125]

Gender plays no apparent role in this case. This woman could not fast as planned, so she sought rabbinic guidance to resolve her dilemma, no more and no less.[126] In other instances, fasting among women became a subject of halakhic discussion when conditions unique to women—be they biological or social—were at the heart of the queries being raised. From the Talmud onward, halakhic texts exempt pregnant, post-partum, and nursing women from fasting on Yom Kippur.[127] This explicit release implies that women were otherwise expected to fast as members of the community. A responsum by Haim Paltiel (thirteenth century) illustrates the nexus of the quotidian nature of women's fasts and the exceptions that may arise. Here a woman took on the obligation to fast, then immediately discovered that she was pregnant. Haim was asked how she could annul her vow and he detailed the procedure for her.[128] Like other medieval texts, this opinion provides a common explanation for the prohibition against fasting during pregnancy— as a potential cause of miscarriages that must be avoided.[129] Unfortunately, it offers no background for the motivation behind this woman's fast.

Fasting, Repentance, and Atonement

The evidence of these Jewish men and women who fasted and their motivations for fasting presented up to this point has been varied. Although fasting was commonly attributed to conspicuously pious individuals,[130] I suggested the qualities that determined piety were often the degree and frequency of practice, rather than the deed being performed. Thus the stringently pious fasted alongside community members who followed more conventional approaches in accordance with the calendar cycle and personal circumstances.

Much as fasting on Yom Kippur was seen as a form of self-denial on the path to atonement, individual fasts were also understood as a means for repentance. Numerous sources describe fasting as a substitute for the sacrifice that would have been offered during the Temple period to atone for a given sin.[131] Penitential fasting was certainly not unique to medieval or Jewish culture. As noted above, fasting had already been linked to atonement in biblical and rabbinical literature. For example, a talmudic interpretation of "When Adam had lived one hundred and thirty years" (Gen. 5:3) in Tractate Eruvin describes Adam fasting after being exiled from Eden: "Meir said, 'Adam was a *hasid*.[132] When he recognized that death was ordained as a punishment on his account, [Adam responded by] fasting, avoiding sexual relations with his wife,[133] and wearing fig leaves for one hundred thirty years. That statement[134] was made to offset semen that he accidentally emitted.'"[135]

According to this passage, Adam tried to atone for having sinned—whether defined as the actions that led to his exile from Eden or the emission of semen—by fasting.[136] In fact, it could be argued that repentance has been a consistent motif in Jewish fasting throughout history, in terms of individual practice and communal observance. For example, on communal fast days such as Yom Kippur, confession is a component of the public prayer service that is understood as a fulfillment of the biblical injunction to recite a personal confession (*vidui*). However, the concept and practice of repentance were dramatically transformed among the Jews of medieval Ashkenaz, much as they were among their Christian neighbors. Before turning to these medieval Jewish developments, I survey medieval Christian approaches to penance.

Penance in Medieval Christian Culture

Fasting was an essential component of Christian penance, along with prayer and almsgiving, as described above,[137] and medieval penance was a subject of scholarly investigation among theologians and legal historians. These scholars defined the thirteenth-century institution of mandatory confession for every Christian by the Fourth Lateran Council as a landmark for Christian society and also examined the founding of schools and universities that developed common curricula and methods for conceptualizing and teaching about penance.[138] Some of these researchers have interpreted this systematization of penance as a battle over doctrine.[139] Over the past decade, scholars have begun to uncover the social contexts where penitential books were used and how penance was practiced. Their examination of liturgies and records of public penance suggest a lack of congruence between doctrinal divisions and contemporaneous religious practice.¹⁴⁰ As a result, some scholars have forged a new approach that interprets debates about penance as attempts by university teachers to provide an overview of this rich tradition for their students, not as efforts to reconcile doctrinal distinctions.¹⁴¹

Two key aspects of penance that have received current scholarly attention are its origins among laity (as compared with its history in monastic communities) and the differences between private and public penance.¹⁴² As the older of the two forms, public penance was reserved for grave sins. This once-in-a-lifetime ritual and would take place during Lent, in response to the call for confession and penance issued to all Christians at that time each year. Driven by penitential piety, individuals would dress in special (often white) garments and perform penance publicly.¹⁴³ Starting in the Carolingian era, some sins, if known to the public, required stricter discipline. In such instances, this ritual was presided over by a bishop rather than a local priest and the penitent was formally separated from the community on Ash Wednesday until being reintroduced on Holy Thursday.

In contrast with the singular nature of public penance, private penance could be practiced multiple times each year.¹⁴⁴ Scholarly understandings of this sacramental ritual have shifted significantly over the past decade. Recent scholarship has challenged Alexander Murray's widely accepted assertion that confession was rare among the laity before the thirteenth century; instead, scholars have identified the ninth century as a pivotal period in the emergence of confession and the rites of penance for laity and members of monastic orders.¹⁴⁵ This new research claims that "private confession" is more anachronistic than accurate as a description of the penitential ritual performed by individuals regarding their own sins, and that confession rarely occurred in private: detailed scholarly descriptions of confession in medieval Europe reveal that penitents were neither alone with their confessors nor concealed from view.¹⁴⁶ In his study of penance in the early Middle Ages, Rob Meens explains that the so-called "private" penance (*paenitentia occulta or secreta*) is best characterized by way of negation. "It is not public penance, in the sense of a highly ritualized form of penance imposed by the bishop," but it did incorporate various elements adapted from public penance (such as wearing special garments, almsgiving, and fasting) that rendered the penitent visible to the community.¹⁴⁷ "These differences should not be overdrawn," writes Karen Wagner; "the actual confession of one's sin was rarely public, and given the communal nature of early medieval society, no penitential satisfaction could remain entirely private."¹⁴⁸ As Sarah Hamilton remarks, scholars have viewed penance and confession from the perspective of clergy more than from that of the laity; changing that focus has revealed the widespread and public nature of this process.[149] These scholars, along with Mayke de Jong and Mary Mansfield, have each demonstrated that "private" penance was far from private in ninth- to thirteenth-century Christian practice.[150]

As private penance developed over the course of the Middle Ages, it came to include the confession of sins to a priest, an assignment of rituals required to achieve absolution—fasting, praying, or almsgiving (with some acts being interchangeable)—and a granting of absolution. While confession was a prerequisite for participation in Mass and receiving the Eucharist, it was also a key component of penance. Fasting was not the province of ascetics alone any more than penance was exclusive to the clergy prior to the Fourth Lateran Council (1215).[151] Throughout the Middle Ages, penance could include fasting for periods ranging from weeks to months or even years to be forgiven for theft, sexual transgressions, or other sins.[152]

Jewish Fasting and Confession in the High Middle Ages

In this atmosphere, amid the growing importance of penance and confession for Christians, the concept and act of repentance were dramatically transformed by the Jews of medieval Ashkenaz. This revolution is exceptionally documented in the writings of Samuel b. Judah, his son Judah, and Judah's star pupil, Eleazar b. Judah of Worms. These innovators developed their teachings building on ideas from ancient sources and integrating them with current practices.[153] The literature that they produced consistently encourages fasting: *Sefer Hasidim* and *Sefer Rokeah*; other compositions by Judah the Pious, such as *Sefer haGematriyot*; and the extensive oeuvre by Eleazar of Worms, known for its focus on mysticism. These works emphasize fasting as a means for achieving atonement, along with prayer and charity. Relating fasting to these other two components—for example, to refrain from eating before praying—was a long-accepted practice.[154] Similarly, Judah the Pious instructed his followers not to eat until they had both prayed and given charity as they had pledged.[155] This medieval pietist's prescription for repentance stands out for the rigor with which it was embraced and its demand that atonement be actively sought in daily practice.

As numerous scholars have demonstrated during the past century—from the work of Yitzhak (Fritz) Baer and the tremendous expansion of this scholarship by Haym Soloveitchik, Ivan Marcus, and others—Hasidei Ashkenaz have been characterized by their belief in the need for repentance, which was founded on long-held customs while also representing significant degrees of innovation.[156] Hasidei Ashkenaz exemplified extreme piety in their relentless search for rituals that would elevate the level of religious devotion in daily Jewish life. Their writings express fresh notions of how to satisfy "the will of the Creator" (*ratzon haboreh*) and express love for God that balanced fear and awe (*yir'ah*).[157] Liturgically, Hasidei Ashkenaz were known for their prolonged prayer services and their meticulous attention to each word therein.[158] A defining feature of their worldview is the conviction that every human is incessantly lured by temptations which must be resisted and that, consequently, everyone is rewarded in proportion to the suffering involved in that struggle.[159] As part of their quest to worship God wholeheartedly, Hasidei Ashkenaz crafted a distinctive system of repentance that Ivan Marcus outlined two decades ago in his book *Piety and Society*. As Marcus and other scholars have noted, certain dimensions of this framework for repentance are drawn from earlier Jewish texts, particularly Hekhalot literature.[160]

Samuel b. Judah, Judah, and Eleazar of Worms constructed a system where atonement was accomplished through penitent actions that corresponded to the sin committed. Samuel b. Judah expanded the talmudic definition of repentance to include the ability to refrain from repeating sinful behavior[161] by prescribing acts of repentance derived from the biblical punishment for a given sin and the pleasure experienced from that behavior.[162] In the course of their writings, Samuel and Judah developed a four-part conceptualization of sin (and, therefore, repentance) that was articulated more fully by Eleazar of Worms. The four categories are known as *teshuvat hagader*—preventative repentance; *teshuvat hamishkal*—weighted repentance; *teshuvat hekatuv*—scriptural repentance; and *teshuvat haba'ah*—anticipatory repentance.[163] Fasting was an intrinsic component of repentance, as sinners sought atonement through fasts that extended over lengthy periods—even weeks, months, or years. Anyone who had committed a grave sin was also expected to wear black clothing and to give charity. In some cases, transgressors were directed to submit themselves to lashings, to shave their heads, and to exhibit other signs of remorse.[164] Sins that involved men having inappropriate sexual contact with women (e.g., adultery and intercourse with a menstruant) are featured prominently among the misdeeds that required harsher forms of repentance. Transgressions such as desecrating the Sabbath, gossip, and murder also demanded more severe expressions of contrition.[165]

In his analysis, Marcus highlights substantive differences between the systems set forth by Judah and Eleazar of Worms.[166] One distinguishing feature of Judah's system is what Marcus describes as its sectarian nature, which required initiation for membership in his circle of Ashkenazic pietists.[167] In contrast, Marcus stresses the personal nature of Eleazar's mode of instruction for pious atonement, channeled through self-perfection rather than a group experience.[168] One of the most explicit modifications is the apparent elimination of the Sage (*hakham*) in the role of confessor, which was introduced in Judah's system but absent from the writings of Eleazar. Instead, admission of sin was transferred to the realm of private prayer and the determination of appropriate punishment was similarly assigned to the individual. Rather than mentioning a sage or guide, Eleazar produced a manual on repentance for individuals to consult.[169] Despite these distinctions, Eleazar maintains the primacy of fasting as an act of atonement.

Let us now survey the circumstances in which these rabbis advised that fasts be undertaken. In *Sefer Hasidim*, Judah recommends fasting in numerous contexts: fasts associated with communal observances and in memory of beloved family members on the anniversaries of their deaths are mentioned alongside fasts by parents of sick children and single individuals in search of a marriage partner.[170] He advises fasting regularly to safeguard an appropriate posture of piety and humility toward God.[171] He further explains that fasting is effective precisely because it "breaks the body."[172]

Judah also mentions other situations that merit fasting. Not all are directly related to repentance, although most probably included a penitential aspect. For instance, "One who witnesses an eclipse—of the moon, for example—must fast. After all, he would fast after a bad dream and this is for the sake of the whole world."[173] Here, fasting is intended to ward off punishment since eclipses were thought to result from sin.[174] Although the practice of fasting is rarely critiqued in *Sefer Hasidim*, the motives for fasts are questioned. For instance, in discussions of parents fasting for the sake of their children: "Witness how many fasts, [expressions of] self-denial,[175] cries and pleas a parent performs when his son falls ill, because of concern for his son's body. Surely he should do at least as much if [his son] sins, for the soul's well-being is eternal."[176] Here neither fasts nor self-denial are being scrutinized, but rather their underlying motives if these practices were performed for the sake of physical welfare rather than spiritual elevation.

In *Sefer Hasidim*, rituals for repentance after committing a grave sin involved not only fasting but also harsh corporal punishment, such as sitting in freezing water in the winter or on hornets' or ants' nests in the summer, or burning oneself with red-hot irons,[177] per the case of an adulterer: "If he inquires about how to repent . . . in the winter and [the river is frozen], he should break through the ice and sit in the water up to his mouth or nose for the same span of time from when he first addressed the woman until the sin's completion."[178] The inclusion of self-inflicted suffering in is an inherent element of the philosophy of Judah the Pious that has textual roots in the interpretation of Adam's repentance in Tractate Eruvin (above).[179]

Eleazar of Worms details physical repentance rituals for many specific sins, such as murder:

> [In the case of] one who struck his companion—man, woman or child—and thus took his life, [the offender] should be exiled for three years. He should be flagellated and declare: "I am a murderer" in every city he visits. He should refrain from eating meat and drinking wine, from shaving his beard and the hair on his head, from laundering his clothes and washing his body. Washing his beard once a month is permitted. He should attach the hand that dealt the lethal blow to a chain looped around his neck.[180] He should go barefoot and mourn his victim, fasting daily until his period of exile is complete. He should then fast on Mondays and Thursdays for an additional year, even though he will already have fasted every day for three years. He should not do evil to any man. Should he be called a murderer, he should not argue. Rather, he should remain silent. Throughout those three years, he should not laugh (rejoice). When he leaves synagogue each day, he should lie down before the entryway; [all who exit] should step over him, never stepping on him. He should honor his wife and all persons and confess daily.[181]

And the case of a Jew who informed on another Jew to Christian authorities:

> [In the case of] one who informs (*malshin*): one who informs against a neighbor, [thus] setting governmental officials against him . . . (the sinner) should pay (the victim) all (losses incurred as a result of his) action, he should also become his permanent servant, publicly ask forgiveness, be flagellated and confess as though [the informer] had killed all (of his neighbor's) sons, daughters and (other) dependents.[182]

Anyone who followed these instructions was inevitably exposed before the entire community. While such severe modes of repentance were related to extreme transgressions, in the communal perception of repentance they shared many features with normative fasts.

As Marcus has shown, Eleazar of Worms often heightened the severity of the penitential requirements set forth by Judah. To name one representative example, whereas Judah prescribed a three-day fast to any Jewish man who had sexual relations with a Christian woman or maidservant, Eleazar required flagellation, refraining from bathing, and fasting for at least forty days.[183] These physical forms of repentance became very popular.[184]

Marcus has argued that in Judah's generation, these penitential rituals were only intended for a discrete circle of pietists. It appears that the effect of these rituals was substantially greater than has typically been assumed. I would claim that Judah and his disciple Eleazar of Worms were successful precisely because they were promoting fasting and repentance in an environment known for its predisposition toward these rituals.

Ashkenazic liturgy also attests to the crucial place of fasting in medieval culture and the interpretation of fasting as the quintessence of teshuvah. As in other religions, the triad of charity, prayer, and fasting was viewed as the most efficacious path to salvation. In medieval Ashkenaz, this belief was most prominently conveyed in *Netaneh Tokef*, the piyyut that became a signature of the High Holiday prayers. This liturgical poem from late antiquity was part of a tale about Amnon of Mainz that was popularized in the late twelfth or early thirteenth century.[185] The apex of the poem, "and repentance and prayer and charity remove the evil decree" (*uteshuvah utefillah utzedakah ma'avirin et ro'a hagezerah*) offers guidance on becoming worthy of a positive inscription in the Book of Life. As some scholars have noted, this formula can be traced to a section in *Midrash Bereshit Rabbah*, a late antique midrash that was composed at approximately the same time as the Augustinian sermon (noted above), which asserts that fasting, charity, and prayer lead to salvation.[186]

Menahem Schmelzer has traced the versions of this most resonant line of *Netaneh Tokef* that have appeared over time, remarking that compilers of medieval mahzorim debated over the correct sequence of these three terms. Some objected to the conventional order that begins with teshuvah, since "prayer, charity, and repentance" is the sequence found in the midrash and in the Palestinian Talmud. Jacob Moellin (Maharil) defended the prevailing liturgical progression by explaining that true teshuvah, repentance that is integrated with prayer and charity, must necessarily follow fasting.[187] Some scribes copied not just these three terms, but their meanings as well: identifying teshuvah as fasting, tefillah as use of the voice, and tzedakah as money. These definitions were further supported by mathematical calculations using Jewish numerology (*gematriah*).[188]

Although the association of teshuvah with fasting (rather than with a broader definition of repentance) in commentaries on the High Holiday liturgy seems to have emerged in the late medieval period, it is based on fasting as a simile for teshuvah and as a consistent component of medieval repentance in sources such as the Crusade chronicles, *Sefer Hasidim* and *Sefer Rokeah*. Thus, despite the central role of Judah the Pious and Eleazar of Worms in the popularization of fasting for repentance, I would argue that this practice had strong currency outside their circle. Moreover, although the Confessor-Sage uniquely featured in the writings by Judah the Pious on repentance was soon replaced by personal confession, many thirteenth- and fourteenth-century responsa mention transgressors who sought rabbinic counsel on how to repent for their actions. While these sources do not describe formal confessions, in some cases it seems that the authority being asked for advice was expected to treat that discussion of sin confidentially.[189]

Eleazar's composition *Hilkhot Teshuvah* was frequently copied in late medieval and early modern Europe, albeit in different formats, yielding distinct versions of the treatise that were copied and disseminated well into the early modern period.[190] Eleazar's writings on repentance reached northern France through Isaac b. Joseph of Corbeil who, as noted above, was known for his stringent fasting.[191] Isaac incorporated ideas from *Hilkhot Teshuvah* into his popular handbook of customs that have been described as "semi-ritual practices," *Sefer Amudei Golah* (known more widely as *Sefer Mitzvot Katan*). This guide was composed for men and women in a style that aims at the less educated reader and attests to the prominence of these practices during the late thirteenth century.

Isaac's *Sefer Mitzvot Katan* features notions from Maimonides's *Hilkhot Teshuvah* and quotations from Moses b. Jacob of Coucy's *Sefer Mitzvot Gadol*. However, Isaac supplements those teachings with verbatim selections from Eleazar's *Hilkhot Teshuvah*, with a recapitulation of his four categories of repentance.[192] Isaac explains:

> The order of repentance is thus: In the case of a public sin, one should request forgiveness publicly. In the case of a private sin, one should request forgiveness from his Creator (lit., "between himself and his Creator," meaning privately). There are four kinds of repentance: *teshuvat hagader, teshuvat hakatuv, teshuvat hamishkal,*

and *teshuvat haharatah*. Repentance is so great and exalted that it reaches the holy throne (*kise hakavod*), as it is written: "Return O Israel, to the Lord your God, for you have fallen on account of your sin" (Hosea 14:1).[193]

In his commentary on *Sefer Mitzvot Katan*, Peretz b. Elijah explains each category in greater detail, quoting examples from Eleazar's work. This supports the claim that French rabbinical scholars in Corbeil were well versed in the penitential system promoted by the German scholars. Ephraim Kanarfogel has suggested that the rabbis of Evreux—the center of learning where Isaac studied—were similarly conversant with these texts.[194] The main contribution found in the northern French sources on repentance is the distinction drawn between two types of confession, for public offenses and for private deeds. While *Sefer Mitzvot Katan* does not describe how such confessions should be conducted, other contemporaneous sources detail that these rituals entailed fasting, along with charity and prayer.[195]

Northern French halakhic compendia discuss fasting in many contexts. For instance, Peretz criticizes those who fasted in response to the death of a family member, scolding anyone whose abstinence was prompted by circumstances unrelated to repentance.[196] Peretz summarizes his position by stating: "Regarding one whose mourning incorporates fasting to atone for his sins, it has been written: 'I note how they fare and will heal them: I will guide them and mete out solace to them and to the mourners among them' [Is. 57:18]."[197] This discussion suggests that some mourners fasted as a means of expressing grief rather than as a way to better their own souls, a practice that contradicts the commonly endorsed motivations for fasting. Peretz also reprimanded anyone whose fast caused bodily harm.[198]

Twelfth- and thirteenth-century halakhic compendia and biblical commentaries from northern France describe men and women performing penitential fasts that corroborate those prescribed by halakhic authorities such as Isaac of Corbeil and Peretz.[199] So, too, a Tosafist commentary on Tractate Avodah Zarah mentions a man who fasted often, without reference to anything else about him.[200] The widespread practice of fasting on Mondays and Thursdays is assumed in another text where Peretz is asked whether a community member who does not observe that pattern of fasts could be called to the Torah; Peretz concludes that this synagogue honor may be bestowed on the condition that the individual in question promises to make up for his missed fasts.[201] In the fourteenth century, Jacob b. Asher (son of Rosh, 1269–1343) remarked that fasting on Mondays and Thursdays was customary for German and northern French Jews, in contrast to the Jews of Spain who only practiced communal fasts that were part of the annual calendar.[202]

Penitential fasts are also mentioned in commentaries on Genesis. By way of illustration, when discussing Reuben's role in selling Joseph, the medieval commentators follow a late antique midrash when they explain that Reuben was absent when Joseph was sold to the Ishmaelites because he was fasting for his sin with Bilhah, his father's concubine. Reuben is literally described as "fasting and wearing his sackcloth."[203] This midrashic explanation is recounted in medieval commentaries from Germany and France.[204]

Although books such as *Sefer Rokeah* and *Sefer Mitzvot Katan* were written with the aim of equipping individuals to determine their repentant actions independently, rabbis were still consulted for guidance on how to atone. Such queries were so common that rabbis are known to have developed standard responses, as witnessed in responsa that prescribe repentant behavior after specific sins. Desecration of the Sabbath is a recurrent topic in the penitential literature by Judah and Eleazar as well as in writings by other thirteenth-century halakhic authorities. For example, relating to behavior required when a fire broke out and was then extinguished on the Sabbath, Isaac b. Moses discusses whether repentance and fasting are required, since putting out a fire constitutes a desecration of the Sabbath. According to Jewish law, this action is permissible if it saved lives, but it is considered a violation of the Sabbath if lives were not at risk, as Isaac explained:

> [In a case] when Jews extinguished a fire (on the Sabbath) where it was unclear whether lives were endangered.[205] [Those who put the fire out] need not fast or give charity because of their deed, for they were acting with [divine] permission. Even if they wanted to give charity on that account, the court does not permit it, for if they did, in the future they might not respond to fires [or other dangers] in the same way. Some say they should fast because of this [deed], and in the event of another fire, they would instruct them to extinguish it and then fast . . . but as I have said, in my eyes the law should instruct that even if they wish to fast because of this [deed], they should be dissuaded from doing so lest they abstain from extinguishing a second fire (in the future).[206]

Here it seems that community members wanted to fast after having put out a fire on the Sabbath, whereas their rabbis ruled this fast unnecessary, lest this expression of repentance deter Jews from extinguishing future fires on the Sabbath.

Fasting as a means to seek atonement after violating the Sabbath is also mentioned in other sources.[207] Samson b. Tzadok reports that Meir of Rothenburg instructed anyone who inadvertently desecrated the Sabbath to fast:

> He says: One who unintentionally desecrated the Sabbath by bringing an object into the public [realm],[208] by manipulating fire or in whatever manner should give five *hallische* dinars to charity to receive atonement . . . and it would also be appropriate if he fasted on Mondays and Thursdays, as is customary throughout the world to fast on the morrow of the Sabbath (Sunday) for desecrating the Sabbath.[209]

This instruction for repentance is outstanding for its exactitude in specifying the exact monetary sum to be contributed, and for its reference to these actions as standard practice, "as is customary throughout the world."

Another case of repentance for desecrating the Sabbath is addressed in a responsum attributed to Samuel b. Isaac (late thirteenth century):[210]

> Once a woman was riding with a certain Jewish man through the city of Barby on a Friday.[211] This Jewish woman could not remain in that city for the Sabbath because she feared that if her presence were known, non-Jews would seize her. So she rode on to Zerbst. It became dark on the way, but they rode on to that city even though they were desecrating the Sabbath. I asked my teacher, Samuel b. Isaac, to give her instructions [on how to repent]. He replied that they should fast for forty days, but they need not be stringent and fast consecutively. Rather, they should fast on Mondays and Thursdays each week—except on the New Moon and other festivals—until they reached [a total of] forty days. This is sufficient since they were coerced.[212]

Here a woman and her male travel companion sought counsel on how to atone for their transgression, indicating their awareness that repentance was needed. Samuel required identical actions for the man and the woman.

In another source, Isaac b. Moses discusses improper conduct regarding Sabbath candles, a desecration that specifically pertains to women. He mentions women who fasted if they had touched the wax of a Sabbath candle during the Sabbath, to repent for their violation of that holy day.[213] A century later, Jacob Moellin (Maharil) was asked how his niece should atone for having forgotten to light the Sabbath candles one Friday evening. He responded: "[On every Sabbath eve] for the rest of her life, she should assiduously add one candle beyond her customary number.[214] When her fast occurs (*ukeshe'era ta'anitah*), she should be sure to confess this sin. [Furthermore,] if she wishes to obligate herself [to] fasts and to torment herself in order be granted atonement, may she be blessed."[215] This responsum integrates individual confession, as promoted by Eleazar of Worms, with normative fasting. Maharil's words suggest that Jewish women and men would customarily adopt additional fasts and other "torments" as components of repentance.

In a responsum of a case that occurred in London, Jacob b. Judah Hazan (thirteenth century) relates the case of a woman who sought guidance from Menahem on how to repent after having committed adultery. She was told that her husband must divorce her, but that she should not receive her *ketubbah*; however, we have no record of penitent actions that Menahem might have recommended.[216] In a different angle on marital strife, Haim Barukh is said to have instructed a woman who had angered her husband to fast for three days.[217]

Another category of responsa relates to women who fasted following what might be termed "crib death." These rabbinic opinions—with many attributed to Meir b. Barukh of Rothenburg and his colleagues—were published in 2012 by Simcha Emanuel. In these cases, after it was discovered that an infant had died in its parents' bed, the rabbis prescribed deeds of repentance based on the talmudic punishments for an intentional killing. Although these medieval texts sometimes cite ge'onic rulings as precedents for their recommendations, there is no extant evidence of such penitent behavior from that era. Here is one response attributed to Meir himself:

> Maharam (Meir b. Barukh of Rothenburg) was asked about [the case of] a woman who lay on her son, causing his death: How she should repent? He required her to fast for a full year, without eating meat or drinking wine[218] with the exception of Sabbaths, festivals, the New Moon, Hanukkah and Purim, when [not only] should she refrain from fasting but she should eat meat and drink wine. For those holidays and New Moons and Hanukkah and Purim that she does not fast, she should fast on the same number of additional days

until she has completed a 365-day fast. From that point onward, she should fast every second week—[that is to say] on a Monday-Thursday-Monday cycle every other week—as her strength allows, though she may eat meat and drink wine. When she is pregnant or nursing, she should not fast. And she should be cautious for the remainder of her days, that her son will never lie with her again.[219]

This case offers a vivid depiction of what constituted penitent behavior and a careful calculation of the fast days required to complete a full course of repentance.

A second responsum, attributed to Elhanan b. Samuel from Magdeburg (late thirteenth century),[220] provides further data on how these fasts were calculated. Elhanan also recommends fifty-two weeks of Monday and Thursday fasts. Knowing that some of those days would coincide with holidays, he explains:

And all the Mondays and Thursdays that she does not fast, she must make up for during the next year. It is recommended that she have a small piece of wood (tablet/stick) that she would mark on each Monday and Thursday when she does not fast until the end of the year, when she should total up the marks. With another piece of wood [as a measure], she should make up for that number of missed Monday and Thursday fasts. Each time she fasts [during that second year], she should mark the [second piece of] wood until it has same number of markings that appear on the first piece of wood.[221]

Elhanan also clarifies his instruction against drinking wine: "Since we drink thick ale, she should not drink thick ale but thin ale instead and she should wash but twice a month." Unique among responsa, this passage reveals an otherwise unknown element of medieval material culture—marking wood as a way to calculate time.

More moderate forms of repentant behavior have been attributed to Haim Paltiel, who recommended that pregnant women should not fast, lest their actions induce a miscarriage. He allows three options for fasting: three consecutive days and nights, forty uninterrupted days, or on Mondays and Thursdays for one year. In addition, he recommends giving charity.[222]

Our third and final example on this subject comes from an anonymous rabbi who raises an important proviso, noting that only healthy women who were neither pregnant nor nursing are qualified to fast: "Only if her husband wishes her to fast. If she is young and she is unaccustomed to fasting, let her fast on Mondays and Thursdays until she fulfills [the equivalent of] a yearlong fast."[223] These instructions suggest that young mothers,[224] as opposed to older women, may not have been accustomed to fasting.[225]

Married women who wronged their husbands might have been advised to fast as a means of repentance; however, these women still needed their husbands' permission to take on any vow, even for a fast of this nature. This provision is evident in the anonymous responsum cited above, which specifies "and only if her husband wishes her to fast."[226] This stipulation originates in the Bible: "If a man makes a vow to the Lord or takes an oath imposing an obligation on himself, he shall not break his pledge; he must carry out everything that his crossed his lips."[227] The passage continues by listing three categories of women and their relative levels of agency when making vows: if a woman is unmarried, her father has the power to absolve her vows; if she is married, her husband can nullify her vows; a widow or divorced woman may bind herself without a man's consent. As the biblical text states:

> Each and every vow and sworn obligation of self-denial may be upheld or annulled by her husband. If her husband offers no objection from one day to the next, he has upheld all of the vows and obligations that she has assumed; he has upheld them by offering no objection when he learned about them. However, if he annuls them after [the day] he finds out [about her vows and obligations], he shall bear her guilt.[228]

The vows of self-denial described here are categorized in the Mishnah and Talmud as "vows that torment the soul" (*nidrei inui nefesh*) and include fasting, abstaining from sexual relations, refraining from wearing brightly colored clothing, and other behaviors considered normative on fast days and in times of danger.[229] In a ruling attributed to Peretz, such an incident is discussed:

> [In the case of] a woman who vowed not to eat on a particular day whose husband did not annul her vow, rather he traveled to another city and, before his departure, he warned her not to fast, but without naming a specific day. Since her husband demonstrated that he did not wish her to fast, the rabbis may permit her (to annul her vow) without her husband [being present]. But had he not revealed

(his opinion), I doubt that her vow could be annulled without her husband [being present].[230]

This passage does not reveal the motivation for this woman's fast, but this was certainly not the first time she made such a vow.[231] It is obvious that her husband had been trying to prevent her from this practice, exercising his prerogative based on the biblical passage above. Once again we see that the community was generally aware of who was fasting and, moreover, that their actions could be considered disruptive.

If we compare this documentation of women who fasted often to descriptions of their male counterparts, gendered qualifications begin to emerge. The Tosafist commentary on Tractate Avodah Zarah recounts:

> A question[232] came before Rabbenu Tam about one who fasted many times without declaring his fasts in advance. Rabbenu Tam determined that he did not "lose" his fasts if he meant to fast, meaning that if he committed himself in his heart . . . even though he had not stated [his intention] with his lips (in prayer). . . . Rabbenu Tam added that, even if he had not decided in his heart [to fast] until the evening before,[233] he was permitted to fast and recite the liturgy for fasts, fulfilling his vow as if he had articulated it on the previous day. . . . It is preferable to publicly declare [one's] fast during afternoon prayers (*minhah*) on the preceding day. When Isaac (of Dampierre) fasted on a Sunday, he would proclaim his fast on the Sabbath during his recitation of the 'Elohai Netzor prayer.[234]

This explanation relies on the same verses in Numbers that spell out the limitations on women's vows, stating that a vow must "cross the lips." Our talmudic selection asks if one could be credited for a fast that had not been declared during the afternoon prayers immediately preceding the fast, as was customary. The text does not specify whether such vows were usually made silently or aloud. Jacob b. Meir (Rabbenu Tam) conceded that pledging to fast in advance was preferable, but he was willing to accept fasts that were not declared beforehand because, as Peretz remarked when discussing this same topic, "decisions made by the heart (and not announced) are also decisions."[235] The divergent attitudes toward frequent fasting by men and women can be explained at least in part by their differing levels of authority to swear vows. Men had the agency to pledge themselves to fasts, whereas single and married women were dependent on approval from their fathers or husbands, respectively.

In sum, the textual evidence resoundingly indicates that medieval Jews fasted often and that piety was commonly attributed to those who fasted with outstanding frequency. While the roots of this practice originate in the Bible and the legacy from late antiquity, the penitential structure that was articulated by Judah the Pious and his followers reinforced the role of fasting, repentance, and the reputation for piety that accompanied it in Germany and northern France.[236] Given that outward displays of repentance were readily visible even if the sin that preceded them was not publicly declared, it is inconceivable that such behavior could go by without being noticed by family and community members.

Those who fasted also added liturgical formulae and supplications to their regular prayers, which might not have been conspicuous in synagogue services, but if they were also flagellated in public or prostrated themselves when leaving the synagogue so others could step over them, the fact that they were fasting would have been self-evident, causing community members to be unavoidably aware and involved as participants in these practices of repentance.[237] Let us now situate these Jewish practices within the majority Christian environment.

Jewish and Christian Fasting: A Comparative View

How might these changes in fasting and repentance practices among the Jews of medieval Ashkenaz be understood vis-à-vis their surrounding Christian society? As noted above, most scholars, whether intentionally or not, have skirted this question by rejecting any such comparison or, more commonly, by avoiding it altogether. For example, in her history of *Megillat Ta'anit Batra*, Shulamit Elizur presents forty-odd fasts that gained popularity in medieval Ashkenaz.[238] Elizur suggests in passing that this list of fast days that commemorates biblical figures and significant events is reminiscent of the medieval Christian calendar, studded with saint's days.[239] However, she does not engage in this comparison in the main body of her study. She instead focuses on the textual tradition of *Megillat Ta'anit Batra* from its origins in late antique Palestine to its transmission and popularity in medieval Ashkenaz.[240] Alternatively, scholars have assumed, much like the statement evident in Nicholas Donin's claim against the Jews in mid-thirteenth-century Paris, that Christians fasted and Jews did not.

Figure 7. A family eating together. © Bibliothèque nationale de France. Ms héb. Paris, 1333, fol. 20b. Haggadah, fifteenth century.

Another group of scholars that has addressed medieval fasting, including Yaacov Gartner, Daniel Sperber, Meir Rafeld, and Ephraim Kanarfogel, analyze halakhic discussions of fasting from medieval Ashkenaz.[241] Their work is largely devoted to halakhic details and the prominence of frequent fasting among pious rabbinic leaders. Like Elizur, these authors attribute medieval Ashkenazic fasting practices to traditions from late antique Palestine. They each attend to internal Jewish routes of intellectual transmission without touching on the cultural milieu that enveloped medieval Jewish life. Grossman and Har-Shefi, along with Elizur, highlight rituals from late antique Palestine that resurfaced in twelfth- and thirteenth-century Ashkenaz.[242] Similarly, many scholars of Hasidei Ashkenaz have turned to late antique Palestinian traditions to explain the centrality of fasting within *Sefer Hasidim* and *Sefer Rokeah*.[243]

Admittedly, there are significant distinctions between Jewish and Christian understandings of penance. It is possible to point to four readily apparent differences. First, Eucharistic theology with penance as a concomitant requirement for participation in Mass lacks any equivalent in Judaism. A second difference concerns to celibacy, which had a role in some forms of penitent behavior among Christians and was an inherent feature of mendicant and cloistered life; however, celibacy had almost no place in the medieval Judaism of northern Europe.[244] Confession is the third contrasting element. In Christian culture, confession has a clear juridical parallel and, as some scholars have shown, ideas of penance are often equated or infused with concepts of legal judgment and medical processes,[245] so much so that developments in penitential theology have been explained by innovations in legal thought.[246] Such similarities are less prevalent in Jewish writings due to the status of Jews and Jewish communities in medieval Europe. A final distinction between the two societies relates to models of approbation and emulation within medieval life. Judaism lacked the categories of saints and celibates who were known for their penance and were so esteemed within medieval Christian culture.

Despite these significant distinctions, I would argue that a comparison is possible nevertheless. While the contrast between extreme forms of Christian asceticism and medieval Jewish fasting practices was great, as I have demonstrated, routine and even frequent fasting belongs to the broader category of repentant practice without being inextricably tied to Eucharistic piety that characterized ascetic fasting and was separate from Jewish culture. That aspect of Christian piety did not impede the development of Jewish fasting practices within medieval Christian society at large.[247]

As outlined in the introduction, I suggest approaching this as a bricolage rather than trying to determine whether fasting practices were "Jewish" or "Christian" per se. Fasting as a religious practice of self-denial has been in wide circulation throughout history. Jews and Christians shared the notion that those who practiced severe self-denial deserved admiration. Jews did not need to accept celibacy, Eucharistic piety, or penitential theology to share this perspective. Medieval Jewish texts define a number of exemplary men and even a few women as pious (*hasidim*), ascetic (*perushim*), or righteous (*tzaddikim*) on the basis of their fasting practices. For instance, Isaac of Dampierre was referred to as a *hasid,* as were other rabbis who fasted regularly.[248] Women and men who fasted during the High Holiday period were called *hasidim* and *tzaddikim* as well.[249]

Jews and Christians saw each other fasting. As demonstrated in Simone

Roux's recent study of medieval Paris, little went unnoticed in urban environments in the Middle Ages.[250] Just as Christians were well aware of their religious peers' comings and goings, so too urban Jews and Christians would have known a good deal about their neighbors' activities, irrespective of their religious identities. Members of these two communities lived in such close physical proximity that Jews would have had effortless access to their neighbors' practices. That is to say, it can safely be surmised that Jews witnessed Christians, from commoners to royalty, confessing as public penitents before their communities.[251] Jews would similarly have witnessed processions through the streets of their cities, where participants in penitential parades would have displayed outward signs of fasting, including special garments and flagellation.[252]

Awareness of Christian conduct is not synonymous with appropriation of its ideology or practices. From an intellectual perspective, this familiarity and the new practices it brought with it were often buttressed by traditional sources. As Haym Soloveitchik noted four decades ago, the penchant for fasting among medieval Jews arose as a consequence of living among Christians,[253] although Jewish texts were used to validate the embrace of these adapted rituals. Along these same lines, David Berger has suggested that familiarity with the Christian system of penance led medieval Jews such as Judah to seek corroboration in earlier Jewish sources for the rituals that he was prescribing.[254]

Asher Rubin and Talya Fishman have also each examined this issue in recent decades.[255] In an article that deserves far more attention than it has received, Rubin emphasizes just how novel active penance—that required deeds in addition to contrition as a means for atonement—was in the medieval context. He suggests that, much like the German word *busse* (that conveys both "penance" and "atonement"), the medieval use of the word teshuvah—in contrast to the term *kapparah*, common in earlier periods—connoted these two meanings as well. Rubin also demonstrates the similarity in prescriptions for penance among both Jews and Christians, such as for adultery and murder.[256] Fishman observes points of congruence between the penitential systems of Hasidei Ashkenaz (as outlined by Marcus) and its Irish and local German parallels (as from Burchard's *Corrector*).[257]

A further look at the Jewish and the Christian texts indicate that medieval writers themselves were well aware of similarities between practices. A fascinating responsum by Isaac b. Mordekhai (late thirteenth century; a contemporary of Meir b. Barukh) indicates that Jews were aware of Christian confession. Isaac told of a certain Jacob that confessed to two rabbis, Jonah and Shemaryah, who promised not to divulge what he had told them. The responsum addresses the question of whether the rabbis could disclose the content of this confession since Jacob seems to have had a history of threatening to set fires and therefore posed a danger to his community. Most remarkably, in his discussion of the rabbis' pledge of confidentiality, Isaac b. Mordekhai comments: "Though they are a thousand times apart (*ulehavdil elef alfei havdalot*), when a non-Jew confesses to a priest (*galah*) [who promises] that he will not reveal [the sin being confessed], he [the sinner] has no fear."[258] In other words, Isaac compares the rabbis' promise to Jacob with respect to his admission of wrongdoing to priestly confidentiality during confession. This source is an exceptional indicator of a Jewish familiarity with the nuances of Christian confession.

Furthermore, even though medieval sources from the generations that succeeded Eleazar of Worms uniformly emphasize the performance of personal confession, textual descriptions also show that certain sins required public admission. In fact, even Eleazar acknowledged transgressions that necessitated public confession, as did Isaac of Corbeil.[259] While no categorical list of these sins exists, *Sefer Rokeah* states that in some cases penitent actions would not suffice without a public admission of wrongdoing and an apology for those deeds.[260] An example of public confession appears in a responsum attributed to Meir of Rothenburg (one of numerous ascriptions of repentant action accredited to him). Here Meir quotes a certain Isaac: "Our rabbi, Isaac, says that whoever reneges on an oath should not do penance (*ya'aseh teshuvah*) in the location where he sinned; rather he should proclaim his sin and repent (*yashuv*) in a different location."[261]

This brief responsum leaves contemporary readers wondering who was intended to hear his confession: the local court? members of his community? representatives of another community? While this format is a far cry from institutionalized penance as practiced by Christians, its structure is sufficiently robust to include conventions for announcing and atoning for sin.

The Yom Kippur liturgy also offers a telling example of confession in Jewish belief and practice. Its longstanding association with confession is especially evident in the content of *Kol Nidrei*, the signature prayer of the opening service in which all vows are collectively absolved, and insertions in the Amidah for this unique day. However, thirteenth-century sources—as in the passage below—explain a line that was inserted in the opening prayers of the evening service that begins Yom Kippur by declaring that with the consent of God and the community, "we are permitted to pray with the sinners." If confession were practiced privately, what is the meaning of this announcement?[262]

This liturgical insertion and its justification first appeared in thirteenth-century German sources and then spread to other Jewish diaspora communities. Meir b. Barukh clarified that this line refers to one who has transgressed against the community, an idea that was reinforced by his student, Mordekhai b. Hillel.[263] This explanation is also included in a polemic between Jews and Christians in *Sefer Nizzahon Vetus:*

> The heretics criticize us in connection with the Beichte (confession) for not confessing the way they do, and they cite proof from the book of Proverbs: "He that covers his sins shall not prosper, but he that confesses and forsakes them shall have mercy" (Prov. 28:13). This is how you should answer him: On the contrary, one should conceal one's sins from another man and not tell him: "This is how I have sinned," lest the listener be tempted to commit that sin.[264] One should rather confess one's sin to God, as David said, "I acknowledge my sin to you and my iniquity have I not hidden. I said I will confess my transgressions unto the Lord and you have forgiven the iniquity of my sin, Selah" (Ps. 32:5).[265]

Here the author of *Sefer Nizzahon Vetus*—which was compiled a century after the lifetime of Judah the Pious—is advocating a Jewish version of confession. This passage bears witness to the shared tradition and heritage of Jews and Christians since the biblical verses cited by the Christian accusers (from Proverbs) and the Jewish respondents (from Psalms) held integral positions in the internal discussions of confession in Jewish as well as in Christian discourse. Similarly, the figure of David was used to champion the cause of those promoting confession within the Jewish and the Christian communities.[266]

Sefer Nizzahon Vetus also demonstrates a high level of Jewish familiarity with Christian customs. In another portion of the passage quoted above, the Jewish interlocutor questions and condemns Christian celibacy by articulating his perception of the evils of this practice and its link to confession:

> It was because of the fact that they wallow in fornication and yet their Torah forbade them from marrying that they agreed to require men to come and tell their sin and publicize their marital affairs so that they might know which women are having extramarital affairs. They then tell those women that they would like to do the same and the women cannot deny anything because the adulterer has already identified them. This is certainly the explanation because otherwise

why doesn't the pope, who is regarded as the vicar of their god and who has the power to forbid and to permit, give nuns the authority to hear the confession of women? It would clearly be more proper and acceptable for women to confess to women and men to men so that they would not be seduced into fornication and adultery.[267]

In this case the Jewish author of the polemic is commenting on an issue that was also being debated among Christians, whether women are qualified to hear other women's confessions.[268] No less significantly, the question of public versus personal confession was being debated both by Jews and Christians at that time, as discussed above.

I would suggest that discussions of common themes, be they harmonious or polemical in content and tone, support situating medieval Jewish practice within the broader culture of Christian ritual and penitential fasting. This contextualization need not infer Jewish adoption of Christian doctrinal beliefs with regard to the significance of fasting or penance. In point of fact, I would argue that precisely because Jews and Christians differed over the role and performance of confession, they were able to maintain contrasting approaches to shared practices, given their religious and social positions.[269]

In order to further examine the similarity between Jewish and Christian practice, let us now turn to two themes that relate to the issues examined above: gender and fasting, and penitential fasts by Jews who contemplated conversion or who converted and then returned to Judaism.

Jewish and Christian Women's Fasting

Women's fasting represents a useful example for assessing Jewish and Christian practices in relation to one another. As the sources analyzed above show, fasting was practiced by both men and women. However, in the previous section of this chapter, we also saw that gendered considerations led the rabbis, the governing authority of the Jewish community, to set different standards of appropriate practice for men and women who fasted. Women's physiology is a primary factor in this gendered perspective. To a certain degree, these directives can be read as an extension of the general guidelines that limit those whose fasts would restrict their availability as caregivers to times when the entire community was fasting.[270] For example, Judah the Pious wrote in detail about who was qualified to fast. Although his instructions follow ancient guidelines,[271] they attest to the frequency of fasting and the piety attributed to those who fasted in his circle:

> When the enemies surround the city, one should not fast lest he be rendered unable to fight. Whoever goes to redeem captives should not fast, for if he becomes weak, he would hinder their journey (of the redeeming group). Likewise, one who may save a soul—such as a midwife or one who attends to an elderly father or mother or one who cares for the sick without additional assistance—should not take on an individual fast;[272] rather (he should fast) only with the community or according to his regular fasting practice, like on the anniversary of his father's death.[273]

This list manifests the tension between fasting and maintaining ongoing activities, underscoring fasting as an interruption from routine commitments. Fasting entailed a degree of separation from service to friends, family, and neighbors for the sake of devoting oneself more intensively to God. Therefore, Judah instructs those who would otherwise be exempt to fast only when the community takes precedence over individual and communal health-related needs.[274] However, in a world where women were responsible for younger children, their households and probably older relatives as well, it is reasonable to assume that they were far more likely to be relied upon by others than were men.[275] Moreover, at times of privation, women were known to abstain from eating so they could provide sustenance for others.[276] The halakhic asymmetry that assigns the agency to make vows according to gender noted above also informs discussions of fasting. As a result, women and men had different levels of autonomy with respect to committing themselves to personal fasts.

The relationship between women's responsibilities in the kitchen and control over their fasts invites reflection on Jewish and Christian comparisons and connections. Over two decades ago, Caroline Bynum published *Holy Feast and Holy Fast*, where she examines fasting practices in Christian Europe, especially among a small group of radical ascetics who abstained from eating except when taking the Eucharist during Mass. In subsequent research on women's fasts in medieval and early modern Ashkenaz, Avraham Grossman, Bitha Har-Shefi, and Yemima Hovav each refer to Bynum's argument as a possible explanation for fasting among Jewish women, noting the similar roles with regard to preparing meals that Jewish and Christian women assumed in their respective societies. However, these scholars of Jewish culture readily dismiss the comparison between Jewish and Christian women explaining that the connection between Christian fasting and Eucharistic piety precludes it.[277]

In contrast, I propose that Bynum's work goes beyond theological

Figure 8. Women cooking. From *Leipzig Mahzor*. © Leipzig University Library. 1102, Kennicott 665, fol. 68v. Mahzor Worms, ca. 1310,

considerations behind medieval Christian women's fasting. Alongside her theological emphasis, her study underscores the social value of fasting, thus presenting the affinity between women and food preparation as a practical application.[278] Jewish and Christian women—and by extension Jewish and Christian societies—shared more than just a similarly gendered division of labor with respect to food preparation. Both communities also held many commonalities that related to gender hierarchy, as can be seen in the following instructions from Thomas of Chobham's (ca. 1160–1236) *Summa Confessorum* that address a clerical readership who heard confession and assigned penance:

"Likewise, it should be noted that a woman is in the power of her husband and cannot make any vow of abstinence, nor can the priest impose some special fast on her for penance, because the husband can alter the vow if his wife vowed some fast, or if the priest imposed a fast on her beyond the common fasts of the year."[279] Even though Thomas is discussing the Christian annual ritual cycle and Christian penance, not only does he follow the same biblical directive on swearing vows that was operative among his Jewish contemporaries, he also promotes an analogously gendered social hierarchy.

As such, it might be concluded that although we cannot equate Jewish fasting to Christian fasts that subordinated common meals to Eucharistic piety, there is a basis for comparison. Although the radical ascetics Bynum studied are without parallel in Jewish culture, Christian laity—both men and women—are more analogous. Whereas lay Christian approaches to abstinence were less radical than those of the ascetics, they too fasted frequently.

An illustration of the resemblance between lay Christians and their Jewish neighbors is found in a story told by the Cistercian monk, Caesarius of Heisterbach (1170–1240). He recounts the tale of a woman who sold iron (possibly second-hand) and made confession to Herman, the priest of St. Martin's Church in Cologne.[280] While the sins pertaining to her trade are his primary interest, Caesarius also recalls her boasts about fasting, charity, and church attendance. She said: "Lord, I am accustomed to fasting on bread and water during such-and-such number of Fridays each year, giving my alms and going to church."[281] Although Caesarius criticizes her inflated claims, this woman was simply overstating practices that were expected of any respectable Christian: fasting, charity, and worship as expressions of penance and piety.

Similarly, the so-called Ménagier de Paris (fourteenth century) who instructed his wife on proper behavior also advised her on fasting. In addition, he enumerated the prayers that she should recite daily before breaking her fast.[282] He remarked that "penance is performed in three ways: by fasting, alms, and prayers,"[283] and concluded his prescription for avoiding sin by emphasizing that a chaste life and a spotless conscience could only be attained by "fasting and keeping always before you the remembrance of death."[284] Despite such injunctions, Christian women, like their Jewish neighbors, were also cautioned against excessive fasting lest their families need their attention.[285] Thus we see that a common gendered ideology ruled these distinct religious practices.

Fasting, Converts, and Conversion

Fasting served as a marker of difference between Jewish and Christian societies in other instances. I now turn to my second comparative example: fasting during the High Middle Ages as a form of repentance for Jews who had converted to Christianity and subsequently returned to Judaism, by analyzing exempla that depict such practice. While these cases may actually be fictitious, as they were designed to ring true to readers and listeners and to reflect reality, they are worthy of consideration.[286] *Sefer Hasidim* contains this story: "A certain Jew entered the courtyard of a church. When he exited, he heard a heavenly voice say: 'And Me you have cast behind your back' (I Kings 14:9). He fasted for the rest of his days."

This teaching is followed by a similar account: "A certain individual entered a house of idolatry (a church) and felt remorse. He asked a Sage to advise him [on how to repent] and [the Sage] said, 'You should fast on that date each year.' And so he did."[287]

These characteristically terse passages raise questions even as they convey a clear message. One could wonder about the difference between these two people that would cause one to be instructed to fast for the rest of his life—likely defined as following a constrained diet and refraining for the most part from meat and wine,[288] whereas the other was mandated to fast on the anniversary of his lapse. One might also question what prompted each of these Jews to enter a church. Given that many Jews participated in business transactions that were conducted in churches,[289] I read the motivations implied here to be out of the ordinary, namely the contemplation of conversion.

Prescriptions for fasting and suffering as means to deter conversion also appear in a unique narrative from medieval England: the well-known story of Yom Tov, a young man who ultimately committed suicide. While its details go beyond the scope of this discussion, it is noteworthy that young Yom Tov was tempted by a ghost bearing a cross who urged him to convert to Christianity. The narrator responds by recommending ascetic and penitent practices in this world to enable proper worship of God: "It is better for a person to repent by fasting, suffering and receiving lashes in this world [so he can then] worship God with all of his heart and soul, and be fruitful, with holy and wondrous seed emerging from him, so his days may be renewed as with Job."[290] In his collection of instructions for repentance after the sin of conversion (or being on the verge of converting), *Sefer Hasidim* recommends fasting until "his teeth turned black" and donning black clothing, presenting a series of warnings about the gravity of conversion.[291]

Penitent fasting after conversion to Christianity appears in another thirteenth-century source as well. On the subject of women who converted under duress, Asher b. Yehiel (Rosh) writes:

> Regarding women who lacked the strength to stand in the king's chamber,[292] and converted during the hour of persecution due to their fear of death, [ultimately] found a way to escape, and then returned to their religion: Surely this is a grave matter for which they must show remorse and repent. [Moreover] they must suffer more intensely than those who converted privately since persecutions took place in public.[293]

This text indicates that repenting after conversion or considering conversion was standard and, furthermore, that the women described here fasted of their own volition.

The process of returning converts to Judaism has been described in additional Jewish and Christian sources, as outlined by Ephraim Kanarfogel.[294] According to the French Inquisitor Bernard Gui (d. 1331), a returning apostate was first required to remove all clothing and bathe. During this procedure, in addition to being washed from head to toe, the convert's fingernails and toenails were cut to the quick, to the point of drawing blood. The convert's head was then shaved. The final step was immersion in the mikveh.[295] This description leaves no doubt that anyone who went through this ritual would be conspicuous to the whole community. William Chester Jordan has also written about this process for converts who returned to Judaism in twelfth- and thirteenth-century France.[296] Although Gui does not mention fasting, contemporaneous Jewish sources do: Simhah of Speyer ruled that such a convert must afflict his body;[297] and Eleazar of Worms, much like *Sefer Hasidim*, specified that a returning convert should abstain from meat and wine, and fast regularly during the next several years.[298]

Beyond serving as a safeguard against conversion and as a mode of repentance upon returning, one purported twelfth-century convert to Christianity, the famed Herman-Judah, reported that he fasted while contemplating conversion.[299] Like the biblical Daniel, Herman fasted for three days in his quest for divine counsel:

> I knew that Jews and Christians did not keep the same rule of fasting. Since Christians eat on fast days at the ninth hour, abstaining

from flesh, while Jews, continuing until evening, are allowed to eat flesh and anything else. But I did not know which of these pleased God the more. I decided to keep both without distinction. And so according to the rite of Christianity I abstained from flesh and extending the fast until evening in the fashion of the Jews, I remained content with a little bread and water.[300]

Herman's account informs us of two features that separated Jewish and Christian fasting. Such distinctions underscore the impact that nuances can have on creating difference. Christians fasted until midday; in fact, the designated time for Christians to break their fasts was scheduled ever earlier during the course of the Middle Ages.[301] Ascetics would exhibit the stringency of their practice not only through fasting, but also with the foods they ate (and avoided) when concluding their fasts. In contrast, according to Herman, Jews fasted until evening and breaking fast with meat was commonplace.

This passage from Herman's autobiography is a reminder of the power of food as a social and cultural influence, and of how seemingly minor variations in dietary norms can set the communities apart. This phenomenon is discernible in comments from several Ashkenazic rabbinic authorities about the custom of fasting on the day before Rosh haShanah. Both Meir b. Yekutiel Cohen (1260–1298; author of *Hagahot Maimoniyot*) and Jacob Moellin note that some Jews were wary of this popular medieval custom lest its practitioners be misconstrued as "observing non-Jewish customs" (*mishum hukat hagoyim*). This discomfort stemmed from the common Christian custom of fasting on the day prior to a holiday; Jews wanted to avoid being perceived as imitating this practice. Thus, they would compromise by rising early and eating before sunrise on the day before Rosh haShanah.[302]

Daniel Sperber has explained the background of this pre-Rosh haShanah fast on the basis of the quarterly Ember Days,[303] a Christian Wednesday-Friday-Saturday fasting cycle observed in the middle of December, March, June, and September.[304] On occasion, the eve of Rosh haShanah corresponded with one of the Ember Days in September, which added complexity to the relationship between these rituals and the impressions that they conveyed. Even more interesting than the effort to separate Jewish and Christian practice is the assumption by Jewish authors that rising early to eat before their fast would distinguish Jews from their Christian neighbors. It is unclear whether this difference would be evident to Jews, Christians, or both groups.

These discussions of Jewish and Christian fasting further inform our knowledge of medieval fasts. They supplement the data from Herman's memoir, showing that both the length of fasts and the foods eaten immediately before and after defined the members of each religion.[305] This dynamic is accentuated by the singular exception to the Jewish norm of fasting until nightfall that applies to fasts that fall on Fridays, be they individual or collective (e.g., the communal fast on the tenth of Tevet that can fall on a Friday).[306] As with the fast on the day preceding Rosh haShanah, some rabbinic leaders instructed their followers to eat before nightfall, prior to leaving for synagogue or at sunset, to signify the holiness of the Sabbath.[307] In contrast, Friday fasts were observed until nightfall in other Jewish diaspora communities,[308] which raises the question of whether this Ashkenazic practice was associated with local Christian customs.

Conclusions: Jewish and Christian Fasting

The similarities between Jewish repentance rituals and Christian penance in medieval northern Europe are striking, especially in connection to the incumbent values that were expressed via fasts, charity, and prayers. A catalogue of what Jews actually consumed and avoided while fasting emerges from Herman-Judah's narrative as well as from our overall examination of penitential fasting. Medieval authors define refraining from all food and drink from sunrise until three stars appear as a full-fledged fast;[309] however, variations on this pattern were practiced and some testimonies mention fasts that ended before nightfall.[310] As we have seen, Meir of Rothenburg distinguished between mature women who were accustomed to fasting and younger women who were not.[311] Moreover, Jacob Moellin demonstrated a similar sensitivity in the reverse direction when he noted that, since fasting could be difficult for older people, they might rise early to eat before the fast started, whereas younger people should not.[312] These exceptions represent just a sampling of the accommodations discussed in medieval sources on fasting. Instructions for penitential rituals in both *Sefer Hasidim* and Eleazar of Worms's *Hilkhot Teshuvah* include fasts of bread and water rather than full fasts.[313] In addition to specifying when to fast, some texts also offer instructions to refrain from eating meat and drinking wine for a period of time (as noted above).[314] No text enumerates the precise details of fasting as they were actually performed, but the extant corpus depicts a variety of practices.

The "moral arithmetic"[315] used here was unique to medieval northern

Europe. Rather than assuming that these common beliefs and customs somehow lowered the fences between Jews and Christians, I am proposing that their congruence fostered the development of boundaries and separate identities. The forty-day fast is an apt example—before Yom Kippur for Ashkenazic Jews and before Easter for Christians—that demonstrates an inward acculturation that harnessed shared rituals to express religious difference.[316]

If fasting was as widespread as I am suggesting, then Jews and Christians would have seen signs of their counterparts fasting not just in the public venues, such as the marketplace, pawnshops, and outdoor spaces. To the contrary, Jews would have noticed that their Christian neighbors and employees were fasting whether during Lent or for individual penance.[317] For example, the author of *Sefer Nizzahon Vetus* indicates that he was quite aware when Christians fasted; in particular, he mentions the forty days from Christmas through February 2, when the purification of the Virgin Mary was celebrated.[318] Interestingly, he errs here, for Christians did not fast forty days between Christmas and the Purification; rather, they fasted from Advent to Christmas and during Lent.[319] In the case of communal Christian fasts, not only did Christian servants who worked and lived within Jewish homes refrain from eating as usual, but public processions also announced the fasts. Furthermore, the fare available at local markets would also have reflected the festival cycles as well as the fasts,[320] and anyone who glanced into a courtyard oven would have known something of her neighbors' diet.[321] This was true as far as smell was concerned as well: the scents of foods or their absence would have been part of everyday life. Even if Ashkenazic Jews had only a partial grasp of the various Christian fasts, they likely would have been aware that fasting was linked to penance. This connection would have resonated with medieval Jews since it was supported by ancient Jewish texts and was reflected in their own religious practice.

Judah the Pious commented on Christian penitential fasts. His remarks hint at his perception of the differences between Jews and Christians: "A person should not say: 'Lest jealousy, lust and pride remove me from the world, I shall distance myself from them (worldly pleasures) as far as possible,' [to such a degree that] he doesn't eat meat or drink wine, live in a fine house or wear nice clothing, but rather [dresses in] sackcloth, harsh wool or other such similar items, as the Christian priests do."[322] In this passage, Judah describes some practical aspects of Christian penance that differed from Jewish fasting, thereby emphasizing distinctions between Jews and Christians. This teaching also reveals that Jews were familiar with modified fasting among Christians, where they refrained from meat and wine rather than abstaining from food and drink altogether.

As Jews were cognizant of Christian fasting, Christians would have had reciprocal knowledge of Jewish fasting since they interacted with Jews in these same situations—in business transactions, and as neighbors or as employees in Jewish homes. As noted above, fasting was manifested publicly through absence from group meals, at times by wearing distinctive clothing or hair. Even though personal fasts among Jews were announced in the community's main public space, the synagogue, it seems likely that their Christian neighbors could have become aware of that vow despite being members of a different religious sphere. Said differently, Christians would have had access to the signals of Jewish fasting since, as in Christian fasting, they were publicly displayed, making possible the accusation of fasting "to show the world her piety."[323]

Ashkenazic Jews would have been quick to cite the differences in practice that distinguished them from their Christian peers: Jewish fasts were not performed in anticipation of rituals akin to attending the Mass or receiving the Eucharist; Christians fasted until midday, whereas Jews continued until nightfall;[324] Jews fasted on Mondays and Thursdays but rarely on Fridays, whereas Christians typically fasted on Wednesdays and Fridays—as a result, Jews and Christians hardly ever fasted concurrently. The disparity between Jewish and Christian activities on Fridays are particularly striking, with Jews cooking meat in anticipation of the Sabbath while Christians fasted and then ate fish, refraining from meat altogether.[325] Some sources suggest that a Jewish custom of eating meat before the Sabbath on Fridays may have started as another way of expressing Jewishness.[326]

Medieval Christians and Jews remarked on the divergence in their fasting practices. While these differences might seem at first glance like variations on a common pattern, especially when the intensive fasting rituals that were embraced by medieval Ashkenazic Jews are taken into account, each practice was intrinsically tied to piety as expressed by its religion. In other words, even when customs seemed equivalent, calendrical and dietary distinctions effectively fortified each community's identity and sense of belonging. As anthropologists have asserted, the cycles of daily and annual observance are instrumental in the construction of identity.[327] Among the Christians and Jews of medieval Ashkenaz, ostensibly minor discrepancies were symbolic of religious, social, and cultural difference.

Although our subject here is fasting, it is noteworthy that wine, meat, and bread—essential fare mentioned in our texts—hold currency whether they are consumed or avoided, albeit with different valence and timing in Jewish and Christian cultures. The repentance rituals assigned to the woman whose child died when she lay upon him is illustrative: she was specifically instructed to eat and drink wine on specific Jewish observances, such as the new moon and holidays; thus, participating in the communal calendar cycle took precedence over her individualized penitential fast.

* * *

This chapter has demonstrated how eating and fasting were one way to epitomize the distinctions between Jews and non-Jews,[328] and were used by members of both groups as a way of expressing piety. These were also aspects of medieval life that demanded constant negotiation. We have seen that Jews and Christians in northern Europe during the High Middle Ages saw fasting as an effective way of practicing piety on many levels.[329] Fasting was a form of bodily control and of torment, and an essential component of penance, a central motif in this chapter. Oftentimes, these different aspects of fasting were intertwined. Both Christian and Jewish leaders and thinkers developed systems of penance during the High Middle Ages. When compared, these medieval approaches reveal ancient roots and, in many cases, divergent values. Yet at the same time, both groups of medieval leaders devised complex structures of repentance whose theoretical and ritual overlap is too extensive to be coincidental. These beliefs and practices reflect their understandings of proper worship of God and *timor dei*—*yir'at hashem* as key concepts—ideas that had redefined and developed since late antiquity, a process that these leaders fervently continued in their own generations. Christian and Jewish cultures both compared fasting to sacrifice, through its respective associations to the Eucharist and to bringing offerings to the Temple. Another commonality between the medieval Jewish and Christian penitential systems was the option of substituting one form of penance for another. This option was well known in Christian Europe from the ninth century onward, as attested in sources that detail suitable alternatives; for example, fasting could be replaced by prayer and alms, and so on.[330] On the whole, the Jewish sources suggest that fasting became the preferred penitential ritual during the thirteenth century.[331]

It is noteworthy that most Jewish sources examined in this chapter are from Jewish centers in Germany, although, as I have indicated, some innovations introduced by German rabbis in the late twelfth century were embraced by their peers in northern France during the thirteenth century and others had earlier precedents.[332] Penitential culture with fasting as a major element maintained a significant role in Christian life until the Reformation, although calls for moderation were raised during the late Middle Ages.[333] Among Jews, one can also see a consistent culture of fasting well into the early modern period.

CHAPTER 3

Communal Charity: Evidence from Medieval Nürnberg

Charity saves from death.
—Prov. 10:2

An epitaph from 1287 in the Jewish cemetery of Worms reports: "[Buried here is] the Mistress Yokheved daughter of Rosh¹—R. Yehiel son of our teacher, Rabbi Ephraim—who excelled (*hefli'ah la'asot*) in building synagogues and cemeteries here and in many communities, and in [contributing to] other charities and also by surrounding this cemetery with a wall."²

This Yokheved³ is being praised for her generous support of community institutions, not only in her home city of Worms but in other locations as well.⁴ Her patronage is noted on her tombstone and attests to the outstanding scope of her contributions. This posthumous acknowledgment of her charity was a means of applauding her deeds in life and commending her smooth passage to heaven, for assurance of a place in the World to Come was understood as one of the enduring benefits of giving charity.⁵

For those who were without extensive means, the charity that would lead them to heaven was often contributed in the form of a donation commonly known as *pro anima* (for the soul). This chapter focuses on this process of giving such charity for the soul, as transmitted by the quantitative data on donations from Jewish men and women in the *memorbuch* (book of commemoration) from medieval Nürnberg.⁶ This chapter also dovetails with Chapters 1 and 2 by tracing a core pious practice that accompanied praying and fasting.⁷ Unlike the other chapters in this volume, where I draw upon what could be called "standard sources"—prescriptive texts that convey procedures as designated by the intellectual elite—alongside exceptional practices that illuminate cracks in the system, this one draws on information that is derived from a unique source that invites close consideration of charitable giving in the medieval Jewish community of Nürnberg.[8]

Material from the Nürnberg Memorbuch is at the heart of this chapter, which begins with an introduction to the Memorbuch followed by five thematic sections. The first of the five provides an overview of Jewish beliefs in the efficacy of charity during late antiquity and the Middle Ages, serving as a background for medieval Jewish interpretations of charity and associated rituals. The next section surveys medieval Christian and Jewish charity pro anima and compares and contrasts them. In the third section, I present the evidence from the Nürnberg Memorbuch for the period before the Black Death to delineate the custom of contributing charity for one's soul and the patterns of donations that emerged as this ritual became more firmly institutionalized. I then analyze the social norms of donating gifts for the soul on the basis of that data, including the participation of Jewish men, women, and children in this custom. As in previous chapters, the final section examines Jewish practice in the context of medieval Christian attitudes toward and contributions of analogous forms of charity and piety.

The Nürnberg Memorbuch

The memorbuch that has survived from the medieval Jewish community of Nürnberg represents the earliest example of a genre that became widespread in early modern Ashkenazic communities.[9] This manuscript contains the liturgy for honoring the dead as well as various lists of deceased community members, including a register of donations that they pledged to the synagogue and affiliated institutions for the sake of their souls. The donation entries in this volume span more than two centuries, from the closing decades of the thirteenth century through the late fifteenth century. I have limited this analysis to entries dated until the onset of the Black Death in 1349,[10] for two reasons: in keeping with the general temporal scope of this study as a whole and because the community itself changed drastically after that crisis.[11]

The Nürnberg Memorbuch was created in 1296 by Isaac b. Samuel Meiningen as a gift to his community when their new synagogue was dedicated in November of that year. Isaac called it a *sefer zikaron* (book of remembrance). The initial folio of the manuscript as it has reached us contains the liturgy that was recited between the Torah reading and Musaf prayers, when donations were acknowledged and their contributors were thanked with words of blessing.¹² This book included two community necrologies—with lists of those who died and gifts for the soul that the deceased had pledged for communal benefit—organized by timeframe: until 1346 and 1375–1392. It also contains a martyrology that names all who perished in attacks on Rhineland communities from 1096 to 1349. In the late nineteenth century, this source was edited in its entirety by Siegmund Salfeld and Moritz Stern;¹³ its contents, especially the register of martyrs, have received considerable attention since that time.¹⁴

Despite its groundbreaking role and exceptional detail, the memorbuch leaves many questions unanswered. After Isaac b. Samuel died during the Rintfleisch attacks in the summer of 1298, several anonymous hands assumed the task of inscribing names and contributions in his stead over subsequent generations.¹⁵ During the modern period, the Nürnberg Memorbuch was owned by Eliakim Carmoly, infamous for having taken liberties with manuscripts in his possession.¹⁶ Due to these codicological complexities, the exceptional social data in this memorbuch have been almost completely ignored, albeit with notable exceptions.

Three decades ago, Israel Yuval mined these lists for evidence of individual and communal praxis. In a fascinating article, he examined the later necrology and late fourteenth-century listing of donations, primarily focusing on charity to the Land of Israel, a common element of *matnat yad* (charity given on the three pilgrimage festivals, each named for an assigned biblical reading). As Yuval has noted, when compared with the earlier material, this register from after the Black Death records fewer donations¹⁷ but includes greater chronological detail, such as a notation that marks the beginning of each year so pledges could be tracked per annum.¹⁸ Michael Toch has studied the memorbuch for its numismatic evidence. These findings contributed to his investigation of the currencies used in Germany during the thirteenth and fourteenth centuries.¹⁹ Judah Galinsky drew on data from this memorbuch in his categorization of the charitable donations given in medieval Ashkenaz, with particular attention to liturgical formulae that commemorate the dead (*yizkor*).²⁰ Most recently, Rainer Barzen has examined the post–Black Death donations, noting the prominence of the *hekdesh* (a communally supported hospital) as a charitable cause during the late fourteenth century.²¹

This chapter investigates the necrologies recorded through 1349 that itemize charitable contributions pledged for the soul by over one thousand individuals. It registers male and female donors by name, the pledged sum, and, in many cases, its declared purpose. As one of the rare extant medieval sources to provide quantitative data, this text is an invaluable resource for assessing charitable giving in medieval Ashkenaz. The entries in this memorbuch represent gifts that were contributed or earmarked for distribution while their donors were still living. Since this source enumerates only bequests dedicated by the Jews of medieval Nürnberg for the sake of their own souls, each name appears once.[22] Presumably most, if not all, community members would have contributed funds to the community occasionally throughout the years, since it is inconceivable that medieval Jews would have donated to their community but once in a lifetime.[23] As I suggest throughout this chapter, the causes toward which charity for the soul was directed were officially recommended by and therefore represented the directives of communal leaders, since this was a formal donation par excellence. As such, these contributions are arguably indicative of prescribed norms rather than personal preferences. While each donor would have determined the size of the gift, a known standard probably guided such choices.[24]

If a preamble introduced the list of donors in the Nürnberg Memorbuch, the pages where it had been inscribed are missing, leaving the mechanism for acknowledging the charitable donations recorded therein open to speculation. Was the whole list read aloud on each Sabbath? Were the names divided into groups that would be read in synagogue but without correlation to the anniversaries of the contributors' deaths?[25] The scribe of the Nürnberg Memorbuch, Isaac of Meiningen, provides a partial answer to these questions. Alongside a list of the Ashkenazic community's most renowned benefactors (e.g., Shlomo and Rachel, who founded the community;[26] Shimon, who was instrumental in rescinding the harsh eleventh-century decrees against the Jewish community; and Gershom Me'or haGolah [Ragmah, d. 1028], among others, concluding with Meir b. Barukh of Rothenburg), Isaac noted that their names were to be mentioned "every Sabbath."[27] Solomon Freehof has echoed this remark by suggesting that a prayer in memory of all who were martyred and the names of key benefactors might have been read on each Sabbath.[28] These names are followed by those of the individual donations from members of the community who were not as illustrious. Freehof already raised the possibility that most of the names were only read at specific times, perhaps according to the anniversary of each death, but that seems unlikely given the absence of dates in the text.[29] Alternatively, on the basis of later memorbücher from Prague, Rachel Greenblatt has recently proposed that names were read in an annual cycle from the earliest to the most recent.[30] Although it is not clear which of these alternatives was practiced, the information in the memorbuch allows an unprecedented familiarity with many people and their charitable donations that would otherwise be unknown.

Charity as a Redemptive Act in Late Antiquity and the Middle Ages

Medieval Jews read "Charity[31] saves from death" (Prov. 10:2) as a teaching on the life-enhancing effects of charity,[32] but the notion of charity as a redemptive act that could facilitate a better life in this world and salvation in the World to Come did not originate with them. This understanding can be traced to late antiquity among both Jews and Christians, as current scholarship demonstrates. Following the work of Roman Garrison and Richard Finn on redemptive charity in late antique Christian culture, Alyssa Gray and Michael Satlow have recently analyzed redemptive charity in late antique Jewish and Christian cultures.[33] Garrison and Finn noted the redemptive attributes associated with Christian charity, claiming that Christians inherited these ideas from their Jewish predecessors and that Christian theologians based their concepts of charity on Jewish texts from antiquity (e.g., Prov. 10 and the Book of Tobias).[34] Ephraim Urbach countered that position by arguing that for Jews, charity was a worldly action aimed at assisting the poor in their midst, whereas Christian charity was meant to sanctify the poor and, more importantly, to hasten the donor's own redemption.[35]

With this scholarly debate as a backdrop, Gray examines the idea of redemptive charity among Jews in Palestine and Babylon and compares the conceptualization of charity among Jews and Christians in Palestine. She finds that Jewish understandings of redemptive charity seem to have Palestinian origins since they are mentioned in texts from the Land of Israel and in Babylonian quotations of Palestinian texts. Further, Gray states that Jews viewed charity as redemptive and, at least according to Palestinian sources, many believed that charity could redeem them from death, rescue them from hell, and ease their entrance to heaven. Gray has proposed that some rabbis—especially in Babylonia—were reticent to consider the impoverished recipients of charity as a keystone of Jewish society. Those very rabbis sought to acquire that pivotal role by positioning themselves as intermediaries between donors and the poor.[36] In his analysis, Satlow remarks on the discomfort conveyed in rabbinic discussions of gain—be it material or spiritual—as an outcome of giving charity. He describes the belief that rewards would be granted in return for charity among Jews and especially Christians in the third century,[37] devoting considerable attention to women depicted in stories of piety and charity.[38]

Medieval Jews were heirs to these traditions. In addition, they witnessed the increasing importance of charitable practices among the medieval Christian majority. Like their predecessors in late antiquity, Christian authorities in medieval Europe continued to stress the value of religious donations in Christian thought and practice. As refined by medieval theologians, charity became an evermore elaborate doctrine that promised donors earthly benefits and a path to God. As the significance of giving grew, so did the institutions that managed the collection and distribution of monies, the modes for expressing appreciation to donors, and the assurance of charity's instrumental role in personal and communal redemption. Local churches and especially monastic houses became key actors in the expanding economy of charity.[39]

The qualms imparted by some rabbis in late antiquity regarding the redemptive features of charity had all but vanished by the medieval period[40] when charity as a means for receiving spiritual and material recompense had come to occupy a vital place in medieval Jewish life. In contrast to the passages from the early centuries of the Common Era cited by Satlow and Gray, where rabbis often acted as intermediaries between donors and recipients, medieval narratives often depict less prominent Jews, men and women, as both protagonists and meritorious recipients in vignettes about charity.[41]

As in Christian society, formal institutions and rituals developed to showcase Jewish donors and their contributions. The Nürnberg Memorbuch represents such a platform for recording and acclaiming gifts for the soul. Charity was routinely collected in times of danger and collective need, and contributions of various sorts were regularly recognized on the Sabbath and during festivals. These donations were intended for community relief and to memorialize the dead; benefactors and recipients alike were understood to merit redemptive effects from these contributions.

The customs relating to matnat yad and yizkor (remembrance of deceased relatives) have been described in recent studies by Eric Zimmer and Judah Galinsky, respectively.[42] Like charity given for the soul (the primary focus of the Nürnberg Memorbuch), those contributions were announced during prayer services and thus formed a component of public ritual: matnat yad contributions were recognized on each of the three pilgrimage festivals, as yizkor donations were on the High Holidays.[43] Within the Nürnberg Memorbuch, these rituals are interwoven in the form of blessings—for charity given by the

Figure 9. Excerpt from *Nürnberg Memorbuch*. Owned by private collector (formerly Mainz 19 Anonymous IR), fol. 44v. Nürnberg, late thirteenth century.

community and by individuals remembering loved ones—that were recited after the Torah was read on Sabbaths and holidays. At this same liturgical juncture, the names of eminent benefactors (i.e., the prominent rabbis and couples noted above who had made substantial donations) were read aloud,[44] presumably with a rotating list of community members.[45]

Besides their redemptive nature, charitable donations also served highly valued societal functions.[46] Public recognition of donors reinforced communal hierarchies while bestowing status on major benefactors.[47] In certain respects, just as fasting was broadly accessible as a pious practice (as discussed in Chapter 2), so too with charitable gifts. Like fasting, donations required neither literacy nor special training. By virtue of belonging to the group and giving charity, one merited blessing. The prayer for the entire community (*kol hakahal*) in the Nürnberg Memorbuch reiterates the inclusive nature of this ritual, rhetorically linking communal membership with support for its collective welfare:

> May the One who blessed Abraham and Isaac and Jacob bless this entire community that volunteers to give charity, and that rises early (each morning) and comes each evening to this house of prayer. May God (haMakom, lit., the place) hear their prayers and accept their charitable contributions (lit., charities), and save and redeem them from all trouble and danger, together with all Israel. And let us say: "Amen."[48]

It could be argued that, based on this blessing, charity was a defining feature of participation in the collective.[49] Yet unlike fasting, which could be practiced by anyone with willpower and a daily routine that allowed for abstaining from food and drink, assets were a prerequisite for giving charity. Contributions, whether monetary or material, were reliant on resources and personal agency. As I address later in this chapter, no dependent had the ability to make a contribution of his or her own volition. That is to say, minors, married women, and other dependents were supposed to be subject to permission from their recognized authority in order to give charity.[50]

The Nürnberg Memorbuch refers to charity of different forms and meanings (to memorialize the dead, to honor the living, or to support the poor) and among these forms was the charity given for the sake of one's soul. This type of donation was a common feature of medieval Christian pious practice as well. Before turning to the gifts enumerated in the Nürnberg Memorbuch, let us consider the Christian custom.

Medieval Charity Pro Anima

Numerous studies of medieval European Christianity point to the mounting importance of charity pro anima that often led to sponsored Masses to be said for the soul of the deceased.[51] These bequests are recorded in wills from the eleventh century onward and in the charters of churches and monasteries. Over time, many of these donations, especially within monastic orders, were chronicled in books known as *libri vitaes* (books of lives) or *libri memoriales* (books of commemoration), as well as in necrologies. In some cases, donors' names were recorded when they pledged their contributions as an assurance that they had secured a place for themselves both in communal memory and in heaven.[52] These communal volumes were kept by the altar, demarcating a symbolic place for the deceased through a physical object that served as a reminder of their continual presence.[53]

Before embarking on a description of the Christian texts that provide points of comparison and contextualization for our study of the Nürnberg Memorbuch, the resemblance shared by the defining features of memorbücher and Christian necrologies and libri memorials must be examined. Indeed, since the Nürnberg Memorbuch became a subject of scholarly interest in the late nineteenth century, most discussions of this volume include a note suggesting that its origin and development would be best understood in the context of medieval necrologia. Yet hardly any systematic effort to compare these genres or related customs has been conducted.[54]

Christian charity at large and pro anima donations in particular have been discussed by scholars as "gifts," using the terminology coined by Marcel Mauss in his seminal work *Essai sur le don* almost a century ago.[55] Mauss and those who followed in his footsteps have articulated a logic of reciprocity that underlies all gifts, to humans and to the gods.[56] More recently, scholars of the Middle Ages and early modern period have developed methods for evaluating patterns of charitable giving that deepen our grasp of economic, social, religious, and political relations in medieval Europe, particularly in its urban centers.[57] As Martha Howell—whose work concentrates on these gifts as indicators of late medieval commerce—has remarked, giving donations was a mechanism for attaining honor. Using the terminology devised by Julian Pitt-Rivers and refined by others, Howell defines honor as "the nexus between ideals of society and their reproduction in the individual through his aspiration to personify them."[58]

Charitable gifts have also been interpreted as a form of sacrifice by scholars such as Arnold Angenendt, who interpreted medieval pro anima donations as analogous to the Eucharist and contended that the increasing emphasis on material components of charity during the Middle Ages was accompanied by rising expectations of reciprocal gestures from God.[59] This concept of mutuality eventually led to the ill-reputed economy of Masses and penance that dominated Christianity in the late Middle Ages;[60] yet this same notion was also a catalyst for a remarkable transformation: the monasteries that received major donations during the High Middle Ages became centers of cultural achievement and social renown.[61]

A review of the philosophy, practice, and societal implications for Christian pro anima charity goes beyond the scope of this study. However, to more fully understand the Jewish memorbuch from Nürnberg in relation to libri memoriales, an introduction to the features and functions of the latter is essential. These Christian volumes usually consist of three sections: a liturgical manual explaining the prayers to recite when reading the names therein, a martyrologium of saints, and a necrologium of donors. Since most necrologia were recorded in and pertained to monasteries, they often include the regula (rule) of that specific community[62] alongside an itemization of the donations that they, their families, and their benefactors had pledged to that monastery and its church over time.[63] Scholars have commented on the motivations that compelled donors to cement their connections with a monastery via charity as a means for "entering" that house.[64]

Now let us examine the content of Christian libri with reference to the Jewish memorbücher introduced above. Selections from Christian necrologia were read daily or weekly during Mass.[65] This liturgical placement correlates to both a similarity and a contrast in the rituals involving these volumes. On the one hand, the Mass represented the pinnacle of Christian prayer, much like Torah reading in Jewish prayer, so commemorating the dead at those moments honors their memory. On the other hand, as a ritual, the Mass was the antithesis of Jewish prayer, having initially been designed as a Christian contra to earlier Jewish liturgy. As an expression of the inward acculturation[66] that typified medieval Jewish life, the decision to remember the dead and their donations between the Torah and the Musaf services—with Musaf connoting sacrifice in the ancient Temple—can be simultaneously read as an appropriation of Christian practice and as a polemic against it.[67] By situating this medieval practice in the established Sabbath liturgy, which had already incorporated the mention of medieval Jewish martyrs,[68] the Jewish character of publicly recognizing its donors was affirmed.

A second distinguishing feature of Christian necrologia is the nature of the donations detailed in them. In contrast to their Jewish counterparts, Christian donors of record regularly bequeathed property to the institutions that memorialized them. That is not to say that candles and monies were not donated, but those contributions were of far lower value—in their explicit worth and the attention that they were accorded. The prevalence of donations of land in Christian necrologies reveals the selectivity behind the choice of who was mentioned in them. Furthermore, membership in monastic communities was often determined to some degree by social status, thereby linking religious orders to affluent families.[69] As a result, necrologies offer a window on the fiscal and relational bonds between monastic houses and their landed benefactors; however, these records lack broader socioeconomic information.[70]

The prioritization of sizeable charitable contributions in necrologies should not be taken to indicate that smaller scale gifts were inconsequential.

On the contrary, charity held an inherent place in the rhythms of parochial life. Parish priests regularly oversaw the collection and distribution of monies, though this was not solely their realm:[71] Michel Mollat has suggested that as the thirteenth century began, charity was no less a responsibility for the laity than for clergy and monastics.[72] With the growth of cities, charity came to supply necessities, as wills attest to in-kind donations of food, cloth, and other basic goods that were frequently pledged to a church and its parishioners. Sharon Farmer has demonstrated that charity was usually distributed as part of communal relief for the poor—residents whose needs had become an ever-present reality.[73] Moreover, heightened theological concern for the afterlife during the twelfth and thirteenth centuries sparked further charitable activity, with a consequent increase in gifts for the soul.[74] The development of female confraternities in urban centers throughout the thirteenth and fourteenth centuries further supported this trend.[75]

The registers in the Nürnberg Memorbuch, counter to the relative exclusivity reflected by those named in Christian libri memoriales, show that Jewish donations for the soul were not only recorded for the elite but also for less prosperous community members. While universal participation cannot be assumed, the large number of donors (relative to the estimated population) suggests that a comparatively high proportion of the Nürnberg Jewish community was inscribed in this record.

Medieval Christian memorbücher include a third feature that the Nürnberg Memorbuch lacks, an obituary section where each entry comprises a brief description of the deceased and an accounting of his or her lifelong gifts to the Church, with stylistic variations depending on the magnitude of an individual's donations.[76] Entries in the Nürnberg Memorbuch are generally uniform, with each donor being mentioned by name ("so-and-so" son/daughter of "father's name") irrespective of the amount contributed. This standard formula can vary slightly. In rare instances names are accompanied by descriptive language that refers to the offspring of martyrs;[77] some women listed as members of a donating couple are named in relation to their husbands alone, while others are also identified in relation to their fathers.[78]

The principal distinction between Jewish and Christian necrologies is theological. Scholars of this Christian genre have documented that the multistage popularization of pro anima donations took place during the early Middle Ages. As votive Masses (offered for special intentions) became common from the sixth to ninth centuries, Christian clergy established themselves as mediators between the laity and God.[79] In this position, clergy essentially became the guarantors of salvation. Moreover, the task of translating donations of earthly goods into what Eliana Magnani defines as "heavenly treasures" fell under their purview.[80] Petitioning saints to intercede in heaven on behalf of donors was a key component of this transformative process. Over time, contributions were described as analogous to the Eucharistic sacrifice, and ultimately the gift itself, like the Mass, assumed the form of a mystery. These beliefs exemplify an expansion of ideas concerning the salvific qualities of charity that are anchored in early Christian texts.[81]

By definition, Jewish charity and memorialization were as distinct from Eucharistic piety as the theology of the Mass and the Eucharist was intrinsic to their Christian parallels. Nevertheless, we again observe that Jews adopted rituals from their cultural surroundings and situated them in the framework of ancient Jewish beliefs and practices while also revising their parameters to fit Jewish thought and to justify the Christian custom being incorporated. Medieval Jewish authors also refer to charity as a sacrifice of sorts, following a comment in the Talmud (at least in spirit).[82] Specifically, these scholars articulate the merit of charity in the next world, a common trope in medieval sources. For example, several narratives in *Sefer haMa'asim*—a thirteenth-century collection of medieval Jewish stories in a manuscript from northern France—present charity as a way to atone for one's sins. As the hero in one of these tales states:

> One who gives a coin (*prutah*) to a poor person receives the *Shekhinah*, for it says: "Then I justified will behold Your face; [awake, I am filled with the vision of You]" (Ps. 17:15). Not only this, but anyone who gives a coin is like one who built an altar and offered a sacrifice when the Temple existed. [Then] a person would give money and receive atonement,[83] and now a person gives a penny and all his sins are forgiven.[84]

Similarly, *Sefer Hasidim* taught: "One who gives charity will earn [an opportunity] to see the face of God (the Shekhinah)."[85]

If charity was seen as a generic means for atonement and seeing the face of God, then charity given prior to death for the sake of the soul was all the more significant, as a mechanism for assuring entry to heaven. The custom of giving charity to redeem one's soul is a logical extension of the earlier practice of making donations for the souls of deceased relatives. As Judah Galinsky has noted, the mention of contributions for one's soul in numerous Ashkenazic sources signals the prevalence of this practice in both Germany and northern France. *Mahzor Vitry* reports: "Then we commemorate the dead (*vezokher et hameitim*), those on whose behalf community members made donations and others that made donations on their own behalf."[86] This source speaks of two categories of contributions for the souls of the deceased—those for whom donations were made (yizkor) and those who donated for their own souls. As Siegmund Salfeld remarked, promising a donation before death is first found in a Rhenish Jewish ordinance dated from 1220–1223, which declares that wherever the compensation paid by the community for children's education is insufficient to cover its cost, a portion of the funds bequeathed by community members in "memory of their souls" may be tapped to supplement teachers' remuneration. However, this contingency plan could not be applied to funds that had been allocated for a designated purpose by one lying on his deathbed. The balance of these gifts—referred to as the community or reserve fund (*kahal*)—could be distributed according to community needs by its leadership unless it had been earmarked by the donor.[87]

As Galinsky has shown, according to some sources these donations were paid prior to death, whereas others indicate that pledges were made during one's lifetime but were fulfilled posthumously. The prescribed timing for this charitable process varies in responsa from this period.[88] Some texts also note that officials from the community were present when deathbed pledges were made.[89] These sources refer to pledges "for the remembrance of the soul" as the Hebrew equivalent of "pro anima" in Latin. As Isaac b. Moses states in his laws of charity in *Sefer Or Zaru'a*, these funds were intended to atone for the donor's sins by preceding his (or her) arrival in the World to Come.[90] Late medieval texts stipulate that these contributions could be declared at various stages in an individual's lifetime, including on the brink of death.[91]

To sum up this comparison: despite the differences between Jewish and Christian necrologies detailed here, their form and function are strikingly similar. Much as libri vitae and necrologies were crafted to emphasize the enduring presence of the deceased in among living Christians and to encourage the prayers that would ensure their place in heaven, so too memorbücher highlighted Jewish themes and rituals relating to communal membership and redemption. As such, memorbücher exemplify another case in which Jewish culture appropriated elements from the Christian majority while tailoring them to harmonize with Jewish frameworks of practice and belief.[92] Let us now examine the data recorded in the Nürnberg Memorbuch.

Donations from the Nürnberg Memorbuch

The list of donations for the soul from the late thirteenth century until the Black Death in the Nürnberg Memorbuch records contributions from individual men and women as well as from couples and, in rare cases, donations by siblings or parents and children who contributed together. This register is divided by the Rintfleisch events of 1298,[93] a series of attacks on Jewish communities throughout Franconia and part of Swabia during the summer of that year, remembered by the name of the German knight who instigated them after ongoing accusations that Jews had committed host desecration. This period of violence was devastating for the Jews of Nürnberg, 628 of whom were murdered.[94] The memorbuch records their names separately from donor listings. Significantly, none of the martyrs from 1298 appear as donors in the necrology,[95] a pattern explained in the liturgical section of this manuscript: whereas those who gave charity were to be remembered on the merit of their contributions, those who died in attacks on the community were to be memorialized on account of their suffering (*ba'avur shesavlu*).[96] Thus, if any who perished in the Rintfleisch events had pledged charity for the sake of their souls, their families presumably would not have fulfilled those vows.[97] This data provides additional evidence that gifts for the soul were intended for the sake of the contributor; once the donor's place in heaven had been assured, no action was necessary and prior oaths for that purpose were seemingly nullified. In a variation on this pattern, the necrology does name a small number of Jews in Nürnberg who died as martyrs in other attacks by Christians (especially before 1298), albeit not due to mass persecutions, but often without mention of a contribution.[98] While the nature of these isolated incidents remains unclear, the record attests to their occurrence.

Salfeld and Stern compiled a complete record of donations in the Nürnberg Memorbuch that was published in a series from 1894 to 1896 (in German).[99] My analysis relies on their work and on a photocopy of the original manuscript at the National Library of Israel in Jerusalem. Of the 515 contributions given before 1298, 43 are credited to couples and the balance is almost evenly split between individual male and female donors (without repetition of names between these categories). The period from the Rintfleisch events until the Black Death is divided into two sections: from 1298 to 1341, with over 600 donations—from six couples and slightly fewer individual women than men;

and over 130 donations from 1341 to 1346, when donations were noted according to year. Women and men are usually referred to by the titles "mistress" (*Marat*) and "mister" (*Reb, R'*).[100]

The vast majority of gifts in the memorbuch seem to have been pledged by donors during their lifetimes, though a small fraction of gifts were contributed by a third party after the demise of the "benefactor-beneficiary." Five such posthumous donations were recorded before 1298 and eight between 1298 and 1346. In each of these entries, the contribution is noted as having been given for the soul of the deceased (*heniah ba'avuro*).[101]

Table 1
Gifts from Individuals and Couples as Recorded in Nürnberg Memorbuch from Its Inception Until 1346

Timeframe	Men	Women	Couples	Total
Period I: Until 1298	238	234	43	515
Period IIa: 1298–1341	329	303	6	638
Period IIb: 1341–1346	63	73	0	136
Period II: 1298–1346	392	376	6	774
Total (Periods I and II): Late 13th century–1346	630	610	49	1289

In Table 1, total donations recorded from the inception of the memorbuch in the late thirteenth century until 1346 are categorized by contributor—men, women, and couples. The damage endured by the Nürnberg Jewish community in the wake of the Rintfleisch attacks is evident from the raw numbers. A total of 515 contributions were given in the years that preceded 1298, in contrast to 774 from 1298 to 1346, a forty-eight-year span. That is to say, donations rose by approximately 50 percent in Period II, though its timeframe is over 2.5 times longer than Period I.

The entries themselves read fairly consistently throughout from the late thirteenth to the mid-fourteenth century, with one central difference that grows more marked over the years: the specification of the purposes of the donations, as illustrated in the following excerpts. The late thirteenth-century format is exemplified by this passage:

> Marat Guta daughter of our R. Urshragu, half a quarter (*ravi'a*); Marat Guta daughter of R. Abraham, half a quarter; R. Isaac b. R. Joseph, half a quarter; Marat Miriam daughter of R. Gershom, half (a *zakuk*); R. Yehiel bar Moses haLevi, half a quarter; . . . R. Isaac b. Abraham and his wife Marat Bat Sheva, one and a half quarters and they [sponsored the] building of the synagogue floor; R. Isaac b. Yo'etz, a quarter; R. Abraham b. R. Solomon, half a quarter.[102]

This excerpt is from the opening section of the memorbuch, which was compiled prior to the dedication of the Nürnberg synagogue in 1296. These donors made undesignated gifts in the form of silver or coins with the exception of the couple Isaac b. Abraham and Bat Sheva, whose substantial, project-specific donation is named. Like the entry concerning Isaac and Bat Sheva, a full two-thirds (165) of the initial 250 donations are general contributions. Until 1298, approximately 60 percent of individual contributions and 50 percent of couples' gifts identify the purposes for which they were bestowed. Given that this record is linked to the construction of a new synagogue, major gifts (which are aggregated toward the beginning of the list) were likely used to build its sanctuary.[103]

The listings between the Rintfleisch attacks of 1298 and the Black Plague in 1349 display a reversal in this pattern: most contributions detail at least one intended purpose, and undesignated gifts appear only occasionally. This tendency toward specifying the goals of charity may have resulted from the completion of the synagogue's construction, perhaps in conjunction with an increasingly ritualized process of giving charity.[104] Although we cannot know the exact reasons, nearly all entries after the Rintfleisch attacks augment the format of earlier entries to include the causes toward which gifts were allocated:

> [R.] Asher b. Shabtai, one and a half quarters for teaching young boys and half a quarter for the sick; Marat Nusshilt daughter of R. Judah, a Torah scroll, one (*zakuk*) for teaching young boys and one for the sick; R. Isaac b. Samuel, half a hallisch pound[105] for teaching young boys; R. Yo'etz b. Menahem, a half for the community and a quarter for the sick; R. Isaac b. Jacob, half a pound for the community; R. Mordekhai b. Joseph, sixty hallisch pounds; Marat Sarah daughter of R. Joseph, half a quarter for teaching young boys and sixty hallisch pounds for the sick.[106]

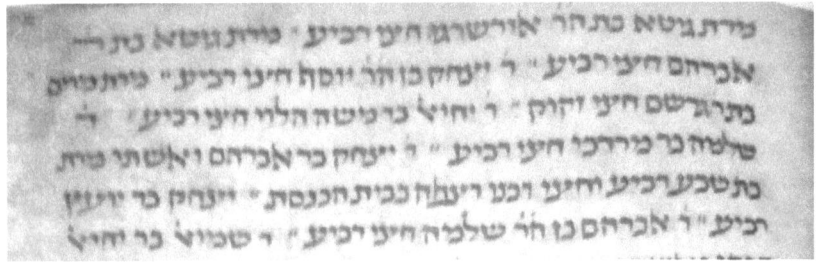

Figure 10. Excerpt from *Nürnberg Memorbuch*. Owned by private collector (formerly Mainz 19 Anonymous IR), fol. 48r. Nürnberg, late thirteenth century.

In addition to monetary contributions, many donors gave ritual objects (e.g., books, Torah scrolls, and silver cups) for communal use. Table 2 enumerates the ritual objects donated. From this tabulation, it is immediately evident that the more substantial gifts came from men and couples. For example, thirty-two Torah scrolls were donated to the community through 1298: seventeen by men (including three who contributed two scrolls each),[107] ten by couples, and five and a half by women. No indication of where the scrolls were stored or who read from them is provided. A comparison of contributions of less expensive ritual objects affirms the community's declining economic capacity: before 1298, on average, individual men donated more than couples and, in turn, couples donated more than women; whereas after 1298, none of the couples gave ritual objects nor did any women donate Torah scrolls.[108] Throughout the entire list, women contributed one-third the number of silver objects men donated and half the books or fewer.

Ritual objects represent one category of specifically designated donations. As indicated above, by 1298, nearly all monetary donations were directed to one or more tangible causes. Gifts contributed for specific purposes are presented in Tables 3a and 3b. Table 3a represents the percentage of contributors who pledged for a specific purpose in each period. Since donors contributed toward multiple purposes, it indicates the proportion of contributions donated toward each cause, rather than the number of people who supported it. Table 3b calculates the percentage contributed to a specific cause (and the number of gifts) according to the gendered distribution of donations for each purpose. This table demonstrates that donations to the cemetery, for instance, were allocated by (essentially) equivalent percentages of men and women.

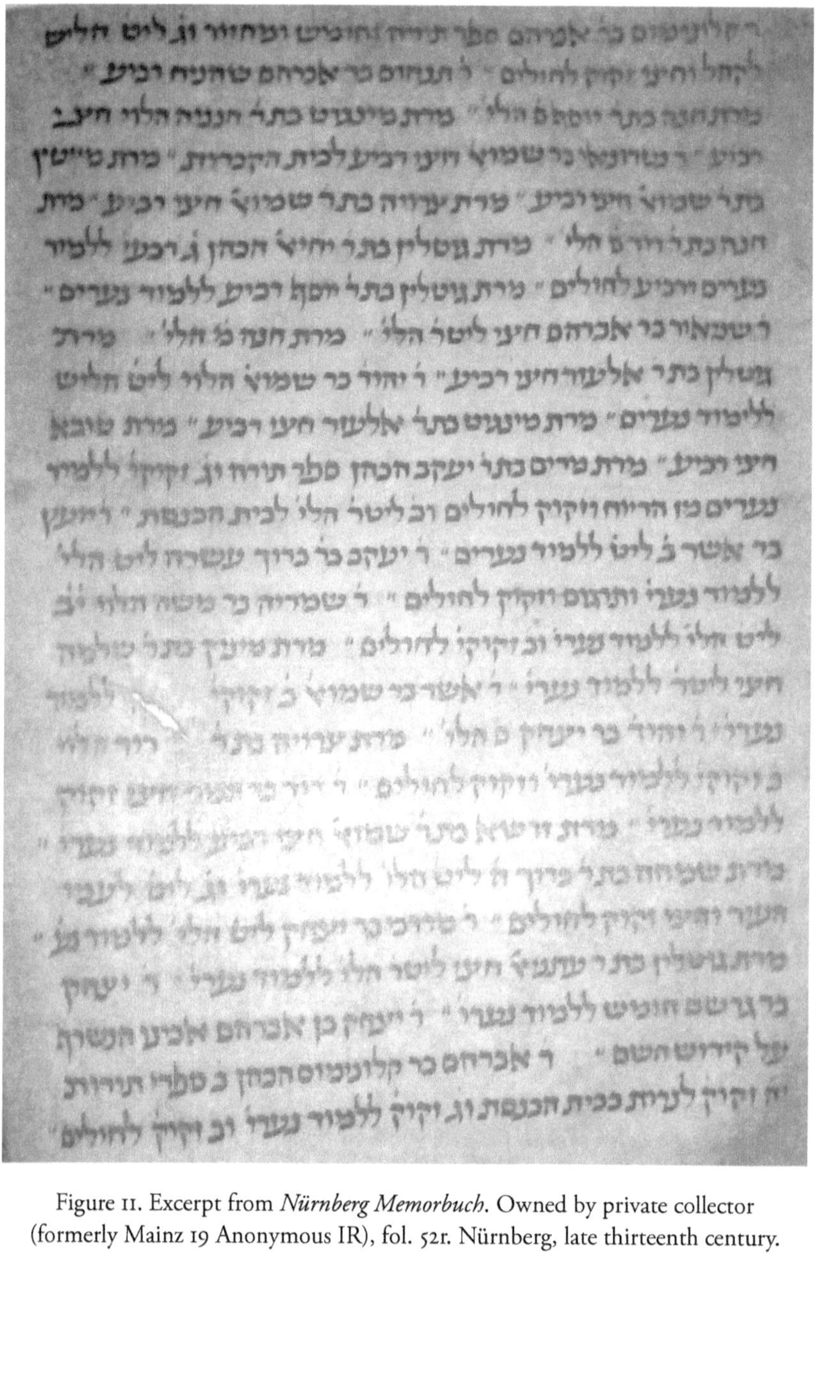

ר׳ קלונימוס בר אפרהם ספר תורה לחומש ומחזור וג׳ ליט חלים
לקהל וחיצי זקוק לחולים ״ ר׳ תנחום בר אכרהם טהניא רביע׳ ״
מרת חנה בתר יוסף מ׳ הלי׳ ״ מרת מינגוט בת׳ר חנניה הלוי חיג׳ב
רביע ״ ר׳ נתרונאי׳ בר שמוי׳ נר רביע לבית הקכרות ״ מרת מי״טין
בתר שמוי׳ חיצי רביע ״ מרת עדויה בתר שמוי׳ חיצי רביע ״ מרת
חנה כתר וריד ם הלי ״ מרת גוטלין כתר יחיאל הכהן ג׳ רכעי׳ ללמיר
נערים ורכיע לחולים ״ מרת גוטלין בתל יסף רביע ללמור נערים ״
ר׳ שמאור בר אכרהם חיצי ליטר הלי׳ ״ מרת חנה מ׳ חלי׳ ״ מרת
גוטלין כתר אלעדר חיצי רביע׳ ״ ר׳ יהוד׳ כר שמוי׳ הלוי ליט חלים
ללימוד נערים ״ מרת מינגוט בתר אלעדר חיצי רביע ״ מרת טובא
חיצי רביע ״ מרת עדים בתר יעקב הכהן ספר תורה וג׳ זקוקי׳ ללמור
נערים מן הריוח וזקוק לחולים ורב ליטר הלי לבית הכנסת ״ ריענן
בר אשר ג׳ ליט ללמור נערים ״ ר׳ יעקב בר ברוך עשרה ליט הלי
ללמוד נערי ותרנום לחולים ״ ר׳ שכודיה כר משה והלוי י״ב
ליט הלי ללמוד נערי וב׳ זקוקי׳ לחולים ״ מרת טרינך בת׳ל שלמה
חיצי ליטר ללמוד נערי׳ ״ ר׳ אשר בר שמוי׳ ב׳ זקוקי׳ ללמור
נערי ״ ר׳ יהוד׳ ר׳ יצדק מ׳ הלי׳ ״ מרת עדויה בת׳ל ...
ב׳ זקוקי׳ ללימור נבערי׳ וזקוק ׳ להולים ״ ר׳ דוד׳ בר מנר חיצי וזקוק
ללמוד נערי׳ ״ מרת זדויאל מת׳ר עומוי׳ חיצי רביע ללמור נערי׳ ״
מרת שמחה כתל פדיך מ׳ ליט הלי׳ ללמור נערי וג׳ ליט לעבדי
ונער וחצי וזקיק להולים ״ ר׳ מרדכי בר יצחק ליט הלי לונמור נע׳
מרת גוטלין כתר עמנצי חיצי ליטר הלי ללמוד נערי׳ ״ ר׳ יצחק
בר גרשם חומיט ללמור נערי ״ ר׳ יצחק בן אכרהם אכינו חמשרה
על קידוש השם ״ ר׳ אכרהם בר קלונמוס הכהן ב׳ ספרי תורות
יה והיה לעיית בבית הכנסת וג׳ זקיר ללמור נערי וב׳ זקיך לחולים

Figure 11. Excerpt from *Nürnberg Memorbuch*. Owned by private collector (formerly Mainz 19 Anonymous IR), fol. 52r. Nürnberg, late thirteenth century.

Table 2
Contributions of Ritual Objects for Communal Use

Ritual Objects[1]	Period I: Until 1298			Period II: 1298–1346		
	Men	Women	Couples	Men	Women	Couples
Torah scrolls	17 (from 14 donors)	5.5 (from 6 donors)	10 (from 10 donors)	11 (from 11 donors)	0	0
Books	9	2.5	5	7	4	0
Silver cups	3	0	1	3	1	0
Cloths (coverings for Torah scrolls or tables)	3	0	0	3	5	0

[1] Some donors gave multiple contributions; e.g., a single contributor gave a Torah and a silver cup.

These two tables provide complementary information about the priorities expressed through gifts for the soul. For instance, data in Table 3a makes clear that after 1298 more individual donations went toward cemetery upkeep than to any other single purpose, and Table 3b shows that men and women gave equally to this cause. Hayim Tykocinski has suggested that the Jewish cemetery of Nürnberg may have been established in the last decade of the thirteenth century, based on its mention as a designation for gifts in the latter portion of the pre-1298 register.[109]

The dedication of the synagogue appears to have been a pivotal juncture for donor patterns for other causes as well. While the synagogue was being planned and constructed, it is likely that most monies were contributed to a general building fund, but, after its completion, donors probably began (or returned to) donating to a specific set of communal projects. As a result, the number of unspecified donations shrank drastically, although the percentages of individual gifts to communal purposes did not change significantly. I would propose another noteworthy factor: given that the distribution of communal funds was directed (or influenced) at the discretion its leadership, as the custom of designating gifts became normative, those in authority may have steered donors toward specific projects, and the synagogue per se might have been deemed less urgent than other causes.[110]

Lighting is a case in point: after 1298, contributions toward lighting the synagogue increased significantly, from one-sixth to two-fifths of donors. Table 3b indicates that men and women contributed equally to this cause after 1298, even though the donor numbers prior to 1298 are inconsistent, a difference I am at a loss to explain. Dramatic increases in the demand for and the cost of lighting are unlikely explanations for this change. Rather, just as tendencies toward giving to the cemetery may have depended on practical need more than personal preference, so too with this category: during its construction, the synagogue may have been better funded, so relatively minor expenses might have been more easily covered; this pattern may also correlate to the overall increase in designated donations after 1298. Under such circumstances, gifts for synagogue lighting were more likely to be recorded.[111]

Table 3a
Donations Toward Ongoing Communal Needs (as a percentage of total contributors in each period)

	Period I: Until 1298			Period II: 1298–1346		
	Men	Women	Couples	Men	Women	Couples
Synagogue structure	16%	20%	36%	1%	< 1%	0
Cemetery upkeep	41%	51%	50%	96%	97%	50%
Synagogue lighting (oil and candles)	11%	<1%[1]	32%	37%	39%	80%
Education[2]	63%	66%	77%	36%	40%	50%
Sick fund	39%	34%	55%	33%	30%	12%
Support for poor	12%	10%	40%	11%	12%	0
Community fund (kahal)[3]	9%	4%	14%	< 1%	1%	0

Note: Since numerous donors contributed toward multiple purposes, the percentages represent the proportion of total donors who gave for each goal.
[1] Only four women donated money explicitly designated for candles: Tzippora bat Menahem (Salfeld and Stern, Die israelitische Bevölkerung, 115); Golda bat Abraham haCohen (ibid., 122); Gutlin bat Kalonymus (ibid., 124); and Esther habahura bat Samuel (ibid., 127). In contrast, most of the couples donated money for candles. See Salfeld and Stern, Die israelitische Bevölkerung.
[2] Theoretically, some categories can be subdivided (for instance, education could be divided between children and adults), although most donations do not provide such details. The lack of consistency in the language of specifically allocated donations prevents a deeper analysis.
[3] As we have seen, these monies were used by the community as needed; see note 84.

While the data in Tables 3a and 3b reveal minor fluctuations in allocated giving, the proportion of designated contributions by individual men and women remain relatively constant for most of the purposes recorded in the memorbuch. Cemetery upkeep received the greatest percentage of contributions, followed by education (despite a slight decline in overall gifts to educa-

Table 3b
Gendered Donations per Cause (as a percentage of total contributions per cause)

	Period I: Until 1298				Period II: 1298–1346			
	Men	Women	Couples	Number of donations	Men	Women	Couples	Number of donation
Synagogue structure	41% (25)	47% (28)	12% (7)	(60)	43% (20)	57% (27)	–	(47)
Cemetery upkeep	50% (62)	51% (73)	6% (10)	(144)	50% (361)	49.6% (357)	0.04% (3)	(721)
Synagogue lighting (oil and candles)	55% (17)	13% (4)	32% (10)	(31)	49% (144)	50% (145)	1% (3)	(292)
Education	46% 93	47% (95)	7% (14)	(202)	48% (142)	51% (149)	3% (1)	(294)
Sick fund	49% (58)	41% (49)	10% (12)	(119)	52% (131)	48% (120)	<0.5% (1)	(252)
Support for poor	40% (19)	32% (15)	28% (13)	(47)	46% (36)	54% (43)	–	(79)
Community fund (kahal)	58% (14)	25% (6)	17% (4)	(24)	90% (9)	10% (1)	–	(10)
Community hospital[1] (Hekdesh)	–	–	–	–	36% (4)	64% (7)	–	(11)

[1] Appears only post-1298; see Barzen, "Meaning of Tzedakkah."

tion after 1298). On the whole, we see that the levels of individual giving to the other listed causes stayed quite stable during our two periods. For example, 30 to 40 percent of men and women contributed to the sick fund and a steady 10 to 12 percent to the poor across the two timeframes. With respect to gendered divisions of charity, men and women gave designated contributions in similar proportions throughout our timeframe. However, a slightly larger proportion of women donated to the synagogue throughout the entire period, whereas after 1298 we see a substantial increase in women who contributed to the poor. More men donated to the sick fund throughout both periods, and the number of men and women who gave to the community (kahal) changes markedly over time.

The greatest differentials revealed by the data from the Nürnberg Memorbuch are in the realm of couples' donations. Before 1298, many couples designated large-scale gifts, but after 1298, not only did the number of contributions from couples plummet (Table 1) but their donations were far smaller. They no longer gave costly artifacts (Table 2) and, as we see below (Table 4), their later donations rarely met the levels given by wealthier individuals (men or women), and in some cases they donated at much lower levels. Tables 3a and 3b demonstrate that the minor significance of couples' gifts were within the total contributions after 1298.

So far we have seen that men and women participated on a par with each other, at least in terms of the numbers of contributions that they designated for specific purposes, but how do their per capita donations compare? Our analysis has already provided some answers to this question. When looking at gifts of more costly ritual items, discrepancies with respect to gender become visible (Table 2): for example, before 1298, Torah scrolls were three times as likely to be donated by a man than by a woman. After 1298, gendered asymmetries in major material contributions to the community after 1298 only intensified: although women and men alike were expected to donate gifts for their souls, based on their designated contributions, men appear to have had greater monetary and especially material wealth at their disposal.[112]

As background for our analysis of the comparative value of donations from men, women, and couples, a brief survey of the currencies mentioned here is in order. Two monetary systems dominated the financial transactions in major medieval urban centers: silver and coin. The currencies commonly used in medieval Nürnberg have been described in detail by Michael Toch, who based his discussion on data from this same memorbuch (as noted above).[113] Toch has explained that numerous currencies were used by the Jews of Nürnberg, from local currencies—namely, silver by weight and coins from Nürnberg, which are the most prevalent in the memorbuch—to coins from as far away as Cologne. Silver by weight (called a *zakuk* in Hebrew and a mark in German) was often registered in smaller units, known as a quarter and half a quarter (*ravi'a* and *hatzi ravi'a*). Coins from Nürnberg were counted in pounds (*litra*).[114] Currency from the nearby city of Schwäbisch Hall (identified as *hallisch*) was also commonly used in Nürnberg; those coins were considered less valuable than local currencies.[115] The currency from Cologne, gold (*zahuv*) and the mancus[116] are also mentioned, but so rarely as to be insignificant for the purposes of this study. Beyond the variety of coins and currencies used for payment, another factor that complicates any assessment of these donations is their fluctuating worth during the sixty-odd-year period examined here. For this analysis, I have assumed that the more affluent gave silver and the poorer dealt in hallisch currency (following the rule that non-local coins which infiltrated markets were neither as strong nor as valuable as local currencies), whereas donations in pounds seem to reflect the middle stratum of Jewish society.[117]

Table 4
Comparison of Average Contributions from Men and Women

Timeframe	Currency	Men's average donation	Women's average donation	Couples' average donation
Period I: Until 1298	Silver	0.74 (140)	0.56 (143)	6.10 (32)
	Pounds	7.30 (47)	2.90 (42)	24.80 (10)
	Hallisch Pounds	44.20 (67)	58.70 (65)	10.75 (10)
Period II: 1298–1346	Silver	1.50 (29)	1.50 (18)	1.25 (3)
	Pounds	4.80 (201)	4.00 (206)	2.00 (2)
	Hallisch Pounds	58.49 (180)	71.23 (162)	0.37 (2)

Notes: The number of contributions for each category is included in parentheses. This table represents a calculation of the average gift by donor category according to each currency rather than an average of each individual's total contribution, because a number of donors gave in more than one currency, rendering them particularly difficult to assess. Since some donors gave in more than one currency, the number of donations in this table exceeds the number of contributions in Table 1.

With these constraints in mind, I have calculated monetary donations according to three monetary units most frequently recorded in the memorbuch—silver (by weight), coins from Nürnberg (pounds), and coins from Schwäbisch Hall (hallisch pounds). I have treated each coin as a separate rubric because of the difficulties entailed in converting their value into a common system.[118] The average donations given by men, women, and children are presented in Table 4 for both our timeframes and for the three coins mentioned frequently in the memorbuch. This table shows that the largest proportion of monetary donations through the summer of 1298 were given in silver, whereas monetary contributions during the first half of the fourteenth century were predominantly given in local pounds and hallisch coin.

A gendered comparison reveals that prior to 1298, men gave larger sums in silver than women, and slightly less than women in hallisch coins. The greatest discrepancy is in local coin, where women donated at 40 percent of the level given by men. These trends change after 1298, when over 35 percent more men donated silver (twenty-nine men as opposed to eighteen women), but their per capita donations were equivalent. Women's contributions in hallisch coin continued to be larger than men's, and the gap between men's and women's donations in local pounds declined, with men giving about 20 percent more than women. This roughly corresponds to the proportion of ritual objects donated individual men and women (Table 2).

These patterns are replicated in the data on donations from couples: just as wealthy couples were more likely to donate ritual objects, so too those with the financial wherewithal often gave silver. For example, Yehiel and Rachel daughter of Shimon donated thirty-four silver coins in addition to funding toward the construction of the women's synagogue and the mikveh, two Torah scrolls, three Torah covers, and a mahzor for the community.[119] By comparison, the monies given in local pounds by forty-three couples before 1298 exceeded the combined donations from individual men and women from that same period, and the total silver from those couples equals more than half the silver given by over 200 men.

Prior to 1298, couples gave an average of three silver coins each, whereas the average individual (man or woman) gave less than one. This gap is even more marked in the case of local coins, where the average couple gave three times the average man's gift and nine times the average woman's. Similarly, donations from couples confirm the relatively low value of hallisch coin, for the majority of couples who gave donations in this currency alone contributed relatively small sums and were not recorded to have contributed other gifts.

Of the forty-three couples listed as donors before 1298, the four who only gave in hallisch coin contributed far less than the average woman or man, another indication of the lesser value of that currency. After 1298, donations from couples nearly ceased and the few couples listed gave modest sums, far below the average individual (male or female) in local or hallisch pounds, indicative of the reduced resources that they must have had at their disposal. Only in silver coin did couples' donations exceed the average individual gift.

One striking reality that the data from these two periods display is the reduced economic means that afflicted the Nürnberg Jewish community after 1298. For example, the enumeration of ritual articles donated to the community (Table 2) reveals significant changes in giving patterns following the Rintfleisch attacks.[120] The elimination of giving by couples in this arena and the prevalence of less expensive objects implies a diminished fiscal capacity.[121] Indeed, most books and silver items and all Torah scrolls came from male donors in that latter period.

Despite the abundant data transmitted in this memorbuch, many questions remain. However, even this partial record offers insight into the fabric of the community as well as the role of gender in charity given for the soul. Men and women are equally represented on this list, indicating that everyone was eligible to pledge such a donation. This is not to deny that some community members, perhaps the most impoverished, were not included in this register. It is plausible that the names of those whose meager resources precluded participation might not have been recorded. However, the nominal donations found in the Nürnberg Memorbuch indicate that community members strove to secure a place in this necrology.[122] The apparent inclusion of the majority of Nürnberg Jewry in this volume—men and women—underscores the social and theological importance attributed to this distinctive form of charity.[123]

These entries also provide information about family relationships, however incomplete in nature. Everyone was listed according to the father's name, a practice that impedes our ability to identify women with complete confidence. Due to the popularity and, thus, repetition of certain names, it is impossible to ascertain connections between individuals.[124] Yet this record offers an outline of certain families, especially wealthier ones. Since Jews in medieval Ashkenaz usually named an eldest son after his paternal grandfather and then conferred other ancestral names on subsequent children, patterns emerge. The family of Abraham b. Kalonymus the Cohen, which features prominently in the list from before 1298, illustrates this point. Abraham donated two Torah scrolls, whereas his wife, Marat Hannah daughter of Isaac the Levi, and their young son, Kalonymus (son of Abraham the Cohen), jointly donated an additional Torah scroll and three silver pieces to the community.[125] This case seems to follow conventional naming practices. However, it is an exception to the rule on two counts. First, this mother-son gift represents one of the few contributions that credits a child with a donation.[126] Moreover, it may be contrary to the standard of each individual being inscribed once in the memorbuch, for in a later section Kalonymus b. Abraham (perhaps the same Kalonymus who is mentioned as a youngster with his mother) was recorded as giving a Torah scroll as well.[127] This family also donated money, silver, and other ritual artifacts.

Due to their format, the entries on this list provide scant demographic information. How old were these community members when they pledged their gifts and when they died? Were they married, single, widowed, or divorced? Some references describe donors as youths (*na'ar* or *na'arah*) or as elders (*hazaken* or *hazekenah*), but most do not. Even these terms provide limited information. For instance, the entries that precede 1298 include twelve references to old women but only one to an old man, four mentions of young girls, two of (female) "virgins," and ten of young boys.[128] Does this vocabulary imply that none of the others named were notably young or old? Similarly, in the listing from 1298 to 1346, seventeen young boys but only five young girls are inscribed, whereas eight elderly men and only one elderly woman are named. Over time it became more customary to remark upon youth in the memorbuch: the entries after the Black Death have many such references, which prompts curiosity whether these young people pledged money while they were ill or if their families made pledges on their behalf, options that may really be two sides of the same coin, for children were unlikely to control assets.[129] Even with this body of unanswered questions, these data attest to a growing commitment to commemorate each and every soul.

Agency and Authority: Gendered Giving

The conspicuous absence of any reference to the marital status of women—with the exception of those who donated with their husbands—raises significant questions. Since individual women are identified by their fathers' names, this record gives no indication of personal status for the great majority of women in this listing. Whether women were single or married, divorced, or widowed has relevance not only for establishing a demographic profile of donors but also in light of the legal norms that governed women's financial agency. Medieval rabbinic authorities debated the permissibility to independently pledge money for two categories of individuals: children under their fathers' authority and married women under their husbands.' I survey these directives below before returning to the donations from Nürnberg.

As in many other areas of Jewish life and practice, medieval Jews inherited guidelines for legal and financial agency of women and minors from the Talmud. Following the Mishnah, the Talmud upholds a patriarchal model where every man was expected to determine the scope of charitable activities for anyone under his authority.[130] "Wives, minors and slaves"[131] are aggregated as a standard category in halakhic texts that address these issues. The talmudic discussion defines wives, minors, and slaves as those who are neither permitted to do business freely with their masters' goods nor to pledge charity of their own volition, for fear that they might steal or distribute monies that did not belong to them, effectively cheating masters.[132]

In her ongoing study of charitable practices in late antiquity and, to a lesser extent, in the Middle Ages, Alyssa Gray has examined aspects of married women's agency for giving charity. Gray focuses on the development of halakhah rather than social aspects of charity, demonstrating how the talmudic ruling that limits married women's ability to autonomously allocate charitable donations developed from late antiquity to the early modern period.[133] As she details, medieval sources (e.g., responsa, talmudic commentaries, and halakhic compendia) follow the Talmud, underlining a woman's personal status as the determining factor for her capacity to engage unilaterally in financial transactions. Single women rarely appear in medieval sources, presumably because most women lived under their parents' auspices—and therefore authority—until marrying at a young age.[134] Widows and divorced women are also absent from this literature—with the exception of widows engaged in lawsuits with other heirs—for they were considered financially autonomous. As such, it follows that widows and divorced women were free to distribute their money as they chose, but married women came under their husbands' jurisdiction.[135]

Charitable giving necessarily depended upon an individual's or a household's level of wealth. Changes can be traced in the laws that regulated Jewish women's finances and fiscal autonomy from late antiquity throughout the medieval period.[136] These developments relate to the monies and properties that women brought into their marriages and directives concerning women's work and their fiscal independence.[137] The Babylonian Talmud[138] permits women to independently sell only a "small amount" (*davar muat*) in business transactions. In contrast, medieval texts (primarily halakhic responsa, but also stories and exempla) suggest that women were intensely involved in family finances; as one text states, "Any man who deposits money does so with the consent of his wife and sons."[139] Women are also depicted as active participants in the workforce and in the monetary exchange system who were often responsible for independent decisions.[140] To the extent that Jews owned land or shares in land, women were counted among them.[141]

Twelfth-century sources from Germany and northern France suggest that women engaged in business with their family members and independently.[142] Women are mentioned as having conducted business as fully authorized proxies when their husbands were traveling and as having journeyed beyond the bounds of their home cities for their own economic activities (as seen in Chapter 2).[143] Some medieval scholars explicitly spell out the range of women's part in business, starting with Ra'avan (Eliezer b. Nathan, first half of the twelfth century), who writes that women "give and take, lend and borrow, pay and are paid, deposit and receive money."[144] Ra'avan extends this logic by asserting that married women could freely give charity, just as they could take part in business without restraint. Later in his discussion of women's financial authority, he quotes the Talmud: "Charity collectors accept small items from them (women, minors and slaves), but not large items that could be stolen, for they (women, minors and slaves) surely steal and sell," and comments: "But from women (as opposed to minors and slaves), they (charity collectors) take even large sums, for they act as their husbands' agents."[145] In this way, Ra'avan underscores the character of the period in which he lived. He acknowledges that the norms "in his days" (ha'idna; lit., in our time) diverged from previous generations, for women acted as partners in their husbands' businesses and they were authorized in commercial and charitable matters.

Women's involvement in financial dealings is evident in sources that document women representing a significant percentage of the Jews who worked in moneylending throughout northern Europe, although they generally handled smaller-scale loans than their male contemporaries did.[146] Women are mentioned as active financial players vis-à-vis the Christian community in reports on various late eleventh- and twelfth-century crises: for example, the 1096 chronicles and the account of the events in twelfth-century Blois remark that Jewish women had close fiscal relationships with ruling Christians.[147] In subsequent centuries, evidence of women's economic activities was recorded in tax documents and in legal discussions of real and theoretical cases.[148] Perhaps the most compelling indication of women's activities are discussions of their ability to give testimony independently before a court of law,[149] which was permitted *de jure* in late antiquity but seems to have become standard practice only in medieval times.

The records of donations from the Nürnberg Memorbuch examined here are from the late thirteenth and early fourteenth centuries, an era that has been identified by some scholars as a period in which a shift in halakhic discourse regarding married women's abilities to give charity at their own discretion occurred. Counter to Ra'avan, a number of thirteenth-century rabbinic authorities returned to talmudic formulations[150] and stipulated that women could not do business or give charity without their husbands' consent, and this grew to be the accepted position over time.[151] By way of illustration, in his *Sefer Or Zarua,* Isaac b. Moses cites the talmudic instructions concerning receiving money from married women verbatim, without acknowledging the more lenient customs of his own generation.[152] Isaac b. Joseph of Corbeil does likewise in *Sefer Mitzvot Katan*; and commentators on the *Semak*, including Peretz b. Elijah and Moses of Zurich, make no mention of alternate positions or practices.[153] Halakhic writings by Meir b. Barukh of Rothenburg and his disciples articulate this same message.[154] Although some medieval sources imply that women were more inclined to give charity than men, the halakhic directives suggest that their ability was limited.[155]

If contemporaneous Ashkenazic texts indicate that a married woman's charitable gifts were contingent on her husband's permission, how might this qualification shape our analysis of the data in the Nürnberg Memorbuch and the community that it represents? Must we assume that the female donors listed were widows or divorced, as the only women who could exercise fiscal independence? While some of the women listed were certainly widowed or divorced, given the near parity of participation among men and women, it seems implausible that female donors were all unmarried. Alternatively, should we presume that all the women named received permission to donate from their husbands?

During the medieval period, men were more likely to be owners of property and goods, whereas women often had limited access to such resources.[156] These norms held true among Jews and Christians, even taking into account that Jews were less likely than their Christian neighbors to possess real property, as corroborated by the material donations in the Nürnberg Memorbuch. From that perspective, perhaps the monetary donations from women in the memorbuch can be classified as the "small amount" that any woman could contribute of her own volition. Or, if it were designated for an officially sanctioned charity, perhaps the community accepted any sum contributed by a woman? If we view these donations as evidence of the mutual standing of men and women—at least when striving to secure a place in the afterlife, then we can understand why every Jewish woman and man, however modest their means, would participate in this ritual.

Although the data from the Nürnberg Memorbuch cannot provide conclusive answers to these questions, it yields some possibilities. As we have seen (Table 4), individual women and men donated similar amounts of silver and currency from Schwäbisch Hall; however, there is a marked difference between men's and women's contributions in local pounds, especially before 1298. If we assume that silver was contributed by more affluent members of the community (as argued above),[157] then wealthier women and men were giving contributions that befit their status, which is to say that class rather than gender played a primary role in determining their gifts. The slightly higher average men's donation in silver before 1298 is indicative of men's stronger financial standing. A similar logic can be applied to contributions in hallisch coin (which women gave at slightly higher levels), as a reflection of the lower economic strata of society reaching to give a minimum donation so they might be acknowledged by the community.[158]

The discrepancy between men's and women's contributions in local coin requires further attention, particularly in relation to research on other aspects of the medieval economy and gifts for the soul. William Chester Jordan has demonstrated that the sums loaned by women were approximately one-third the level of men's, based on judicial records from Picardy.[159] In his work on wills and especially gifts for the soul from Genoa, Steven Epstein has found that large donations were contributed by twice as many men as women, medium-sized gifts were equally likely to be given by women as by men, and a higher proportion of women than men gave very small donations.[160] These figures suggest that the women's monetary contributions recorded by the Jews of Nürnberg are surprisingly higher than might normally be expected. The difference between men and women's donations narrowed over the period examined here, perhaps because of the precarious situation of the community after 1298, indicating that community-specific standards were at work here.

As mentioned above, the relatively high sums donated by women may signal that these were gifts made by married women with their husbands' consent and by widows and divorced women who lacked such contingencies.[161] However, a number of medieval responsa address circumstances where women's contributions for their souls were contested by surviving family members[162] (usually by their children), suggesting that while some gifts were surely sanctioned by the donors' husbands, it is improbable that they all were.

Although the entries in the Nürnberg Memorbuch are insufficient to convey the economic responsibilities exercised by Ashkenazic women, they affirm that women contributed significant sums of money, autonomously or with their husbands' agreement. Moreover, the Memorbuch indicates that women gave fairly large sums of money for over sixty years, with no signs of diminution in the late thirteenth century,[163] an era when rabbinic authorities were reconsidering their view of women's independent charity.[164] At the same time, the evidence consistently indicates that women had less money at their disposal than their male peers, even if they had greater access than might have been expected—a point that is driven home by the donations of ritual objects (Table 2).[165] No less significantly, men's and women's gifts were inscribed with identical formulae and women's names were recited in synagogue rituals on a par with the men in their communities. Such parallel treatment confirms that charity for the soul as a formal ritual that expressed communal norms preserved a record of membership and assured a legacy of remembrance for men and women alike.[166]

Gender and Charity: A Comparison of Jewish and Christian Practice

The same challenges that surface when assessing whether the women named in the Nürnberg Memorbuch donated gifts for their souls independently or with their husbands' consent arise when scholars seek to analyze the charitable gifts from married women that are recorded in contemporaneous Christian sources. That is to say, much as married women's subservience to their husbands was a common feature of medieval Jewish and Christian life, so too women in both communities shared similar pecuniary circumstances within the urban economies that they inhabited. Many medieval sources reveal that Christian women were ready to donate generously in response to appeals by local preachers and community leaders. In fact, almsgiving was the most popular outward form of expiation that Christian clergy recommended to female penitents,[167] even though patriarchy was the norm in medieval society, placing married women, their property and monies, under their husbands' control. While women were encouraged to give charity, they were supposed to act with their husbands' consent.[168]

The extent to which Christian women could allocate monies without explicit permission from their husbands is addressed in medieval confessors' manuals and penitential compositions. Dyan Elliott has explored this subject in her research, and her findings are highly relevant to comparisons of Jews and Christians. For example, she describes Raymond of Penafort (d. 1275), a prominent thirteenth-century Spanish jurist who studied in Italy and whose writings were influential throughout northern Europe, who declared that a married woman could give alms against her husband's wishes from her own possessions and from the household provisions under her care, in accordance with her husband's resources and the needs of the poor. He offered the following justification:

> And she should always shape her conscience so that she would not displease her husband in his heart although perhaps he would sometimes prohibit an act by mouth: for husbands are accustomed to make a prohibition to their wives absolutely. . . . Also she can shape her conscience according to the condition and the misery of the poor, knowing that if her husband saw them it would please him in every way that she had made alms for him. If, however, consciousness should proclaim utterly and precisely to the wife that an act displeases her husband and thus would scandalize him, let her put aside that consciousness if she can, if not however, she ought not to and let her grieve that she cannot give these alms.[169]

In effect, Raymond granted Christian women the latitude to give charity despite the knowledge that, if asked directly, their husbands would likely have forbidden such contributions. Nevertheless, he counseled women against making donations that would provoke their husbands' disapproval. In such situations, women were to obey their husbands while grieving because they could not give charity at that time.

Other authors also suggest that moderate sums were accepted from women, even without their husband's consent. The instructions given to confessors by Thomas of Chobham (d. ca. 1233) in his *Summa Confessorum* are of particular interest in this context:

> If he is avaricious she should arouse generosity in him, she should secretly give alms from their common property, supplying the alms that he omits. For it is permissible for a woman to expend much of her husband's property without his knowing in ways beneficial to

him and for pious causes. . . . Therefore this ought to be the first and foremost concern of the priest, that he instruct the wife in this way.[170]

Similarly, his contemporary Caesarius of Heisterbach recounts the story of a priest who convinced the wives of avaricious men to give their husbands' goods to charity.[171] Sharon Farmer has underlined this connection between priests and women and the encouragement of female charity in her research.[172]

Thomas of Aquinas discusses this same issue in his writings by asking to what extent women and servants could give charity from their husbands' or masters' property. Basing himself on Augustine, he asserts that "alms should come out of what a man has honestly earned by his own toil, not out of other people's property." As a result, a wife could give alms from her own resources, but she "should exercise moderation in the matter so as not to reduce her husband to penury."[173] Miri Rubin has noted that fifteenth-century Christian authorities questioned if women had a duty to give charity, in contrast to earlier sources where their contributions were expected.[174]

It would seem that shared social norms and dynamics are at work here. Rabbis and Christian clergy were similarly caught between adhering to patriarchal authority and obtaining desired funding. Whereas Ra'avan openly stated in the twelfth century that women could give any amount they wished, over the next hundred years Jewish authorities reclaimed the talmudic stance that women could give but small donations without their husbands' permission, a directive that resonates with Christian norms from that era. Both Jewish and Christian texts imply that women gave charity more willingly than men, rendering them more easily swayed to donate than male householders.

Once again we see that the gendered norms of Jewish society matched the broader European fabric of women's relationships with religious authorities and subservience to their husbands.[175] Although the data in the Nürnberg Memorbuch cannot fully articulate the workings of this patriarchal system, they attest that married women donated substantial sums—at times even at parity with men. Viewed within the formal framework of gifts for the soul, these donations reflect accepted and respected practice. This remained true until the Black Death, despite the modifications in rabbinic teachings. These donations also indicate that the Jewish community recognized the importance of commemorating women alongside men.

Scholars of medieval Christian society have suggested that economic norms for women began to change during the fourteenth century, with the establishment of guilds (exclusive to men) and legal revisions of women's authority over family property as catalysts for wider changes in women's economic standing.[176] Patricia Cullum's research on charitable bequests to Christian communities in medieval Yorkshire provides compelling evidence of this phenomenon. Studying the donations of men, women, and clerics who bequeathed monies to charity in their wills, Cullum has noted that women donated at higher levels than both laymen and clerics. However, looking at pro anima donations pledged in wills from the fourteenth and fifteenth centuries, she tracked changes in women's charitable promises. Using samples from 1389 to 1398 and from 1440 to 1459, Cullum has demonstrated that women's giving declined precipitously during the half century that had elapsed between the two time frames.[177]

A comparison between Cullum's evidence from the fourteenth and fifteenth centuries and the Jewish memorbücher from the early modern period merits further research. While the data from Nürnberg before the Black Death is a rarity among medieval Jewish texts, subsequent memorbücher that record different categories of communal contributions were compiled in German-Jewish communities through the nineteenth and twentieth centuries. An assessment of early modern memorbücher would be of great value, though it goes well beyond the scope of this study.[178]

* * *

To conclude this chapter, let us draw together the different material under discussion. Medieval Jews in Ashkenaz, like their Christian neighbors, formalized a mechanism for assuring redemption and commemoration after death by pledging or donating charity as a gift for the soul during their lifetimes. This practice became part of an economy of piety that was widespread among Christians and Jews in northern Europe during the High Middle Ages. In addition to their commonly held desire to guarantee a heavenly destiny, shared understandings of social hierarchy emerge from this study of gendered donation patterns. Nonetheless, despite the overlapping conceptual and communal features of the charitable practices outlined above, fundamental differences existed between Jewish and Christian memorial volumes that related to theological distinctions and cultural dissimilarities. Any medieval Jew or Christian, if asked about the two practices, would have been quick to point to the unique features of each religion's practice.

At the same time, as elsewhere in the book, gender serves as a measure for comparing and contrasting religious singularity. This chapter's discussion of gendered giving and the similarities between the expectations and constraints on Jewish and Christian women's contributions provide evidence that both societies were working within a common social construct despite their differences. As much as pro anima contributions and necrologies provide keys for understanding Christian society, gifts for the soul and the ritualized recitation of contributors were symbolic of Jewish communal needs, values, and dynamics. Thus, reading names as a component of prayer became a status symbol when donations were announced in synagogue and became known to all. Individual giving was thus expressed in communal terms, with personal donations and social position being publicly and concurrently acknowledged. The memorbuch itself held a role for the whole community, as a record of deceased members whose names were recalled during prayer services.

Noteworthy differences between later Jewish memorbücher and the one from Nürnberg highlight the uniqueness of this source. The equal number of donations by men and women noted in the Nürnberg register sets this first Jewish memorbuch apart from the genre that it initiated. Although it seems certain that the entries in the Nürnberg Memorbuch are not inclusive of the entire community, male or female, I would claim that it is as all-encompassing as any medieval source might allow. In contrast, the representation of women in memorbücher from subsequent centuries falls far below that of men.[179] As reading names from memorbücher became more and more ritualized, only donors of major gifts were mentioned. As we have seen, records of gifts from women were far less valuable than men's, although there were exceptions to this rule as well. Parallel trends among male and female contributors have been demonstrated in the case of medieval European Christian pro anima donations.[180] Thus charity given before death in each community reinforced social status and power in this world while preserving connections between the living and the deceased. Jewish and Christian communities each emphasized the aspects of these practices that reflected their collective sensibilities and religious principles.

CHAPTER 4

Positive Time-Bound Commandments: Class, Gender, and Transformation

The rabbis taught: Beloved are the Jewish people, for the Holy One, Blessed be He, has surrounded them with commandments: tefillin on their heads and their arms, tzitzit on the four corners of their garments, and a mezuzah on [each of] their doorways.

—BT Menahot 43b

One of the most commonly noted forms of medieval Ashkenazic piety featured in scholarly and popular literature is women's adoption of commandments that have traditionally been seen as specifically male obligations.[1] This category, known as positive time-bound commandments,[2] was delineated in late antiquity and throughout the Middle Ages.[3] These commandments, whose performance is determined by a precise timeframe, include daily as well as annual observances, like hearing the shofar on Rosh haShanah and precepts related to Sukkot.[4]

Whether or not a given precept was defined as time-bound has direct implications for determining who was halakhically obligated for its observance.[5] The complexity involved in determining which commandments belong to this group was first recorded in the Talmud, where this category is debated from theoretical and practical perspectives. A consensus had developed over the rituals classified as time-bound by the High Middle Ages and it had been established that these acts were incumbent on men but not women.[6] The designation of this category and its gender-related norms should not be mistaken for unanimous practice among men who performed them or women who refrained from them. The "lived religion" of Ashkenazic communities dictated neither consistent observance of these precepts nor, as we will see, absolute gendered divisions for their enactment.

Figure 12. Man holding a lulav and etrog, woman holding another object. © Universitäts- und Landesbibliothek Darmstadt. Cod. Or. 13, fol. 326v. Mahzor, Germany, 1348.

Explanations for this lack of uniformity abound. In some cases, the precepts themselves were hard to fulfill: for example, obtaining the four species needed to satisfy the commandments for Sukkot, including two that are not native to northern Europe (a lulav [a palm branch] and an etrog [a type of citron]), was no small feat.[7] Other commandments—such as those concerning tefillin and tzitzit,—were less commonly practiced due to their lack social acceptability, as Ephraim Kanarfogel has demonstrated.[8] In the case of tefillin, economic realities must also be acknowledged, since the acquisition of these objects required a substantial expenditure, in addition to the more common

Figure 13. Man holding a lulav and etrog. From *Leipzig Mahzor* © Leipzig University Library. 1102, Kennicott 665, fol. 181v. Mahzor, Worms, ca. 1310.

factors that prevented other ritual observances, namely fear of impurity and a lack of interest in fulfilling them. To a certain extent, the norms in Ashkenaz resembled the patterns of observance in other diaspora communities, where evidence indicates that in late antiquity and the early Middle Ages, most Jews did not keep the commandment of tefillin.[9] In contrast, other commandments seem to have been practiced without interruption throughout the ages, such as hearing the shofar on Rosh haShanah.[10]

One feature shared by many positive time-bound commandments is the need for objects in order to carry them out. These articles are quintessentially Jewish, with few parallels in Christian practice.[11] Consequently, many accouterments of positive time-bound commandments became symbols of Jewishness within Jewish society and in the eyes of other religions.[12] This notion initially appears in the Talmud and is repeated in medieval compendia:

> The rabbis taught: Beloved are the Jewish people for the Holy One, Blessed be He, has surrounded them with commandments: tefillin on their heads and their arms, tzitzit on the four corners of their garments and a mezuzah on [each of] their doorways. Concerning these commandments, David said: "Seven times a day I have praised you for your righteous commandments" (Ps. 119:164). When David entered the bathhouse and saw [that he was] naked, he said: "Woe is me, that I should stand naked without a single commandment [to perform]." But once he remembered the mark of circumcision on his flesh, he felt comforted.[13]

By emphasizing the visible nature of these commandments, this passage underscores the connection between individual practice and religious identity, on the body and in public. The intrinsic link between these rituals and related symbols augmented the personal and collective investment of adhering to these practices, including the production of ritual objects and proficiency in using them.[14] Wearing or holding ritual objects, such as tefillin and the lulav, also provided Jews a tactile means for connecting with God. While tactile rituals would not have held universal appeal, they resonated with those who sought additional ways to express their piety.

With its focus on positive time-bound commandments, this chapter provides an opportunity to explore public expressions of piety from yet another perspective. The piety represented by these commandments is overt, given their material and symbolic nature and their performance in typically public settings. Moreover, gender represents a central motif in classic halakhic discussions of these practices and in the evolution of individual and communal norms in medieval Ashkenaz. As I demonstrate, observance of positive time-bound commandments changed during the High Middle Ages, and this transformation provides a window into the dynamics of gender, piety, and community in that period.

In the remainder of this introductory section I present a survey of research on medieval women's observance of positive time-bound commandments to date, a subject that, since the nineteenth century, has often been coupled with their instrumental role in the mass suicides committed during the First Crusade.[15] These studies have been significantly influenced by contemporary sensibilities and concerns.[16] On the one hand, like medieval authors, these modern scholars view adherence to these commandments as a sign of piety. From that angle, their performance by women in medieval Ashkenaz has been singled out as an outstanding occurrence.[17] This modern reading echoes medieval sources that refer to women who perform positive time-bound commandments as *tzadkaniyot* (righteous) and *hasidot* (pious).[18] Most contemporary scholars have also assumed that all medieval Jewish men performed these customs, per the norms of Orthodox men today. However, medieval evidence does not support that hypothesis.[19]

These medieval Ashkenazic women and their religious observances, in times of stability and crisis alike, have attracted scholarly attention as Jewish feminist scholarship has expanded over the past two decades. The research of Avraham Grossman, Israel Ta-Shma, Judith Baskin, Bitha Har-Shefi, and, most recently, Simha Goldin—to mention just a few scholars who discuss women's observance of positive time-bound commandments—has described the sources that outline women's practice and sought to elucidate this phenomenon.[20] This growing corpus has addressed several core themes. First and foremost, scholarship has focused on the reasoning exercised by rabbis who granted women permission to perform these commandments, especially since women were technically not obligated to observe them; indeed, in some diaspora communities, women were prohibited from doing so.[21] The reason for such a prohibition derived from the blessings said in conjunction with these religious acts, which included the standard formula "Blessed are You . . . who has sanctified us . . . and *commanded* us. . . ." Given that women were not halakhically commanded to carry out these practices, how could they say these words?[22]

Two additional issues have been raised, one quantitative and the other qualitative: How many women performed these commandments? And what circumstances led to such an exceptional practice? These questions have been engaged most notably by Grossman, as well as Ta-Shma, Har-Shefi, and Mordechai Friedman.[23] I concur with these researchers that, though it is impossible to calculate the number of women who performed these commandments, their observance does not seem to have been an isolated phenomenon.[24]

In the discussion of positive time-bound commandments that follows, I build on existing research by taking a somewhat different approach.[25] Prior scholarship has presented women's practice in a vacuum, operating from the above-mentioned premise that (all) men performed time-bound commandments whereas women did not. I suggest that these assumptions skew our perspective on medieval Jewish life and texts. Furthermore, this inquiry closely examines changes in rhetoric and practice with regard to positive time-bound commandments, whereas previous scholars have been more intent on describing the peak of women's observance in the twelfth and thirteenth centuries rather than tracing modifications over time.[26] As a result, the medieval texts that critiqued those women have not been as thoroughly examined. Finally, scholars have focused on local Jewish custom and only briefly pointed to the context of medieval urban Christian spirituality in explanations of how and why women began to perform positive time-bound commandments, a matter I undertake toward the end of the chapter.[27]

Etrog, Lulav, and Shofar: The Eleventh Through the Fourteenth Century

The question of precisely who performed specific commandments cannot be easily answered on the basis of medieval sources since most discussions of religious observance appear in books that were written by and geared toward highly educated men.[28] While their authors occasionally comment on the details of religious practice, their primary objective was to expound ancient sources and harness their teachings to inform contemporaneous issues. Moreover, due to the prescriptive nature of much of this literature, adherence is often taken as a given. Even custom books, which might be expected to provide guidance for correct observance, were intended to serve as instruction manuals rather than to describe standard practices.

As a result, investigating women's observance of positive time-bound commandments is far from a straightforward project. As we have seen in previous chapters,²⁹ it is often difficult to know if medieval Hebrew sources are describing men and women or referring to men alone. Only where women are mentioned explicitly can the gendered aspects of texts be treated with certainty. In some cases, women's actions are mentioned only in the context of an objection being raised to their participation without any previous information. Thus, I begin here with sources that clearly discuss women.

Perhaps the earliest source from medieval Ashkenaz to address women's observance of positive time-bound commandments treats the permissibility of women performing precepts related to Sukkot. This discussion appears in *Mahzor Vitry*—the early twelfth-century compilation attributed to Rashi's student, Simhah of Vitry (d. 1105)³⁰—in a passage that transmits teachings associated with Isaac b. Eliezer haLevi and Isaac b. Judah (eleventh century),³¹ with whom Rashi studied in the Rhineland,³² and conveys a mid-eleventh century perspective:

> And R. Isaac instructed against preventing women from reciting the blessing for [waving] the lulav or [dwelling in] the sukkah, for it is said: "Women are not obligated to perform positive time-bound commandments" (BT Kiddushin 34a), meaning that they are not compelled so need not [perform them], but if they wish to take on those obligations, they are permitted to do so and they should not be reprimanded (*ein mohin*), after all, they are no different from [a man] who is not obligated [to perform these commandments]. Therefore, when these [women] perform a commandment, they cannot do so without [saying the accompanying] blessing.³³

Isaac b. Judah further explains his position by referring to another instance when women would say a blessing and perform a mitzvah that they were not formally obligated to perform: when a woman was called up to the Torah, even though she was not required to study Torah, she still ought to recite the customary blessings.³⁴ This is an interesting case since the custom of calling women up to the Torah became nearly obsolete during the High Middle Ages, so one can only wonder how common it was during the eleventh century, when it is mentioned as matter of course. The passage quoted here appears in the earliest manuscripts of *Mahzor Vitry*. In the London manuscript it is followed by an addendum, asserting that Rashi or one of his contemporaries³⁵ objected to this practice and argued that women were not permitted to recite blessings when carrying out commandments that were taken on voluntarily.

Nonetheless, they could participate in the ritual activity without saying the blessing.

Despite these conflicting opinions, as in the case of the women who refrained from entering the synagogue when menstruating, it seems that the rabbis were responding to the women's initiative and attempting to regulate their practice. Though we have no indication of how many women observed these commandments, this text from *Mahzor Vitry* refers to "women" in the plural form, without specifying a discrete group or one unusual individual. Neither opinion voices doubts regarding the women's intentions when performing the commandment. Moreover, the fact that Isaac compares women to men who were not obligated to perform specific commandments, such as blind men, but did so rather than to minors or slaves departs from talmudic rhetoric, where the latter comparison was standard.

The point of reference employed by the rabbis is of great import as it hints at the gendered conceptions and associations held by the halakhic authorities whose opinions have reached us. While I would not argue that these eleventh- and twelfth-century rabbis were positioning women as equal to men—this is a modern feminist idea, not a medieval one—considering women's religious praxis relative to men's is important especially in light of later discussions, as we shall see. This parallel between women reciting blessings and men who chose to fulfill precepts for which they were not obligated is expressed unapologetically in eleventh-century sources. For example, in one of the earliest discussions of women's performance of positive time-bound commandments attributed to Isaac b. Asher (Riva, eleventh century, Mainz), he is reported to have said: "It is permissible for them (women) to perform them (the commandments for Sukkot), meaning they are doing something good and they will be rewarded for their actions, like men."[36] Thus we have evidence from both northern France and Germany that this practice was current in the late eleventh and early twelfth centuries, at least among some women.

This analogy remained prevalent in the mid-twelfth century and was most famously communicated in a ruling by Jacob b. Meir (Rabbenu Tam) that women *must* recite blessings when performing positive time-bound commandments. This opinion, which has earned him the reputation as a champion of women's status, draws on the talmudic passage which recounts that the sages did not reprimand women to whom rabbinic legends attribute typically male ritual practice: Michal, the daughter of Saul, who wore tefillin, and the wife of Jonah, who made pilgrimage to Jerusalem.[37] Rabbenu Tam also likens women to blind men, who were exempt from certain commandments but performed them nevertheless.[38] The classification of women portrayed by Rabbenu Tam and his twelfth-century contemporaries echoes the eleventh-century opinions described above: a woman is akin to a man, albeit a physically impaired man. Like their physically restricted male peers, women were not obligated to perform positive time-bound commandments, but neither should they be rebuked for practicing them.[39] This opinion is echoed by R. Eliezer b. Joel haLevi (Ra'aviah) as well, and he notes that there are some who object to women performing these commandments. He quotes Rabbenu Tam and also suggests that this was a common custom and that women were not being presumptuous or arrogant when performing these practices as they were doing what everyone (*kulei alma*) did.[40]

An unprecedented explanation from medieval Provence highlights the comparison between women and men that emerges in the halakhic discussions. In his thirteenth-century compilation *Shut min haShamayim* (Responsa from Heaven), Jacob of Languedoc tacitly accepts Rabbenu Tam's position while proffering a new argument to justify women performing positive time-bound commandments. This book and its author are considered quite unusual but nevertheless offer an interesting example. He explains that the verse where God tells Abraham to act according to Sarah's instructions ("Whatever Sarah tells you, do as she says" [Gen. 21:12]) should be interpreted as a precedent for allowing women to take on these commandments with their corresponding blessings. This biblical passage, regarding Abraham and Sarah deciding Ishmael's fate, is not simply cited as a halakhic source but presented to teach about women's motivations and divine guidance for men's responses to them. Jacob then states that women were party to the same miracles as men (as with Purim and Hanukkah), so they too need God to remember them when the shofar is sounded on Rosh haShanah.[41]

In contrast to Jacob's affirmation of women taking on blessings and commandments, a number of his fellow thirteenth-century halakhic authorities began to revisit and resist Rabbenu Tam's position on women's recitation of blessings and observance of positive time-bound commandments. Over time they increasingly question how women could say blessings that refer to them as having been "commanded" to perform precepts that they were not obligated to practice. The view of Isaac of Dampierre (R"I), which exemplifies this position,[42] is summarized well by Friedman:

> None of these sources advances to the next step and disagrees with the popular practice and Rabbenu Tam and forbids women from

reciting *berakhot* (blessings) on positive time-bound commandments. This being the case, a halakhic paradox emerges.... The scholarly elite, from Rabbenu Tam to R"I and his followers, all agree that a woman has no obligation whatsoever, and the R"I and his followers supported the theoretical distinction between a blind man and a woman, that whereas a blind man could recite a blessing based on a rabbinic obligation—a woman should not be able to. Despite this strong and convincing argument, no one dared to take this to its logical conclusion and challenge the ruling of Rabbenu Tam and the popular practice.[43]

This analysis suggests that, out of deference to Rabbenu Tam, thirteenth-century rabbinic authorities refrained from openly contradicting his instructions. It also underscores the likelihood that these French scholars were not only acting out of respect to Rabbenu Tam's stature but deferred to his view because it reflected actual practice.[44] Friedman also cites objections raised by later German scholars to Rabbenu Tam's position, where they undermined the endorsement of Michal the daughter of Saul by citing talmudic versions where sages did rebuke her for wearing tefillin. Despite their objections, most of these scholars leave Rabbenu Tam's instructions intact,[45] a rhetorical decision that I return to later in this chapter.

Twelfth-century discussions of women's performance of the commandments of shofar, lulav, and sukkah also discuss whether a man who had already fulfilled his obligation is permitted to help women perform that same commandment. For example, could a man who has already heard the shofar sounded on Rosh haShanah then blow the shofar for a woman? As Friedman explains, responses to this query varied throughout the Middle Ages, and it is hard to find a single system of reasoning that unites these opinions. In this context, as with respect to women performing commandments independently, Rabbenu Tam permits men to help women. But by the thirteenth century, not all rabbis were willing to accept his reasoning.[46] Modern scholars have argued that Rabbenu Tam's rulings stem from the norms of women in his community, which he was unwilling to contest.[47]

Before moving on to the changes that took place in the thirteenth century with regard to women and their performance of positive time-bound commandments, let us consider men's (and therefore general) observance of this category of holiday-related commandments. Medieval teachings on this subject appear in four main genres: biblical and talmudic exegesis, books of customs and commandments, rabbinic responses to specific questions posed by individuals, and sources of moral counsel (provided in compositions such as *Sefer Hasidim*). This corpus implies that men typically observed the commandments related to the High Holidays and Sukkot. Although it is reasonable to assume that not all men fulfilled these commandments, those who didn't go unmentioned.[48]

In sum, according to eleventh- and twelfth-century sources, the precepts for shofar, lulav, and sukkah were generally practiced by men and to some extent by women. Much as "men" represent a category that practiced these commandments, so too "women," who are mentioned without qualification. Indeed, neither Isaac haLevi, Riva, Ra'aviah, nor Rabbenu Tam depicted women who practiced shofar or lulav as especially pious.[49] As noted above, these discussions compare women to men who perform commandments despite being exempt or simply doing what everyone is doing.

One remarkable change is revealed in thirteenth-century writings on these commandments. Prior to the late twelfth century, texts rarely mentioned elevated levels of observing commandments known as *hiddur mitzvah* (adding splendor to the commandment) and *hibbuv mitzvah* (fondness for the commandment).[50] By the thirteenth century, many sources from northern France and Germany emphasize this new mode of performing select commandments. Drawing on the term "*hibbuv mitzvah*," texts regularly note the heightened devotion exemplified by the most prominent and pious members of the community.[51] This approach to ritual practice is also lauded in several late thirteenth- and early fourteenth-century sources. For instance, *Sefer haMaskil* (fourteenth century, Germany; also known as *Sefer Hasidim Katan*) praises those who perform the commandments of Sukkot with splendor, asserting that selecting a beautiful etrog is more important than any other commandment.[52] This text recalls a year when it was especially cold during the High Holidays, so nary an etrog could be found in Ashkenaz. In response, "the pious were deeply saddened" and eventually they spent a small fortune to obtain one small, green etrog.[53] This Ashkenazic approach is mentioned in the writings of Asher b. Yehiel (Rosh), who emigrated from Germany to Spain; he comments on the Spanish Jews' aversion to the extreme measures that were commonplace in Germany.[54]

While women who perform the holiday precepts are not described in terms of *hibbuv mitzvah*, there is evidence that women too were expected to observe these commandments despite the reticence expressed by some rabbis in reference to their participation. For example, women's roles are delineated in one discussion of a late thirteenth-century practice, where each family would contribute to a communal fund in order to hire someone to blow the shofar and to obtain the four species for Sukkot. This text indicates that women who were the heads of their families were expected to contribute on a par with men.[55] Indeed, over time, it became customary for women as well as men to carry out observances of shofar and the four species.

A concluding point that must be emphasized in relation to the observance of lulav, etrog, and shofar is that these practices were equally accessible to men and women. Since the shofar was sounded during synagogue services, all women and men in attendance could hear it. Although some thirteenth-century scholars debated whether a man who had already heard the shofar could sound it for women who had not,[56] most women could have heard the shofar along with the men, avoiding any need for men to repeat this ritual specifically for women. Sources suggest that women came to synagogue especially to ensure that they heard the shofar,[57] so this question may have been more theoretical than practical. As for the lulav and etrog, blessings related to these objects were recited in public spaces since medieval communities usually had a limited quantity of them, if not a single set of the four species for all to share. If each man queued up for his turn to say the blessing and perform this ritual, one can assume the women did the same. Most communities were not too large to allow this individual performance, as is evident in other ritual activities.[58] In other words, due to their enactment in shared space—and, in the case of lulav and etrog, using shared objects—the conditions for access were relatively balanced between men and women. This factor is significant when compared with observance of tefillin and tzitzit.

Tefillin and Tzitzit: The Thirteenth Through the Fifteenth Century

Men and the Observance of Tefillin and Tzitzit

In contrast to the eleventh- and twelfth-century sources that focus on the holiday-related observances, early thirteenth-century sources pay greater attention to tzitzit and tefillin. Before returning to women's practice, let us examine what these texts reveal about men's performance of these commandments. At the outset, defining these key terms in their medieval context is essential: while scholars are quite confident of the items under discussion when medieval rabbis write about tefillin, it is far more difficult for us to determine what exactly they had in mind when they considered tzitzit. In some cases, they are referring to a garment known as a *tallit katan*, equivalent to tzitzit in modern sources, a small, rectangular article of clothing, one fringe tied on each of its four corners, with head hole or slit for the head to pass through, so the wearer can pass it over his head to cover the tops of his shoulders plus his chest and back, either under or over the shirt. In other cases, a *tallit gadol* is intended, known today as a tallit, worn by prayer leaders and participants in prayer (the latter during appropriate times of day), a large square or rectangular shawl-like garment, also with fringes on each of its four corners. A lack of precision characterizes the treatment of these ritual garments in medieval sources, rendering ambiguity that cannot necessarily be clarified to modern readers.[59] Eric Zimmer has recently addressed this complexity, indicating the difficulties in resolving this issue. For the purpose of this discussion, I read tzitzit as tallit katan unless noted otherwise.

Mahzor Vitry echoes the Talmud, noting that God loves Israel on account of its observance of positive time-bound commandments, specifically tefillin and tzitzit, as quoted at the opening of this chapter.[60] This oft-cited sentiment could be read as an affirmation of these practices as having been regularly observed; however, it also could be read as evidence that a common standard was not firmly established. The section of *Mahzor Vitry* on tefillin presents elementary instructions including numerous ways of putting on tefillin. By offering a variety of options, perhaps the author was attempting to persuade his readers of the importance of this practice. As Ephraim Kanarfogel has outlined, numerous medieval sources suggest that men refrained from wearing tefillin for a variety of reasons: due to their desire to avoid ridicule, their inability to buy tefillin, or their religious reasoning, such as a fear of impurity or a belief that they were not obligated in the commandment if they did not study Torah.[61]

Evidence that wearing tefillin was less than normative reaches back to the rabbinic and ge'onic periods. In a responsum attributed to Sherira Ge'on (d. 1006), the author considers whether the commandment of tefillin was ignored due to concerns about purity or fear of seeming arrogant, issues that appear in the Talmud.[62] In his survey of current practices, Sherira notes that Jews in the Land of Israel were less fastidious about tefillin than were their Babylonian contemporaries.[63] He also explains that rather than being viewed as self-important, those who wear tefillin should be considered pious![64] This discussion and others confirm that those who wore tefillin and tzitzit were not necessarily perceived as pious and at times were seen as arrogant or overly righteous.[65]

This concurs with Kanarfogel's and, more recently, David Malkiel's claims that the commandments of tzitzit and tefillin were not commonly observed in twelfth- and early thirteenth-century Ashkenaz.[66] Malkiel even goes so far as to define this non-observance as "deviance."[67] While the decision against wearing tefillin certainly departed from halakhic prescriptions, I would take issue with classifying this behavior as deviant. If the majority of men did not observe this commandment, how can they be labeled as deviant? Studies in the social sciences have used the concept of deviance as a tool for demarcating boundaries and determining group membership.[68] In the case of positive time-bound commandments, if wearing tefillin and tzitzit was not the dominant practice, then one who behaved accordingly was not deviant but following conventional behavior.

Interestingly, this lack of adherence does not seem to have disturbed twelfth-century rabbinic authorities, who saw their communities as pious and holy. On the one hand, Ra'avan (Eliezer b. Nathan, d. 1170) wonders why "most Jews" did not wear tzitzit but, as Malkiel has observed, he also formally excuses them from this duty.[69] This twelfth-century rabbi certainly did not claim that Jews who didn't practice tzitzit and tefillin were less worthy or less pious. Building on this foundation, I would argue that thirteenth-century rabbis attempted to change Jewish practice and thought by encouraging piety, not by condemning laxity. Rather than castigate community members for the commandments that they did not uphold, these rabbis preached in an effort to raise the collective standard. This tendency can be seen in German and northern French sources. Thus, Moses of Coucy encourages the wearing of tefillin and tzitzit.[70] Drawing support from numerous prooftexts, he recommends each and every individual to put on tefillin, emphasizing them as fundamental symbols of Jewish identity. Moses recalls having preached in Spain that "each and every person is obligated by tefillin and mezuzah."[71]

Sefer Hasidim is replete with passages that impart similar messages. The many instances where the author praises those who observe tefillin and tzitzit attest to a desire to encourage these practices in an atmosphere where they were unpopular. The following passage encapsulates his message:

> "It is for Your sake that we are slain all day long" (Ps. 44:23). These are people who are subject to embarrassment, shame, and humiliation[72] for observing the commandments. [When] one comes forward to perform the commandments of tzitzit, tefillin, and others, his blood is then spilled [while being] shamed or [he] is humiliated

as if his blood had been spilt.[73] This [type of ridicule] prevents them from fulfilling the commandments.[74]

This passage suggests that the observance of these commandments was not standard practice. Judah dramatically invokes a biblical verse that is usually quoted in reference to martyrdom[75] to convince his readership to adopt these daily religious practices. In fact, the trope that a pious individual must suffer humiliation and embarrassment occurs regularly in connection with tefillin and tzitzit. Moreover, the idea that performing these commandments would cause such shame reinforces the assertion that one who did not perform them was not an outlier but represented the norm.

Textual evidence in *Sefer Hasidim* and subsequent sources suggest that Judah the Pious, Moses of Coucy, and the generations that followed them were waging a campaign to promote observance of the precepts of tefillin and tzitzit. This example from *Sefer Hasidim* is a case in point:

> One man wanted to wrap himself in tzitzit. They said to him: "Wait until the Sabbath to begin." He said: "With any other garment, I would postpone it until the Sabbath. But I will not postpone tallit and tzitzit. Rather, even on a weekday I will wrap myself for the sake of the commandment, as it says [in Scripture]: 'I have hurried and not delayed in keeping Your commandments' (Ps. 119:60)."[76]

The first line of this quotation illustrates the difficulties in distinguishing between a tallit katan and a tallit gadol that can arise in medieval texts. It only becomes clear that *Sefer Hasidim* means both tallit and tzitzit in the subsequent lines, which make clear that both garments are being discussed.

Elsewhere, *Sefer Hasidim* explicitly tries to induce the pious to observe these commandments in public:

> Any commandment that can be done in private should be [done that way]. But in order to teach others on the basis of his deeds, he should carry out [commandments] such as tallit and tefillin [in public]. Lest people say: "This [or that commandment] need not be performed." Therefore he should do them in public. Even if people mock him, he should perform them [publicly]; for [ultimately] he will receive a reward for the shame and the sorrow.[77]

This passage is fascinating since it suggests that the pious were encouraged to perform certain (otherwise private) deeds in public for educational purposes, even if they were shamed.[78] *Sefer Hasidim* applies the same principle in sections that promote the commandments related to lulav, shofar, and sukkah. With regard to lulav, Judah emphasizes the importance of fulfilling this commandment with as much splendor as possible, invoking the values *hiddur mitzvah* and *hibbuv mitzvah* (mentioned above).[79] Here, in the case of tallit and tefillin, he does the same, suggesting that both were mocked.

The importance of wearing tzitzit and tallit in public is also conveyed in a thirteenth-century French addendum to *Mahzor Vitry*:

> Whoever fulfills the commandment of tzitzit is like one who has carried out all of the commandments in the Torah, for it says: "Thus you shall be reminded to observe all my commandments" (Num. 15:40). What does this teaching illustrate? [It is analogous] to a servant who wears the king's insignia wherever he goes.[80] Everyone recognizes it as the mark of the king. Similarly, the blue [thread in tzitzit] resembles the sea, and the sea resembles the sky, and the sky is the abode of the holy throne.[81]

Moses of Coucy includes a similar notion when discussing the significance of tzitzit: "And one should not wear them in the synagogue alone, but also at the markets and on the streets, where the need for caution is even greater, 'So that you do not follow your heart and eyes' (Num. 15:39)."[82] In the case of tefillin, Moses taught that a man who neglected this commandment was missing an essential sign of Judaism, thus placing this observance on a par with keeping the Sabbath, a pillar of medieval Jewish identity. With this analogy, he asserted that wearing tefillin should be central to Jewish life.[83] In this passage he is pointing to the importance of tzitzit as well.[84] The emphasis on public observance in each of these sources—from Germany and northern France, as well as those imported to Spain by Moses of Coucy—stresses the role of open displays of piety associated with *hibbuv mitzvah*. A response attributed to Simhah of Speyer (1140–1225) similarly states that one who wears tzitzit should do so over his shirt rather than under it, for the sake of *hibbuv mitzvah*.[85] Rabbenu Peretz notes in his comments on the *Semak* that some young men wear their tzitzit all week without removing them, a testimony to the success of this campaign.[86] So, too, this principle is featured prominently in late fourteenth-century instructions for carrying out the commandments of tefillin and tzitzit. For example, the author of *Sefer haMaskil* claims that all religious practices should be performed with splendor, fulfilling the verse "This is my God and I will praise him" (Exod. 15:2).[87]

The precepts of tzitzit and tefillin appear with increasing frequency in thirteenth-century sources, a pattern that seems to be correlated with heightened levels of observance.[88] As noted above, two options existed for fulfilling the commandment regarding tzitzit: fringes could be worn on any four-cornered article of clothing, or a tallit (a square or rectangular prayer garment with tzitzit tied on each corner) could be worn during prayers or all day. Regarding tallitot, Ivan Marcus has discussed Hasidei Ashkenaz as catalysts for the introduction of tallitot that were designed to be worn during prayers, an issue that emerges from the sources examined above as well.[89] More recently, Katrin Kogman-Appel has demonstrated that tallitot started appearing in Jewish art and became a symbol of Judaism during the thirteenth century, and that only then did wearing tallitot became a common part of Ashkenazic practice, having previously been worn by prayer leaders in synagogue. An illustration from the Leipzig mahzor (Worms, ca. 1310), for example, portrays only the prayer leader with a tallit (see Figure 14) but other men without one.[90] Adult men were further prompted to wear tallitot through the custom of each man being given a tallit on his wedding day, a custom that appears in thirteenth-century sources as well, first mentioned by Eleazar of Worms and then in later sources.[91]

Not surprisingly, twelfth- and thirteenth-century sources also transmit debates over making and wearing tzitzit,[92] as for example the question of whether fringes should be tied on garments that did not require them according to the Torah.[93] These topics could only be raised in a climate where wearing tzitzit was becoming widespread. Two other long-debated topics—whether it was appropriate to wear tzitzit when being interred or when attending a funeral—were also reevaluated. Whereas the eleventh- and twelfth-century sources advised against burying the dead with tzitzit, following the talmudic reasoning that this garment would embarrass the deceased if he had neglected that commandment in life, texts from the late thirteenth and fourteenth centuries advocate burial with tzitzit, not only for community leaders but for every man.[94] With respect to the living wearing tzitzit when accompanying the dead to burial, by the late Middle Ages the rabbis had articulated a distinction according to the gender of the deceased: it was not permitted to wear tzitzit at a man's burial, harkening to the talmudic sensitivity of possibly embarrassing

Figure 14. Prayer leader with tallit, other men without. From *Leipzig Mahzor.* © Leipzig University Library. 1102, Kennicott 665, fol. 27r. Mahzor, Worms, ca. 1310.

the dead, but since women are not commanded to observe this precept, wearing tzitzit was permitted when burying a woman because she would not be so disgraced.[95] Thus, this practice of wearing tzitzit that Judah the Pious, Moses of Coucy, and others had ardently advanced was ultimately adopted.[96]

As should be evident, I am not extrapolating from these texts that men ignored the commandments of tefillin and tzitzit during the eleventh and twelfth centuries. I trust that members of the rabbinic elite that read and produced halakhic texts would have observed these practices, at least to some degree. Indeed, some discussions suggest that tefillin was only a scholarly obligation while studying Torah.[97] My argument is that, beyond this circle of highly literate males, this commandment became popularized during the thirteenth century.

Women, Ritual Production and Practice

Now that we have examined the thirteenth-century popularization of tzitzit and tefillin among adult men, let us proceed to examine women's relationships to these commandments. Some of these developments have been outlined by Aliza Berger and Aviva Cayam and others, and most recently by Bitha

Har-Shefi.²⁸ Discussions of women appear in two contexts: the production of these ritual objects, especially tzitzit, and personal observance. As noted above, general discussions of tzitzit and tefillin in eleventh- and twelfth-century sources are modest in number and scope, and women are barely mentioned in them. Although Rabbenu Tam quotes the Talmud that "Michal the daughter of Saul donned tefillin and the rabbis did not rebuke her" (BT Eruvin 96b) as a prooftext supporting women's performance of the commandment of lulav, he does not comment on tefillin and tzitzit specifically. In light of what we have seen concerning men's practice of these commandments, this omission seems unexceptional.⁹⁹

Although few writings from the eleventh and twelfth centuries mention women's performance of the commandments of tefillin and tzitzit, texts from the eleventh and twelfth centuries do refer to women who made ritual objects, among them tefillin and especially tzitzit. Discussions of the blessing that should be recited as part of their production assume male actors, with women as noted exceptions. *Mahzor Vitry* mentions Marat Belle (or Bellette), the sister of Isaac b. Menahem (eleventh century; LeMans, France), as an authority on making tzitzit.¹⁰⁰ So, too, the pious twelfth-century figure Dulcia (d. 1196), the wife of Eleazar of Worms, is depicted as having zealously made tzitzit, tefillin, and other ritual objects.¹⁰¹ The wife of Judah Sirleon (early thirteenth century, Paris) is also described as an authority on this issue.¹⁰²

The involvement of women in making tzitzit is not self-explanatory. Tzitzit were tied onto the corners of a four-cornered garment, often woolen, and worn under or on top of one's clothes. In the medieval context, women did most of the spinning to make thread; in some places they also wove.¹⁰³ Women are referred to throughout the Middle Ages as making tzitzit. The permissibility of women's involvement is queried only in the final stage of "sanctifying the garment," when the fringes were tied. In a singular opinion for his generation, Rabbenu Tam ruled that women could not make tzitzit, a stance that seems to contrast with his opinion that women must recite blessings when performing positive time-bound commandments. The report on Rabbenu Tam's position makes it evident that this was not a theoretical issue. Rabbenu Tam is reported to have disqualified tzitzit that were tied and sanctified by a woman from Troyes.¹⁰⁴ His logic, following a principle enunciated by the Talmud, was that only one who is obligated to wear ritual objects may make them and recite any blessing that could be said during that process. Even though this position is unprecedented among the generations before and after his, it was often cited due to Rabbenu Tam's stature.¹⁰⁵

Rabbenu Tam's prohibition of women manufacturing tzitzit was met with objections. For example, Judah Sirleon (d. 1224), the teacher of Moses of Coucy and whose own wife made tzitzit, suggested that a different talmudic interpretation allows tzitzit to be made by any member of the Jewish people, irrespective of their level of obligation.[106] In the fourteenth and fifteenth centuries one sees a compromise approach. Rather than ruling against women engaged in this task, Jacob Moellin (Maharil) states: "In a place where a man who knows how to affix tzitzit is present, a woman should not tie them."[107]

The position put forward by Rabbenu Tam is pivotal in our current discussion, for it demonstrates that performing a commandment and producing its corresponding ritual object did not necessarily go hand in hand. Indeed, Rabbenu Tam's prohibition of women tying tzitzit stands in contrast to instruction for women to recite blessings for positive time-bound commandments.[108] Some scholars have tried to argue that Rabbenu Tam's approval pertained to the precepts of lulav and shofar but not tefillin or tzitzit. Indeed, one of the texts that he cites in his ruling in favor of women reciting blessings for positive time-bound commandments is in his commentary on Tractate Rosh haShanah. However, as David Golinkin has noted, the position that Rabbenu Tam articulates is not directed toward a specific example.[109] Rather, Rabbenu Tam presents a broad statement that affirms the capacity of women to recite blessings when performing positive time-bound commandments, which he supports with the talmudic tale of Michal wearing tefillin. He then compares women to male slaves who are also exempted from performing these commandments but still observe them, much as women were compared to blind men in an earlier discussion.

Let us now consider the textual evidence of women performing the precepts of tefillin and tzitzit beyond merely producing the ritual objects. While there is evidence that women performed the mitzvot of lulav and shofar, neither *Mahzor Vitry* nor *Sefer Hasidim*, texts that repeatedly encourage men to wear tzitzit and tefillin, mention women observing these commandments. I also note that despite the modern legends, there is no medieval evidence that Rashi's daughters wore tefillin.[110] However, the late twelfth and early thirteenth century halakhic compendia discuss the permissibility of women performing tefillin and tzitzit with unprecedented frequency. The late twelfth-century *Sefer Yere'im* by Eliezer of Metz as well as the thirteenth-century compendia that contain lists of the commandments (from *Semag* at the beginning of the century to *Semak* at the century's end), as well as halakhic compendia such as *Sefer Tashbetz,* all acknowledge the issue of women performing the commandments of tzitzit and tefillin in some way, a topic that had not even been mentioned in early twelfth century sources.[111] These thirteenth-century documents each categorize women as exempt from positive time-bound commandments. For example, Moses of Coucy also writes:

> R. Isaac ruled that women are exempt from tzitzit[112] since this is a positive time-bound commandment . . . much like they are exempt from tefillin . . . and one cannot reason that women took this obligation upon themselves as in the case of *matzah* (eaten on Passover) for in the case of matzah this is a holiday festivity. . . . Nevertheless a blind man is obligated to perform the commandment of tzitzit even though he cannot see them.[113]

Here Moses of Coucy addresses women's lack of obligation and contrasts them to blind men following the Talmud, but he does not comment on actual practice.[114] Subsequent thirteenth-century compositions reiterate women's exemption alongside a grudging acknowledgment of their practice. Isaac of Corbeil states that blind men and boys should wear tzitzit, but on women's observance he remarks: "Women are also exempt but if they wish to say the blessing, they should; and women are allowed to make tzitzit."[115] Isaac concludes his comments by affirming tzitzit as one of the most important commandments.

German scholars voiced more opposition to Rabbenu Tam's approval of women reciting these blessing.[116] For example, Isaac b. Moses details different arguments that concern women making blessings, then closes by summarizing his opinion, which counters the position of Rabbenu Tam.[117] In a brief comment on the observance of tzitzit, Moses Parnas (second half of the thirteenth century) states from the outset that women are exempt whereas blind men are not and does not note whether they may perform the obligation.[118] Regardless of these differences, thirteenth-century German and northern French sources indicate that the question of whether women could perform positive time-bound commandments, including tefillin and tzitzit, was receiving unprecedented consideration.[119]

While it is tempting to argue that the omnipresence of this subject resulted from widespread thirteenth-century practice, these halakhic deliberations lack clear information about women's actual observance. However, some indications of women's practice can be gleaned from other sources. A Tosafist commentary (thirteenth century, northern France) on Tractate Berakhot[120] includes a discussion of the interruptions that are permitted when reciting the Hallel psalms. In this context, when explaining who is obligated to recite the blessings, the Tosafist quotes Samson b. Samson of Coucy (thirteenth century), also known as the Master of Coucy (*haSar meCoucy*), who taught that even if one is not obligated, it is permissible to recite a blessing, as "some women (*hanei nashei*) make a blessing on lulav and tefillin." Although some later copyists would write "tefillah" (prayers) rather than "tefillin," following scholars who amended it based on local practice in which women did not wrap tefillin, this does not seem to have been the original wording.[121] For example, Meir b. Yekutiel, author of the *Hagahot Maimoniyot*, following the Tosafot, states in a number of places that women can perform "lulav and tefillin": "The Master from Coucy concurred with Rabbenu Tam, that women can make the blessing for lulav and tefillin and other such things. R. Simhah also did, concerning the blowing of the shofar: a woman can blow shofar for herself and recite the blessing, and one should not protest."[122]

In one of its reiterations, Meir b. Yekutiel includes the phrase that appeared in the Talmud, "*hani nashei*"[123] ("these women" or sometimes "the women of our place"), often used in the Talmud to discuss women's practices, whether permitted or discouraged.[124] Alternatively, perhaps this can be read as specific women observing this practice. Avigdor haTzarfati (thirteenth century, Vienna) states that righteous women observe the commandments of tzitzit and tefillin,[125] and Meir b. Barukh suggests that some women performed this observance as well, as we see below. This comment on women's observance of lulav and tefillin is accompanied in at least one reiteration of a phrase we saw in our discussion of women observing the commandment of lulav. Isaac b. Asher, who permitted women to take the lulav, stated his agreement subtly, using the phrase "*ein mohin*" (one does not reprimand) rather than a stronger formulation.

The presentation of women's practices is often most vivid in sources that wish to curtail them. One objection to women wearing tefillin, unrelated to positive time-bound commandments but to the specific precept of tefillin, is raised in Isaac of Dampierre's (R"I) commentary on the Talmud. He notes that women encountered a distinct obstacle with regard to this ritual, for it was difficult for them to ensure that their bodies were clean (pure). In this discussion of the cleanliness required to properly fulfill the commandment of tefillin, the Talmud focuses on the permissibility of sleeping or passing wind while wearing tefillin,[126] but without mention of women performing this commandment. That is to say, corporeal cleanliness was also understood as a challenge already in the Talmud as well as in the medieval period. Indeed, some modern scholars posit that many medieval Jews may have refrained from wearing tefillin due to the recognition that they could not adequately regulate their level of purity and cleanliness.[127]

The Tosafists pick up this trope by commenting on the cleanliness of women's bodies in their consideration of women and tefillin. R"I remarks: "Women are not quick to be careful about the cleanliness of their bodies."[128] As Har-Shefi has argued, these words could be read as having theoretical rather than practical intent,[129] meaning that R"I is not categorically stating that women could not ensure their physical cleanliness, but emphasizing this as a distinct challenge. During the thirteenth century, some rabbis built on this discomfort communicated by Isaac of Dampierre by casting further doubts on women's abilities to maintain their hygiene. Moses of Coucy, who as we saw is known for his active promotion of tefillin, also raises cleanliness as an issue, but he battles its negative ramifications. He stated that tefillin need not be worn all day long, but that "all Jews can remain pure for one hour of the prayer service."[130] He sees this as especially important because of his belief in tzitzit and tefillin as crucial to Jewish identity.[131] A generation earlier, Barukh b. Isaac of Paris (1140–1200) expressed similar views in his extensive section on the laws of tefillin in *Sefer ha Terumah*. Twice he recommended that boys should put on tefillin from the moment they could take responsibility for personal hygiene; further, he asserted that anyone observing this commandment would merit a long and pleasant life.[132] One can assume that, since he advised that tefillin be given to minors, he concurred with Moses that cleanliness was required only during prayer services. Isaac of Corbeil followed suit. He stressed the importance of a clean and pure body, and remarked that most people can exercise care for bodily cleanliness for an hour each day and therefore observe this practice. However, he did not mention women. It would seem that a different gendered standard was being applied to men and women in respect to cleanliness and/or purity.[133] Only the later commentaries on the *Semak* engage the question of women wearing tefillin explicitly, prohibiting them from doing so.[134]

A similar growing interest in women and tefillin and discussion of cleanliness and purity can be traced, moving from northern France to Germany. Eleazar b. Judah's early thirteenth-century composition, *Sefer Rokeah*, discusses the blessing recited on tefillin briefly and does not mention women.[135] However, Isaac b. Moses discusses tefillin at length in his mid-thirteenth century *Sefer Or Zaru'a* and includes sayings attributed to previous authorities—from the Talmud through the Ge'onim—about the importance of tefillin.

According to Isaac: "Every upstanding person[136] should observe this (commandment)."[137] He underscores the roles of physical status and intention by declaring that anyone wearing tefillin was obligated to uphold purity and holiness.[138] Not only is the section devoted to tefillin in *Sefer Or Zaru'a* longer and more detailed than comparable texts from the previous century, it offers practical advice for making tefillin and copying their parchment insertions.[139] Isaac does not comment on women and tefillin at all, but it would seem that all his "upstanding people" are men.[140]

Only in the late thirteenth century is this matter addressed directly by Meir b. Barukh of Rothenburg:

> Women are exempt from tefillin and tzitzit because both are positive time-bound commandments. After all, tefillin are not donned on the Sabbath and tzitzit are not worn at night. However, one should not protest if [women] wrap themselves in tzitzit and recite the blessing for them (because [women] can take on obligations, as stated in BT Kiddushin [32a–b]).[141] However, they should not put on tefillin because they don't know to keep themselves pure.[142]

Meir permits women to wear tzitzit but he objects to women putting on tefillin, taking the talmudic passage on the exemption of women from positive time-bound commandments to its logical extreme, and categorically stating that women are incapable of maintaining their bodies in a state of purity, rather than casting doubt on women's purity and cleanliness from a theoretical perspective, as per R"I. Meir discusses purity (*toharah*) rather than R"I's term, "cleanliness" (*guf naki*), perhaps subtly shifting his focus to menstrual impurity. Interestingly, those who later draw on Meir's opinion, along with copyists of his writings, inserted a selection from the Palestinian Talmud in his teaching. That addition refers to Michal as *bat kushi* (daughter of a black man), not as the daughter of Saul, and adds: "Why was she called 'daughter of a kushi'? Because she was strange in her deeds, as he was strange in his skin [color]."[143]

This position represents a considerable shift from the *bon ton* during the twelfth and early thirteenth centuries. Rather than comparing women to blind men, Meir b. Barukh mentions what he views as an intrinsically female feature, their inability to remain pure.

Meir b. Yekutiel Cohen, author of the *Hagahot Maimoniyot* and student of Meir b. Barukh, follows suit. He states that he found an unnamed authority (*matzati beshem gadol*) who forbade women to wrap tefillin because of their hair, which is *erva* (nakedness), and he seems to be suggesting that by extension hair is considered impure.[144] These new opinions were being expressed during the second half of the thirteenth century, a period for which there is evidence that some women were wearing tzitzit and putting on tefillin, and that they were considered especially pious. Thus we saw Samson of Coucy remarking matter-of-factly that "our women" make the blessing on tefillin and lulav,[145] and Avigdor haTzarfati stating that righteous women observe the commandments of tzitzit and tefillin.[146] Other late thirteenth- and early fourteenth-century scholars comment on the disparity between Meir's instructions and accepted practice.[147]

However, a survey of fourteenth-century halakhic literature reveals that Meir b. Barukh's opinion concerning tefillin became standard as part of an increasing concern for purity. Not only did his student Meir b. Yekutiel follow in his footsteps, so did Moses b. Menahem of Zurich (fourteenth century) who comments on the permission granted to women to perform the precept of tzitzit in Isaac of Corbeil's *Sefer Mitzvot Katan*:

> And Yehiel (of Paris) ruled that *every* [emphasis added] Jew (lit., son of the covenant) who can say the Shema [prayer] should put on tefillin. He brought proof from the Palestinian Talmud. As for boys who are frivolous (*kalut rosh*) even when saying the Shema, they should not put on tefillin. . . . They should not (put them on) and treat them [without proper attention, like when they are] distracted with desire for women. Similarly, women should not put on tefillin because they do not know how to maintain [their] purity.[148]

Moses incorporates Meir's opinion in his commentary. Here, women are grouped with frivolous boys who were not yet able to control their sexual desires. Notably, these opinions correspond with the attitudes toward men's and women's impurity analyzed in Chapter 1. Imbedded in this passage is an implicit comparison between men's capacity to manage their impurity, at least for the brief duration of prayers, and women's involuntary bleeding (and therefore an unpredictable source of impurity).

One composition takes a noted exception to Meir b. Barukh of Rothenburg's view. In his book, known as the French (rather than German) *Sefer haMaskil*, Solomon Simhah of Troyes (late thirteenth century; a student of Meir b. Barukh and Rabbenu Peretz) includes several remarks on women's observance of positive time-bound commandments. First he suggests that widows (who, by definition, were unhampered by male authority) and married women who had obtained their husbands' permission should perform positive time-bound commandments. He then explains that, unlike men, women are exempt from punishment if they did not perform positive time-bound commandments; however, "if they received permission and obligated themselves, they should be praised and they should say the blessing 'that we have been commanded' just as men do."[149] Admittedly, this opinion is sui generis and does not comment on actual practice, but it does indicate a positive approach toward women who wanted to perform these rituals.

If we move from the fourteenth to the early fifteenth century, further changes emerge: on the rare occasions when women and tefillin are discussed, the authors univocally assert that women cannot put on tefillin due to impurity. Jacob Moellin (Maharil) applies similar reasoning in his recommendation against young boys donning tefillin since they cannot yet control their passions, so only married men should be obligated.[150]

Interestingly, none of the discussions cited above refer to a classic justification of women's exemption from positive time-bound commandments that appeared as early as the twelfth century and that was articulated more forcefully over time. This reasoning appears in non-legal compositions but could have been used in legal texts as well. In the twelfth century, Joseph of Orléans (known as Joseph Bekhor Shor) stated that women could not elect to take these commandments upon themselves because they are subservient to their husbands. He suggested that a "double loyalty" would result; to avoid this conflict of interest, God released women from this category of commandments.[151] *Sefer Hasidim* provides a similar rationale: "A woman should serve her husband so he can study Torah. This is why men were given dominance. [Moreover] whoever serves [one master] day and night cannot set time aside for another; therefore women are exempt from positive time-bound commandments."[152]

This explanation for women's exemption gained currency in the early modern period,[153] but with the exception of these passages it hardly appears in sources from the High Middle Ages.

Another position that becomes more pronounced over time is threaded through medieval discussions of tzitzit, namely the talmudic concern that one who wears tzitzit might be regarded as arrogantly (*yohara*) parading his piety. Throughout the Middle Ages, and especially during the thirteenth century, rabbis countered the link between wearing tzitzit and arrogance when discussing the importance of men taking the practice upon themselves. So, too, when women and tzitzit were discussed as in the writings of Meir b. Barukh, he did not mention arrogance.¹⁵⁴ In the fifteenth century this concept was reintroduced in relation to women and tzitzit. Jacob Moellin (Maharil) discusses this matter by weaving together several of the issues we have considered above:

> Wherever a man who knows how to fix (finish ritually) tzitzit, a woman should not fix them. He has said that it is not clear to him why some women take on the obligation of tzitzit. They asked him why he does not reprimand Rabbanit Bruna [who lives] in his city for wearing tzitzit at all times. And he said: "Perhaps she will not listen to me." On such matters it has been said: "It is better to err accidentally than intentionally" (BT Bava Batra 62b).¹⁵⁵

It seems Maharil is discussing tallit katan, as he states explicitly elsewhere, outlined below.¹⁵⁶ In a separate responsum, he begins by explaining that women are unaccustomed to performing the commandment of tzitzit. He then compares tzitzit with other commandments, emphasizing the relative passivity of tzitzit as an artifact that becomes part of another garment, in contrast to more active obligations.¹⁵⁷ He sums up his opinion as follows:

> It seems that the main purpose of the commandment of tzitzit is to remember all of God's commandments. . . . And one remembers all 613 commandments, those we understand and those we don't. But women are not obligated by [the full complement of] 613 commandments because they are exempt from all positive time-bound commandments and from a number of negative ones [lit., the "do nots"], such as "You shall not round off the side-growth on your . . . beard" (Lev. 19:27). But in the case of men, even though there are select commandments that only pertain to priests, men all comprise a single category. A court populated by Israelites is responsible for priests, and if they (the priests) do not adhere (to a verdict) they [the Israelites] can punish them. This is not the case with women. Since they are not included in [the full obligation of] 613, they are a people unto themselves.¹⁵⁸ For all these reasons, although I have seen women wearing four fringes—as a woman in our neighborhood does—to this very day, this arouses incredulity and is considered arrogant.¹⁵⁹

The major effort invested by Maharil is readily apparent. He is battling with someone, a woman in his neighborhood, identified elsewhere as Rabbanit

Bruna.[160] Since he notes that "I have seen women," his comment may apply to more than one such woman; however, he is undoubtedly mentioning specific examples rather than a general trend. Although Maharil does not forbid women from practicing the commandment of tzitzit, he voices a forceful objection in the form of his inability to comprehend why women would wish to take on this observance.

Several noteworthy conclusions can be drawn from a critical reading of Maharil's comments about Rabbanit Bruna. Unlike the general references to women who practiced tzitzit and the seemingly casual remarks by thirteenth-century scholars that mention "pious women" or simply "women" who observe this mitzvah, here one specific woman, known to all her neighbors, is mentioned by name. Moreover, Maharil suggests that it would be futile to reprimand her for this "misdeed" since she would not heed him. Maharil's efforts were successful, for this opinion reverberates in later rabbinic writings, including the most important early modern code, the *Shulkhan Arukh,* where it is stated and then further emphasized by commentators that women should not wear tzitzit because it would be arrogant.[161] That is not to say that women immediately ceased to observe this commandment, but those who continued were unusual enough to be mentioned as outstanding individuals, much like Rabbanit Bruna from Maharil's neighborhood.

The gendered definitions presented by Maharil provide a significant linguistic and conceptual prism. By classifying all men as being of the "same type" and women as a "separate people," he directly states concepts that are only hinted at in earlier writings. In this passage, he refers to a talmudic debate about women's jewelry and whether it could be worn on the Sabbath (BT Shabbat 72b). In the Talmud, the rabbis suggest that women have a distinct attitude toward jewelry that is not shared by men. Maharil's statement is admittedly derived from his reading of the Talmud[162] but at the same time is quite unique. Indeed, few medieval deliberations on women's performance of positive time-bound commandments—certainly not those dated from before the early thirteenth century—classify women and men as mutually exclusive categories. As we saw, some rabbis presented women as analogous to men who were fully commanded and as having agency to take commandments upon themselves, while others understood women as akin to "deficient" men, such as the blind. Still others advocated women performing positive time-bound commandments for the sake of their contentment (*nahat ruah*).[163] Even R"I did not claim that women were universally incapable of managing their own cleanliness; he merely stated that women were not, as a rule, sufficiently careful.

Although the authors of these opinions each cited support for their positions in the Talmud, a survey of these comparisons yields a transformed definition of gender differences over time. The trend toward presenting men and women as increasingly different was a deliberate choice. Ultimately, an integral explanation of gender difference relating to women qua women surfaced toward the late thirteenth century and emerged more starkly over time.[164]

Maharil's depiction of men and women appears in a discussion concerning tzitzit and mirrors Meir of Rothenburg's unmitigated claim in his consideration of women and tefillin (notwithstanding the fact that these two rabbis arrive at opposing practical recommendations, as Meir permits tzitzit) that women cannot maintain their physical purity. Meir's statement takes the opinion of R"I one step further: whereas R"I states that it is difficult for women to exercise sufficient care with regard to their physical purity, Meir declares it impossible. We saw Meir's students followed his opinion as well. Each of these statements is a far cry from Riva's eleventh-century assertion that women who perform positive time-bound commandments by their own free will resemble men who take on commandments for which they are not obligated.

I am not arguing that twelfth-century rabbis did not see women as halakhically or socially distinct from men whereas fifteenth-century men did. Rather, I am suggesting that even within a hierarchal and patriarchal society (adjectives that aptly describe all pre-modern societies despite the differences between them), variation and change are also evident. When Rabbenu Tam ruled that women could not tie the fringes on tzitzit since, unlike men, they were not commanded to make them,[165] he too was placing men and women in different categories; this did not, however, prevent him from ruling that women, like men, could perform positive time-bound commandments and recite blessings when performing them.

Performers and Practice: Continuity and Change

By examining the rulings and rhetoric of medieval Ashkenazic rabbis, we witness changes in both thought and practice. Some researchers who have delved into these issues have chosen to ignore the constriction of women's practice after the thirteenth century by pointing to the purported open-mindedness of medieval rabbis.[166] Others have presented these rabbis as less broad-minded or have argued that discussions of women and positive time-bound commandments applied less to the realities of women's religious concerns than to philosophical and exegetical ones.[167] As an alternative, I have analyzed the role of gender rather than that of women and argued that transformations can be found in rhetoric and in practice.

We have seen that in the eleventh- and twelfth-century texts the initiative to perform positive time-bound commandments connected to holidays was attributed to the women themselves, and they continued these practices well after the thirteenth century. As elements of daily life, tefillin and tzitzit differed in nature from observances that were tied to a specific day or festival. That these deeds were considered pious and righteous is reflected in the superlative language used by medieval authors to laud their observance when performed by men and women and to depict the shame and humiliation suffered by those men who performed them.

It is likely that the women who practiced these commandments were relatives of the male religious elite. As we saw, several women who made tzitzit and tefillin had familial connections to prominent rabbis. The sources, however, do not portray specific women actually performing the precepts linked to these ritual objects; rather, they note that "women" wore tzitzit and "pious women" put on tefillin, with the exception of Rabbanit Bruna in the fifteenth century who was mentioned by name.

As tefillin and tzitzit gained popularity, even men who were impure due to seminal emissions were considered clean enough to put on tefillin for the duration of prayers, whereas women were considered impure because they might begin to menstruate while wearing them; this mirrors the conditions (discussed in Chapter 1) in which all men could enter the sanctuary but women who were menstruating could not. As observance of tefillin and tzitzit became more commonplace, the issue of gender was addressed outright, in contrast to the early stages of the process when the popularization of these practices was of the highest priority. Not until the late thirteenth century were these observances sufficiently widespread for Isaac of Corbeil to assert that "every Jew" should perform them.[168]

Although distinctions between men and women were critical for the development of ritual norms during the second half of the thirteenth century and in subsequent decades (and centuries), gender was not the only contributing factor in these changes. With respect to tefillin, other hierarchies were also at play: whereas tzitzit was a widely observed precept that even children were qualified to perform, tefillin became the domain of adult men to the exclusion of young boys; some even recommended that this commandment be reserved for married men.[169]

In later centuries, references to pious women who donned tefillin or wore tzitzit are rare. A sixteenth-century source from Siena mentions "two women who put on tefillin like Michal" and who were called upon as trustworthy witnesses.[170] In the late seventeenth century, women who belonged to pietistic-hasidic circles—such as that of Nathan Adler (1741–1800)—are said to have worn tzitzit.[171] In this instance, the decision that women could wear tzitzit is attributed to the male leaders of their local community. Yemima Hovav has noted the skepticism of rabbinic authorities (such as Benjamin Selnik, 1550–1620) concerning the intentions of women who wore tzitzit or put on tefillin.[172] In short, women who practiced tefillin and tzitzit after the medieval period became even more rare.

As we saw, one line of reasoning that became a standard explanation for why women should not wear tzitzit in early modern halakhic guidebooks, such as that of Benjamin Selnik quoted above, is based on the final lines of a responsum by Maharil, who asserted that a woman who wore tzitzit should be considered arrogant (*yoharah*).[173] This idea of perceived arrogance in relation to tzitzit was first discussed in the Talmud, where wearing tzitzit was considered comparable to a demonstration of piety, whether in this life or in the World to Come.[174] In accounts of the First Crusade, tzitzit were also presented as a symbolic affirmation of Jewish adherence. For example, when Count Emicho and his troops entered the bishop's courtyard in Mainz, they encountered a group of Jews wearing fringed garments—perhaps in anticipation of their imminent deaths (and burial), perhaps as a declaration of piety.[175] The propriety of burial with tzitzit was debated in the Talmud but also became the norm for men.[176]

Women are not mentioned in the talmudic discussion of arrogance in the context of wearing tzitzit. However, the subject of women, commandments, and perceived arrogance does arise in talmudic discussions of other positive time-bound commandments, such as the sukkah.[177] When medieval commentators considered this issue, they affirmed that women could perform positive time-bound commandments without fear of displaying arrogance. This theme was addressed by Ra'aviah, and his remark was cited verbatim by rabbis of later generations, among them Moses Parnas (late thirteenth century; a student of Meir b. Barukh of Rothenburg):

> Women, slaves, and children are exempt from [dwelling in] the sukkah and any boy that no longer needs his mother [for succor] and is already four or five [years old] is obligated by [the commandments

relating to the] sukkah. It is not arrogant (*yoharah*) for women to sit in the sukkah and make the [applicable] blessing. Although one who is obligated and performs a commandment has done a greater act than one who performs [the same commandment] without being obligated, in either case, a commandment [has been fulfilled].[178]

The theme of women's arrogance or impudence was current in thirteenth-century halakhic writings, albeit in a different context, that of marital law. Meir of Rothenburg ruled strictly against a woman demanding a divorce in response to a scholar from Regensburg who sought his advice on how to reduce the frequency of women demanding divorces. This scholar implored him: "Since the women of Regensburg have always elevated (*higbihu*) themselves above their husbands and even more so in these times. Therefore, you (R. Meir) must stand in their way."[179] Meir responded to this plea by employing similar vocabulary to affirm that women in his times were not as "modest" as women had been in the past and ruled that women should "treat their husbands with respect" (Esther 1:20).[180]

Some of Meir's sstudents repeated his ruling, in an effort to limit women's ability to divorce their husbands and especially to exercise their financial rights after the divorce, by claiming, "In our generation of immoral women, they should not be believed."[181] Meir's student, Asher b. Yehiel, described the women of his generation as *shahtzaniyot* (haughty).[182] Both "arrogant" and "haughty" are indicative of a growing critique of women, one in the realm of ritual, the other in the realm of law.

These expressions concerning the haughtiness of women from the thirteenth century and their arrogance in the late fourteenth century are suggestive of gradual social changes. This dynamism not only shows how gender constructed religion but also how religious politics constructed gender and led to transformed definitions of man and woman and their traits.[183] These altered views of gendered religious practices did not result from trauma and exile, as some have suggested, for they pre-date the tumultuous events at the turn of the fourteenth century, nor were they the fruit of a new type of halakhic logic.

Medieval Christian culture represents an invaluable resource for understanding these religious phenomena because Christian society was also deliberating many similar issues regarding women's expressions of spirituality and their place in the social order, specifically during the course of the thirteenth century. Although positive time-bound commandments are an inherently

Jewish construct, the revised approaches to gender and redefinitions of gendered practice cannot be explained by internal logic alone, for, as others have argued, no single line of reasoning can fully explain these medieval developments.[184] If we consider these dynamics not only within Jewish society but as part of medieval processes that involve gender and the politics of gender, how might they be explained?

The thirteenth century has been identified as a period when Christian women's participation in religious and social ritual rose markedly, as documented by their involvement in religious groups and orders, be they female monastic houses or groups of lay women such as the Beguines. Similar transformations have also been situated in the broader context of post-Lateran definitions of membership in the Church. These shifts have also been presented as outcomes of a revolution in the hegemonic attitudes held by the ruling elite—in this case, male leadership within the Church and royalty—toward women.[185]

Numerous scholars have demonstrated that the thirteenth and fourteenth centuries were characterized by unprecedented demands for Christian women to prove their faith and piety in new and complex ways. Dyan Elliott has detailed how women were accused of heresy with increasing regularity while also being required to prove their fidelity to Christianity.[186] Walter Simons has shown how church authorities demanded the right to supervise the Beguines more closely because it could sometimes be difficult to discern whether they were pious women or prostitutes.[187]

The accusations voiced against these women had two main themes. First, they were portrayed as unsupervised and thereby out of control. In contrast to the prevailing customs of the medieval world, they were not subordinate to any man. Second, they violated the accepted division of gender roles by assuming positions that were considered the purview of men. When preaching and speaking about the Bible and other holy texts in public, these women were often accused of being haughty and vain. These condemnations were repeated in many thirteenth- and fourteenth-century texts, which led to women being prohibited from preaching, and, as many scholars have claimed, their influence was directed toward the realm of mysticism.[188] The sanctions and suspicions of the Christian hierarchy[189] differed little from the rabbis' concerns. Without minimizing the differences between Jewish and Christian society and the paths available to women within each religion, the reactions led by these male authorities to women's more active agency in religious life are remarkably similar, whether following Meir b. Barukh or Jacob Moellin and their reasoning.

Positive time-bound commandments provided a means for expressing belonging and identity as well as for externally manifesting religious identity within the medieval city. In the mixed neighborhoods where Jews lived, the construction of a sukkah would have been witnessed by Christians as well as Jews. Similarly, sounding the shofar and carrying palm branches were activities that would have been heard and seen publicly, irrespective of the specificity of their meaning and community of observers. These rituals embodied tangible expressions of belonging and enmeshed the body with God's words and commandments. Tefillin and tzitzit became more popular and more visible conventions for enacting piety. During the thirteenth century, some women, like men, chose to fulfill these commandments. These observances would have complemented longer-standing religious actions that also conveyed identity—observing the Sabbath and holidays, fasting, and culinary rituals, to name a few.

Tefillin, tzitzit, lulav, sukkah, and shofar were all exposed via sight and sometimes sound to community members and neighbors alike. One who wore tzitzit and tefillin communicated piety through visible symbols. Such tangible codes were part of medieval society much like they are part of modern society today. The male nature of these conventions was well established. As we saw at the opening of this chapter, much as King David was lauded for his tefillin and tzitzit, when he was naked he found his connection to God through circumcision, the ultimate male symbol. Yet we have also seen that ritual objects, like other non-verbal signs, must be interpreted according to the time and place in which they are displayed. Visual codes and their medieval contexts are the focus of the last chapters of this book.

CHAPTER 5

Conspicuous in the City: Medieval Jews in Urban Centers

> Their offspring shall be known among the nations, their descendants in the midst of the peoples. All who see them shall recognize that they are a stock the Lord has blessed.
> —Isaiah 61:9

Many of the pious practices that we have analyzed in this study draw attention to specific codes that were broadcast daily by medieval Jews to one another and to their Christian neighbors. Such actions often elicited comments and praise from religious leaders or fellow community members, although when praxis breached social conventions, these same behaviors could be reprimanded and even forbidden, as exemplified in the cases of positive time-bound commandments when gender lines were crossed and fasting when religious boundaries were blurred. Together with the ritual objects used to express devotion (e.g., tallit and tefillin), which became especially popular during the thirteenth century (see Chapter 4), piety was also communicated via dress. Anyone who adopted the distinctive garments worn on a daily basis by those repenting for sins or those who were impure was displaying religious devotion.[1]

The extent to which clothing conveyed religious identity as well as a specific position in one's own community is discussed in medieval texts. In his commentary on a talmudic passage about women who behaved improperly by "going out with their dresses unfastened and spinning cloth in the streets with exposed armpits," Rashi compares them to the Christian women in his environs, describing the behavior as "customary among the Christian women (*edomiyot*) of France, whose flesh is visible from the side."[2] This observation differentiates Jewish and Christian women's modes of dress while assessing the propriety of these norms. Rashi implies that Christian women wore gowns that exposed more skin than those that Jewish women wore. This remark and others like it provide glimpses of basic details of medieval life that were taken for granted by the individuals and groups that are examined in this volume. Our restricted abilities to reconstruct what medieval Jews and Christians witnessed daily represents a serious limitation for modern scholarship, but this difficulty in no way diminishes the intrinsic relationship between clothing and religious expression.

As the quotation from Rashi indicates, medieval Jewish sources do not readily divulge the dress codes and conventions of their time. Consequently, this chapter presents initial steps in the process of gathering evidence concerning pious and ordinary Jewish dress in an effort to discern how appearance signaled piety and belonging among the Jews of Ashkenaz. I begin this analysis with a discussion of medieval Christian clothing because of the relatively abundant available data on this subject and the reality that medieval Jews would have been keenly aware of the dress codes of the majority culture. I then address four examples of how appearance enabled medieval Jews and their Christian neighbors to transmit social and religious messages within their communities and to one another:[3] three normative choices, namely, garments and accessories, grooming hair and beards, and the fabrics used to make clothing; and one made under duress, cross-dressing as a mechanism for protection through disguise. While each of these topics deserves further investigation, my purpose here is to provide a survey of the social codes that informed the pious practices of medieval Ashkenaz. This chapter concludes with a general discussion of appearance as it relates to piety.

Clothing and Coiffure as Markers of Piety in Christian Europe

The use of dress codes as an expression of religious affiliation and values pervades all cultures. As anthropologists have demonstrated from a variety of perspectives, clothing is far more than merely a protective or stylish covering for the body; it is a key manifestation of belonging that often reflects collective definitions of purity and identity.[4] Medieval Jews and Christians were certainly not exceptions to this rule, for their modes of dress broadcast significant messages. Indeed, recent studies by scholars of medieval Christian Europe have pointed to the many ways that clothing conveyed religious identity, social status, and piety, as Dyan Elliott summarized: "Because clothing is an essential tool in social semiotics—an invaluable shorthand for describing the wearer's condition to the outer world—the way in which a saint chose to dress is an expression of this discrepancy."[5]

Scholars who research medieval dress have remarked on the continuity in clothing styles from the eleventh to thirteenth centuries (relative to the period after the Black Death) that was concurrent with the fierce arguments concerning dress and physical presentation that raged during that period. As Giles Constable outlined, the color of cloth was a source of bitter debate among twelfth-century reformers.[6] Following Constable, Gabor Klaniczay elaborated: "The controversy was caused on the one hand by the fashions prevalent at royal and aristocratic courts and on the other hand by the symbolic attire of the ascetic religious movement which opposed in equal measures the opulence of the church and of the laity."[7] The quality and quantity of fabric in a garment as well as the presence (or lack of) ornamentation were each indicators of economic and religious status. Fur and fine cloth, embroidery and jewelry all bespoke status and wealth.[8] Analogously, the simplicity of monastic apparel signified the renunciation of material possessions and insignia distinguished military orders. Color generally carried broadly recognized cultural meanings, and select colors were associated with seasons in the liturgical calendar, as reflected in clerical vestments.[9]

The attire worn by men and women in religious vocations conveyed messages that corresponded to their communities' principles and beliefs.[10] Françoise Piponnier and Perrine Mane have described the twelfth- and thirteenth-century revolution of religious orders through the galvanization of the relationship between their clothing and their convictions, with each house identified by its distinctive garb: Benedictines donned black and pinned emblems on their robes to indicate their precise affiliation; Dominicans wore white robes and black caps; and Cistercians wore white or undyed wool. Certain orders minimized the number of garments worn by their members to maximize simplicity and austerity. Echoing the broader trends mentioned above, color served as an identifying feature of many groups. Orders associated their distinctive attire with Christ, the Apostles, angels, the cross, and other Christian symbols.[11] Some houses were nicknamed according to their attire, the most evident being the Franciscans, who were called "Cordeliers" (and its Hebrew equivalent, *hovlim*, among Jews) because of their belts of knotted rope and also *frères du sac* because of their robes of rough fabric.

Members of lay Christian groups also communicated piety with their wardrobes by wearing unadorned attire. For instance, beguines, who were not affiliated with any order, wore distinct gray or black garments that functioned as a uniform and that became well known.[12] The *filles de Dieu*—who later joined the Cistercians in France—were known for their signature white clothing.[13] As the mendicants became increasingly popular, laity independent of any order were known to have adopted a religious-ascetic system of symbols as well.[14]

Much as pious practitioners used simple garments to communicate many aspects of their social and religious positions, the higher echelons of lay Christian society exercised similar strategies. The aristocracy employed jewels and choice fabrics as central means of expressing social and material capital. And, of course, knights and soldiers externalized their roles as well. Thus, for Christians, dress was determined to a significant degree by religious season, individual commitments, and communal practice, as well as social and economic status.

In addition to publicly demonstrating membership in pious communities or promoting related values, clothing could also be a mechanism for communicating within a more exclusive circle. As Anne Lester has remarked: "A noble wearing undyed cloth, a young girl in a loose shirt tied with a leather cord, an old matron in coarse woolen hose were all modest variations on mundane attire that by disguising the human enriched the sacred."[15] Following these conventions in medieval society, clothes functioned on two levels. Some messages were obvious to all (e.g., clothing that denoted membership in a religious order or participation in a religious observance), whereas subtle variations on a common practice could transmit messages that were only accessible to a select audience.

Living among Christians, Jews were presumably familiar with some of the signs communicated among their neighbors, although others were likely outside their realm of familiarity.[16] As outside observers, they would have been cognizant of clothing as a defining symbol of Christian groups and movements,[17] since such dress codes were an omnipresent aspect of daily social and cultural encounters.[18] Even if medieval Jews could not read nuances of these internal Christian conversations, they certainly could have known some rudiments of their outward manifestations.[19]

Reconstructing Jewish Dress in Medieval Ashkenaz

To date, the subject of apparel in Jewish society during the High Middle Ages has received scant attention.[20] I suggest that outward appearance could convey piety and religious identity simultaneously, with varying inflections, depending on the setting. In order to bridge the intricacies of pious garb within Jewish society, I first examine to what degree Jews could be differentiated from Christians on the streets of medieval cities and then discuss how piety was displayed in that context.

The event that has often been identified as pivotal in the history of Jewish dress is the Fourth Lateran Council of 1215, where it was decreed that Jews must wear a symbol that rendered them visible as Jews.[21] Although Jewish scholarship typically focuses on the implications of this injunction for Jews living in Christendom, the Fourth Lateran Council concerned itself with attire at large, devising guidelines for Jews and Muslims, Christian laity and clergy.[22] In fact, the Church's motivation for defining Jewish attire is perhaps more meaningful than the results of that attempt. The Lateran Council was attempting to institute unmistakable distinctions between religious groups in order to eliminate any barriers to readily identifying their members. These regulations not only aimed to separate Jews, Muslims, and Christians, but were also an effort to make divisions among Christians easily recognizable.[23] Scholarly research on the effects of legislation from local or higher-ranking Christian authorities to compel Jews and other non-Christians to wear distinctive signs has concluded that these efforts were not particularly successful, at least not initially.[24] Nevertheless, such directives substantiate the claim that dress was a major factor for indicating religious belonging and status. Moreover, the impetus for this demand suggests that without such dictates it would have been nearly impossible to ascertain one's religion at a glance, which is to say that it was hard to tell Jews and Christians apart.[25]

Let us now consider a variety of symbols that are associated with Ashkenazic Jews in medieval texts.

Jewish Hats and Jewish Hair

The subject of this section—prescriptions for hats, haircuts, and facial hair from Jewish and Christian authorities—overwhelmingly focuses on Jewish men. The required accessory par excellence that has been investigated in scholarly studies is the so-called "Jewish hat" (Juden hutte) that first appears in illuminated manuscripts in the eleventh century and becomes a standard feature in graphics from the thirteenth century onward.[26]

Despite its frequent mention in popular medieval literature, scholars have argued that this hat was not as typical as later texts suggest, especially the pictorial sources. The *Sachsenspiegel* (written in 1221) states that some Jews elected

Figure 15. Jewish men with Jewish hats. From *Leipzig Mahzor*. © Leipzig University Library. 1102, Kennicott 665, fol. 40r. Mahzor, Worms, ca. 1310.

to wear the Juden hutte even before it became a legal requirement, first by decree in Germany and then in other regions.[27] Neither Christian nor Jewish texts indicate that Jews in thirteenth-century France wore hats that marked them religiously.[28] The process by which this hat became associated with Jews was not rapid; in fact, some scholars maintain that it had been favored by others—be they Muslims in Spain or Christian clergy in Europe—before becoming a symbol of Jewishness.[29] While Jews were commonly described as "male, bearded and hat-wearing" in late medieval European writings, medieval Christian art does not begin to portray Jews differently from Christians until the late thirteenth and early fourteenth century.[30]

Not only do we lack any reports of specific headwear worn by Jews, we have no conclusive evidence that Ashkenazic men covered their heads in any ritual manner during the eleventh and twelfth centuries. In his study of the male practice of wearing headpieces during prayer in medieval Jewish communities, Eric Zimmer writes that even in the late thirteenth century, only the especially pious covered their heads.[31] Zimmer's claim is supported by a passage from the fourteenth-century *Sefer haKushiyot* that asks why men would go out in public without head covering: "Why does a man go out with his head uncovered but a woman goes out with her hair covered? The answer is that this should be compared to a man who sinned then feels embarrassed (*mitbayesh*) when he goes out to the market, so he covers his head. So too in the case of a woman who transgressed the commandment 'From the fruit of the garden' (Gen. 3:3)."[32] This teaching operates from the premise that Jewish men neither covered their heads nor saw a need to do so. Given its early fourteenth-century authorship, it would seem that even in this period when Jews are said to have regularly worn the "Jewish hat," the prevalence of this custom was far from decisive. Thus while some Jewish men may have been identifiable by their hats during the High Middle Ages, this was by no means universal.[33]

As another mutable feature of personal appearance, hair was also a critical factor in communicating religious identity and piety.[34] The decision by some Jewish men to grow beards, as opposed to most of their peers, was praised by certain medieval rabbis who remarked on the piety of that choice.[35] While some medieval manuscripts (in Hebrew and in Latin) portray Jews as bearded, others do not.[36] Elliott Horowitz's study of the medieval beards has asserted that in medieval Christian Europe (and especially in northern France and Germany), most Jews, like their Christian contemporaries,[37] were clean-shaven; this pattern stands in contrast to Jews who lived under Muslim rule, where beards were the norm for men in both religions.

Medieval rabbinic discussions of beards were not preoccupied with whether or not men were clean-shaven, but rather with the implements used for shaving.[38] This theme relates to the biblical instructions concerning male facial hair: "You shall not round off the side-growth on your head or destroy the side-growth of your beard" (Lev. 19:27). Among medieval Jews in northern Europe this verse was understood as a prohibition against using a razor to shave the hair on one's head or face; therefore, some authorities recommended using scissors.[39] Thus, a clean-shaven Jew might have looked exactly like his Christian counterpart even though he achieved the same effect with a different instrument.[40] "Jewish shaving" exemplifies a culturally specific custom that was commonplace among Jews but was neither discernible nor necessarily meaningful to members of other communities who were not privy to this religious nuance.

The importance of this matter of shaving is evident in medieval communal ordinances that discuss how beards should be cut and groomed and that deliberated over which areas of the face, neck, and head could be shaved with a razor. The late twelfth- and early thirteenth-century texts that weigh these questions reveal that, as a rule, Jewish men in that era were clean-shaven. Abraham b. Ephraim (early thirteenth century) cites Jacob b. Meir (Rabbenu Tam), who cautioned that the chin should not be shaved completely. Abraham b. Ephraim concludes his remarks by stating: "All who are stringent should be blessed."[41] Isaac of Corbeil also advised that it was "better not to use any razor whatsoever on the beard."[42]

Advocacy for growing beards is attributed to Judah the Pious, whose writing from Germany predated those of Abraham and Isaac in France by several decades. An account of Judah that was recently analyzed by Eli Yassif is indicative of beards as a symbol of medieval Jewish piety and even as fuel for confrontations among Jewish groups. The following anecdote is attributed to Zalman, Judah's son:

> Once there was a rich man in Speyer who would cut his beard with scissors. My father (Judah the Pious) came to rebuke him but [the rich man] did not heed his scolding. Rather, he said: "I am an *istenis*[43] and I cannot stand having a beard." My father said: "You should know that your fate will be dire. After your death, demons that resemble cows (*parot*) will stamp on your beard. This is the lot of those who destroy their beards. You should know this, for it is written [in Scripture]: 'You shall not destroy the side-growth of your beards' (Lev. 19:27), the words [of this biblical instruction] form the acronym 'parot.'"[44] When that rich man died, the prominent people of Speyer were all sitting (*shivah*) in his home. My father was there (too). He wrote a name[45] and flung it on the corpse of the rich man that then stood up. Everyone (else) ran away. The corpse began to pick at his head and tear his hair. My father asked him: "What are you doing?" He said: "I regret not having listened to you."[46]

Yassif has considered the literary conventions and symbols in this narrative, which concludes with Judah helping the rich man redeem himself from hell. In our inquiry, more important than the specifics of this story is the window that it provides on conventions and convictions regarding men shaving their beards, even with scissors, and the tremendous efforts exercised to dissuade them from cutting their beards, even by invoking demonic cows to deliver the message. Given that the source for this tale postdates the thirteenth century, it may be somewhat anachronistic, representing a later time when beards were more typical. Fourteenth-century texts indicate that Jewish men who had regular contact with Christian nobles often copied their haircuts and beard styles.[47] Overall, medieval Ashkenazic sources indicate that most Jewish men were clean-shaven, with the exception of the most pious; this phenomenon had a Christian parallel, where men who dedicated their lives to religion, such as hermits, anchorites, and ascetics, were often noted for their beards.[48]

Research on medieval Christian Europe confirms that hairstyles and grooming facial hair had social and religious currency in Christian society as well, as outlined by Giles Constable over thirty years ago. During the eleventh century, many young men had their hair ritually cut to ensure their "decent" and "respectful" appearance in church.[49] In certain orders, hair and beards were ritually cut with accompanying blessings at regular intervals during the year.[50] By the twelfth century, Christian clergy were uniformly expected to be clean-shaven.[51] In the thirteenth century, clean-shaven faces and short hair had become normative. At the same time, some noblemen began wearing long hair, a practice that caught the attention of Jews in their midst,[52] as attested in the Rhineland Statutes (*Takanot Rheinus*) that caution Jews against growing their hair long, as Christians did.[53] The potency of hair as a symbol was further underlined in the fourteenth century, when members of the so-called "modern devout" wore their hair in a singular style.[54]

In medieval rabbinic sources, Jewish hairstyles are frequently raised in conjunction with discussions of beards, following the two-fold biblical injunction against shaving the "side-growth" (*pe'ah*) of the beard and head in Leviticus (19:27). By late antiquity, certain haircuts and, more to the point, specific rituals related to cutting hair were deemed inappropriate for Jews since they were viewed as cultic activities, often dubbed the "ways of the Emorites,"[55] and so were to be avoided.[56] The Talmud specifically names two men's hairstyles as unacceptable: *komi*, described as the haircut of magicians, and *blorit*, long hair. Numerous medieval commentators describe their Christian contemporaries as models when explaining these talmudic categories. Rashi, for instance, defines komi as having the crown of the head shaved while the sides and back are kept long, reminiscent of tonsure;[57] he explains that some Jews adopted this style to conceal their religious identity.[58] In his *Sefer haGematriyot*, Judah the Pious characteristically introduces a more stringent position by stating that no man who grows his hair long, cuts his beard with scissors, or wears non-Jewish clothing should be called to the Torah in synagogue.[59]

The prohibition against ritual haircutting, which had been considered idolatrous in antiquity, was extended to Christian customs during the Middle Ages. A number of rabbinic commentators equated these customs with tonsure, a hallmark of Christian clerics, which was therefore prohibited among Jews. Medieval Jewish texts also highlight ritual hair cutting as questionable. Echoing our discussion of "Jewish beards," the technique for cutting hair became an intrinsic criterion for determining the acceptability of hairstyles.[60]

Despite the desire of some rabbinic authorities to regulate grooming of facial hair and hairstyles, it seems that most medieval Jewish men followed their neighbors (with the noteworthy exception of tonsure, which was indeed excluded from Jewish custom). Some rabbinic passages imply that Jews went to non-Jewish barbers; if that was the case, then the resemblance between hairstyles[61] among men in these two medieval communities is even less coincidental.[62] In addition, Eric Zimmer has argued that Jewish sideburns as instructed in the Bible were not normative among Jewish men in medieval Europe.[63] Amid this cultural environment, as noted above, the Rhineland synods in the early thirteenth century issued warnings against Jewish men cutting their hair in a komi style, shaving with a razor as non-Jews did, and growing excessively long hair. This rebuke suggests that these were common practices that the rabbis sought to deter.[64] An apt demonstration of how beards and hats came to epitomize images of Jewish men after the thirteenth century—irrespective of the heterogeneity in practice documented by texts from that time—is presented in the Bird's Head Haggadah in the portrayal of Jews going to heaven (see Figure 3 in Chapter 1). All the men there have Jewish hats and beards.

Before leaving this theme, a word about women's hair and head coverings is in order. The medieval sources examined here are nearly silent on this subject.[65] This lack of attention can be attributed to the reality that men are the focus of biblical directives about hair[66] and to longstanding cultural norms. Like their Christian counterparts, married Jewish women covered their heads when they left their homes and yards, as verified by illuminated manuscripts from the period.[67] This was the case even when some of the men were depicted bare-headed. For example, in this picture of matzah preparation in the

Figure 16. Jewish women with head coverings, men with and without hats. From *Birds' Head Haggadah*. © Israel Museum, Jerusalem. B46.04.0912; 180/057 fols. 25v–26r. Southern Germany, ca. 1300.

Bird's Head Haggadah, some men are with hats and some are without, but the women all have their heads covered. During the thirteenth century, some rabbis emphasized that women should cover their heads whenever they were outdoors, which may suggest that this practice also was not always strictly followed. One of the Tosafists explains that women were obligated to cover their hair because they were born with the burden of their sins.[68] Asher b. Yehiel conveys an exceptional degree of severity when discussing this matter: he attributes the absence of a head covering to (women's) "impudence and the lure of sexual immorality (*znut*)."[69] Few comments of this nature exist; to the contrary, discussions of women's head covering generally lack the religious fervor found in texts on analogous men's issues.

Cloth and Clothing

The fabrics and thread used to make clothing also broadcast religious messages. As with men's hair and head covering, medieval discussions of cloth and clothing address distinctively Jewish approaches to these matters and contrast majority practices with stringent piety. The topic of clothing is often mentioned in relation to the biblical prohibition against wearing garments from mixed threads called sha'atnez (Lev. 19:19, Deut. 22:11). Especially from the late twelfth century onward, medieval rabbinic texts feature detailed descriptions of what did and did not constitute mixed cloth,[70] including examinations of the process of making fabric and of the elements being combined.[71] While the exact materials used when making a garment might not be readily apparent, as with shaving versus clipping the beard, the cloth could look identical even though the process differed, as we will see below.[72]

The subjects of permissible (and forbidden) fabrics were often inseparable. The existence of a common culture of dress in northern Europe is evident in medieval responsa on the question of whether Jews could wear clothes being held in pawn for Christians.[73] Examples of this practice often refer to women's garments, though it was also relevant for men's. Interestingly, the primary reservations stem from a fear that Jews might dress in fabrics that violate halakhic guidelines or that they would be acting without the consent of the items' Christian owners, rather than the concern that these Jews could be mistaken for Christians. The general consensus was that Jews were allowed to wear clothing left with them in pawn, provided it was not made from prohibited cloth.[74]

An additional concern was that Jews might dress in clothing that had been worn during Christian rituals by their owners. In such circumstances, Jews were advised to wash the garments, to rid them of any ritual impurity before wearing them.[75] Women sometimes asked how to proceed if they had worn a dress that belonged to a Christian woman and then noticed a spot of blood on it—would they need to declare themselves menstrually impure (niddah) on account of a stain that came from its Christian owner? Here, too, rabbis counseled them simply to wash the clothes in question. Thus, with the possible exception of cloth that Jewish law declared forbidden (see below), the distinctions mentioned in these responsa would not have been easily discernible. Rather, the determination of whether Jews could wear clothing that belonged to Christians depended on intention and prior ritual use rather than the garments per se.

Medieval European attitudes toward silk offer an instructive case study of shared Jewish and Christian perspectives on clothing as a symbol of piety, propriety, and status. Within Christian circles, silk was one of the fabrics worn by clergy and aristocrats to emphasize their rank; however, by the fourteenth century, donning this luxurious material was often condemned in the sumptuary laws. Women in particular were impugned for excessive vanity for wearing silk.[76] Jewish texts also attest to lively debates over silk during the High Middle Ages. By the end of the thirteenth century, numerous sources demonstrate Jewish familiarity with and regular use of silk. These discussions center on its properties in halakhic terms and, especially, whether it was imperative to tie fringes on silk clothing to fulfill the biblical instructions regarding tzitzit.[77] Asher b. Yehiel (Rosh) summarized these issues: "Nowadays silk clothing is common and all recognize it, therefore one should not forbid the use of silk threads in a wool garment."[78] However, just a few decades earlier (in the late twelfth and early thirteenth centuries), queries over silk and its uses were still being posed. Piety informed the objection articulated in *Sefer Hasidim*: given the cold German winters, such thin fabric would be insufficient to keep synagogue-goers warm for the duration of services; therefore, he instructed that the pious should refrain from wearing silk to synagogue, lest they be tempted to leave before prayers were over.[79]

It may not be coincidental that *Sefer Hasidim*'s reasoning coincided with the appearance of Jewish and Christian texts that mention ascetics who renounced silk. Whereas Christian clergy wore silk, penitents and mendicants—by way of distancing themselves from luxury—did not.[80] Nor did Jews who had vowed asceticism or were repenting. Thus the Jews of Trier and Blois pledged not to wear silk after their cities were attacked.[81] The embrace of silk as a luxury item was also shared by medieval Jews and Christians, as illustrated by certain silk garments being associated with specific positions of Christian authority and silk vestments with Jewish and Christian religious leaders.

This overview of the use and meaning of silk supports the assertion that Jews and Christians categorized clothing with a common measure of values and preferences. From another angle, if Jews wore Christian clothing held in pawn, we see how difficult it would have been to tell Jews and Christian apart, as various texts make plain. Notably, in discussions of extinguishing fires, many decisors mention the difficulty involved in identifying Jews from Christians; consequently, they instructed Jews fighting fires to try to rescue everyone, not only fellow Jews.[82]

Up to this point in our analysis it would seem that—despite subtle differences in appearance that enabled Jews and Christians to be distinguished from each other only by members of their own communities—for the most part Jews and Christians dressed alike. This idea is not novel but deserves further emphasis when assessing Jewish appearance in Christian Europe during the High Middle Ages, a period when Jewish distinction in attire has been so consistently emphasized. We have also seen that pious individuals in each religion, particularly men, could readily signal stringent observance through external choices—such as clothing, hats, and coiffure. Nonetheless, medieval texts also send clear messages that Jews and Christians could be identified by appearance, as indicated by considerations of when, where, and why Jews might dress in the guise of Christians. It is to these sources that I now turn.

Dress and Pretense

A number of discussions concerning distinctive Jewish clothing interpret the verse that opens this chapter: "Their offspring shall be known among the nations, their descendants in the midst of the peoples. All who see them shall recognize that they are a stock the Lord has blessed."[83] One midrash expounds this verse by stating: "As a rose stands out among the grasses, so is Israel distinct among the nations."[84] Many medieval commentators explain that Jews stood out among the nations because of circumcision.[85] Others claim that Jews have been distinctive since the Exodus from Egypt, naming that event as their defining experience.[86] Still others posit that wearing tzitzit,[87] the ultimate way to counter any resemblance to non-Jews, was a symbol whose meaning was augmented by refraining from clothing and haircuts that mirrored Christian styles.[88] For example, *Sefer Hasidim* too cites Isaiah 61:9 and its talmudic commentary multiple times, listing a variety of uniquely Jewish customs: reciting Hebrew blessings on food, abstaining from eating or drinking with non-Jews, marrying other Jews exclusively, avoiding non-Jewish garments (*malbush nokhri*), and wearing tefillin and tzitzit.[89] These passages do not define non-Jewish clothing, but they highlight tefillin and tzitzit as counterpoints.

The topic of Jewish patterns of dress also arises in discussions of travel.[90] When on the road, Jewish men and women often tried to hide their religious identity by wearing garb that typified monks and nuns, despite the contravening halakhic principle against donning non-Jewish religious symbols.[91] This need for monastic dress signals that, despite the commonalities between their Christian peers' appearance and their own, Jews were still recognizable and therefore vulnerable when journeying between urban centers. Travel constitutes an intriguing example since it was a dangerous undertaking in the Middle Ages and as such required extra precautions.[92] Even *Sefer Hasidim* declared it imperative for Jews to dress with the intention of concealing their religion when traveling, and that anyone who chose not to would likely cause havoc by raising the chance of being captured and held for ransom, thus creating an extra burden for the Jewish community.[93]

These instructions notwithstanding, *Sefer Hasidim* criticizes Jews who took this camouflage too far:

> One man told his friend: I walked among the non-Jews wearing priestly garb until they (the non-Jews) assumed that he (the narrator) was a priest and did not harm him. Another man said: "I studied the books of monks and, when among gentiles recited Psalms in their language to fulfill the saying: 'Wisdom preserves the life of him who possesses it' (Eccl. 7:12)." And the Sage said: "It was about you that it was said 'Laws that were not good and rules by which they could not live' (Ezek. 20:25)." This is why R. Eliezer said: "I acknowledge the Judge as right,"[94] and then regretted it, and this is why he was saved.[95]

In this complex tale, one of a number of depictions of traveling in Christian dress in *Sefer Hasidim*, Judah the Pious cites various biblical and talmudic passages to critique a case when imitating Christians exceeded reasonable limits. While he objects to extreme levels of masquerading as a Christian, the practice of Jews taking on Christian trappings under these circumstances seems to have been normative.[96] These comments also imply that without a Christian disguise, Jews would have been easily recognized.

Not only were Jewish men instructed to wear "non-Jewish clothing" when traveling, but women were to dress as men and pre-pubescent boys as women.⁹⁷ *Sefer Hasidim* directs Jewish women to dress as Christians in times of danger, for fear of sexual assault:

> If a woman is walking on the road and hears that she might encounter gentiles and is worried that they might rape her, she should disguise herself as a female religious woman (*komeret*, lit., priestess)⁹⁸ so they won't rape her. And if she heard that Jewish thugs might harm her, she may dress like a gentile woman, threaten to betray them, and cry for help before they (the Jewish thugs) attack. [All of these actions are permitted] so the gentiles will help her, even if they kill the (Jewish) thugs.⁹⁹

This teaching stands out for granting Jewish women agency to avert rape by any means necessary, even if it leads to the deaths of the Jewish men who had threatened them. Furthermore, it assumes that the clothes worn by Christian women made them known as Christians, even if they did not belong to a religious or lay order. However, this quote offers no details about the features of Christian women's attire, whether explicitly religious symbols (e.g., a cross) or the cut of their clothing, as depicted by Rashi (above).¹⁰⁰

Elsewhere in *Sefer Hasidim,* the conditions of duress when women could present themselves as Christians and the parameters for those options are delineated:

> During a time of persecution, some (women) were killed and others converted with the intention of returning to Judaism when they had the opportunity, for they had converted due to fear of the sword. From among the women whose husbands were killed and those who were single, some said: "Lest the uncircumcised contaminate us." And those [women] said that they wished to become religious women (*komrot*) But the young (girls)¹⁰¹ were not sent there. Because they (the older women) said that if they escaped, they would not leave the young ones (the girls behind in the convent) with them [in other words, if the young girls were put in a convent they would not be released].¹⁰² Others wore black clothes in their homes.¹⁰³ Since they [the women who wore black] said if they would be like nuns, they wouldn't be able to easily escape. The gentiles said to them: "Either you should be in the convent (*komriyah*)¹⁰⁴ or you should wear white clothes."¹⁰⁵ So they wore

white clothes. Because they [the Jewish women] said: "Perhaps if we are in the komriyah, we would be unable to escape." And the wise [women] among them[106] said: "If they are contaminated against their will by way of prostitution, it is not as grave a sin as those who enter the komriyah and are guarded for years that eat impure food and desecrate the Sabbath without escaping. But if the uncircumcised urge her to marry an uncircumcised man, she will not be able to escape from the husband who watches over her; so it is preferable for her to be in the komriyah rather than becoming contaminated by the uncircumcised."[107]

Here we see the intricate choices faced by Jewish women who were forced to convert to Christianity along with ample evidence of Jewish awareness of Christian dress codes and lifestyles. This text also underscores the distinction between a volitional journey and a forced masquerade. Jewish women were permitted to pose as Christians but not if it entailed joining a religious institution. If it was a time-restricted event, enduring rape was preferable over feigning a Christian life; alternatively, it was preferable to enter a religious house than to be compelled to marry a Christian. Apparently, the authorities were negotiating the tension between protecting sexual propriety and upholding religious identity. The concern for physical and sexual safety is the justification for advising Jewish women and young boys to dress as Christian women.[108]

It is striking how discussions that center on Jewish women who disguised themselves as Christians gloss over the fact that some of them dressed as Christian men. This strategy and its parallel, young men dressing up as Christian women, are problematized by a ban that originates in Deuteronomy: "A woman must not put on man's apparel, nor shall a man wear women's clothing for whoever does these things is abhorrent to the Lord."[109] The severity of this interdiction is signaled by the word *to'evah* (abhorrent). This prohibition also applied to cross-dressing among Jews without any connection to Christian norms, namely during festivities such as Purim and weddings.[110] Discussions of this commandment in texts from medieval Germany and northern France usually follow the talmudic passages that prescribe how women should groom their hair, particularly pubic hair.[111] However, in the context of travel, these restrictions were downplayed, especially for women.[112]

As the passages cited in this section show, exceptional circumstances that led to a relaxing of strictures offer insights on standard practice. The contrast in precautions recommended for travel versus times of danger at home broadens our knowledge of distinctions between Jewish and Christian appearance while providing the logic that informed rabbinic instructions. For example, another teaching in *Sefer Hasidim* interprets Isaiah 61:9 to highlight the differences between pretending to be Christian while traveling and hiding one's Jewish identity on home turf, even in times of peril. This text conveys a hierarchy of piety, marked identity, and security concerns, as well as evidence of how religious identity was revealed in everyday contexts and how Jews affirmed their belonging using commonplace materials:

> "All who see them shall recognize that they are a stock the Lord has blessed" (Isa. 61:9). How so? Israel (a Jew) should say: "Even if soldiers come they (the Jews) should not stitch crosses on their clothes nor make themselves look like priests, nor place crosses in their homes, nor shave their heads in the manner of priests and monks, so non-Jews might think that they are not Jewish." And if the non-Jews come through (the area) to hurt Jews and the non-Jews go to a house of idol worship, the Jews should not join them, so they will think that they (too) are gentiles. For it says [in Scripture]: "If we forget the name of God and spread forth our hands to a foreign god" (Ps. 44:21).[113]

These instructions for Jews under duress where they reside differ significantly from the preventative measures that we saw prescribed for Jews in transit. Whereas Jews on the road were directed to reduce the likelihood of random attacks by concealing their identity, they were not to shield themselves with pretense in their home communities.

Two core issues undergird discussions of Jews dressing as Christians. The first involves literally wearing garb that typified Christians. Since constructing a false identity was the purpose of such a choice, it would have been counterproductive to forbid this behavior. In this situation, the most that could be hoped for was avoidance of explicit Christian symbols. The less visible principle at hand was the avoidance of mixed cloth. Even in times of great threat, *Sefer Hasidim* advises that this commandment be observed meticulously. Judah the Pious recommends that the pious keep a set of "Christian clothes" from permissible fabrics to ensure observance of Jewish dress codes despite the menace:

> During a persecution, one (Jewish) man donned Christian garb and escaped, since they (the non-Jews) thought he was a Christian. He

(later) asked if he needed to repent for [the sin of wearing] mixed cloths (sha'atnez). They told him: "Since you [should have] considered this in advance by purchasing [Christian] clothes and repairing them with threads that were not linen, you should repent."[114]

A different section explains that one who travels "should prepare clothing with hemp or silk threads, so that he won't be [wearing] mixed cloths; [these clothes] should be prepared before he embarks on a journey."[115] This was a rigorous demand since, by definition, times of peril do not lend themselves to the preparation of special clothing; thus the specification for such advanced provisions.[116]

As noted above, these discussions of mixed cloths give the impression that the uninitiated would not have been able to distinguish sha'atnez from halakhically acceptable fabrics. To the casual observer the garments worn by Jews who followed this advice looked like Christian clothes, but in fact were singular to Jews. Indeed, in some cases only Jews from specific locations could see the difference. This held equally true under safer conditions. Thus rabbis who traveled between France and England wrote about regional differences in the costs and methods of cloth production and instructed their followers to exercise caution in their selections.[117] These sources further indicate that the distinguishing features of "Jewish fabrics" were imperceptible to non-Jews but functioned as an internal code of sorts that contributed to Jewish self-definition, akin to wearing a hair shirt or metal braces beneath a cloak for pious Christians.[118] A fifteenth-century passage attributed to Jacob Moellin (Maharil) captures this notion: "One who makes wool clothing should not use white hemp thread, but only colorful thread, so that no one should be given the impression that he has mixed materials by using linen threads."[119] Jacob's recommendation implies a tremendous investment whenever Jews purchased clothes from Christians, for travel or any other purpose, since Jews are portrayed as disassembling then reassembling each garment. Samson b. Tzadok suggested that Jewish clients should personally supervise their tailors to witness the use of permissible thread.[120] If thorough re-stitching was necessary before donning a garment that had been purchased from Christians, this concealed ritual translates into another task that reinforced religious identity.

The textual evidence from this section yields contradictory impressions: Jewish identity was so explicitly manifest that Jews took shelter in Christian clothing as a means of protection when traveling; however, only exclusively Christian symbols were sufficient for confident identification of Christians. What additional elements signaled religious belonging?

Apparel, Piety, and Religious Distinction

As we have seen, the process of discovering expressions of piety and religious belonging that were imparted through clothing is made more complex by the similarities between medieval Jewish and lay Christian apparel, especially prior to the late thirteenth and early fourteenth centuries. With the exception of the standard dress worn by Christian religious and lay orders and distinctive objects associated with each community (e.g., a cross or relic for Christians; tzitzit, tefillin, or the absence of mixed cloths for Jews), a wardrobe that conveyed piety for Jews and Christians in medieval Ashkenaz shared many features due to their common understanding of what constituted unadorned garb. In a milieu where simplicity was a key tenet of piety, this value took form in similar codes of asceticism and festivity as shown through dress. Nevertheless, Jewish knowledge of Christian codes also led to the rejection of particular garments or fashions. Eleazar of Worms remarked that "the clothing of Jews should not be like the arrogant garments worn by knights,"[121] as also reflected in this statement by Maharil: "When one young man sat before him, the Maharil noticed that he was wearing a nice jacket: with a white body and black sleeves all made from linen. And Maharil told him that it is forbidden (to wear such a garment) because this is in the manner of gentiles (*hukat hagoyim*)."[122] What exactly was wrong with this jacket? Perhaps it was too much like a style worn by a specific order? Maharil solves this dilemma by recommending that the stitching be removed and its components be sewn back together so its Jewish tailoring details would be visible. Interestingly, Maharil does not outright condemn wearing this garment; perhaps his incremental approach indicates the popularity of such clothing precisely because of its resemblance to "Christian" fashion. Thus a single article of clothing could set Jews and Christians apart due to its stitching; and, based on their ability to detect such nuances, the Jewish minority could manage to wear Christian-influenced styles and still avoid being mistaken for non-Jews.

This survey of pious practice as manifest through wardrobe choices can be elaborated upon by considering the styles of dress described in earlier chapters of this study: Women who carefully monitored their menstrual purity often wore distinctive clothing to announce their status.[123] *Sefer Hasidim* counseled men to always go to synagogue in especially clean clothing; moreover, the strictly pious were instructed to designate a particular article of clothing for trips to the outhouse, to demarcate pure and impure clothing.[124] When fasting, neither Jews nor Christians wore their finery; rather, they seem to have worn sackcloth or black to signify severe repentance, then white to symbolize purification.[125] Christian penitents wore specific clothing and men remained unshaven to proclaim their process of repentance, and they would don black and white to represent physical purity.[126] On a communal level, Jews took on practices related to clothing and outward appearance at times of danger and persecution. For instance, during and after the Crusades, some Jewish communities disavowed fancy attire and, more specifically, silk for extended periods.[127] Individuals also took on similar vows as part of personal repentance.[128]

Not only was the adoption or avoidance of specific clothing associated with religious devotion, but religious identity and piety could sometimes be deduced on the basis of dress for major communal observances. To cite one example for each community: white clothing was worn by all Christian women for the celebration of the Purification of the Virgin Mary each year (on February 2), and all Jews would wear white on the Day of Atonement. On each of these holy days, white and "non-white" clothing each projected potent messages.[129]

Clothing was also linked to participation in life-cycle events that would have been noticed by neighbors of either religion and could carry messages of piety and belonging for community members and outsiders. For example, when discussing circumcision ceremonies, some texts state that certain garments were worn not only by family members but by others in attendance.[130] In this way each celebration was communicated to the wider circles within and beyond the Jewish community. In their weekly routines, Jews and Christians wore different attire on their Sabbath days than during the rest of the week.[131] In both communities, designated garments were essential in their mourning customs;[132] while such clothing did not necessarily signal an unusual level of piety, it symbolized their religious affiliation and collectively embraced values. In some cases, mourners' garb also represented pious practice.[133]

As we have seen, clothing served similar functions in both societies. Akin to our discussion of fasting in Chapter 2, I would suggest that, at least in urban settings, differences in dress could more often be attributed to each community's own patterns than to clothing itself. Jews and Christians lived according to cycles of sacred and common time—Sabbaths, festivals, weekdays, and life-cycle observances—each of which required appropriate attire. While the days, dates, and significance distinguished these religious cultures, their sensibilities regarding the dress codes for these occasions may not have varied meaningfully. Jewish and Christian ritual cycles, whether annual or occasional, communal or personal, were instances when distinctions were signaled across religious divides. In short, mutual concepts of respectability and humility and their manifestation through dress are evident in medieval Jewish and Christian sources.

Our discussions of apparel and coiffure as expressions of religious practice yield gendered inferences as well. Jewish men were more consistently marked by their religious identity than their female counterparts, starting from the most private physical imprint, circumcision during infancy, and continuing in adulthood with adaptable external features like beards, haircuts, and hats. We have seen that these outward signs became more prominent during the thirteenth century, prompted in part by ecclesiastical insistence. Few Jewish texts from that era mention visible differences, but this paucity should not be taken as proof against their presence; rather, I would suggest that authors saw little need to record details perceived as obvious, even if they were small nuances.

Medieval sources that engage with the specifics of female dress point to striking similarities between the wardrobes of Jewish and Christian women. Illuminated manuscripts from the Middle Ages further affirm this impression.[134] For these women, decisions about clothing represented far more than a display of piety. They were subject to a complicated chain of command that determined their dress codes and was consequently reflected in their appearance. Women were not accountable to God alone, but were also subservient to male authorities in their families and in the community.[135]

Even from the limited data outlined here, it is evident that for medieval Jews, like their Christian counterparts, dress was an essential instrument for expressing membership and piety. In many respects, this medieval reality echoed a statement that originated in late antiquity: "Such is Israel: wherever one of them goes, he cannot say he isn't a Jew. Why? Because he is recognizable."[136] In connection to this matter, in his work on Jewish identity in late antiquity Shaye Cohen has argued that "the diaspora of Jews in antiquity were not easily recognizable—if indeed they were recognizable at all. Jews looked like everyone else, dressed like everyone else, spoke like everyone else, had names and occupations like those of everyone else and in general closely resembled their gentile neighbors."[137] Here Cohen suggests that a Jew in late antiquity, particularly a man, could not be identified on the basis of appearance alone, but by inferences that could be drawn from a constellation of readily observable factors, including where he lived, whom he married, and his overall social network. Logically, if an individual performed Jewish rituals, his religion could reasonably be surmised. However, as Cohen remarks, in that era: "Each of these conclusions would have been reasonable, but neither would have been certain because gentiles often mingled with Jews and some gentiles even observed Jewish rituals."[138]

While medieval Ashkenazic Jews typically wore clothing that mirrored their Christian neighbors' wardrobes, the blurring of religious behaviors that characterized late antiquity was not operative in medieval Europe.[139] Being half-Jewish and half-Christian had ceased to be an option, and it seems that one who contemplated conversion would have kept all deliberations private unless an affirmative decision had been reached.[140] Furthermore, as we have seen, over the course of the thirteenth century the Christian emphasis on outward appearance as a reflection of piety intensified, as the regulation of material signals of religious identity demonstrates. In other words, the Church was committed to eliminating whatever remnants of ambiguity survived in medieval Europe.

Given this backdrop, it is hardly surprising that during the thirteenth century, when Christian groups were vying with one another to communicate their ideologies, practice, and membership through distinctive apparel, Jews would have begun to prioritize the commandments regarding tzitzit, tefillin, and mixed cloths. The increasing adherence to these pious practices coincided with greater attention to them in the writings of rabbis who promoted heightened religious observance; for example, thirteenth-century books of commandments (*sifrei mitzvot*) all include discussions of mixed cloths.[141] As we saw in Chapter 4, *Sefer Hasidim* led this trend.[142] Once again we can trace how Judah and Eleazar's writings were spread to northern France via Isaac of Corbeil and others who passed through Evreux. Since piety was accorded respect in medieval society and learned men were at the apex of Judaism's religious and cultural hierarchy, perhaps their clothing and customs were outstanding and therefore received greatest textual attention as a means of reinforcing their importance.

* * *

This chapter has demonstrated how attire, coiffure, and the grooming of facial hair functioned as markers of identity in medieval Europe, or to be more precise, the extent to which medieval texts present personal appearance as a linchpin for defining identity among and within religious groups. This discussion also exposes the limitations of the sources that have reached us. The majority of passages cited here came from medieval narrative collections and *Sefer Hasidim*; as such, they do not represent a full spectrum of medieval Ashkenazic writing. Yet given that Judah the Pious was considered zealous in his desire to differentiate between Jews and Christians, his resolute efforts at distinguishing the clothing of lay Christians and Jews can lead us to understand that, on the whole, Jews and their neighbors had remarkably similar norms for dress. Nevertheless, Jews seem to have desired and preserved real differences. The desire to make religious distinctions vivid is also evident in medieval Christian writings, and it is well known as a central project of the Fourth Lateran Council. The relative absence of physical signs to distinguish Jews from Christians cultivated a deepening significance of symbols that underscored belonging and piety, as visible difference became increasingly valued in both societies.

Reading between the lines, we see that medieval texts hint at the phenomenon of "Jewish clothes" and "Christian clothes," such that the owners of ostensibly identical garments could be identified by religion. Much as Diane Owen-Hughes has pointed to subtle distinctions between Jewish and Christian women in Renaissance Italy in her study of the earrings worn by Jewish women, similarly nuanced markers of Jewish and Christian dress codes likely existed in Ashkenaz, although the corresponding documentation has not been transmitted.[143] Both visible and hidden distinctions would have been intimately familiar to medieval Jews and their Christian neighbors when looking at themselves and at one another. Their meaning is concealed from modern eyes, but they were intuitively obvious to those who inhabited medieval Europe.

CHAPTER 6

Feigning Piety: Tracing Two Tales of Pious Pretenders

> I looked up again and saw two women approach, soaring with the wind in their wings—they had wings like the wings of a stork.
> —Zachariah 5:9

> "Like the wings of a stork": That is hypocrisy (*hanupah*) for they (those women) were pretending to be pious.
> —*Rashi, BT* Sanhedrin 24a, s.v. "kekanfei hehasidah"

The analyses in the preceding chapters have each highlighted visible aspects of medieval Jewish piety. Whether fasting, giving charity as an expression of penitence and piety, performing time-bound commandments, attending synagogue for prayer services, or stringently adhering to the laws of impurity, these rituals were easily recognizable to members of the Jewish community and, on some level, to the Christians among whom they lived. Although medieval Jews would have readily acknowledged that God alone can judge and determine piety, our study thus far has demonstrated the prevalence of external signs of practicing piety and the roles of these signals of devotion within and beyond the medieval Jewish community.

This chapter examines displays of piety from a different angle. Rather than studying a specific practice, here I investigate depictions of Jews who mimicked or were alleged to have mimicked piety. This complicates the meaning of piety, for piety was not defined simply by action but also by the intent of each actor.[1] A close reading of sources that discuss the exposure of "pretenders" and the details of their "deceptions" enables a more nuanced understanding of piety in medieval Ashkenazic culture.[2] The degree to which strict adherence to ritual raised suspicions or was accepted at face value provides an additional measure of the social capital accrued through piety.

Much as this subject represents a complementary line of inquiry to the prior chapters in this volume, so too the texts discussed here and their literary genres reflect this distinctive focus. This chapter traces two stories of pious pretenders, with male and female subjects respectively, from their talmudic origins to their medieval Ashkenazic versions, with attention to these tales as reflections of the changing definitions and developing views of pious practice.[3] Most of these passages are found in narrative material rather than the literature of halakhah and praxis. The last section of the chapter contextualizes this material in Christian culture.

Visible Piety as a Sign of Trust

The vignette examined in this section first appears in a discussion on wearing tefillin throughout the day from Tractate Berakhot in the Palestinian Talmud. This story of pretense and piety can be read as an explanation of why tefillin need not be worn for the entire day and as a warning against blindly trusting those who did so.[4] The Talmud recounts: "Why does one not wear [tefillin] (lit., hold on to them) all day? On account of imposters. Once a man deposited something with another (who was wearing tefillin) who then reneged [on his promise to keep the other's property]. He (the first man) said to [the one wearing tefillin]: 'It wasn't you whom I deemed trustworthy, but those on your head.'"[5]

This brief tale, expressed in a single talmudic line, highlights tefillin as a symbol of piety and the practice of constantly wearing tefillin as a marker of outstanding piety. Such men, following the logic that we have seen in previous chapters, were so pure in body and spirit that they could wear their tefillin all day long without fearing for their sanctity. In this case a man who performs this pious practice is actually a fraud. The Talmud thus cautions its readers against conferring trust solely on the basis of this outward sign.

This tale is repeated in numerous medieval sources, starting with *Midrash Pesikta Rabbati* (a ninth-century compilation originating in Islamic lands), which expands on the terse talmudic prose by describing a traveler who wanted to place his money in safekeeping before taking a journey. At a synagogue, he saw a man wearing tefillin and left his money with him. Upon returning to collect his deposit, the man wearing tefillin denied ever having received it. The traveler prayed to God: "You know that I only left my money with that man because your name was on him [on the tefillin, whose parchment scrolls contain God's name]."[6]

The story then appears in compilations from North Africa and Spain.[7] In *Sefer haYafeh min haYeshu'ah,* an eleventh-century North African source by Nissim of Kirouan (990–1062), the narrative is localized and told of a man who was about to embark on a journey to Iraq. Just before his departure, he deposited money with a man wearing tefillin. Upon his return, the traveler was denied his money. Elijah the Prophet then appeared and advised him: "Go to the wife of this crook and say to her: 'On Passover you ate bread and on the Yom Kippur you ate pork.' You will then receive your money."[8] In this telling, partaking of forbidden foods is the definitive mark of impiety, whether bread during the festival when it is prohibited or non-kosher meat during Judaism's most sacred fast. Moreover, after being confronted with their sins, the pretender and his wife in this source are said to have converted to Christianity. Nissim concludes with a warning to beware of those who look like penitents but whose character contradicts their appearance.[9] Nissim goes on to outline several prototypes of falsely pious individuals, based on talmudic descriptions in Tractate Sotah. He concludes his treatment of this topic with a quotation concerning pretenders: "Don't fear those who are ascetic (*perushim*)[10] or those who are not ascetic, rather [be wary of] pretenders that seem like *perushim*, for their deeds are [the deeds] of Zimri[11] and they seek a reward as Phineas did."[12]

Our narrative also appears in two compositions from twelfth-century Spain: Joseph B. Meir ibn Zabara's *Sefer Sha'ashu'im*[13] and *Disciplina Clericalis* by Petrus Alfonsi (who converted to Christianity in 1106).[14] In his rendering, Ibn Zabara (b. 1140) comments on "hypocrites who pretend to be pious," exemplified by the man wearing tefillin who was exposed as an idolator when it was discovered that he possessed a figurine with a cross in its hands. Here, too, a Jew who feigns piety is associated with Christianity.[15] Petrus Alfonsi's (1062–1110) adaptation of this story follows the contours of the talmudic original and Nissim's version more closely; however, as part of a Christian collection of moral exempla, some features of piety are altered and there is no mention of tefillin.[16] Alfonsi recounts the tale[17] of a Spaniard who decides to put his money in safekeeping before journeying to Mecca.[18] Rather than choosing the guardian himself, this traveler consulted local residents who "pointed out an old man whose trustworthiness and righteousness were famous."[19] This traveler finds himself to have been deceived when he returns to collect his deposit. As in the eleventh-century North African Jewish version, he receives assistance, not from Elijah the Prophet but from an old woman who is "dressed in the trappings of a holy hermit" (*cuidam vetulae pannis heremitalibus indutae*). At this point the narrative departs from the Jewish versions: the deceiver is exposed when he is lured to surrender the traveler's money after being led to believe that he would receive even greater riches after returning the original deposit. This literary ending is commonly found in Latin and Arabic tales from this era, though it is absent from the Hebrew tellings of this story.[20]

In medieval Ashkenaz, this tale is recounted with startlingly different emphases. For instance, in *Sefer haMa'asim*,[21] the largest collection of stories from medieval Ashkenaz (first half of the thirteenth century, northern France), the traveler's tale depicts the man who accepts the deposit not as a pretender but as genuinely pious.[22] As in its earlier versions, this tale opens with a man in search of a trustworthy guardian for his monies just before he goes on a journey:

> There once was a man from the Upper Galilee who made pilgrimage to pray in Jerusalem, [where] he prayed and vowed to journey to Babylon. He had 200 gold dinars that he wished to deposit with one whom he could trust. He went to the synagogue and saw a very pious local man. The pious man was praying and even after he finished, he didn't move from his place.[23] [The Galilean] said to him, "Rabbi, I can tell that you are pious. I would like to deposit something with you because I'm going away." [The local man] replied, "What is it?" He said to him, "Money." He said: "Go in peace and in health.[24] If it is God's will, I will not touch them (the coins) until you return in peace and I see your countenance." Immediately [the Galilean] took out his money (lit., pocket) and placed it in [the pious man's] hands. He then went to Babylon, where he stayed for eight months.[25]

When the traveler returns to Jerusalem, he enters the synagogue and notices a man who looks exactly like his trustee sitting in the very same place. He was "identical in countenance, traits and piety."[26] When prayer services ended, the traveler follows this look-alike out of the synagogue and greets him; however, the look-alike offered a weak response since he didn't recognize him. When the traveler demands the return of his money, the man denies knowing him. The traveler gives him an ultimatum: either take an oath that he had never met him or to return his deposit. The look-alike pious man refuses to take a pledge and states: "Go in peace, for I owe you no oath. Even if you had given me all the money in the world, I would not agree to an oath."[27]

This exchange is followed by a roughly described sequence that echoes the Book of Esther, where the traveler knots a rope into a noose that he loops around the look-alike pious man's neck and then marches him through the city while declaring, "Anyone who takes a deposit and then denies it should receive this treatment." The narrator emphasizes that the local merchants know that the man being paraded through the streets is indeed righteous and they are all in tears as they witness such ill treatment. After that scene, which the narrative voice describes as a humiliation or mortification (*herpah*), the man removes the noose from his neck and goes home deeply shamed.

This medieval French narrative departs from prior versions, particularly as the narrator makes clear that the disgrace suffered by the falsely accused pious man was unwarranted. Yet the story from northern France does not end there. Sometime later, the actual guardian arrives at the synagogue and, according to his custom, takes his regular seat. Upon seeing him, the traveler wonders if in fact he had been mistaken previously. He then decides to follow this man, at which point the trustee immediately recognizes the traveler and greets him. He even asks: "You weren't worried, were you? After all, your money was always visible to the One who created the world. Since the day you gave it to me, no [other] hand has touched it. Come and collect it."[28] After the traveler receives his money, he starts to weep and he wonders how God could ever forgive him for debasing the man whom he had falsely accused. He approaches that man and offers financial recompense for the embarrassment that he caused.[29] This man refuses the money and declares that God will be the judge of that incident. The traveler then hires three men to loop a rope around his own neck and parade him around the city as he had forced on the innocent man, to show remorse for his unjust accusation and for the shame that he inflicted on a righteous man.

This version of the traveler's tale is appended with another incident. The pious man who had been unjustly accused and humiliated is later approached by friends wishing to console him. One of them brings a fish, wherein the pious man and his wife discover a treasure that they accept as a reward.[30] The story closes with the verse "For He pays a man according to his actions" (Job 34:11)[31] and an explanation that the pious man was repaid threefold for his goodness. Concluding with the traveler's repentance and the pious man's compensation reinforces the notions of penance and the belief that sin must be nullified by a comparable gesture of atonement, hallmarks of medieval Ashkenazic repentance.[32]

A number of manuscripts from medieval and early modern Ashkenaz transmit our story with this ending.[33] The moral lesson conveyed in this Ashkenazic genre takes a new direction: the trustee who appears pious is not fraudulent, he is sincerely pious! Moreover, the Ashkenazic telling paraphrased above depicts two pious men: one who agrees to keep the money safe and one who is falsely accused of theft. This stands in contrast to the versions from late antiquity, North Africa and Spain, where piety is legitimately questioned and hypocrisy is plausible.

The characterizations of piety in this narrative from *Sefer haMa'asim* mirror features of Ashkenazic piety conveyed in other medieval texts. Staying in synagogue for extended periods without moving from one's place is a pious custom found in sources from northern France and Germany that is predicated on a passage in *BT* Berakhot that articulates the merit of praying from a fixed location.[34] In the medieval context, for example, Isaac of Dampierre (R"I) was reputed to have always occupied the same synagogue seat, "and if someone else entered the synagogue while he was there, he would read a book until (everyone) had finished their prayers."[35] The practice of maintaining a fixed seat in synagogue is mentioned in numerous other tales in *Sefer haMa'asim*. In one story[36] the pious protagonist is said to have "sat in the synagogue and prayed at length."[37] Another narrative speaks of a man who was always the first to open the synagogue door and the last to close it. He lost all his assets when he discontinued this custom.[38] A third tells of a young, talented, and handsome protagonist who received a deathbed instruction from his father that he never leave the synagogue from the moment when the cantor begins to pray until the recitation of the final kaddish. The father explains that this had been his lifelong custom and he had known success. He added that whenever his son would pass by a synagogue and hear praying, he should enter and remain until the services concluded. Adherence to these directives eventually saved the protagonist from grave danger.[39]

Turning from northern France to medieval Germany, *Sefer Hasidim* also expounds the merits of permanent seats and lengthy prayers at synagogue. Judah the Pious (d. 1217) counseled the pious to ensure that they were praying beside God-fearing neighbors in synagogue.[40] *Sefer Hasidim* includes a narrative of a traveler who leaves a deposit with a pious stranger. Here, rather than being en route to Babylon, the traveler arrives from Babylon. Judah's version concludes as follows: "A pious man commanded his sons, saying: 'These books and objects were my father's, but they did not belong to him. Rather they belonged to a man from Babylon who died. And now, if possible, give (a donation that equals) their value to decent poor people[41] for the sake of his (my father's) soul.[42] Afterward you will bear no guilt.'"[43] Although this differs from the conclusion in *Sefer haMa'asim*, it demonstrates true piety yet again, rather than disingenuous behavior from the pious figure's family (as an extension of himself).

In the version from *Sefer haMa'asim*, having a permanent synagogue seat and engaging in lengthy prayer are two factors that inform the traveler's selection of a trustee who will safeguard his money. However, the text also states that "appearance, traits, and piety" contributed to the traveler's decision. What outward indicators were at play? Unlike the talmudic original and later narrations of this story that presented wearing tefillin throughout the day as a sign of piety (particularly from late antiquity and, to a limited degree, from Spain), none of the twelfth- or thirteenth-century Ashkenazic texts describe this as a common practice. In light of the laxity in observance of this commandment before the thirteenth century (detailed in Chapter 4), the omission of tefillin from the main attributes of piety seems unremarkable.

As an apparent replacement for tefillin, some medieval Ashkenazic sources from the thirteenth century indicate that wearing a tallit throughout the day was a sign of piety.[44] Non-Ashkenazic authors still mention the practice of wearing tefillin for the entire day. Their discussions highlight the contrast between Ashkenazic and non-Ashkenazic versions of this story. In their versions of the tale of the betrayed traveler, Nissim of Kirouan and Ibn Zabara cite Tractate Sotah (noted earlier) where those who wore tallitot all day are mentioned as one type of pious imposter. However, commentaries on that talmudic passage from twelfth- and thirteenth-century Germany and northern France reject earlier interpretations of this practice. Whereas Rashi expresses doubt regarding the piety of men "who cover themselves with tallitot,"[45] a century and a half later Judah the Pious not only praises this practice but instructs his followers to wear tallit and tefillin in public, despite the taunts they might experience. As I have suggested, such rhetoric was part of his concerted effort to encourage these observances. Judah girds his directives with proof from King David who, according to tradition,[46] would play a musical instrument late at night, awakening his household. Prompted by the king's music, the royal attendants would emulate his model by hurrying to carry out commandments and study Torah.[47]

Judah promised that whoever performed commandments in public would be granted double or triple the standard divine reward to compensate for the shame he might suffer.[48] He acknowledged that these observances were uncommon in his generation and that some might take on pious customs without sincerity: "Even though some of them might do this (perform these commandments) for inappropriate reasons, rather as 'the zeal among scribes increases wisdom,'[49] so too 'the zeal for the commandments' will increase [observance of the] commandments."[50] As this text conveys, Judah was willing to risk an increase of pious pretenders for the sake of encouraging public demonstrations of personal piety. Furthermore he used the term "zeal for the commandments" to parallel the rabbinic concept of "zeal among the scribes," a principle that he harnessed to argue that even if adopting these commandments led some to arrogance, that would be preferable to accepting the status quo in a community that neglected these practices.[51] This notion resonates with the value of *hiddur* or *hibbuv mitzvah* (as seen above).[52]

Sefer Hasidim and the manuscript of *Sefer haMa'asim* were written at approximately the same time in Germany and northern France, respectively. The versions of our traveler's tale in these sources affirm that wearing tefillin (and to a certain extent tallitot) was relatively uncommon among medieval Ashkenazic Jews.[53] These texts also praise pious behavior while recognizing the ridicule that could result from stringent observance. Admittedly, the humiliation endured in these two accounts differs: in the northern French text, pious practice was not the source of shame but rather the punishment that the traveler unjustly imposed on a pious man. Yet both teachings suggest the belief that disgrace as an outcome of piety would eventually be rewarded, perhaps by double or triple measures.

These German and northern French adaptations of this story bring a novel understanding of a shared motif by validating public manifestations of piety, whether practiced by community leaders or anonymous individuals.[54] Whereas its prior versions suggest that outward signs of religious devotion were not necessarily reliable indicators of character, in this Ashkenazic literature a pious appearance indicates pious intentions. I expand on this idea later in this chapter.

Excess as a Destructive Force: Women's Piety, Women's Gossip

Let us turn from our tale of fraudulent and genuine piety with male protagonists to a story about piety and pretense centered on female characters. Its earliest version appears in Tractate Sotah of both Talmuds[55] in the passage that warns against those who appear pious but are in fact disingenuous.[56] These talmudic texts explain the mishnaic teaching that "a praying (BT) or fasting (PT) virgin and a gadabout widow destroy the world"[57] by exploring the identities of these two types of women accused of causing global destruction. In the Mishnah, these women are cited as examples of persons who might inadvertently be viewed as pious.

The Palestinian Talmud clarifies who destroys the world: "A virgin (or girl) who afflicts herself by fasting to such an extent that she ruptures her hymen and a gadabout widow who constantly gossips and thus earns a bad name for herself." According to this interpretation, a woman or girl who fasts so intensively that she loses her hymen[58] and a widow who wanders freely should both be censured.

In contrast to the Palestinian Talmud's condemnation of these women, the Babylonian Talmud abrogates these accusations by defending the praiseworthy aspects of their behavior:

> But it is not so, for Rabbi Yohanan has said: We learned fear of sin from a maiden [who gave herself up to prayer] and [confidence in] the bestowal of a reward from a [gadabout] widow. *Fear of sin from a maiden*—For R. Yohanan heard a maiden fall prostrate herself and exclaim: "Lord of the Universe! Thou hast created Paradise and Gehinnom; Thou hast created righteous and wicked. May it be Thy will that men should not stumble because of me." *[Confidence in] the bestowal of a reward from a widow*—A certain widow had a synagogue in her neighborhood; yet she used to come daily to the school of R. Yohanan and pray there. He said: "My daughter, is there not a synagogue in your neighborhood?" She answered him: "But Rabbi, I have not (merited the) reward (of even ascending) its steps!"[59]

This passage suggests that Yohanan dismissed the accusations against "praying virgins" and "gadabout widows." Rather, he found merit in their actions, arguing that neither had sinned. The discussion in the Babylonian Talmud concludes that only one specific widow, Yohani bat Retivi, brought destruction to the world: "When it is said (that they bring destruction upon the world) the reference is to women like Yohani the daughter of Retivi."[60]

The figure of Yohani bat Retivi was well known among Jews in Muslim lands and in medieval Ashkenaz, for her tale was recounted in many texts.

These sources portray Yohani as having earned a reputation for piety due to her prayers for the welfare of women, especially during pregnancy and childbirth. However, despite her seemingly pious behaviors, Yohani was actually a witch whose prayers caused trauma, suffering, and protracted births among the women she was purportedly assisting.[61] According to Nissim of Kirouan's version, Yohani was mistaken for being pious because, after bewitching the parturient and causing her prolonged labor, she would then release the spell and receive credit for relieving the woman's birthing process through her prayers. Nissim concludes by acknowledging the existence of pious women who pray with sincerity, despite the case of this deceiver.[62]

In medieval Ashkenaz, numerous commentators recount the tale of Yohani, stressing her dishonesty.[63] For example, Judah the Pious casts her in the category of dangerous and evil women who should be approached with caution.[64] More interestingly, when discussing this passage in the Talmud, Ashkenazic commentators severely criticize not only Yohani but also the gadabout widow and the praying (or fasting) virgin.

Rashi explains that these women each adopted righteous behaviors to dissuade anyone from monitoring their deeds and discovering them to be adulterers or witches.[65] Rashi's words closely resemble the writings of his contemporary, Nathan of Rome (1035–1110), author of *Sefer Arukh haShalem*, who describes a "gadabout widow":

> [The term] *sevavit* describes a woman who is constantly visiting her neighbors . . . [the phrase] "gadabout widow" (*almanah sevavit*) describes one who is mischievous at heart. Rather than stay modestly at home, she strolls through the markets and streets. According to the Palestinian Talmud (she is called sevavit) because she wanders around/roams.[66] Another interpretation—She stated: "I have repented and will not marry (again). Rather I will devote my life to God." She cannot live up to [this promise]. When things become too difficult for her, she acts with deceit and sins often.[67]

The Tosafists also follow this trope, providing negative accounts of this seemingly pious virgin. As in the Palestinian Talmud, they claim that she fasted so intensely that her physiology was altered and she lost her virginity. A supplementary explanation in the name of Meir b. Kalonymous (thirteenth century, Germany) states that such a young woman would have been feigning piety by praying and fasting only to disguise her activities as a prostitute.[68]

Doubt about female piety is evident in other Ashkenazic texts from the High Middle Ages as well.[69] As with writings on fasting virgins and gadabout widows, those sources too were influenced by earlier sources. In this context, let us revisit the passage in the Palestinian Talmud about the matron who boasted about her fasts to gain social status: "Once a righteous man traveled to the netherworld, where he saw a woman named Miriam hanging by her ear from the hinge of hell's door[70] because 'she fasted and announced her fast publicly.'"[71] This talmudic vignette is repeated in a medieval Ashkenazic story of a virtuous man who wonders why some apparent evildoers are treated as righteous at the time of their deaths whereas others who always seemed pious are treated as sinful. In response to his query about divine justice, this protagonist is brought to tour heaven and hell so he can observe various figures and their rewards and punishments. At hell's entrance he encounters a number of women: a woman hanging from her breasts because of immodesty and the same woman mentioned above, whose ear is pierced by the ever-burning hinge of hell's door.

At that station on his journey, he is told: "There once was a righteous woman who was without sin, but for one exception: she would suffer then fast to show the world her piety in order to be considered important and respectable."[72] This medieval account follows the pattern of its late antique precedent by identifying the woman's desire to publicize her fasting as her sin; however, this later version offers a more nuanced description. While it expresses discomfort with actions intended to "show the world her piety," it does not critique this woman for publicizing her fasting. Rather, the disapproval in this narrative comes from her use of religious ritual to gain stature and respect.[73] The visible and praiseworthy nature of her fasts remain undisputed. Indeed, the traveler in this story is surprised to find this woman in hell.

This woman endures the same punishment, albeit resulting from a slightly altered history, in *Darkhei Teshuvah* (Paths of Repentance) by Eleazar b. Judah of Worms. He explains: "She fasted all her days, then she would say: 'My heart aches from this fasting.' When people would talk slanderously and gossip about others, she would listen and repeat it to her husband in order to instill hatred for them within him. For this reason, her ear is punished (with a hinge) in hell."[74] Rather than criticize the publicity of this woman's fasts, Eleazar of Worms condemns her motives. In his view, her penalty fits her deeds since the ear that listened to gossip was punished in hell.

To bring our consideration back to the censure of the "praying virgin" and the "gadabout widow" in BT Sotah, one can say that the negative Ashkenazic

Figure 17. In an illustration of the Hanukkah story, women hang from their breasts as a form of punishment by the Greeks. © Staats- und Universitätsbibliothek Hamburg. Cod. Heb. 37, fol. 79r, detail, Siddur, fifteenth century.

assessment of these women and their deeds stands out not only by comparison with the Talmud and retellings of this story from late antiquity, but also with texts written elsewhere during the Middle Ages. As mentioned earlier, in his depiction of Yohani, Nissim of Kirouan summarizes his discussion by underscoring the reality of women whose piety was genuine and instructing his readers: "One should seek out pious women and stay far from the evil ones."[75]

Even traditions that were more temporally and geographically proximate to medieval northern France and Germany show a more generous understanding of women's piety. For example, the fourteenth-century Provencal rabbi Menahem haMeiri (1249–1310) comments on this passage in BT Sotah by explaining: "A *perushah*—not meaning just any woman, but a witch who feigns piety so she can deceive the world with her magic while claiming that she does so through (genuine) prayers and piety. The Talmud refers to her as a 'gadabout widow'—to say that she continually goes around bearing her claws to her neighbors."[76] Menahem fuses the female personae in the talmudic narrative into one woman. He then tells the story of Yohani bat Retivi, who exemplifies this hybrid figure. He concludes that such women "destroy the world" and that "these traits are more commonly found in women." However, he ends with a qualifying remark: "But any woman who is properly pious, heaven forbid that we hold her piety suspect. What is more, some women are more fearful of sin and more scrupulous in their observance than me."[77] Like Nissim, Menahem refrains from globalizing his negative assessment of disingenuous women who tried to appear pious. He explicitly allows for the possibility of genuine piety among women, thus taking a contrasting stance to his northern French and German counterparts, who suggest suspicion of all virgins and widows who displayed pious practices.

These accounts of the traveler seeking a trustee and of female pretenders all take the form of instructional tales rather than actual events. The adaptations in their tellings and content as they wind their way from ancient texts to medieval Ashkenazic sources are noteworthy, especially when viewed through a gendered prism. In each tale, men and women are described performing similar pious actions (e.g., prayer as a defining expression of piety appears time and again).[78] However, medieval revisions of these ancient stories effectively transform the meaning of their deeds. In the story of the traveler, not only are pious men praised but, over time, its trajectory takes a positive turn, where even the "classic" pretenders are seen as pious. The opposite trend is operative in the narratives of the "praying virgin" and the "gadabout widow." Women who had previously been viewed as pious are portrayed in a negative light in twelfth- and thirteenth-century texts.[79]

How can these divergent developments in the presentation of men and women be explained? By tracing the history of these retellings, what attitudes toward male and female piety led these disparate emphases to emerge? This question has particular import since versions of these stories from Kirouan, Spain, Provençe, and other regions beyond the geographical boundaries of medieval Ashkenaz barely stray from the content and overarching message of their talmudic sources. The shifting perceptions can best be understood by investigating these same themes in northern European Christianity during the High Middle Ages.

Piety and Pretense in Christian Europe

The consideration of feigned piety invites reflection on a broader topic that was at issue in medieval Christian Europe: hypocrisy.[80] Given that the question of the extent to which exterior piety reflected interior piety was under tremendous debate,[81] efforts to deter hypocrisy held a crucial place in discussions of penitential piety. For instance, medieval clergy were instructed to help the parishioners who would come to them for confession by ensuring that they themselves and the laity avoid hypocrisy.[82] One means of enacting this injunction was for confessors to require that repentance be performed publicly. Writings on penance from the early Middle Ages through the thirteenth century reveal that significant attention was devoted to monitoring and directing the emotions displayed by penitents to gauge their authenticity.[83] Scholars have argued that visible piety was increasingly considered dubious over time. Namely, displays of piety that had been accepted at face value in the eleventh and twelfth centuries were more liable to be questioned during the thirteenth,[84] leading to extended discussions of exteriority and interiority.[85] From the twelfth to the fourteenth century, outward expressions of piety became more and more extreme, not just among members of religious orders but among lay Christians as well.

As we have seen, medieval Jews were well aware of the pious rituals practiced by Christian men and women, for their distinctive clothing and behavior stood out in their shared urban landscape. As in the Hebrew stories examined above, beyond praying and fasting, being paraded through the city with a noose around one's neck was a common form of public penance.[86] Thus the punishment dispensed to the pious man who was falsely accused as well as the penance that the traveler took upon himself would have been familiar sights in the cities of medieval Ashkenaz. Moreover, the growing presence of religious individuals and groups featured prominently in this environment. Suspicion toward these pious men and women rose, especially toward the end of the thirteenth century.

One group of pious women that became widespread in northern Europe in the twelfth and especially thirteenth century, the beguines, provides an illustrative case. Although they did not take vows of celibacy, these women lived in separate housing and enacted pious devotion through their dedication to good deeds. Constant prayer was another signature of their religious practice.[87] One of the frequent accusations against them was that their piety was not genuine, despite their visible engagement in fasts and murmured prayers.

During the twelfth and thirteenth centuries, objections to the beguines intensified and they were pressured to abandon their urban independence by joining religious orders. They were often alleged to be praying and fasting while whoring and prostituting themselves. As Bruce Venarde has argued, these represent classic misogynist claims, and they were voiced loudly and with rising frequency[88] in northern France and in Germany during the thirteenth century. For example, Nicholas of Bibera (Erfurt and Mainz), the thirteenth-century author of *Carmen Satiricum,* writes: "There are others of whose habits I shall speak who, like matrons under false religiosity, seek idleness and wander about all kinds of places. Abhorring the spindle, they walk everywhere to play: now going to the market, then seeking the cloisters of monks, then again visiting the choir of clerics and perhaps even their beds."[89] In his poem *Dit de beguines,* Rotbeouf of Paris (thirteenth century) accuses these women of glibly proclaiming that all their actions were pious, whereas none of them really were. He disparages the absence of supervision in their lives and the fact that they made vows to no one—neither man nor God:

> Whatever a beguine says, listen only to what is good. All that happens in her life is religious. Her speech is prophesy; if she laughs, it is good companionship; if she cries, it's out of devotion; if she sleeps, she is ravished; if she has a dream, it is a vision; and if she lies, don't think of it. If a beguine marries, that is her vocation, because her vows or profession are not for life. Last year she wept, now she prays, next year she'll take a husband.[90]

Such sentiments toward the overtly pious behaviors of religious women were expressed not only in literary compositions but also in various statutes and decrees. For instance, the Synod of 1244 in Fritzlar (Germany) discussed Cologne's large beguine community that some described as disruptive.[91] As the critique of *filles de dieu* was growing in northern France, it was also spreading throughout Europe, as documented in the ecclesiastical and regional legislation of that time.[92] Although Tanya Stabler-Miller has shown that some clerics assessed beguines positively, these negative tropes were evident throughout the thirteenth and fourteenth centuries and became more pronounced over time.[93]

Other scholars have demonstrated that the harshest allegations were voiced against women who lived piously in their homes without affiliation with a specific framework.[94] Distrust of pious women grew concurrently with the idealization of male piety and celibacy. As Dyan Elliott documents, during the thirteenth century pious women were ever more pressured to verify their piety and their credibility, a challenge that was less typical in discussions of male piety, though suspicion of pious men grew over the course of the thirteenth and fourteenth centuries as well.[95]

As such, the suspicions toward external piety that we saw in the medieval

Hebrew stories echo a central concern in medieval European Christianity. Many Christian sources articulate a distrust of outward displays of piety despite the fact that Christian practice during the late Middle Ages became increasingly dependent on externals (such as rosaries, indulgences, and relics).[96] Scholars of Christian piety have confirmed that deep suspicions were directed specifically toward women's external acts of piety.[97]

Given this religious evidence from Christian northern Europe, I would suggest that the attitudes toward male and female piety and pretense seen in the Ashkenazic retellings of talmudic stories analyzed here concur with those held by their Christian neighbors in Germany and northern France. Piety that was practiced outside of clearly defined institutions—especially by women—was likely to be held suspect. The commentary on Zachariah 5:9 that opens this chapter encapsulates this view. In its biblical context, this verse ("I looked up again and saw two women come soaring with the wind in their wings—they had wings like those of a stork") has positive connotations, but the Talmud transforms this pair of women into a metaphor for the Babylonians.[98] Several centuries later, Rashi augments the case against these women by stripping the verse of its metaphorical quality and reading it as a literal reference to the women themselves.[99] He states that they merely feign piety, a stance that rings consistent with the quotations from Rashi discussed earlier in this chapter.

On the basis of the narratives studied here, the women who were criticized by medieval Ashkenazic rabbis may have been linked to their Christian peers by more than actions that were construed as pious pretense. Their religious activities bore a suspicious resemblance to those performed by their Christian counterparts. Nathan of Rome hints at this in his definition of the "gadabout widow." He describes her as one who has said: "I have repented and will not marry (again). Rather I will devote my life to God."[100] This phrase resounds of Christian culture! Similarly, Christian women who engaged in constant praying and fasting, like the Jewish virgin and widow mentioned in the Talmud, were accused of insincerity and, not surprisingly, this critique was often imbued with tones of sexual impropriety.[101] One contributing factor to the disapproval voiced toward Jewish women who fasted or prayed continuously may have been that their piety was too familiar, too reminiscent of pious Christian women in their midst.

The resonance between Jewish and Christian women's prayer and fasting rituals becomes more evident if we compare these practices according to gender within each religion. No ritual garments externally define a woman's prayer as Jewish. Moreover, since many of the Christian women who were considered pious did not belong to religious orders but lived in their own homes, one can wonder to what degree these Jewish and Christian women could be distinguished from one another. Murmuring prayers, perhaps in the vernacular rather than Hebrew,[102] could have been another source of ambiguity. In contrast, if a Jewish man prayed continuously, he was likely to wear uniquely Jewish ritual items, such as tefillin and a prayer shawl. Thus a Jewish man who prayed constantly would have stood out from his Christian counterparts more dramatically than a Jewish woman from her Christian peers. Once again, a world of shared gender values comes into play, where religious distinction could be manifest by each community in its own way.

Yet gender does not encompass the entire story. As I have noted, the issues at stake here—hypocrisy and distinctions between inner and outer piety—were key issues in medieval culture. The ongoing reconfiguration of the narratives examined here, about both men and women, are evidence of the importance attributed to these questions that allowed a story of intentional fraud to become centered on feigned piety, a very different matter indeed. Within the medieval context where these topics were especially fraught, these stories indicate the degree to which the Jewish narrators reworked materials to engage with the issues of their day. Like their Christian counterparts, these rabbis endorsed external displays of piety despite their reservations. Judah's commendation of pious rituals that were publicly visible even if the performer did not have the correct intentions indicates the importance attributed to outward signs of piety in a community that was surrounded by Christians who externalized their own religiosity.

This discussion of pious imposters underscores the centrality of external cues in medieval societies. The stories analyzed here suggest that designated acts lent an air of piety to their performers. Prayer, fasting, and retaining a seat in synagogue were all such indicators. One Ashkenazic version of the traveler's tale notes a man who was distinct in his "countenance, traits, and piety." Yet that narrative does not detail how that piety was displayed. Given that visible piety is the connective thread of this entire study, we now move toward a concluding examination.

CHAPTER 7

Practicing Piety: Social and Comparative Perspectives

> She set her mind to fulfill the commandments, all who see her praise her.
> —Eleazar b. Judah, poem about Dulcia of Worms (d. 1196)[1]

"This is the tombstone of the important and respectable [woman] Marat Rivkah, who was bound by her fear of the Torah and who was also modest and . . . to all precepts and loyal with all her heart to her creator."[2] This epitaph describes Mistress Rivkah, who died in Worms in 1160. In this sole record of her life, she is described as God-fearing and loyal to her creator and her piety is emphasized in the adjectives chosen for her gravestone. Jews like Rivkah, who left little mark of their individuality behind, populate this study of personal and communal pious practices in medieval Ashkenaz. The sources examined here employ specific terminology to depict those who took on these observances. For example, menstruant women who refrained from attending synagogue were described as "practicing stringent and ascetic piety" (*nahagu silsul be'atzman u'ferishut*);[3] men and women who fasted from the beginning of Elul through Yom Kippur were called "pious individuals" and "righteous women" (*yehidim hasidim; nashim tzadkaniyot*) in some sources,[4] although others state that "the entire community" (*kol ha'am*)[5] fasted during that forty-day period. Still other texts on fasting portray men who fasted as pious (*hasidim*) or righteous (*tzaddikim*) and women as respectable (*hagunot*).[6] This vocabulary of piety[7] also appears in discussions of men and women who took on positive time-bound commandments.[8] Medieval tombstones use this vocabulary frequently as well.[9]

Additional descriptions of individuals who observed these same rituals exist without language that portrayed them or their actions as pious or otherwise praiseworthy. In some cases this difference can be ascribed to the context in which the rituals were being considered. I have suggested throughout this book that a certain measure of quotidian piety was expected from reputable community members in medieval Ashkenaz. In other instances, these very customs were assessed critically, as when women were taken to task for fasting too frequently and for performing commandments that were not required of them, per some thirteenth- and fourteenth-century discussions of women wearing tefillin or tzitzit. The closing chapters in this book establish that, although it is difficult for present-day historians to define how Jews displayed their religious identity and devotion during the Middle Ages on the basis of textual evidence, medieval authors and their readership shared codes that allowed such messages to be conveyed and readily grasped. Indeed, the effort to achieve greater knowledge of the subtleties of medieval Jewish life by attempting to decipher these very codes is central to this inquiry.[10]

In many chapters, I have highlighted the synagogue as the primary gathering place for the community and as a constant site for the production and reinforcement of identity and culture. The rituals that individuals experienced in synagogue cultivated personal devotion as much as collective coherence, to such an extent that the synagogue itself was often perceived as an extension of the community and its values. In Christian Europe, the synagogue signified the unity and status of Jews as a holy community (*kehillah kedoshah*). Medieval Ashkenazic Jews saw their synagogues and their presence therein as manifestations of their resistance to Christianity and of Judaism's inherent validity.[11] Consequently, many personal observances took place in synagogue in an effort to augment the community's status before God, in their own eyes and among their Christian neighbors. Thus the synagogue served as a locus for standardizing pious practices that became communally embraced and for affirming the position of less common expressions of devotion.[12]

This study also emphasizes the possibility of constructing history on the basis of popular piety, not only from accounts of high-profile figures as pious exemplars.[13] By analyzing rituals that did not require in-depth halakhic or textual knowledge, I have shown that the quest for piety was a common feature of daily life among many Jews in medieval Ashkenaz. The likelihood that less educated Jews did not necessarily comprehend or act on the basis of highly nuanced rabbinic formulations neither diminishes nor devalues their search for means to express devotion to God or their place in the community. As the thirteenth century progressed, these examples abound.[14]

The demonstration of the validity of attributing certain religious practices that have generally been associated with specific personae or discrete groups more broadly supports my assertion that it is incumbent on scholars of medieval Ashkenaz to widen their accepted scope of inquiry.[15] I have argued for an analysis based on practices and widely held beliefs in addition to the well-established focus on the history of ideas and ideals in Jewish studies.[16] This diversified approach would assign religious practice and piety a place beside—not beneath—theology, law, and spirituality. In support of this position, I have highlighted the essential role of sociocultural contextualization for research on medieval Ashkenazic Jews, namely the urban landscape of the High Middle Ages.[17] The remainder of this conclusion is dedicated to the elucidation of my claims through the lenses of two distinct (yet ultimately intertwined) categories that have been underscored throughout this volume: social and comparative perspectives.

Social Perspectives

My primary goal has been to read medieval rabbinic texts with attention to the information that they yield about the lives, attitudes, and pious observances of the medieval Jewish community which apply beyond the scholarly circle that authored them. This venture has required a shift in emphasis for relating to the medieval Hebrew literature that provides the most enduring record of these communities and their practices: I approach these sources with the assumption that social realities served as catalysts for fresh readings and applications of earlier teachings at least as much as textual heritage guided communal observance.[18]

Each chapter has documented how customs were introduced and practiced in medieval Ashkenazic communities. In many cases, rituals that were presented as innovations or adaptations that required explanations were clarified with citations from the Bible or rabbinic literature. Whereas scholars of medieval halakhah often endeavor to identify earlier textual sources that might provide the background for modifications in religious practices, I have argued that such prooftexts could also have been sought at a later stage of the process, when a halakhic rationale was being formulated for explaining a practice that had already become customary or was being promoted.

These contrasting approaches have practical implications for research methodologies: whereas scholars of the history of halakhah debate the role of texts composed during late antiquity in Palestine within medieval Ashkenaz and credit shifts in practice to the influence of Palestinian or Babylonian traditions, I have searched for praxis-oriented bases for the appearance of particular customs.[19] For example, increased levels of concern with menstrual purity—in the synagogue and in other settings—have often been attributed to rabbis who encountered *Baraita deNiddah* during the High Middle Ages.[20] According to this position, this exposure to older Palestinian observances via textual traditions led to changes in scholarly perspectives and subsequently in communal norms. This chain of causality could also explain the precipitous rise in fasting among medieval Ashkenazic Jews.[21] Despite its reliance on the learned elite, the notion that the introduction of these and many other customs in medieval Ashkenazic society was motivated by the arrival of halakhic sources from the East has become a standard narrative in modern scholarly literature. In contrast, I have documented how women initiated change in the relationship between menstruation and synagogue attendance as the medieval texts themselves indicate. Furthermore, I have reasoned that this mechanism could not have been textually driven since women lacked access to halakhic sources and argumentation, but it could have stemmed from Jewish women's familiarity with the views of purity held by their Christian neighbors and the common ideas circulating within society. Although similar Jewish understandings of purity existed at other times, I contend that texts that are rooted in Palestinian materials did not become a contributing factor until rabbinic authorities were motivated to elucidate and standardize these new rituals. At that stage, textual proof was harnessed to affirm (or reject) emergent practices. In another case examined here, Jewish women began to take on the commandment of lulav, leaving the rabbis to endorse or rebuke their behaviors.[22] Earlier halakhic materials were undeniably integrated into rabbinic teachings that responded to new modes of observance, but that fact alone does not adequately explain the inception of these social and religious phenomena.

A second common category used as a prism for explaining shifts in practice during the Middle Ages in Ashkenaz has been scholastic, distinguishing between *minhag* (custom) and halakhah.[23] Scholars of halakhah have often examined the tendency for societies to move from practice-based norms to more text-based and legalistic structures by outlining the trends and patterns of categorization in medieval legal thought and reasoning. Yet, as studies of this dynamic have confirmed time and again, the boundaries between custom and law are far from obvious, being largely dependent on the textual choices exercised by rabbinic authors.[24] By taking the vantage point of those who performed rituals rather than those who penned their descriptions and prescriptions, I question whether the less educated practitioners of piety could plausibly have been aware of the scholarly distinctions dividing law from custom.

With an eye to practice rather than textual transmission and to the religious observance of Jews as a social group rather than the behaviors modeled by learned figures, I have investigated how daily rituals helped cultivate a pious Jewish identity that stood in contrast to the surrounding Christian society and sustained the commitment that Jews felt for their community and faith. As part of that effort, this study has examined the place of women and gender conventions in order to identify a broader spectrum of participants who shaped medieval Jewish identity.

This investigation has been deeply informed by the writings of Judah b. Samuel (known as Judah the Pious) and Eleazar b. Judah of Worms, two leaders of the group known as Hasidei Ashkenaz. As noted in the introduction, modern scholars have presented these medieval innovators in various ways: as leaders of a sect-like group or community subset, or as pious outliers who embraced a unique theology. Their writings have been subject to a similar range of interpretations.[25] Scholarly discourse on the ideology and identity of Hasidei Ashkenaz has led to differentiation of pietism and piety on the basis of core ideas and doctrines concerning God that are prominent in many of their writings.[26] Pietists have been defined by their adherence to specific doctrines concerning the relationship of God and humanity, the will of God (*retzon haboreh*) and the dedication required for worshipping God (*la'avod et Hashem beyira'ah*), thus constituting an exclusive and sectarian group. Proponents of this reading have admitted that many Jews may have acted piously, but they could not be classified as Pietists if they did not fully hold the worldview presented by Judah and Eleazar. Further research has suggested that only men could be Pietists, and that they were often ridiculed by the communal majority.[27] Not surprisingly, the impact of Pietist doctrine on medieval Judaism has likewise been subject to debate.[28]

My query into medieval popular piety in pursuit of what can best be conveyed by the German term *frommigkeit* has not been aimed at a specific group of Pietists[29] but at the pious and their practices.[30] Toward this goal, I have read the directives of Judah and Eleazar of Worms as a window onto the repertoire of Ashkenazic Jews who wished to elevate the practice of piety in their lives. Together the Pietists (if such a group actually existed) and the pious constituted the broad fabric of medieval Ashkenazic communities.[31]

I have argued that many pious practices, as well as the beliefs and explanations that were associated with them, originated in Germany and northern France and radiated from there. Despite my efforts to distinguish between the practices and beliefs that were recorded in Germany from those in northern France, as is evident in many instances throughout this volume, there was tremendous overlap among observances and ideas in these centers.[32] A prime example of this is fasting practices which were central in the writings of Judah and Eleazar and widespread in Germany and northern France. Fasting was a key issue in the system of repentance Judah and his disciple Eleazar conceived of and promoted. It was designed to facilitate their followers in reaching their spiritual goals.[33] However, as I have shown—and as even those who call for a strict distinction between the Pietists and the pious have admitted—this penitential structure spread far and wide and became an essential framework for European Jewish practice and piety.[34] So, too, the efforts by Judah and Eleazar to encourage observance of tefillin and tzitzit, as mirrored in northern France as well, gained currency in the thirteenth century, and these rituals became elements of standard observance.[35] The relative lack of textual evidence from the Jewish community of northern France is certainly an effect of their expulsion and dispersion in the early fourteenth century.[36]

Many of the practices examined here have underscored the thirteenth century as a period of marked change. In this context, *Sefer Hasidim* is an invaluable source for facilitating our understanding of how piety was defined in that era. For instance, in a departure from Rashi's definition of the pious (hasid) by association with a stork (hasidah) who performs acts of kindness for her friends, *Sefer Hasidim* states that "hasid" is derived from the Aramaic term *havaritah*, meaning pale. Referring to the verse "No longer his face grows pale" (Isa. 29:22), Judah relates that despite being taunted to the point of his face becoming blanched (*malbin panav*), the hasid remained loyal to God.[37] Judah emphasizes this trope throughout *Sefer Hasidim* (with tefillin as the primary example), emphasizing that taking on pious practices was not normative, and that the adoption of conspicuous religious rituals required the resilience to withstand social critique and resulting feelings of humiliation.

Eleazar of Worms further developed this line of thought when explicating a line from "Nishmat Kol Hai," a liturgical poem that was reportedly recited daily by the members of Judah and Eleazar's circle. Eleazar expounded: "'By the language (lit., tongues) of the pious (*hasidim*) you shall be sanctified': Whenever he (a hasid) hears [words of] humiliation and does not respond, he is behaving like David, who said: 'Preserve my life for I am steadfast (hasid)' (Ps. 86:2). Thus [the Hebrew] stork (hasidah) was translated as hivartah (pale) [in Aramaic], like a hasid who is shamed but does not respond [to insults]."[38] In the writings of Judah and Eleazar of Worms, piety is synonymous with steadfastness in the face of social condemnation[39] in response to observance, but not doctrine or belief. Insults were directed at visible rituals, and the pious were praised for placing loyalty to God over social acceptance.

This religious and social backdrop is the same environment in which gender has been investigated here. Gender as a conceptual framework has served in multiple capacities in the chapters of this book.[40] At its most basic level, gender directed the examination of the rituals carried out by women, as a distinct communal subset of those performing pious acts, and the comparison of their practices to those of men. Much as Dulcia, the wife of Eleazar b. Judah is described in his eulogy of her as having dedicated her life to performing the will of her creator, we have abundant evidence that many medieval women and men were active agents who sought ways to further their piety.

Gender has also provided a lens for seeking representatives from sectors of Jewish society who were outside the learned elite. In this realm, women's deeds serve as reminders that, despite the authority held by rabbinic leadership—as witnessed by their authorship and preservation in medieval texts, rabbis alone did not determine practice. While rabbis may have directed and at times censured popular practice, community members also acted on their own initiative without requesting guidance or permission, leaving rabbis to respond if they wished. Moreover, rabbis could prescribe behavior, but it took time for their teachings to become implemented, if they were at all. By definition, the practices examined here all required enactment to become recognized as expressions of religiosity and piety. Confession and repentance, entering or keeping a distance from the synagogue, as well as giving charity, all required concrete effort.

In this context, we have seen that participants in pious practices were often more diverse than the population implied by halakhic literature. We have clear evidence that an admittedly indeterminate number of women wore tzitzit and tefillin, irrespective of rabbinic disapproval. With regard to charitable giving, women gave significant donations without necessarily involving their husbands in their decisions. The data from the Nürnberg Memorbuch represent a rare treasure for historians of medieval Jewry, offering quantitative proof that women were more active and rabbinic guidelines less strictly observed than the halakhic texts suggest. Even when their instructions were followed, the rabbis could not unilaterally ordain acceptance of their rulings; for instance, rabbis could not enforce dress codes without cooperation from community members. These are the circumstances in which I have presented women's and men's agency with regard to ritual conduct,[41] rendering a more detailed portrait of their own positions and of Jewish society at large. The comparisons of men and women and their religious observance throughout this book offer a more complete view of the complexities and gender inflections of medieval religious practice.[42]

At certain points, I have suggested that women from scholarly families may have been eager to adopt newly promoted pious practices such as tefillin and tzitzit[43] because of their greater exposure to halakhic principles and practices, despite their own lack of formal education. The "Nishmat Kol Hai" prayer cited above provides a relevant example, since Eleazar of Worms reports that his wife, Dulcia, recited this prayer daily, as did his other followers.[44] In this instance, gender did not factor into the equation; men and women were viewed as members of a single group, related to class and education. This parity between men and women is also evident in the discussion of charity for the soul, in which I argue that donor patterns illustrate the importance of ensuring a peaceful death and transfer to heaven for men and women alike.[45]

Third, gender has been considered a dividing factor that cut across class, education, and religion in medieval life. Patriarchy was a pervasive feature of mundane daily activities, as conducted in the domestic and public spheres.[46] Masculine hierarchy typified medieval Jewish and Christian societies on ideological and pragmatic levels alike, especially in the realm of piety, where the suspicion of women and sexuality motivated religious behaviors, such as the anxiety over impurity in the synagogue or church that dissuaded women and men from full participation in communal prayer. Attempts to ensure proper repentance for sexual sins (as mentioned in Chapter 2) could also be included in this category. The tension between normative and pious gender relations is encapsulated in the counsel provided to a pious man who was learning to tolerate public scorn when practicing piety, as recorded in the fourteenth-century *Sefer haMaskil*: "If you are still but a lad and you are ashamed to retreat completely from looking at a women's face lest you be scorned, train yourself to look at a woman's face in a single glance when you talk with her."[47] Gender analysis, therefore, provides an essential tool for tracing the contours of Ashkenazic history and social categories that relate to class and piety in medieval Jewish society. Most importantly, gender has served as a point of comparison for considering medieval Ashkenazic communities amid the Christian majority, the perspective to which I now turn.

Comparative Perspectives

The position of Jews as an intrinsic part of the social landscape of medieval Ashkenaz while being discrete from Christian society provides the setting for this volume. As I spelled out in the introduction and in each subsequent chapter, Jews understood themselves and were viewed by their neighbors as a distinct religious group, separate from the Christian majority. At the same time, they were participants in medieval society who resided in a Christian environment where church bells tolled the hour and where public spaces were adorned with statues and figurines, constant reminders that they were members of a (persecuted) minority. In this entangled existence they were connected yet detached, much as the boundaries between Jews and Christians were simultaneously omnipresent, porous, and ever-changing.[48] Contemporary medieval historiography has been intently investigating the borders between Jews and Christians in medieval Europe, and this work joins the chorus of scholars.[49] I have used gender as a benchmark, not to determine which society influenced or copied, adapted or borrowed from the other, but to expose areas of contrast and commonality.[50]

Scholars have recently suggested that even the distinctions in practice and belief among Jews and Christians were less crisply delineated than previously believed. In contrast to other works, this book focuses on how belief and practice relate to social norms rather than to religious thought. We have repeatedly seen shared gender conventions, whether concerning a married woman's ability to give charity or the potential for men and women to resemble angels. Despite their different understandings of God and the nature of prayer, pious Jews and Christians were united in their stance on women's place in the social hierarchy. This was a fundamental premise, much like the acceptance of patriarchal authority. Gaining an understanding of a societal order that was common to Christians and Jews enables a more intricate comprehension of both Jewish minority culture and the areas where distinctions between Jews, Christians, and their beliefs are less clear.

I have suggested that gender provides a useful template for gaining a more comprehensive understanding of how Jews in medieval European society defined their community, organized themselves, and interacted with the Christian majority. Beyond their shared notions of gender hierarchy and of the authority that men held over women, it is significant that women in Jewish and Christian societies were central to medieval piety and that medieval women actively pursued pious practice whether within Christian orders and laity or in daily Jewish life. My analysis also shows how views of gender were transformed over time and how the religious role of women was reinterpreted, with changes that often resulted in the exclusion of women from pious rituals.[51] These revisions serve as reminders that halakhah has not always addressed women with a single standard over time.[52] The dynamics that caused alterations in women's ritual observance differed in Judaism and Christianity. Christians debated over how impressionable women who heard confession might be, whereas Jews deliberated about the appropriateness of women committing themselves to specific time-bound commandments. Pious Christian women sought celibate lives, whereas pious Jewish women did not. Despite the different topics of deliberation, I have claimed that a common trajectory can be mapped.

The changes in women's roles and status represent but one of the societal shifts that occurred during the High Middle Ages, with new modes of expressing piety prominent among them. The historical processes regarding piety that I have outlined here converge with parallel developments in medieval politics and religion, including the intensification of Jewish-Christian polemics. Thus we have seen indications that augmented displays of Jewishness (and by extension piety) appeared as medieval Christian authorities began requiring Jews to broadcast their religious identity with visual symbols. The Fourth Lateran Council in 1215 was an attempt to reorder medieval Christendom that represented a culmination of preceding events as well as the beginning of a new era. Alongside this landmark in Christian thought, changes in medieval economies and monarchies affected the Jews, whose standing in medieval Europe deteriorated during the closing decades of the thirteenth century and the early fourteenth century.[53] As Jews and Jewishness were becoming more rigidly defined and as legal limitations were being imposed, Jewish communities in turn seem to have been electing new ways to present themselves, as with the adoption of Jewish beards and hats. The task of teasing apart the voluntary and coercive aspects of these visible signs of Jewishness is persistently challenging, perhaps due in part to the likelihood that internal and external factors were at play simultaneously.

My emphasis on practice is intended to prescribe an antidote of sorts to the common inclination to flatten out past realities according to the texts that describe them. Practice offers a glimpse of the three-dimensional world of people acting and changing, commenting and objecting. Through my attempts to capture how Jews presented themselves and the seemingly minor particularities that they used to project their distinctiveness, I strive to draw closer to this vitality. Piety was not limited to words of prayer or expressions of belief; it was visible and even tactile at times,[54] and it is this tangible quality that I have sought to understand and convey.

I have suggested that practice was one means by which Jews preserved their uniqueness and further fostered a separate ethnic identity, despite the resemblances to praxis and belief among their neighbors that I have documented here. By zooming in on these subtleties, I have examined the Jewish and Christian systems as competing pieties, in which distinctions were paramount. This observation is closely related to one of the most important social characteristics of defining and practicing piety: while being directed toward God as the object of devotion and as ultimate judge, piety was assessed and evaluated by the men and women who witnessed its observance. Returning again to Dulcia of Worms, not only was she pious but "all who saw her praised her."[55] Each chapter of this book has demonstrated the extent to which piety was visible, being performed by its practitioners in their cultural surroundings. These explicit displays also help elucidate the social tensions and divisions that developed around piety—on the personal level, within a given religious community, and in the competition between religions.[56] Critical consequences of piety included the sharpening of distinctions and the reinforcement of divisions within and between religions.[57]

With regard to the system of small differences that I have argued was intrinsic to the Jewish-Christian environment, especially as seen through the eyes of the Jewish minority, this study of pious practice aims to discern a more complex understanding of the medieval world. Thus Herman-Judah could weave together Jewish and Christian modes of fasting, stressing their unique features while operating on the basis of their shared meanings and belief in the efficacy of this ritual.[58] Perhaps even more telling is the fact that according to the medieval narrative—be it historically accurate or fabricated, but nevertheless written in the Middle Ages—when Herman decided to convert, he was not ultimately swayed by rational arguments but by the impressive piety displayed by two Christian women.[59]

Jews in medieval Europe undoubtedly adopted and adapted beliefs and ideas that were prevalent in their surroundings. As Ivan Marcus has phrased it, this was effectively "inward acculturation."[60] This process was guided by the Jewish exegetical and legal traditions that sought proof and reasoning based in ancient texts for new ideas, which gave medieval Jews license to explain their current practices by drawing on the Bible and classical rabbinic literature in creative ways. In this manner, Jewish leaders were able to "translate" practices that had been adapted from their surroundings into Jewish terms.[61]

The inward acculturation was also facilitated by the connections between Christianity and Judaism that had existed since the inception of Christianity from within Jewish culture. As many scholars have remarked, the historical tables were partially turned in the urban centers of medieval northern Europe, where Jews lived as the minority and Christian authorities were dominant and their rituals most prominent.[62] Here, too, the economy of minor but meaningful difference was regularly on display and noted for its social and identifying factors. No less important, the proximity and constant engagement between Jews and Christians, and each group's ongoing observations of the other, facilitated the promotion of shared values and beliefs as well as competing narratives. As demonstrated in Chapter 6, some Jews were able to read at least a selection of Christian pious codes, and it appears that Christians could follow some portion of internal Jewish ones.

To reiterate the obvious, I do not contend that these processes were exercised consciously, at least not for the most part.[63] The religious divide between Jews and Christians was so enormous that it overshadowed many common facets of life. When Jews and Christians feared that that distinction was not sufficiently robust, they responded by shoring up their differences and emphasizing the need for practices that underlined group coherence; at the same time they may have failed to perceive some of the broad similarities that were signs of their era. I am convinced that some of the seemingly common practices among medieval Jews and Christians actually encompassed differences that strengthened both groups' abilities to maintain their religious and social identities. Medieval Jews and Christians operated in two registers simultaneously: sharing ideas, beliefs, and practices while also carrying messages of religious singularity. The realm of practice included less tightly defined aspects that were fastened to each community through particulars that made them meaningful to those who performed them. As such, the slippage that I have suggested between Judaism and Jewish piety was constantly being negotiated.

Returning to Judah and Eleazar's explanation of the etymology of the hasid as relating to the stork, let us look at another symbol of medieval piety, the pelican. In medieval literature, the pelican was thought to be especially attentive to her young, to the point of wounding her breast to provide her own blood for her offspring when no other nourishment was available.[64] In medieval Christian society this devotion was equated with the passion of Christ, for which the pelican became a symbol.[65] Remarkably, the dramatic expressions of piety that Judah and Eleazar attributed to the hasid are traits that were also associated with Jesus. The hasid had to be prepared to shoulder scorn from his fellow community members without responding or being defeated by humiliation.[66]

Rather than submit that these rabbis were proffering Christian values, I would suggest that this interpretation of the etymological link between the hasid and the stork was founded on contemporaneous ideas of piety, bolstered by earlier prooftexts. Indeed, this medieval definition of a hasid as one who could withstand ridicule resonated not only with Christian notions of piety but also with the earlier midrashic formulation suggested by Huna b. Pappa and Simon, that a stork is named hasidah because she allows herself to be trampled by her neighbors.[67] Instead of attempting to discern whether Judah based his formulation on Jewish sources or the medieval Ashkenazic milieu, I would posit that he was a product of both cultures and he would have operated from his immersion in both. Much like the definition of piety itself, this book claims that medieval Jewish piety can only be fully apprehended in the context of practice that was grounded in religious beliefs and social realities, textual heritage and teachings, gender hierarchies and the close quarters of the medieval cities where Jews and Christians displayed their beliefs and practiced everyday rituals throughout their lives.

ABBREVIATIONS

AJS Review	*Association for Jewish Studies Review*
BT	Babylonian Talmud (standard editions)
JQR	*Jewish Quarterly Review*
JSQ	*Jewish Studies Quarterly*
PL	*Patrologia, series latina,* ed. J. P. Migne
PT	Palestinian Talmud (standard editions)
REJ	*Revue des études juives*
Moses b. Jacob, *Semag*	Moses b. Judah of Coucy, *Sefer Mitzvot Gadol*, 2 vols. (Venice, 1547; repr. Jerusalem: Defus S. Monzon, 1961)
Isaac b. Joseph, *Semak*	Isaac b. Joseph of Corbeil, *Sefer Amudei Golah haNikra Sefer Mitzvot Katan* (Kapost: Israel Yafe, 1820; repr. Jerusalem, 1979)
SHB	Judah b. Samuel, *Sefer Hasidim* (Bologna, 1538)
SHP	Judah b. Samuel, *Sefer Hasidim (Das Buch der Frommen),* ed. Jehuda Wistinetzki (Frankfurt: M. A. Wahrmann Verlag, 1924) based on MS Parma, Biblioteca Palatina 3280, de Rossi 1133

NOTES

INTRODUCTION

1. Rashi provides two translations for "hasidah": *cigogne* in French and *ciconia* in Latin; see Greenberg, *Foreign Words*, 52.

2. Deer were also considered kind animals, and their hasidut was explained as their mercy on their offspring and neighbors; see the commentary on Psalms, *Midrash Tehillim*, chap. 22, #14. Many human qualities were ascribed to animals in the Middle Ages; see http://bestiary.ca/beasts.

3. So, too, the midrashim on Psalms provide three etymological explanations for the stork's name: she allows others to tread on her; she shows mercy to her friends; and she is kind to her neighbors. See *Midrash Tehillim*, chap. 104, #14, which was well known in medieval Ashkenaz.

4. See, for example, Büchler, *Types*; Diamond, *Holy Men*; Kanarfogel, *Peering*.

5. Vauchez, "Réligion populaire," 91–107; Delaruelle, Piété populaire; Schmitt, "Religion populaire," 941–53; Davis, "From Popular Religion," 321–42; Biller, "Popular Religion," 221–46, esp. 222; Brodman, Charity and Religion, 178–244; Pullan, Poverty and Charity, 288–90; Tanner, "Least of the Laity," 395–423; Ryan, "Some Reflections," 961–71. I do not mean the sort of two-tier analysis that Peter Brown and others have rejected, as I am aware of the problems with assuming a popular/elite divide, since the practices of the people are always influenced by elite strictures and elite strictures are always shaped by what people are doing. My attention to the popular is meant to overturn the tendency in Jewish studies to focus only on the elite.

6. For comparison, see Kamaludeen, Pereira, and Turner, *Muslims in Singapore*, 11–13.

7. Historical scholarship on Christianity has emphasized practice much more than studies on Judaism have; see M. Rubin, *Medieval Christianity in Practice*. For Jewish history, see Fine, *Judaism in Practice*, especially his introduction, 1–38. This has been a common feature of scholarship on gender as well; see n. 93 below. This trend is ironic, given that Judaism is more practice-oriented than Christianity; however, that tendency is more strongly driven by historiography than by the religions per se.

8. Recent scholars have noted that when men are included in discussions that focus on gender, the mention of women is often obliterated. I make an effort to include both perspectives. See Bennett, "Forgetting the Past," 669–74.

9. Although much of the scholarship that uses the word "gender" focuses on women, gender is intended to be a category that compares between men and women rather than presenting women in a vacuum. See J. W. Scott, "Gender." This point has been presented in numerous ways over recent decades: see Bynum, *Holy Feast*; M. Rubin, "Identities," 383–412, and recently Kelleher, *Measure of Woman*. For a comment on the limits of agency, see Mahmood, *Politics of Piety*, 5–10.

10. I have not adopted a two-tier approach to society, dividing the elite and non-elite community at large; see n. 5.

11. Scott, "Gender," 41–50; Scott, "Unanswered Questions," 1422–29.

12. Baskin, "Male Piety, Female Bodies," 11–30; McLaughlin,"Women and Men," 192–95. For example, men who refrain from looking at women are an example of an expression of piety. This is a prominent theme in medieval texts; see, for example, *Sefer Hasidim* (*SHP*), #14, 18, 43, 52, 55, 775, 978, 980, 986, 1137, 1177, 1500, 1907. In this case, piety was practiced as a male behavior with regard to women. In other cases, women actively practiced piety by fasting, praying, and giving charity, as demonstrated in this book.

13. Weinstein and Bell, *Saints and Society*, 143–60; Brodman, *Charity and Religion*, 179–81; Bynum, *Jesus as Mother*, 88, 104–5, who comments on each individual's need to express personal piety within a community setting. Kramer, "Priest," 149, notes that twelfth-century spirituality is known not only for personalism but also for its emphasis on communal harmony between exterior and interior. This understanding has been noted with respect to Hasidei Ashkenaz and their ideology as well. See Baer, "Religious-Social Tendency," 20–36, and Soloveitchik, "Three Themes," 326–29, who both emphasize the responsibility that those who identified themselves as hasidim felt toward their communities.

14. This comparison provides data that can benefit those interested in medieval Christian society, given that the status of Jews (much like women in what follows) often served as a type of litmus test; Bonfil, *Jewish Life*, 6–8, 43–50, 101–24. Some scholars of Christian society have noted this phenomenon as well: Moore, *Formation of a Persecuting Society*; in the context of gender see McLaughlin, "Women and Men," 195–99.

15. Baron, *Jewish Community*, 1: 210–15; Bonfil, *Jewish Life*, 50–51.

16. This issue has been discussed by various scholars in recent years. While some have argued for drawing a stark distinction between these two areas, others have defended the advantage of studying these regions together. For a discussion of this issue, see Ta-Shma, *Early Franco-German Ritual*, 14–16, 22–27. See further discussion of this point in Soloveitchik, *Wine in Ashkenaz*, 123–36; Kanarfogel, *Peering*, 189–250, 256–57. Although Grossman distinguishes between Germany and France in his histories of the lives of the sages, he treats them as a single region in his study of women: Grossman, *Pious and Rebellious*. Others have argued for greater differentiation: Zimmer, *Society and Its Customs*, and reviews of this book, including Soloveitchik, "Review Essay of *Olam keMinhago Noheg*," 223–25, and most recently, idem, "Piety," 455–93. For a discussion of this issue in broader terms, see Brühl, *Deutschland-Frankreich*.

17. See Toch, "Economic Activities," 181–210, and Soloveitchik, *Wine*.

18. For settlement in France, see Grossman, *Early Sages of France*, 13–21; Stow, *Alienated Minority*, 41–64; Schwarzfuchs, "Mekomam," 251–67.

19. Grossman, *Early Sages of Ashkenaz*, 27–48.

20. An additional geographic area that could theoretically have been included in our frame of reference is Poland, where many German Jews emigrated during the High and Late Middle Ages. However, the current state of research about medieval Jewish life in Poland precludes a detailed examination for the purpose of this study.

21. In relative terms, there are substantially more transmitted Christian sources than extant Hebrew texts on medieval Jewish communities in England. See the volume edited by Skinner, *Jews in Medieval Britain*, as well as Chazan, *Jews of Medieval Western Christendom*, 154–67, for a survey of the sources available for medieval England.

22. See n. 16 (above) for some examples of regional and local contexts.

23. Baumgarten, *Mothers and Children*.

24. I emphasize the term "relatively" here because there are far more extant sources on Christian society in comparison to the dearth of Jewish sources dated prior to the twelfth century.

25. For an overview of the events of these years, see Chazan, *Jews of Medieval Western Christendom*, 129–97. As a result of the events of the First Crusade, which mainly effected northern Jewish communities, attitudes toward martyrdom differed considerably between northern and southern Europe; for an analysis of this as a particularly northern issue, see Soloveitchik, "Bein Hevel Arav leHevel Edom," 149–52, and idem, "Religious Law and Change," 205–21.

26. The literature on this topic is tremendous; see E. Haverkamp, *Hebräische Berichte*, 1–23; J. Cohen, *Sanctifying the Name of God*, 31–54. For a somewhat different understanding, see Malkiel, *Reconstructing Ashkenaz*, 73–94.

27. The literature on this topic is also abundant. For overviews, see Urbach, *Tosaphists*; Grossman, *Early Sages of Ashkenaz*; idem, *Early Sages of France*; Yuval, *Scholars in Their Time*; Kanarfogel, *Peering*.

28. See, for example, Aptowizer's *Mavo leSefer Ra'aviah*, as representative of scholarship from the late nineteenth and early twentieth centuries, and the many articles by Israel M. Ta-Shma as examples of recent scholarship, in his *Studies in Medieval Rabbinic Literature*. Also see Malkiel, *Reconstructing Ashkenaz*, 5–43, 148–49, for a historiographic survey of this issue.

29. For two classic formulations of this idea, albeit decades apart, see Graetz, *History of the Jews*, 3:169–74, 297–310, and Urbach, *Tosaphists*, 17–21, esp. 20–21. For a very different take on this matter, see Elukin, *Living Together*. See also Chazan, *Reassessing Jewish Life*. These emphases on martyrdom and internal Jewish cultural achievement also contributed to what historians, following Salo Baron, have called the "lachrymose conception of Jewish history"; see Baron, "Plenitude," 308–22; idem, *Social and Religious History*, 11:13–76; and for discussions of this idea, see M. Cohen, *Under Crescent and Cross*, 201–2n.1, 283n.1. I have been especially influenced by Bonfil's discussion, *Jewish Life*, 1–3.

30. Examples of this idea are found in Bonfil, *Jewish Life*, 1–9; Marcus, *Rituals of Childhood*; idem, "Jewish-Christian Symbiosis," 449–518, esp. 461–63.

31. The works of Moritz Güdemann and Israel Abrahams contributed significantly to this process in the late nineteenth century; see n. 53. Also see H. Liebschutz, "Relations Between Jews and Christians," which provides an assessment of the field during this period; for a recent discussion, see D. Berger, "Generation of Scholarship," 4–14.

32. For a concise overview of the period and the changes within it, see M. Rubin and Simons, *Christianity in Western Europe*, 1–9.

33. Goodson et al., "Introduction," in *Cities, Texts, and Social Networks*, 1–17; Kowaleski, *Medieval Towns*; Nicholas, *Growth of the Medieval City*; idem, *Later Medieval City*; A. Haverkamp, "Jews and Urban Life," 55–70; idem, "Concivilitas," 103–36.

34. Breuer, "Black Death," 139–52; Rokéa, "The State, the Church and the Jews," 99–126; Jordan, *French Monarchy and the Jews*, 214–38.

35. For settlement of Jews in Germany, see Grossman, *Early Sages of Ashkenaz*, 9–18; Ziwes, *Studien zur Geschichte der Juden;* Toch, "Formation of a Diaspora," 55–78.

36. Toch, *Die Juden im mittelalterlichen Reich*, 55–67; Fram, *My Dear Daughter*, 22–36.

37. D. Bell, *Sacred Communities*, provides an overview of coexistence in the fifteenth century, a period when the norms that typified earlier centuries had already changed due to increasing ghettoization. Also see Kaplan, *Beyond Expulsion*. Although a number of regional studies have appeared, we lack detailed local studies of specific communities during the High Middle Ages, a subject that remains a desideratum. Given these limitations, to study specific locales I have used the classic Elbogen,

Freimann, and Tykocinski, *Germania Judaica I*, Avneri, *Germania Judaica II*, and Gross, *Gallia Judaica*, as well as the studies produced by the so-called "Trier school": A. Haverkamp, *Geschichte der Juden*, 2 vols.; Mentgen, *Die Juden des Mittelrhein-Mosel-Gebietes*; idem, *Studien zur Geschichte der Juden*; Ziwes, *Studien zur Geschichte der Juden*, along with the maps produced by this same group of scholars. Archaeological studies have also been fruitful; see Wamers and Backhaus, *Synagogen*.

38. This was clearly formulated by Marcus, "Jewish-Christian Symbiosis," 461; and also see Nirenberg, *Communities of Violence*, 7–11, 242–43.

39. Soloveitchik distinguishes between assimilation and acculturation, with the first being a conscious adaptation and the second being an unconscious one. I have benefitted greatly from Marcus's definition of inward acculturation; *Rituals of Childhood*, 11–12. This has also been called syncretization and particularization; see, for example, Sabar, "Childbirth and Magic," 671–722. For a helpful discussion of this matter, see Malkiel, "Vision and Realization," 135. Other studies have discussed appropriation as a near parallel term; see Sponsler, "In Transit," 17–39. For a recent discussion of how ideas, values, and practices move from culture to culture, see Flood, *Objects of Translation*.

40. Kaplan, *Beyond Expulsion*, 26–48; Bonfil, *Jewish Life*, 68–77.

41. Biale, *Cultures of the Jews*, esp. xvii–xxxi; Rosman, *How Jewish*, 82–130; Fredriksen, "Just Like Everyone Else," 119–30.

42. See, for example, Yuval, *Two Nations*.

43. This point is nicely manifested when the medieval period is compared to late antiquity; see S. Cohen, *Beginnings of Jewishness*, esp. parts I and II; S. Schwartz, *Imperialism and Jewish Society*, 101–76. One could argue that medieval converts to Christianity were in an intermediary category of sorts, since they were often treated with suspicion by both Jews and Christians, yet this is quite different from the blurred definitions of antiquity. Moreover, although Ashkenaz witnessed many individual converts, it lacked the mass conversions that characterized Spain and other locations. As a result, groups that could be seen as intermediaries were essentially absent from Ashkenaz.

44. I am not denying the presence of factions and groups within the Jewish community, yet I assume that the Jews were a congregation that maintained face-to-face relationships, acknowledged the same traditional rules, and shared a sense of solidarity; and that this latter notion was furthered by their definition as a Jewish community *vis-à-vis* their Christian surroundings. I am indebted to Talmon-Heller's lucid discussion of this issue in the Muslim context: Talmon-Heller, *Islamic Piety*, 22–24. Also see Burke, *History and Social Theory*, 56–58.

45. Freud, *Civilization and Its Discontents*, 58–63. I am borrowing this term from Freud but am not alluding to the Freudian baggage that comes with it.

46. I thank Judah Galinsky for suggesting this term to me.

47. I have benefitted significantly from the ideas of historians of early modern and modern contexts who have used the terms *histoire croisée* or "entangled histories" in order to explain these complexities. See Zimmerman and Werner, "Beyond Comparison"; Wolf, *Entangled Histories*; Subrahmanyam, "Connected Histories"; idem, "Holding the World in Balance." David Ruderman has recently used this term to characterize early modern Jewish history: Ruderman, *Early Modern Jewry*, 285nn.28–29.

48. For a discussion of this question, see D. Berger, "Generation of Scholarship"; Fishman, "Penitential System"; J. Cohen, *Sanctifying the Name of God*; Marcus, *Rituals*; and my "Shared Stories," 18–36. For example, attitudes toward the spiritual rewards that may be gained in this world as a means for arriving in a better world after death offer a fascinating additional topic for research in this context. See Perry, *Tradition and Transformation*, 230–53.

49. I have chosen the term "social history" over "cultural history" despite the fact that they are treated synonymously in numerous studies; and, as outlined by Peter Burke, cultural history has been

seen as a replacement for "social history." Burke, *History and Social Theory*, 118–26; idem, *What Is Cultural History?* Yet, as Burke notes, the terms can be used somewhat interchangeably. My choice of "social" rather than "cultural" stems from my interest in multiple segments of society and their various practices; also see Chartier, *Cultural History*.

50. This approach has been especially prevalent among the Annales School; see Burke, *What Is Cultural History?*, 51–76. See also Latour, *Reassembling the Social*; De Certeau, *Practice*; and Bourdieu, *Outline*; idem, *Logic*, whose contributions in anthropology have all influenced the realm of history.

51. The bibliographies related to these topics are vast. Detailed references to specific publications are featured throughout this book. For recent surveys of many of these subjects, see M. Rubin and Simons, *Christianity in Western Europe*.

52. Goitein, *Mediterranean Society*.

53. Berliner, *Aus dem inneren Leben*; Güdemann, *Geschichte des Erziehungswesens*; Abrahams, *Jewish Life in the Middle Ages*.

54. Baron, *Social and Religious History*.

55. The medieval period in Europe was central to Baron's work. Whereas his volumes on the period before 1200 are organized thematically (philosophy, Hebrew language and letters, magic and mysticism), his works on 1200–1600 are arranged by specific locations or prototypes (the infidel, the apologist, the citizen, etc.). The latter focus led to a blurring of geographical distinctions in many discussions. Baron's chapters on geography were first and foremost a history of the relations between the ruling class and the Jews; thus women, a central group in the present study, are almost absent from his oeuvre.

56. J. Katz, *Tradition and Crisis*; idem, *Out of the Ghetto*. Herman Pollack's work on early modern Europe, *Jewish Folkways*, should also be noted in this context.

57. J. Katz, *Exclusiveness and Tolerance*. See D. Berger, "Jacob Katz on Jews and Christians," 41–65.

58. Bourdieu, *Logic*.

59. J. Katz, "Law, Spirituality and Society," 87–98, 105–8; Weissler, "Missing Half," 99–105, 108–115. For a discussion of this dialogue, see Rosman, *How Jewish Is Jewish History*, 168–81; Carlebach, "Early Modern Ashkenaz," 80–82.

60. Bonfil, *Jewish Life*; Marcus, "Medieval Jewish Studies," 113–42.

61. See Shoham-Steiner, *Involuntary Marginals*; Baskin, "Jewish Women"; Grossman, *Pious and Rebellious*; Baumgarten, *Mothers and Children*; Nirenberg, *Communities of Violence*.

62. Some scholars have viewed Jewish society through the prism of timeless minds speaking to each other. Clearly, this is not the historical approach being applied to the questions here. For an examination that privileges context and chronology, see Soloveitchik, *Pawnbroking*; idem, *Wine in Ashkenaz*. For the early modern period see Fram, *Ideals*, 48–50. Fram notes that custom and piety were learned "on the street," but the examples he brings are connected to impiety more than to piety.

63. Kanarfogel, *Peering*, 118–19; Goldberg, *Crossing the Jabbok*.

64. Kanarfogel, *Peering*, 118–19.

65. Kanarfogel explicitly states that he is not searching the catalyst for piety within Christian society; ibid., 127n77. He relies on Schäfer, "The Ideal of Piety," 9–23; Marcus, *Piety and Society*; idem, "Hierarchies," 7–26. Both of these authors have presented slightly different views recently: see Marcus, *Rituals of Childhood*, and Schäfer, "Jews and Christians in the High Middle Ages," 45–59. It is interesting to note Urbach's comment on this issue in *Tosaphists*, 745–48, where he resolved the similarity between Jews and Christians in the medieval world with a quotation from Job 32:8.

66. See above, n. 10. Neither of these terms is straightforward. For elucidation, see Brooke and

Brooke, *Popular Religion*, esp. 46–103; Biller, "Popular Religion," 221–46; Shinners, *Medieval Popular Religion*; and, most recently, Bynum, *Christian Materiality*, 129–30, 224–27. The social uses of learning represent another closely related subject, though it is not a central theme of this book. See Chamberlain, *Knowledge*, 1–4.

67. Vauchez, "Religion populaire," 91–107; Van Engen, "Practice," 150–77; Biller, "Popular Religion," 222.

68. This applies to Jewish historiography as well. See Güdemann's presentation of folk practices, among them those of women, *Geschichte des Erziehungswesens*, 1:199–238.

69. Ibid. See Brown, *Cult of the Saints*, who has emphasized the small distance between the "popular" and the "elite"; see also Chartier, "Culture as Appropriation," and idem, "Culture as Appropriation," 229–53, esp. 233–34; Shinners, *Medieval Popular Religion*, xvii–xix; M. Rubin, *Medieval Christianity in Practice*, 1–5; Jaritz, *Zwischen Augenblick*, 127–92. These studies of practice note that the evidence at hand is often fairly messy, and that, rather than solid intellectual consistency between doctrine and practice, a more complex relationship should be sought. See Van Engen, *Sisters and Brothers*, 9. Similar observations have been made concerning Muslim society; see Talmon-Heller, *Islamic Piety*, 22–23, and Berkey, "Popular Culture," 133–46.

70. Ginzburg, *Night Battles*; Scribner, *For the Sake of the Simple Folk*.

71. Malkiel, *Reconstructing Ashkenaz*, 148–99, uses this definition as the basis for an entire chapter. For a fascinating illustration of deviance in late antiquity, see Schremer, *Brothers Estranged*, 16–17, 69–70; yet Schremer does not emphasize practice as much as belief.

72. Deviance is often presented as the opposite of orthodoxy, and thus, by extension, it could be seen as a challenge to piety. See King, *What Is Gnosticism?*; Erikson, *Wayward Puritans*. However, while piety and deviance occupy opposite ends of a spectrum in many respects, they can also be seen as two terms that are closely related. The boundary between the pious and the deviant can be far more nuanced than that between the pious and non-pious.

73. See Erikson, *Wayward Puritans*, 6–7; Schremer, *Brothers Estranged*, 69–70.

74. This idea, as formulated by Lara Deeb, has proved very helpful to my thinking, despite the differences in our areas of focus; see *Enchanted Modern*, 7–9. I do not view public piety as a new phenomenon; rather, piety has always had public aspects. However, the medieval world differs from Deeb's specific topic, Muslim modern piety, in *Enchanted Modern*, 5.

75. As Victor Turner has remarked, ritual expresses belief and belief is expressed on the body; therefore, individual and communal practice each require the individual body. See Turner, *Dramas, Fields, and Metaphors*; Ashley, *Victor Turner*.

76. The historiography of Hasidei Ashkenaz represents more than a prime example of the scholarly debates over the connections among Jews residing apart from one another, albeit in relative proximity, with shared customs, norms, and traditions. This literature offers a representative overview of the disputes among scholars regarding how Jewish and Christian lives were related, with some seeking to isolate Hasidei Ashkenaz from both their fellow Jews and their Christian neighbors, and others attempting to entwine them. The debates concerning Hasidei Ashkenaz also reflect contrasting approaches within the larger field of Jewish-Christian relations. Some scholars have asked to what extent Hasidei Ashkenaz were a distinct group within Jewish society, whereas others have focused on the relationships between Hasidei Ashkenaz and Christian society as a case study for medieval Jewish communities at large.

77. Scholars have debated to what extent Hasidei Ashkenaz were a sect-like group or individuals. Whereas twenty years ago they were often seen as a sect, recent scholarship has a somewhat different approach. See Marcus, "Introduction," *Religious and Social Ideas*. We await his new review of recent scholarship. Also see Chapter 7.

78. For a history of Hasidei Ashkenaz, see Marcus, *Piety and Society*. Following Marcus, I have treated Judah as the central author of *Sefer Hasidim* although I am well aware that the book originated with his father Samuel and was edited and added to by Eleazar b. Judah and others.

79. For the different perspectives, see the collection of articles in Marcus, *Religious and Social Ideas*. Especially noteworthy is Yitzhak (Fritz) Baer's postion, "Religious-Social Tendency," 1–50. Baer was severely criticized after the publication of this article. See also Fishman, "Penitential System," 201–29, and for a more recent discussion see the articles in the *JQR* forum, vol. 96 (2006), on Sefer Hasidim in the wake of Haym Soloveitchik's article, "Piety," 455–93.

80. For a summary of some of this literature, see Wolfson, "Mystical Significance" and more recently Shyovitz, "He Has Created."

81. Ta-Shma, "Mitzvat Talmud Torah," 112–29, and Kanarfogel, *Peering*, 251–57, presented one view, whereas Haym Soloveitchik has argued that Hasidei Ashkenaz were not particularly influential beyond their teachings that were reformulated and circulated in the popularly named *Sefer Hasidut*, an abridged version of *Sefer Hasidim*; Soloveitchik, "Piety," 455–93.

82. Both Marcus, *Piety*, and Soloveitchik, "Piety," set out with the assumption that there were specific people who were part of a pietist group.

83. Soloveitchik, "Piety."

84. Indeed, I would argue that Hasidei Ashkenaz were a far less uniform group than some scholars have assumed. See Chapter 7, 216–18.

85. Compare Soloveitchik, "Piety," 477.

86. See Noble, "Jewish Woman," 347–55; Einbinder, "Jewish Women Martyrs," 105–27; Grossman, *Pious and Rebellious*, 198–211.

87. Berliner remarked on this in the late nineteenth century in *Aus dem inneren Leben*, 51.

88. Baskin, "Jewish Women," 94–113.

89. Grossman, *Pious and Rebellious*. I have referred to the English version of this book throughout the notes; when I refer to its far more detailed Hebrew original, I have noted it accordingly. Also see Loewe, *Position of Women*. Despite their substantive differences, these studies share the tendency to judge medieval Jews and their practices as "negative" or "positive" with regard to their effects on women. My approach, following the formulation suggested by Merry Weisner, has been to refrain from such judgments. See Weisner-Hanks, "Do Women Need the Renaissance," 545.

90. Har-Shefi, "Women and Halakhah"; Ta-Shma, "Ma'amad haNashim haMitnadvot," 262–79.

91. Heschel, "Jewish Studies as Counterhistory," 101–13.

92. Scott, "Gender," 41–50; also see her essay, "Unanswered Questions," 1422–29; West and Zimmerman, "Doing Gender," 121–51.

93. See, for example, earlier works in religious studies whose authors attempted to locate women in the sources and made attempts to overcome the absence of theoretical and practical texts written by women. For a classic example, see Falk and Gross, *Unspoken Worlds*.

94. Indeed, the role of sexuality in religious life is one of the most commonly stressed differentiating features. Nevertheless, this central factor does not eliminate all similarities. See Baumgarten, *Mothers and Children*, 7–13.

95. This idea has been stressed in many sociological studies; see Kandiyoti, "Bargaining with Patriarchy," 274–90; Sered, *What Makes Women Sick*, as well as in specific medieval works: D. Elliott, *Proving Woman*; Furst, "Conversion," 179–201.

96. Quoted by Biller, "The Common Woman," 140. Biller refers to a thirteenth-century tractate from Strasbourg, where the same idea was suggested, "De Rebus Alsaticis ineuentis saeculi XIII", ed. P. Jaffé, *MGH* SS 17 (Hanover 1861), 232–37. On a certain level, this statement identifies an enduring

truth regarding women and religion; however, as Katherine French has stated in *Good Women*, 1–17, this is a point worth pursuing and documenting.

97. Güdemann, *Geschichte des Erziehungswesens*, 232, asserts this, and see the story in MS Oxford Or. 135 (1466), fol. 307a–b, about Nathan de Tzutzita where his wife is portrayed praying.

98. This is a subject of ongoing examination and debate. See Bynum, *Holy Feast*, 23–30; Evergates, *Aristocratic Women*, introduction; D. Elliott, *Proving Woman*; Howell, *Commerce*, 1–48; and, in Jewish contexts, Grossman, *Pious and Rebellious*, 273–82; Baumgarten, *Mothers and Children*, 185–88.

99. Borrowing a formulation from Abrams, "Germanic Christianities," 114, where she asks, "Are they like two cards from the same pack or like the same card from separate packs?"

100. The corpus of literature on this subject is extensive. See, for example, Swanson, *Religion and Devotion*; Vauchez, *Laity*; Tanner, *Ages of Faith*.

101. Biller, "Popular Religion"; Goering, *William de Montibus*, 58–99.

102. As Bynum comments in "Perspectives," 79, "Objects are hardly objective."

103. Gauvain, "Ritual Rewards," 336n.8, discusses the importance of investigating how ritual practice is prioritized and framed in daily life; I have adopted this approach. See also C. Bell, *Ritual Theory*.

104. Bock, "Challenging Dichotomies," 1–24; Kerber, "Separate Spheres," 9–39; Newman, "Critical Theory," 59. For a general discussion on the public and private domains using feminist methodology, see the articles in Landes, *Feminism*. The prism of space is not central in my inquiry since the available evidence is not sufficiently robust to justify a place-based approach. Nevertheless, some discussions herein provide a foundation for future studies that use location or space as their primary template. I have relied on Michel de Certeau's definition of space as "practiced place"; de Certeau, *Practice*, 125–30. See also McDowell, *Gender, Identity and Place*, 22; Rose, *Feminism and Geography*, 41–51.

105. In the vein of social historians and of anthropologists such as Pierre Bourdieu, I am resisting the tendency to privilege logic over practice; see Bourdieu, *Logic*. For a discussion of this issue in the context of early Christian practice, see Shaw, *Burden of Flesh*, 23, 219–20.

106. See the epitaphs recorded in the Steinheim database: http://www.steinheiminstitut.de:50580/cgi-bin/epidat.

107. Schmelzer, "Penitence."

108. See Zahavy, "Politics of Piety," 42–68; Epstein Weinberg, *Piety and Fanaticism*.

109. I make use of endnotes to detail specific comparisons that support the local identifications that I suggest, especially examples that apply to Islam and Jewish communities within Islamic societies. I hope that future studies will further these cross-cultural comparisons beyond the scope of this current work.

110. For a compelling discussion of the sights and sounds witnessed and recorded in medieval cities, see Symes, "Out in the Open," 279–302.

CHAPTER I

1. Israel Ta-Shma has discussed the problems involved with attributing these words and passages to Rashi, arguing convincingly that Rashi's students must have recorded his teachings. Nevertheless, whether transmitted by Rashi or his students, this text indicates that this custom originated with medieval Jewish women. Ta-Shma, "Minhagei Harhakat haNiddah," 284–86. Hereafter I refer to this text as attributed to Rashi by way of shorthand, despite the likelihood that it was recorded by his students.

2. This text continues with the case of an individual who could not become purified despite his

immersion in a ritual bath, but then entered the Temple nevertheless; as a result, he received the most severe punishment possible, *karet* (lit., cutting off, referring to being denied entry into Paradise).

3. Simhah b. Samuel of Vitry, *Mahzor Vitry*, Horowitz edition, #498 (p. 606). This passage appears in parallel texts: Solomon b. Isaac, *Sefer haOrah*, 167–68; idem, *Sefer haPardes*, 3; and idem, *Sefer Likutei haPardes*, 4a. For a discussion of these variants, see Roth, "Sefer haPardes," 95–98.

4. Jewish prayer has a long history of change and adaptation in response to the conditions experienced by Jewish communities, depending on when and where they lived. By the Middle Ages, the structure of the Jewish prayer service was fairly stable. The introduction of piyyutim and other supplementary liturgical compositions represent contributions by medieval writers and rabbis to their inherited public prayers. Many private prayers were also composed and recited during the Middle Ages, including some *tehinot* that have reached us today. For a history of Jewish prayer, see Elbogen, *Jewish Liturgy*; Reif, *Judaism and Hebrew Prayer*, 153–206. Also see Hoffman, *Canonization*, 84–89; Isaacs, "Anthropological and Historical Study," introduction.

5. This applies to *siddurim* (prayer books) and especially to *mahzorim* (prayer books used on the High Holidays and on the pilgrimage festivals). Abundant commentaries on prayer books and poetry are extant: for prayer books, see Kanarfogel, "Prayer"; also see Hollender, "Introduction," in *Clavis Commentariorum*, 1–5; Elbogen, *Jewish Liturgy*, 271–84; and Zunz, *Die Ritus*.

6. At first glance, physical presence seems to represent the lowest common denominator. After all, literal attendance at synagogue prayer services did not require literacy, liturgical or otherwise. Nevertheless, physical presence can be measured with greater ease than acts that left no historical trace. Many forms of devotion expressed by Jews who prayed in synagogue went unrecorded (e.g., the choreography of their physical gestures and the sounds of their pleas, cries, and songs). In light of such limitations, discussions of attendance offer a quantifiable element. I address other aspects of prayer during times of impurity in Chapter 5.

7. This idea of avoiding impurity is related to ensuring that nothing unclean enter the synagogue. While impurity and uncleanliness are related, they are not synonymous; see Douglas, *Purity and Danger*, 7–28. For an example of discourse on dirt in the synagogue, see the material on infants and their diapers in Baumgarten, *Mothers and Children*, 158–61. See also the recent archaeological finds from Cologne, where a special chute for bathroom refuse was found, a structure that is congruent with practices prescribed in *SHP*, #432, #1064.

8. Admittedly, male and female purity represents but one issue among others that determined the presence of men and women in the synagogue. The laws on prayer articulate a gender bias that places adult men in pivotal roles as prayer leaders and as members of the quorum required for public prayer, a standard that dictated the way men's presence was viewed and ordered. This chapter focuses on praxis and attitudes in the synagogue that are associated with personal and communal concerns for purity, while acknowledging the gendered framework for prayer responsibilities as part of the cultural milieu.

9. This idea was initially discussed by Berliner, *Aus dem inneren Leben*, 37; Abrahams, *Jewish Life*, 13–48.

10. The question of whether non-Jews regularly entered synagogues during the Middle Ages arises in this context. Written accounts from times of attack and peril report that Christians entered synagogues in search of Jews in a given community. Evidence from Italy indicates that Christian preachers entered synagogues in the fourteenth century and later; Ruderman, *Preachers of the Italian Ghetto*. Many sources mention Jews who visited churches for reasons relating to business; see Shatzmiller, "Church Articles," 93–102. Similar accounts also appear in Christian stories of conversions; M. Rubin, *Gentile Tales*, 89–92.

11. For these practices, see Finkelstein, *Jewish Self-Government*, 15–18; Grossman, "Origins," 199–221; and, more recently, Bonfil, "Right," 145–56.

12. In medieval Ashkenaz, the evening prayer service (*ma'ariv*) immediately followed afternoon prayers (*minhah*); thus, prayers were held in synagogue twice rather than three times a day.

13. Kanarfogel, "Prayer," 256–60.

14. Krinsky, *Synagogues of Europe*, 44; Baron, *The Jewish Community*, 2:144–45. Alick Isaacs has suggested that ideological or perhaps theological reasons could explain the lack of uniformity among medieval synagogues, "Anthropological and Historical Study," 41–51. On synagogues located in private quarters, see Urbach, *Tosaphists*, 92; Meir b. Barukh, *Teshuvot, Pesakim* (Cahana ed.), 1:50; Meir b. Hillel, Mordekhai, *Shabbat*, 228; see also *SHP*, #493, #535; #1227.

15. Not only were life-cycle rituals (e.g., weddings) held in the synagogue, but other gatherings also took place there; see Abrahams, *Jewish Life*, 13–48.

16. Ibid.

17. Katz, *Tradition and Crisis*, 148–55, esp. 153–55.

18. Bonfil, *Jewish Life*, 215–30.

19. In Isaacs's dissertation "Anthropological and Historical Study," he compares his approach to that of Jacob Katz. See *Tradition and Crisis*, 148–52, where Katz hints at the many sociological groups that were present in the synagogue.

20. Goldin, *Uniqueness and Togetherness*, 102–15, esp. 111–15. The social activities that typified the synagogue extend beyond the scope of this chapter.

21. Woolf, "Medieval Models," 263–80; Ta-Shma, "Synagogal Sanctity," 351–64, esp. 359–64.

22. Kanarfogel, "Prayer."

23. For a discussion of Jews who did not attend synagogue, see Kanarfogel, "Rabbinic Attitudes," 3–35.

24. *SHP*, #442, #447.

25. Baumgarten, *Mothers and Children*, chap. 2; Samson b. Zadok, *Sefer Tashbetz*, #397.

26. *SHP*, #442, #447. These statements suggest that Hasidei Ashkenaz were not a sect, as some scholars have asserted.

27. BT Berakhot 6a, 7b–8a. This is stated clearly in *Sefer haMaskil* (late thirteenth-century France); see Stahl, "Inyanei Tefilla," 50.

28. Woolf, "Medieval Models," 266–78. It is noteworthy that one remnant from the Temple hierarchy endured, namely the preservation of priestly and Levitical descent. This distinction in lineage remained operative in certain liturgical settings, such as Torah reading. Though peripheral to the topics addressed in this chapter, this practice is part of the bigger picture.

29. The difference between the washing required of men and immersion for women is significant.

30. Lev. 12 and 15:16–30.

31. These statutes are attributed to Ezra in the Amoraic period: BT Bava Kamma 82b; BT Berakhot 22a. See Dinari, "Profanation," 17–37.

32. BT Bava Kamma 82b.

33. The limited application of such ancient principles in medieval life is exemplified by the acceptance of physically impaired individuals who would have been considered impure, and therefore banned from entry and service in the Temple, such as lepers or maimed individuals. Medieval sources make no mention of lepers in the synagogue; see Shoham-Steiner, *Involuntary Marginals*, 211–12.

34. See, for example, *Sefer haOrah*, #2. Here the author notes that if a man remembers his state of impurity while praying, he need not stop; rather he should quickly conclude his prayers, then go to immerse. For a survey of sources on male impurity, see Dinari, "Profanation," 17–37.

35. Dinari, "Profanation," 17–37. Dinari has commented on the unusual nature of this definition in light of other Ashkenazic customs, and even more so the prohibition against women praying while impure (26). I find Sharon Koren's suggestion (which follows the work of Charlotte Fonrobert) convincing, that male impurity was externalized whereas female purity was considered physically inherent. See Koren, *Forsaken*, 9–12. For discussion of these matters in medieval Ashkenaz, see Moses b. Jacob of Coucy, *Semag*, Aseh, #3, Asher b. Yehiel, BT *Sukkah*, chap. 2; Haim b. Isaac, *Drashot Maharah*, #31. Meir b. Barukh of Rothenburg recorded the customs from both his native Germany and from France, where he lived for a period; see *She'elot uTeshuvot* (Crimona), #37. Many of these statements relate to wearing tefillin, a practice addressed in Chapter 4.

36. *SHP*, #48; Isaac b. Joseph, *Semak*, #25. This relates directly to BT Avodah Zarah 20b, where men are warned against gazing at women by day, which could cause impurity by night.

37. Judah did encourage ritually impure men to wash. For example, he recounted men of meticulous piety who, after having sexual relations, would wash before going to synagogue; *SHP*, #1064, #1066, #1944. These texts discuss extraordinary piety, as most men did not wash themselves after sexual relations. *SHP*, #1611, contains a fascinating story of a man who practiced what could be considered "reverse purity." When his wife was impure, he immersed in the mikveh to ensure his own purity. The text suggests that when she was sexually available, he was not as stringent.

38. Following the destruction of the Temple, matters of purity steadily diminished in importance. Scholars of late antiquity differ over the mechanism and timeframe of these changes. For a summary of this literature, see the recent work of Noam, *From Qumran*.

39. For a summary of this scholarship, see Marienberg, *Niddah*; idem, "Menstruation in Sacred Spaces," 17–27; S. Cohen, "Purity and Piety," 103–15; Har-Shefi, "Women and Halakhah," 187–98; and, recently, Koren, *Forsaken*.

40. Dinari, "Impurity Customs," 302–24. For changes in these customs, see Ta-Shma, "Minhagei Harhakat haNiddah," 280–88; Har-Shefi, "Women and Halakhah," 163–68.

41. See, for example, Rashi, BT Ketubbot 72a, s.v. "huhzeka niddah beshkhenuteh"; Eliezer b. Joel, *Sefer Ra'aviah*, #936; Isaac b. Moses, *Sefer Or Zaru'a*, 1: #672; Meir b. Hillel, *Mordekhai*, Yebamot, #61.

42. See n. 167 below.

43. *SHP*, #440, #648, #1064, and especially #1612, which recounts the story of a pious man who would only wear white clothing in synagogue.

44. Israel b. Petahyah Isserlein, *Terumat haDeshen*, #245, #248.

45. Simhah b. Samuel, *Mahzor Vitry*, Horowitz edition, #498. This passage appeared in other parallels: Solomon b. Isaac, *Sefer haOrah*, 167–68, idem, *Sefer haPardes*, 3, and idem, *Sefer Likutei Pardes*, 4a. For a discussion of the variants, see Roth, *Sefer haPardes*, 95–98.

46. A baraita is a passage attributed to the early centuries of the first millenium that was not included in the Mishnah. The Tosefta is comprised of baraitot; however, other baraitot have been recorded in independent collections. Evyatar Marienberg is currently preparing a new edition of *Baraita deNiddah*.

47. *Baraita deNiddah*, 30.

48. See *Otzar haGe'onim, Massekhet Berakhot*, #121, p. 49. My thanks to Dr. Sol Cohen of Philadelphia for this reference.

49. Ta-Shma, *Ritual, Custom and Reality*, 280–88. Woolf, "Medieval Models," 271, has argued that this baraita was known to Rashi and his students, but the text itself counters his position; see p. 39 below. Ephraim Kanarfogel and others have argued that Rashi and his students were familiar with the *Hekhalot* literature that can be linked to *Baraita deNiddah*; see his *Peering*, 127–30, 149–51, 253–54. Also see Schäfer, "Ideal of Piety." Nonetheless, I find Rashi's inquiry into the reasoning behind this practice

and the absence of references to *Baraita deNiddah* in writings from his school to be more convincing than their potential familiarity with *Hekhalot* literature.

50. Here I differ with Pinchas Roth, *Sefer haPardes*, 96, who claimed on the basis of Christian practice that this topic of discussion was not unusual; rather, I posit that if this issue were self-evident, it would not have been raised.

51. Eliezer b. Joel haLevi, *Sefer Ra'aviah*, ed. Deblytski, Hilkhot Berakhot, #68.

52. Simcha Emanuel spoke about this topic at the World Congress of Jewish Sudies held in Jerusalem in 2013. His work is forthcoming, "Niddah," and I thank him for sharing it with me.

53. This idea is also reinforced in one manuscript of *Sefer haPardes* where the copyist notes that some women "prevent themselves"; Roth, *Sefer haPardes*, 96.

54. With the exception of Dinari, who focused on both male and female impurity, in "Impurity Customs."

55. In fact, from the Mishnah to the Shulhan Arukh (sixteenth century), nearly all halakhic discussions of bodily purity address men and women together, with the exception of *Takanat Ezra* and its exclusive male focus. Perhaps the lack of attention to this pattern comes from a lapse on the part of the modern scholars who have discussed these sources over the past decade, and whose interest in women's status led them to read these medieval sources as if they pertain to women alone. Or perhaps discomfort with regard to this topic led male scholars to avoid it.

56. This is contrasted to some extent in *Sefer haOrah*; see there, #2.

57. Ibid.

58. This follows biblical instructions in Lev. 15; see n. 40.

59. *SHP*, #1609.

60. Eleazar b. Judah, *Sefer Rokeah*, #318. In MS Paris héb. 363, fol. 119b, it is noted that this tradition first appeared in *Ma'aseh haGe'onim*.

61. Emanuel, "Niddah"; Roth, *Sefer haPardes*, 96.

62. Solomon b. Isaac, *Sefer Likutei haPardes* (Bnei Berak), 84; see Roth, *Sefer haPardes*, 98.

63. Isaac b. Moses, *Sefer Or Zaru'a*, 1: #360. I have purposely left the language gender-neutral, as it is a general statement.

64. Haim b. Isaac, *Drashot*, Drashah #22.

65. Isaac b. Meir of Düren, *Sha'arei Dura*, Hilkhot Niddah, #18. The existence of numerous manuscript copies attests to the popularity of this book. See, for example, MS Oxford Bodl. Opp. Add. fol. 34 (641), fol. 80a, where Isaac b. Meir remarked that the laws of niddah were more strictly observed during his lifetime than in previous generations.

66. Jacob Barukh b. Judah Landa, *Sefer haAgur*, #1388.

67. *Sefer haMiktzo'ot* is comprised of writings by many Ge'onim. Scholars have dated this book to the mid-eleventh century. Selections from this volume were quoted by Ashkenazic rabbis in the twelfth and thirteenth centuries. See Assaf, *Sefer haMiktzo'ot*, 6–10.

68. Emanuel, "Niddah." This is an especially powerful argument, since sources on this topic from the Ge'onic period advocate that women attend synagogue; see n. 50.

69. Fishman, *Becoming the People*, 194–98.

70. *SHP*, #1184, refers to this practice of intermediary bathing: the pious are instructed to take special care during the days from a woman's intermediary bathing until her immersion, when she was able to resume sexual relations with her husband. See S. Cohen, "Purity, Piety and Polemic."

71. It is noteworthy that numerous stringencies were innovated and enforced for the "white days" during the twelfth and thirteenth centuries; see n. 41.

72. Haim b. Isaac, *Drashot Maharah*, #22; Isaac b. Meir of Düren, *Sha'arei Dura*, 18.

73. *Sefer Rokeah*, #217.

74. Due to the expulsion of Jews from France in 1306, the latest medieval source material from that region is from the early fourteenth century.

75. Some of Isserlein's prooftexts are far from exact: Rashi did not include the phrase "spiritual pleasure" (*nahat ruah*) in his writings on the laws of niddah; rather, he used this concept to explain why women were allowed to perform other commandments related to the holidays. See Chapter 5.

76. Lit., "sadness of spirit and illness of their hearts."

77. Yuval, *Scholars in Their Time*, 59–71, esp. 66n.61.

78. He is referring to the abridged version of this book, known as *Sefer Or Zaru'a Katan*.

79. Israel b. Petahyah Isserlein, *Terumat haDeshen*, part 2: 132; S. Cohen, "Purity and Piety," 110–11.

80. Solomon b. Isaac, *Sefer Likutei haPardes*, 84.

81. Moses Isserles (Remah), as translated by S. Cohen in "Purity and Piety," 104.

82. This practice is already evident in literature from the Rashi school and continues consistently throughout the Middle Ages. The literature is brought by Dinari, "Impurity Customs," and Har-Shefi, "Women and Halakhah," 92–102.

83. See n. 71.

84. Zimmer, *Society and Its Customs*, 220–49.

85. For a summary of this stage of its development, see Rosman, *How Jewish*, 149–52.

86. It is of particular relevance to consider post-partum customs for comparison, since they too included specific features that were correlated to bleeding. See Baumgarten, *Mothers and Children*, 101–5.

87. This immersion is noted in many medieval sources; see, for example, Simhah b. Samuel, *Mahzor Vitry*, Goldschmidt edition, 3: Hilkhot Erev Yom haKippurim, #1; *SHP*, #1182; Eleazar b. Judah, *Sefer Rokeah*, #214. It was common in Italy as well; see Tzidkiyah b. Abraham haRofeh, *Sefer Shibbolei haLeket*, #283.

88. For a discussion of the significance of nocturnal emissions on Yom Kippur, see Eleazar b. Judah, *Sefer Rokeah*, #217. This belief is based on BT Yoma 73b.

89. See Chapter 3.

90. It is noteworthy that Jewish men immersed on other occasions as well; see n. 103 and Kanarfogel, "Returning to the Community," 1:69–98.

91. *Pirkei deRabbi Eliezer*, chap. 45; *Midrash Wayyikra Rabbah*, 30:7, p. 705.

92. Eliezer b. Joel haLevi, *Sefer Ra'aviah*, 2: Hilkhot Rosh haShanah, #549; Isaac b. Moses, *Sefer Or Zaru'a*, 2: Rosh haShanah. See also Abraham b. Azriel, *Sefer Arugat haBosem*, 1:127, where the author explains that one who does true penance is closer to God than the angels.

93. See n. 118.

94. For information about these scholars, see Yuval, *Scholars in Their Time*, 63–68, 72–73, 122–23, 188.

95. Shalom b. Isaac of Neustadt, *Decisions and Customs*, 117–118, #337. Although other opinions were written on this issue, it was Judel's position that held long-term ramifications; see *Magen Avraham*, *Orah Hayim*, #610, (5); *Mahazit hashekel*, ad loc. I thank Prof. David Berger for this reference.

96. This seems to be the traditional understanding. See Isaac b. Moses, *Sefer Or Zaru'a*, 1: #112, where this opinion is attributed to Simhah of Speyer, who stated that all who repent should immerse. Also see Abraham b. Azriel, *Sefer Arugat haBosem*, 2:110; Tzidkiyah b. Abraham, *Shibbolei haLeket*, #283, #210, where he noted both nocturnal impurity and teshuvah as reasons for immersion; and Kanarfogel, "Returning to the Community," 82–83.

97. In some locations it was also customary to immerse before Rosh haShanah, see ibid.

98. MS Paris héb. 363, fol. 31b. Men immersed on other occasions as well. For example, ritual immersion was also customary for apostates returning to Judaism; see Kanarfogel, "Returning to the Community." MS Oxford Bodl. Opp. Add. 34 (641), fol. 93a: "On the day before the circumcision ceremony, the father and the ba'al brit bathe for the sake of enhancing the commandment (*hidur hamitzvah*), and the community also bathes with them to show respect for circumcision." Jacob the circumciser reports the same practice (*Zikhron Brit*, 63–64). A fourteenth-century manuscript of *Sefer Tashbetz* reports on immersion in the mikveh (MS Paris héb. 643, fol. 34a).

99. Medieval texts regularly discuss the immersion of women. However, one must ask to what extent this was a normative practice. Bitha Har-Shefi has discussed this in "Al Tevilat Niddah," 4:65–76.

100. This passage offers a rare case wherein women seem to have immersed during the day.

101. *SHP*, #1182; Eliezer b. Judah of Worms, *Sefer Rokeah*, 214; Samson b. Tzadok, *Sefer Tashbetz*, MS Paris héb. 380, fol. 185c, notes explicitly that this is an immersion without a blessing (*tevilah be'almah*).

102. Tzidikiyah b. Abraham also implied that women immersed: *Sefer Shibbolei haLeket*, #283.

103. Jacob b. Moses Moellin, *Sefer Maharil: Minhagim*, Hilkhot Erev Yom haKippurim, #3, s.v. "tevilat."

104. *Genesis Rabbah* (Albeck), 29:9; Schäfer, *Rivalität*. My thanks to Daniel Abrams for discussing this issue with me. A parallel Christian source that was central to Christian discussions of this matter is particularly relevant here, Mark 12:25: "For when they rise from the dead, they neither marry nor are given in marriage but are like angels in heaven."

105. Isaac b. Joseph, *Semak*, #24.

106. Avraham b. Ephraim, *Compendium*, 30, quoting and paraphrasing Moses b. Jacob, *Semag*, introduction to *Mitzvot Aseh*, 10.

107. Galinsky, "Rabbenu Moshe meCoucy," 32–35, and idem, "And to Be a Loyal Servant," 13–31. It is possible that there is also a French-German distinction in this case.

108. The Hebrew is *yitzro*, "his desire."

109. *SHP*, #980. This idea is echoed by Isaac b. Joseph, *Semak*, #24.

110. *SHP*, #981.

111. Har-Shefi, "Women and Halakhah," 190–95.

112. Ortner, *Making Gender*, 21–27; J. W. Scott, *Gender and the Politics*, 41–46; Buckley and Gottlieb, *Blood Magic*.

113. Fishman has recently summarized selections from this literature in *Becoming the People*, 176–81, and see her arguments against this line of research.

114. Har-Shefi, "Women and Halakhah," 118–26, and Ta-Shma, "Minhagei Harhakat haNiddah," 280–88, both suggest this direction. For a similar interpretation in the context of women's involvement in another religious role, as ritual slaughterers, see Micha Perry, "Female Slaughterers," 127–46.

115. Susan Sered has suggested that practices innovated by women were more easily accepted by the male hierarchy when they could be readily linked to a prooftext from traditional sources on which the rabbis could base their reasoning: *Women as Ritual Experts*, 132–41.

116. Meens, "A Relic of Superstition," 281–93; idem, "'Ritual Purity,'" 40–43; Bynum, *Wonderful Blood*, 210–15, 271n.117.

117. My emphasis.

118. Colgrave and Mynors, *Bede's Ecclesiastical History*, 90.

119. It should be noted that these instructions differ from the biblical guidelines, which discuss immersion and not just washing.

120. Payer, "Early Medieval Regulations," 368, and see Miramon, "La fin d'un tabou?," 163–81; idem, "Déconstruction et reconstruction," 79–107.

121. Miramon, "La fin d'un tabou?," 163–81;

122. "*Intellegant ergo quod ecclesiam Christi ingressi, corpus et sanguinem eius non nisi mundo corpore, puroque corde percipere debeant*": Jonas Aurelianensis Episcopus, "De institutione laicali," 187–88.

123. Burchardus, *Decretorum, PL* 140, chap. 19, c. 5.

124. Anderson, "Ritual Purity," 73–94.

125. Meens, "A Relic of Superstition," 290–93, noted that although Gregory is universally cited, his instructions were not adopted.

126. Ibid., 291.

127. Miramon, "La fin d'un tabou," and see Browe, *Beiträge zur Sexualethik*, 10–14. For a comparison to a similar Jewish ritual, see Baumgarten, *Mothers and Children*; Rieder, *On the Purification of Women*.

128. Elliott, *Fallen Bodies*. See also the articles in the collection edited by Cullum and Lewis, *Holiness and Masculinity*, esp. J. Murray, "Masculinizing Religious Life," 24–42.

129. The popularity of this concern can be attributed in part to the spread of Aristotelian ideas among medical professionals during that era.

130. See Brakke, "Problematization of Nocturnal Emissions," 416–19; Leyser, "Masculinity in Flux," 103–20; Diem, *Das monastische Experiment*. My thanks to Prof. Rob Meens for referring me to these works.

131. Elliott, *Fallen Bodies*, 14–34.

132. Ibid., 2–7; J. Murray, "Gendered Souls in Sexed Bodies," 79–93.

133. Elliott, *Fallen Bodies*, 35–45.

134. Swanson, "Angels Incarnate," 160–77.

135. J. Murray, "Gendered Souls in Sexed Bodies," 80.

136. See the sources quoted below, n. 149, which are from northern France.

137. Eleazar b. Judah, *Sefer Rokeah*, #317.

138. Emanuel, "Introduction," 5.

139. See n. 41 and Biale, *Blood and Belief*, 103–4.

140. Joseph Bekhor Shor on Genesis 17:11, in Nevo, *Commentaries*, 29. Translation from S. Cohen, *Why Aren't Jewish Women?* 192; *Sefer Tosafot haShalem*, Gen. 17:11, 2:90, #7.

141. D. Berger, *Jewish-Christian Debate*, #237, 224.

142. This example reveals a fascinating continuation of an earlier stage in Christianity, when some Christian observances developed from Jewish practices.

143. Haym Soloveitchik has demonstrated the extent to which Jews depended on Christian workers within their homes: *Wine in Ashkenaz*, 177–78 [Hebrew].

144. McLaughlin, "Women and Men," 191.

145. Soloveitchik, "Religious Law and Change," 205–21, suggests this concept of a "ritual instinct," where rituals are observed more strictly than halakhic instructions might mandate.

146. This practice was also recommended among Muslims with regard to entering a mosque, but in fact it remained the lot of the most pious women. See Talmon-Heller, *Islamic Piety*, 60; M. Katz, *Body of Text*; and see Koren, *Forsaken*, 127–43.

147. It is noteworthy that medieval Christian theologians mention Jewish observance of menstrual purity; see n. 157.

148. Biller, *Handling Sin*, 17, notes several confessors who warned women to refrain from sexual intercourse during menstruation.

149. This was a well-known concept; see Shoham-Steiner, *Involuntary Marginals*, 68–69, where he detailed its popularity among medieval Christians and Jews. Also see Baumgarten, *Mothers and Children*, 203n.96.

150. This passage appears in the manuscripts of *Sefer Rokeah*, but not in its printed versions. See MS Paris héb. 1408, fol. 138a.

151. Firey, *Contrite Heart*, 79.

152. Biale, *Blood and Belief*, 105.

153. As noted above, it can be argued that the need for ten men in a quorum compounded by the relatively lax biblical stance pertaining to male impurity led to greater flexibility regarding male impurity; however, the contrast in the Christian context also carries great weight, in my view.

154. For a recent summary, see McLaughlin, "Women and Men," 191, who quotes a statement by Honorius declaring that women who had engaged in sexual intercourse with their husbands while menstruating had to stand outside the church as public penance.

155. Some thirteenth-century authorities identified lust as the cause for segregation. See Aston, "Segregation in the Church," 241, and Guilliame Durandus, *Rationale divinorum officiorum*, 18, lib. 1, cap. 1, sect. 46.

156. For example, see Solomon b. Isaac, *Sefer haOrah*, 2: #1, pp. 167, 169–70, where appropriate clothing is detailed; Eleazar b. Judah of Worms, *Sefer Rokeah*, #317, p. 199, for a discussion of clothing; and, for the case of a neighborhood where some women "reported" one among them who was not sufficiently careful in her observance of ritual purity, see Ta-Shma, "Synagogal Sanctity," 1:162–64, who quotes a manuscript response from Isaac b. Moses.

157. See n. 41.

158. See n. 165 as well as *Answers and Rulings*, ed. Kupfer, 250.

159. *SHP*, #981.

160. Baskin, "Mabat Hadash," 79–84.

161. Woolf, "Medieval Models," 279–80, has asked why menstruating women were singled out without any explanation beyond the need to preserve the sanctity of the synagogue, particularly when no other community members or types of impurity were thus scrutinized. I would suggest that in this instance, a "ritual instinct" linked to fear of blood, combined with the idea that women who observed the laws of niddah embodied Jewish distinctiveness, was operating.

162. Isaac b. Joseph, *Piskey Rabenu R"i MeCorbeil*, ed. Sha'anan, 25, #65. For the relationship between Isaac of Corbeil's and Peretz's writings, see Emanuel, *Fragments*, 199–210. This same idea was suggested by Eleazar of Worms in *Sefer Rokeah*, #317, and by Samson b. Tzadok, to whom this practice was also attributed, in *Sefer Tashbetz*, MS Paris héb. 380, fol. 185b.

163. As stated in the introduction, mandates for women's participation in prayer were more lenient than men's. Conversely, women's purity was regulated with greater strictness than men's. Taken together, these two factors could produce a multiplier effect that undermined the importance of women's presence in communal prayer services. However, as we have seen in this chapter, the level of women's participation in communal prayer was neither an automatic nor static outcome of these asymmetrically gendered teachings, as evidenced by dynamic changes that took place during the Middle Ages.

164. *SHB*, #506.

165. For a summary of this issue, see Baumgarten, "Gender."

166. Ibid.

167. Solomon b. Isaac, *Responsa Rashi*, #155; Eliezer b. Joel, *Sefer Ra'aviah*, ed. Deblytski, 4: #1050.

168. Isaac b. Moses, *Sefer Or Zaru'a*, 1: #653; For a discussion of this case and other parallels, see Baumgarten, *Mothers and Children*, 34–36; Shoham-Steiner, *Involuntary Marginals*, 236–40.

169. *SHP,* #463–65.

170. Ivan Marcus has translated the term *hasidah* as "pietist," as belonging to the Pietist "sect." Judith Baskin has understood *hasidah* as an adjective, "pious" or "saintly," "Dolce," 435. While I would reject the translation of "saintly," the other understandings are plausible, since that text portrays Dulcia as "*hasidah* and *hasudah,*" which are both adjectives of piety.

171. Dulcia lived before the establishment of a woman's synagogue in Worms. For treatment of this subject, see Baumgarten, "Gender."

172. Grünwald, "Le cimetière," 104. Given that the epitaph is poorly copied and can no longer be deciphered, I have followed Grünwald's transcription. I thank Rami Reiner for his help with this epitaph.

173. Hovav, *Maidens Love,* 466–85.

CHAPTER 2

1. For a survey of this matter, see Counihan and van Esterik, *Food and Culture*; Mintz, "Food and Eating"; following the work of Mary Douglas, see her *Purity and Danger,* 67, 115–41; and for fasting in the medieval context, see Bynum, *Holy Feast,* 1–5; L. Elliott, *Food and Feasts*; Friedenreich, *Foreigners and Their Food.*

2. Lévi-Strauss, "The Culinary Triangle," 28–35; Douglas, "Deciphering a Meal," 36–54.

3. This is very clear in migrant communities. See, for example, Diner, *Hungering for America.*

4. J. Katz, *Exclusiveness and Tolerance,* 37–47. There is no comprehensive history of the observance of the laws of *kashrut.* See Resnick, "Dietary Laws," 1–15. For a survey of these laws in late antiquity, see Friedenreich, *Foreigners and Their Food.* It is also important to note that early medieval Christianity was also preoccupied by food regulations; see Meens, "Pollution," 3–19. This topic is beyond the scope of this study, but it has hardly been addressed to date and certainly deserves further attention.

5. Caroline Bynum brought this aspect of food practices to the forefront in her *Holy Feast and Holy Fast,* 31–69; Shaw, *Burden of Flesh,* follows Bynum by discussing late antiquity. Abrahams also made this point in *Jewish Life in the Middle Ages,* 137–39, 150–53; and see J. Katz, *Exclusiveness and Tolerance.* Joel Hecker has documented the roles of food in the Jewish mystical experience in *Mystical Bodies,* especially chap. 1.

6. However, fasting practices should not be mistaken for being uniform within any given religion, social group, or locale; see Bonfil, *History and Folklore,* 172, who made this point concerning bathing.

7. Shaw, *Burden of Flesh,* 17–26; Hamilton, *Practice of Penance,* 13–23.

8. Douglas, *Purity and Danger,* 114–29; Bourdieu, *Logic,* 66–80; C. Bell, *Ritual Theory,* 94–117.

9. Shaw, *Burden of Flesh,* 220–54. Bourdieu discusses how the body both reflects and creates meaning;in *Logic,* 66–80.

10. As I noted in the introduction, I am examining the practical aspects of fasting and some of the basic beliefs associated with it rather than the mystical beliefs that were understood only by the learned.

11. On fasting in Christianity, see LeClercq, "Jeunes," 2483–2502; Clancy, "Fast and Abstinence," 847–50; and, more recently, Hundsbichler, "Fasten," 304–12, and Grün, "Fasting," 295–96, where the author talks about the triad of devout life—prayer, fasting, and alms.

12. The claim that provides the conceptual groundwork for this chapter stems from the brief statement by Israel Abrahams in *Jewish Life in the Middle Ages*: "The medieval Jew's calendar was so

studded with fasts, indeed some must have abstained from food for quite half the year." Abrahams did not document the fasts; rather, he made a quick transition by remarking, "But the feasts were more popular than fasts" (*Jewish Life*, 141), and then proceeded to outline medieval Jewish holidays. Abrahams's comment about the prevalence of fasting has been almost completely ignored to date. I would suggest that one of the reasons for giving scant attention to the fasting habits of medieval Jews was their resemblance to some of their Christian neighbors' practices, the topic of this chapter.

13. Goitein, "Ramadan the Muslim Month of Fasting," 151–71, and Vajda, "Fasting in Islam and Judaism," 133–49, discuss many fasting parallels. Muslim fasting was similar to Jewish fasting, in that Monday and Thursday fasts were also customary and no food was eaten from sunrise to sundown.

14. Greenup, "Fast and Fasting," 203–14.

15. Additional fasts have been observed to varying degrees by Jews from late antiquity to the present. Lambert, "Fasting as a Penitential Rite," 477–512; Brongers, "Fasting in Israel," 1–21.

16. Saul decreed a fast, 1 Sam. 14:24; David fasted after death of Saul, 2 Sam. 1:12; David fasted when children were ill, 2 Sam. 12:16; Moses fasted when receiving the Ten Commandments, Exod. 34:28; Daniel fasted when awaiting revelation, Dan. 10:3.

17. For example, 1 Sam. 14:29–30; Isaiah 58:3–6. The latter passage has a major liturgical placement, traditionally being read on Yom Kippur.

18. For example, among the numerous passages that praise fasting in *Sefer Hasidim*, I have found only one that quotes verses that discourage fasting in the Bible, *SHP*, #1284. It tells of a person who approaches a sage in great sorrow and suggests taking upon himself a tremendous burden (or penance) with the hope of being saved after the penance is completed. The sage does not advise against penance but rather seems to imply that penance will not help in this case. This selection is unusual since it implies that the petitioner is mentally ill. Even though the verses against fasting from Isaiah are quoted, fasting is not actually the subject of objection.

19. Mishnah Ta'anit outlines this procedure, and see Hacham, "Ta'aniyot Tzibur"; Levine, *Communal Fasts*.

20. See Tropper, "Motivations for Fasting."

21. These fasts were permitted on the Sabbath as the ultimate solution for a dream that held a bad omen. BT Ta'anit 12b states that "fasting is as efficacious for a bad dream as fire is for straw" and then explains that one who fasts on the Sabbath must fast an additional day because fasting on the Sabbath was not viewed favorably.

22. This fast was hinted at in BT Shevu'ot 20a and is explicitly mentioned in medieval sources; see *SHP*, #292. For fasting in the Talmud, see Büchler, *Types of Jewish-Palestinian Piety*; Zimmels, "Nach Talmudische Fasttage," 599–614; Greenup, "Fasts and Fasting," 203–14.

23. Zimmels, "Nach Talmudische Fasttage," 599–614.

24. *Megillat Ta'anit*, 19–36.

25. Diamond, *Holy Men*.

26. BT Berakhot 17a. This passage was repeated by medieval authors; see, for example, Solomon b. Isaac, *Siddur Rashi*, #544.

27. BT Berakhot 32b.

28. Tropper, *Motivation for Fasting*, 92–94.

29. Diamond, *Holy Men*, 121–32.

30. For discussions of women fasting on Yom Kippur and other fasts, see BT Yoma 82a and BT Megillah 14b.

31. This story is mentioned in several texts, for example PT Sanhedrin 6:6, but none of the texts include an explanation of why this woman was hanged.

32. Another detail in the description of Miriam is that she was hanging by her nipples.

33. PT Hagigah 2:2. The issues of hypocrisy and pretension are discussed at length in Chapter 6.

34. One was supposed to declare a fast as part of the daily supplication included in afternoon prayers. This is evident in medieval siddurim as well; see, for example, MS Paris héb 326, fol. 30a.

35. A lengthy prayer accompanied this. See Eleazar b. Judah, *Sefer Rokeah*, MS Paris héb. 363, fol. 58b; and in print, #21.

36. Thus Mordekhai is described wearing sackcloth in Esther 4:1–2. The expression "his sackcloth and his fast" (*sako veta'anito*) appears numerous times; see n. 203. *Midrash Shoher Tov* on Psalms suggested that the most important aspect of a fast was its public nature; see 22:5.

37. There was a mechanism to cancel a fast after it was taken on, in the event that it was forgotten or a legitimate reason to postpone it arose; see BT Ta'anit 12b and discussions of this issue in medieval commentaries on the Talmud.

38. Lev. 16:29–34.

39. Beer, "On Penances of Penitents," 159–81 and see n. 15.

40. PT Hagigah 2:2.

41. BT Berakhot 32b; BT Ta'anit 11a (and see Chapter 3).

42. BT Ta'anit, 12b; Diamond, *Holy Men*, 121–32.

43. See Gartner, "Fasting on Rosh haShanah," 125–62; Gilat and Gartner, "Fasting on the Sabbath," 1–15. As both of these authors demonstrate, fasting on the Sabbath was a hallmark of some Jews during the third and fourth centuries; also see Williams, "Being a Jew in Rome," 8–18; Zilberstein, "Role of Jews," 35–39; Bonfil, *History and Folklore*, 125–27.

44. For this connection, see Arbesmann, "Fasting and Prophecy," 50. Fasting was a typical method for chasing away demons and a sign of mourning. Musurillo, "Problem of Ascetical Fasting," 23–24, points out that the words "fast" and "mourn" are often used interchangeably in fourth-century texts.

45. Shaw, *Burden of Flesh*. Shaw argues that medieval Eucharistic piety replaces virginal piety. See also Grimm, *From Feasting to Fasting*. This relates to the discussion in Chapter 1 about angels and women.

46. See Augustinus, Sermones 198.2 *PL* 38:1025; idem, *Sermo 400 De utilitate ieiunii*, 3,3 PL 40, 708; Musurillo, "Problem of Ascetical Fasting," 23–24; Downey, "Too Much of Too Little," 89–127; Bynum, *Holy Feast*, 35, 42–47, 78–85, 96–100, 237–44; and within Jewish sources, see Jonah b. Abraham Gerondi, *Sefer Sod haTeshuvah*, 314; and idem, *Sefer Sha'arei Teshuvah*, 4, #12.

47. Vauchez, *Sainthood*; Bynum, *Holy Feast*.

48. Bynum, *Holy Feast*, and see below 91–94.

49. Vauchez, *Sainthood*, 191, 204.

50. This is not to say that there weren't bishops who were typified by their lavish practices, but such ascetic behavior also represented useful social capital. Ibid., 288, 301–2.

51. D. Elliott, *Spiritual Marriage*, 195–265.

52. Interestingly, no history of lay fasting in medieval Christian Europe has yet been written, probably because fasting was just a single component of the penance and confession, longstanding areas of scholarly inquiry. For the early modern period, see Fagan, *Fish on Friday*, where the author suggests the far-reaching consequences of these eating practices. For a history of penance and confession, see Delumeau, *L'aveu et le pardon*; Judic, "*Confessio*," 147–68; Bériou, "La confession," 261–82; Gy, "Les définitions," 283–96; Mansfield, *Humiliation of Sinners*; Biller and Minnis, *Handling Sin*; Hamilton, *Practice of Penance*; and the recent collection of articles in Firey, *New History of Penance*.

53. This practice provides evidence of a shared tradition since it is based on the biblical narrative about Mount Sinai in Exodus 20.

54. Hamilton, *Practice of Penance*, 180–81; Mansfield, *Humiliation of Sinners*, 152.

55. Hundsbichler, "Fastenpraxis," 306.

56. For a discussion of this trio—fasting, prayer, and almsgiving—in Judaism, see Schmelzer, "Penitence," 291–90; and in Christianity, see nn. 11 and 46.

57. Loeb, "La controverse," 1:247–50; Merchavia, *Church*, 249–90. These accusations led to what Amos Funkenstein has defined as a revolution in Jewish-Christian relations that resulted from the discovery of Jewish reliance on the Talmud rather than the Bible; see Funkenstein, *Perceptions*, 172–200. For a recent discussion of this dispute, see Galinsky, "Different Hebrew Versions," 109–40.

58. For a description of this event, see Merchavia, *Church*, 227–315, esp. 249–81. For other discussions of the Paris dispute of 1240, see J. Cohen, *Living Letters*, 317–30.

59. Loeb, "La controverse," 3:53–54, quoting MS Paris, Lat. 16558, fol. 217v.

60. BT Ta'anit 11a.

61. Merchavia, *Church*, 282. I have not found a discussion of this accusation in other scholarly works.

62. *Otzar haGe'onim*, Yom Tov, #20–24.

63. Ibid., #47; *Otzar haGe'onim*, Ta'anit 11b, #20–25.

64. *Otzar haGe'onim*, Taan'it 13b, #45; *Otzar haGe'onim* Berakhot 32b, #196.

65. Hacham, *Ta'aniyot*, 98. See also Elizur, *Wherefore Have We Fasted?*, 1–3, 41–44.

66. Soloveitchik, *Wine in Ashkenaz*, 321–27.

67. Elizur, *Wherefore Have We Fasted?*

68. Elizur catalogs all liturgical manuscripts where these lists appear; ibid., 50–58. See, for example, *Siddur Rashi*, #541; MS Paris héb. 644, fol. 30a, fourteenth century. See also Leiman, "Scroll of Fasts," 174–95.

69. Kanarfogel, *Peering*, 38–39, summarizes the references to this practice. As he demonstrates, almost every medieval Ashkenazic source discusses this issue. It seems the eleventh- and twelfth-century rabbinic practice of fasting on Rosh haShanah became less accepted over the course of the Middle Ages. See also Grossman, *Early Sages of Ashkenaz*, 287.

70. Kanarfogel suggested that these ascetic rabbis were all connected to the Mainz Yeshiva; *Peering*, 40.

71. Abraham of Bohemia was also known for his pious fasting. See Urbach, *Tosaphists*, 402, and also Eleazar b. Judah, *Sefer Rokeah*, #130. Urbach proposes that this Abraham may be Abraham Hildik, whose customs informed fasting in many communities. See Spitzer, "Minhagei R. Avraham Hildik," 196–202.

72. Kanarfogel, *Peering*, 43. Yom Tov of Joigny (d. 1191; England) was also known for pious fasting; Kanarfogel, *Peering*, 40.

73. Isaac b. Moses, *Sefer Or Zaru'a*, 2: #257; *Responsa of R. Meir*, ed. Emanuel, #40.

74. For an anecdote about a woman who could not fast, see Yuval, *Scholars in Their Time*, 54.

75. See a discussion of this in Eleazar b. Judah, *Sefer Rokeah*, Ninth of Ab, #310. Eleazar calls his predecessors "holy ones" (*kedoshim*); see also #311.

76. Kanarfogel, *Peering*, 110–15.

77. The expression he used originates in late antiquity; see n. 27.

78. Samson b. Tzadok, *Sefer Tashbetz*, #121. He attributes this comment to an unnamed ga'on but tempers its force by noting: "I have also found written in another responsum that one who eats for the sake of heaven (*leshem shamayim*) should be blessed and also one who fasts for the sake of heaven so that he will not become frivolous from excessive eating and drinking should also be granted all blessings."

79. See Chapter 7 for further discussion of the presence of Palestinian customs in medieval Ashkenaz.

80. Fasts were undertaken in three-day cycles of a consecutive Monday-Thursday-Monday series. An interval would be taken until the next round of fasting started. Instructions for fasting during a drought are detailed in Mishnah Ta'anit, chap. 2.

81. Evidence of this can be seen in Peretz's discussion of a man who did not participate in these public fasts: MS Paris héb 406, fol. 14, #28.

82. Eliezer b. Joel haLevi, *Sefer Ra'aviah*, 2:#206 (in Elul), p. #561 (part 3). See also Isaac b. Moses, *Sefer Or Zaru'a*, 2: #257, where he mentions women fasting during Elul, as well as Moses b. Yekutiel, *Sefer haTadir*, #38, 250; and *Responsa of R. Meir*, ed. Emanuel, #365. For additional references, see Har-Shefi, "Women and Halakhah," 200–212.

83. These weeks roughly coincide with the reading of the first portions of Exodus according to the annual Torah reading cycle in synagogue. It was customary to say special prayers and fast in Monday-Thursday-Monday (*bahab*) cycles during this season.

84. This prayer is appended to the New Moon blessing in the Nuremberg *Memorbuch*, MS Mainz 19, fol. 44b.

85. This prayer belongs to a genre that became popular during the Middle Ages, known by its common opening phrase, "*mi sheberakh*." For the history of this little-studied liturgical category, see Menahem Ya'ari, "Mi Sheberakh," 118–30, 233–35. This genre originated in the ge'onic period and was developed and expanded in the Middle Ages; it appears often in siddurim.

86. See n. 84.

87. For example, MS National Library Heb 34°1114, (1419), fols. 190a–241b, contains multiple poems of this sort. This manuscript can be accessed online: http://dlib.nli.org.il/R/-?func=dbin-jump-full&object_id=239270&silo_library=GEN01.

88. For example, MS National Library Heb 34°1114, (1419), fol. 24a.

89. The Hebrew here is *tallitot*, but the author may be discussing generic shawls rather than ritual garments.

90. E. Haverkamp, *Hebräische Berichte*, 473.

91. Ibid., 483. The report about Prague explains: "And those three days they fasted and cried and their prayer was received and they were saved by the merciful God."

92. *Sefer Gezerot Ashkenaz*, 126; this source is discussed in Urbach, *Tosaphists*, 1:112.

93. After the Blois murder accusation, Urbach, *Tosaphists*, 112; after the burning of the Talmud, Shalom b. Isaac of Neustadt, *Decisions and Customs*, 165, #515; after the Black Death, Urbach, *Tosaphists*, 616. And Eleazar b. Judah mentioned the communal fasts that were customary in Worms, *Sefer Rokeah*, #212, including the fast of Rosh Hodesh Sivan and its liturgical insertions.

94. I thank Pinchas Roth for introducing me to this text, found in MS Vienna Nationalbibliothek 152, fol. 2a. See Kanarfogel, *Peering*, 171.

95. *SHP*, #292, 295, 296, 301, 302, 960, 1025; Shalom b. Isaac of Neustadt, *Decisions and Customs*, #457.

96. Jacob b. Judah of London, *Sefer Etz Hayim*, Hilkhot Ta'aniyot, 371.

97. MS Paris héb. 644 fol. 21a is a nice example of this ritual; see also MS Jerusalem, National Library, 34°1114, fols. 23a–b. It is noteworthy that the biblical examples of Saul and Jonathan are included in the prayer for this occasion.

98. BT Shabbat 11a.

99. This was already noted in the Talmud, BT Ta'anit 12b, and it was customary in North Africa as well; see Maimonides, *Mishneh Torah*, Hilkhot Ta'anit, chap. 1, halakhah 12. And see n. 209.

100. Eleazar b. Judah, *Sefer Rokeah*, #353, and see MS Paris héb. 363, fol. 170a, where it is noted that brides, grooms, and their family members would fast on the couple's wedding day, in contrast to the printed version where only the bridegroom is mentioned as fasting. On the popularity of this custom, see Stahl, "Inyanei Nissuin," 57–70.

101. *Responsa of R. Meir*, ed. Emanuel, #308.

102. Ibid., #331.

103. Ibid., #139; Kanarfogel, "Returning to the Community," 71, 75–78.

104. See MS Oxford Bodl. Or. 135 (1466), fol. 307a, for the story of Nathan deTzuzita, where they fast for three days, and see Kushelevsky, *Penalty and Temptation*, 142–68.

105. Although early modern sources refer to women fasting before immersion in the mikveh, I have not found evidence for this practice in medieval texts. For the early modern period, see Rivkah bat Meir, *Meneket Rivkah*, 89. It is noteworthy that there is significant evidence of early modern Jewish women fasting as well; see Hovav, *Maidens Love*, 148–49, where she also notes the critique of this practice in the seventeenth-century *Brantspiegel*. See also the early modern epitaph on the tombstone of Mikhele, daughter of Seligman Horowitz (sixteenth century, Prague), which reads: "Here a decent women is buried, she tortured her soul with fasts and abstinence." Monlash, *Epitaphs*, 179–80, #76, and compare to Gluckel's tombstone as described in Davis, *Women on the Margins*, 48; Hovav, *Maidens Love*, 253. See also the epitaph of Rachel, daughter of Manoah, that records that "she fasted most of her days, except for Sabbaths and holidays" (1541). Monlash, *Epitaphs*, 43.

106. *Sefer Gezerot Ashkenaz*, 47, and see n. 91 above.

107. The talmudic discussion of this subject contains a disagreement about when children become obligated to fast, from ages 10–11 or 8–9; BT Yoma 82b and *Massekhet Sofrim*, chap. 18, halakha 5.

108. Rashi, BT Arakhin 2b, s.v. "shehigi'a lehinukh"; Rashi, BT Megillah, 19b, s.v. "bame devarim amurim lekatan shelo higi'a."

109. They are noted as *hamitparshim betahara ubeprishut yisrael*—literally, "they who separate themselves for the sake of purity and the distinctiveness of Israel." The fact that these individuals remain unidentified seems to suggest that such pietists were not limited communally or geographically to Hasidei Ashkenaz.

110. Jacob b. Meir, *Sefer haYashar*, Helek haTeshuvot, #51b and 52b, 108, 111.

111. See Eleazar b. Judah, *Sefer Rokeah*, #217, 108, and Aaron b. Jacob haCohen, *Sefer Orhot Hayim*, Hilkhot Yom haKippurim, #15, 233; Tosafot, BT Nazir 28b, s.v. "bno," where the discussion differentiates between the education of young boys and girls, but addresses fasting for both in equivalent terms.

112. Aaron notes in the laws of Yom Kippur that parents who force their children to fast are mistaken and should be reproached, but when discussing children's education this same author mentions (without criticism) that three- to five-year-olds were trained to fast in select circumstances. The custom is attributed to the Jewish community of Jerusalem, in Aaron b. Jacob haCohen, *Orhot Hayim*, 2: #3, 25. Interestingly, Judah the Pious objects to parents who force their children to fast, *SHP*, #1931.

113. At a graduate student presentation in the winter of 1999, I included women's fasting in the context of women's piety. Subsequently, Avraham Grossman and his student Bitha Har-Shefi have also presented their findings on fasting among medieval Jewish women. As will be evident, my analysis is somewhat different. I am indebted to both authors and especially to Har-Shefi for the list of sources they provided: Har-Shefi, "Women and Halakhah," 200–213; Grossman, *Pious and Rebellious*, 192–94. (The Hebrew version of Grossman's book contains a more extensive section on this topic, 334–37.)

114. Har-Shefi, "Women and Halakhah".

115. Solomon b. Isaac, *Sefer Likutei haPardes*, 3b; Eliezer b. Joel, *Sefer Ra'aviah*, 2: Rosh haShanah, #529, p. 206, and #547, p. 245.

116. Simhah b. Samuel, *Mahzor Vitry*, Horowitz edition, 372; *Responsa Rashi*, #128; Moses Parnas, *Sefer haParnas*, #113; MS Paris héb. 363 includes numerous mentions of women and men fasting, fols. 56b, 58b, 60a–b, 98a; MS Paris Héb. 326, 29b–30b.

117. There are several exceptions: see Meir b. Barukh, *She'elot uTeshuvot* (Lvov), #442, and idem, *Teshuvot, Pesakim uMinhagim*, Cahana edition 2: #113, p. 105.

118. For example, fasting after birth, see Simhah b. Samuel, *Mahzor Vitry*, Horowitz edition, 372; and, for a female convert on the day of her conversion, Jacob and Gershom the Circumcisers, *Sefer Zikhron Brit*, 136.

119. Simhah b. Samuel, *Mahzor Vitry*, Horowitz edition, 210.

120. This kind of fasting continued into early modern times. See Goldberg, *Crossing*, 158.

121. *SHP*, #1722. Parents who fast are also mentioned in *SHP*, #343, 942, 1283, 1284.

122. Isaac b. Joseph, "Piskey R. Isaac of Corbeil," #57.

123. Samson b. Tzadok, *Sefer Tashbetz*, #107–17.

124. Meir b. Baruch, *She'elot uTeshuvot* (Lvov), #442. Maharil writes about a similar case: Jacob b. Moellin, *Sefer Maharil: Minhagim,* Hilkhot Tish'a beAv, #10.

125. *Mordekhai*, Shabbat, "Yetziot hashabbat," Remez 229.

126. A woman fasting in response to a dream is also mentioned by Shalom b. Isaac of Neustadt, *Decisions and Customs*, #456.

127. BT Yoma 82a.

128. Meir b. Barukh, *She'elot uTeshuvot* (Lvov), #161.

129. This is mentioned in numerous sources; see, for example, Jacob b. Moses Moellin, *Shut Maharil*, #45.

130. See the discussion p. 61.

131. *Midrash Tehillim*, #25; Solomon b. Isaac, *Siddur Rashi*, #544.

132. Soncino translates *hasid* as "saint," a term that I do not use as it is not directly applicable to medieval Jewish life; and see Raspe, "Jewish Saints," 26–35.

133. It is noteworthy that this midrash does not depict Adam as having been celibate during that period.

134. Attributed in the text to Jeremiah.

135. BT Eruvin 18b; Beer, "On Penances"; Levinson, "Conceptualization of the Yetzer," 21.

136. See Fishman, *Becoming the People*, 196.

137. See n. 56.

138. Goering, "Scholastic Turn," 219–37; idem, *William de Montibus,* 58–99.

139. Lea, *History of Auricular Confession*; Vogel, *Pecheur et la penitence*; and a discussion of several other works in Goering, "Scholastic Turn," 219–20.

140. Biller and Minnis, *Handling Sin*, 4–13.

141. Goering, "Scholastic Turn," 219–37.

142. Meens, "Historiography of Early Medieval Penance," 89–94; Biller, "Popular Religion," 231.

143. Lester, *Creating Cistercian Nuns*, 36–43, 107–10.

144. Wagner, "Cum aliquis," 204–6.

145. Murray, "Confession as a Historical Source," 275–322; and especially idem, "Confession before 1215," 51–81. Much of Firey's volume, *New History of Penance*, responds to this essay.

146. Hamilton, *Practice of Penance*, 173–206; Biller, "Confession," 13–23.

147. Meens, "Frequency," 52.

148. Wagner, "Cum aliquis," 204.

149. De Jong, *Penitential State*, 245–49; Firey, *Contrite Heart*, 206; Judic, "Confessio," 169–90.

150. Mansfield, *Humiliation of Sinners*; De Jong, "What Was Public," 863–902; Hamilton, *Practice of Penance*, 207–10.

151. A number of scholars have sought to emphasize that some of the changes that were formally introduced by Lateran IV were in place beforehand; see Goering, "Scholastic Turn," 236–37.

152. See, for example, the varieties of penance detailed by McNeill and Gamer, *Medieval Handbooks*, as well as in the compilation presented by Vogel, *Pecheur et la penitence*.

153. Schmelzer, "Penitence," 291–99.

154. BT Berakhot 10b. The notion that prayer, charity, and fasting were substitutes for sacrifice was inherent to both of these instructions.

155. Judah b. Samuel, *Sefer Gematriyot*, Vayakhel, #10, 535.

156. Baer, "Social-Religious Tendency," 18–20; Soloveitchik, "Three Themes"; and Marcus, *Piety and Society*, 2–17, who summarizes these ideas.

157. Marcus, *Piety and Society*, 21–36; Soloveitchik, "Three Themes," 311–25.

158. Marcus, *Piety and Society*, 98–100; Kanarfogel, *Peering*, 26, 54; Fishman, "Rhineland Pietist Approaches," 313–31.

159. Soloveitchik, "Three Themes," 311–25; Marcus, *Piety and Society*, 29–35.

160. Hekhalot literature was written in the Byzantine context and resurfaced in Italian and then in German settings. See Schäfer, "The Ideal of Piety," 9–23; and see Chapter 7.

161. BT Yoma 86b.

162. Marcus, *Piety and Society*, 46–48; Dan, *Safrut haMusar*, 129–33.

163. Eleazar calls the fourth kind of penance *teshuvat haba'ah*, though it is not described here. This is the only mode of penance Marcus did not translate into English (*Piety and Society*, 42). It means one should challenge oneself by seeking an opportunity to repeat the same sin in order to avoid it, to prove that repentance is complete. See Dan, "Note on the History," 224–25.

164. See, for example, formulae for penance recommended by Judah b. Samuel, *SHP*, #18, 19, 37, 38–39, 43; by his disciple Eleazar b. Judah, *Sefer Rokeah*, Hilkhot Teshuvah, #1–29; and by Rabbi Judah in manuscript as well, MS héb. Paris 1408, fol. 140a, where the duration of penance ranges from forty days to multiple years for various sins. This manuscript also emphasized that the penitent should wear black clothes, a feature that I did not find in the printed versions of *Sefer Hasidim*. Such fasts are also attested in late medieval sources; see, for example, Israel b. Petahyah Isserlein, *Terumat haDeshen*, #180, 194.

165. Eleazar b. Judah, *Sefer Rokeah*, #23; *SHP*, #176.

166. In addition to Marcus, *Piety and Society*, 109–32, see Dan, "Note on the History," 221–29. Dan emphasized the differences between Spanish atonement and Ashkenazic penance.

167. This position has been debated by scholars for over a century. Some recent studies have returned to debate the extent to which Hasidei Ashkenaz represented a separatist group or an intrinsically Jewish phenomenon. See the introduction.

168. Marcus, *Piety and Society*, 109.

169. Marcus, "Hasidei Ashkenaz Private Penitentials," 57–83. As noted above, this matter was also debated by Christians, although confession to a confessor remained central in Christianity. See nn. 52, 148–50.

170. *SHB*, #387. The practice of fasting when children were sick or in danger has continued into modernity; see Hovav, *Maidens Love*, 242–46.

171. *SHP*, #280. This same idea comes across in *SHB*, #387, which notes the efficacy of fasting. Compare to *SHP*, #225, where the recommended fast period is eight days. This directive was adopted by Eliezer b. Samuel of Metz, *Sefer Yere'im*, #102; see the discussion of this passage in Soloveitchik, "Piety," 466.

172. *SHP*, #43. It is noteworthy that if a fast did not achieve the desired effect of breaking the body, then it was considered sinful; see MS Paris héb. 363, fol. 59a.

173. *SHP*, #289.

174. Muslims also fasted on eclipses; see Talmon-Heller, *Islamic Piety*, 263.

175. This text uses two words that each mean "fast," *tzom* and *ta'anit*, that seem to be used interchangeably in the medieval texts. In practice, however, only some fasts required complete abstinence from food and drink, whereas others were defined by refraining from specific comestibles. The inclusion of both Hebrew words may be intended to stress this distinction.

176. *SHP*, #301 and parallel, #962.

177. *SHP*, #1566.

178. Marcus, *Piety and Society*, 79; *SHP*, #19.

179. See Marcus, *Piety and Society*, 79.

180. See Chapter 6, p. 199.

181. Eleazar b. Judah, *Sefer Rokeah*, Hilkhot Teshuvah, #23. Compare this recommendation to one instruction of penance for murder from twelfth-century Provence: *Sifran shel Rishonim*, #42. I thank Judah Galinsky and Pinchas Roth for bringing this text to my attention.

182. Eleazar b. Judah, Sefer Rokeah, Hilkhot Teshuvah, #27. My translation is based on Marcus, *Piety and Society*, 127.

183. Eleazar b. Judah, *Sefer Rokeah*, Hilkhot Teshuvah, #12.

184. Marcus, *Piety and Society*, 121–29; Elboim, *Repentance*, 48–49.

185. Marcus, "Kiddush Hashem BeAshkenaz," 131–48.

186. See n. 46 above and *Genesis Rabbah*, ed. Albeck, 44.12, 434. See also *Midrash Tanhuma*, ed. Zundel, Noah, #8, and Spiegel, "Berur beDivrei haPaytan," 271–90.

187. Jacob b. Moses Moellin, *Sefer Maharil*, Seder Musaf shel Rosh haShanah, #1 (294).

188. Schmelzer, "Penitence," 296–99.

189. For a discussion of Hasidei Ashkenaz's conception of sin, see Kiel, "Moral and Religious," 85–101.

190. Marcus outlines many of these manuscripts in his article; see n. 169. In their studies, Marcus and Elboim documented the far-reaching effects of these penitential prescriptions well into the early modern period; see Elboim, *Repentance*, 48–49, as well as Fram, *Ideals*, 62. For example, the late thirteenth-century German composition *Sefer haMaskil* (often called *Sefer Hasidut Katan*) exemplifies the prominence of penitential ideas in Ashkenazic culture in that era. See also Honig, "Al Mahadurato haHadashah," 196–240.

191. Kanarfogel, *Peering*, 43. And see MS Camb. Add. 3127 fols. 165b–166b, and MS Parma 407, fol. 236d.

192. This has been noted by Kanarfogel in "German Pietism"; Urbach, *Tospahists*, 387; J. Katz, *Exclusiveness and Tolerance*, 102–5. This framework was further detailed by his followers, Peretz and Yonah of Girondi. We await Judah Galinsky's work on this topic.

193. Isaac b. Joseph, *Semak*, #53.

194. Kanarfogel, *Peering*, 59–63. Another student from Evreux, Jonah Gerondi, was also known for his piety and his support for ascetic practices. For further discussion, see Ta-Shma, "Hasidut Ashkenaz beSefarad," 165–73, and the contrasting interpretation presented by Soloveitchik, "Piety," 455–93.

195. This is especially evident in Peretz's instructions, and see his "Piskei Rabbenu Peretz," 10–15.

196. Ibid., #8, 9, 28.

197. Ibid.

198. This was a common theme; see Isaac b. Joseph, *Semak*, #175 and n. 41 above.

199. "Piskei Rabbenu Peretz," #8, 9, 28; Isaac b. Joseph of Corbeil, "Piskey R. Isaac of Corbeil" (Lange), #13, 40, 57, 65.

200. Tosafot, BT Avodah Zarah 34a, s.v. "mit'anin lesha'ot."

201. For this practice of Peretz, see n. 81 above. This idea is related to the custom that one who was not fasting could not serve as a prayer leader (*sheliah tzibbur*).

202. Jacob b. Asher, *Arba'ah Turim, Orah Haim*, #292.

203. *Genesis Rabbah* (Vilna), #84; see also #85 where all are repenting. *Bamidbar Rabbah* 13 states: "For Reuben was a repenter (*ba'al teshuvah*) who wore sackcloth and fasted." This description is quoted in many midrashim. And see Rashi, Gen. 37:30, s.v. "veyashav."

204. BT Bava Kamma 82a, s.v. "mi garam," and *SHB*, #167.

205. Extinguishing fire violated the laws against manipulating flames on the Sabbath.

206. Isaac b. Moses, *Sefer Or Zaru'a*, 2: Hilkhot Erev Shabbat, #38; see also *SHP*, #1777.

207. MS Oxford Bodl. Mich. 84 (784), fol. 24a: "And some instruct them to atone for this (extinguishing a fire on the Sabbath) and then when there is a fire instruct them to extinguish it." This source also transmits the story of a fast that was declared in Regensburg following a death. See also MS Paris héb. 380, fol. 26c.

208. Meaning that this individual was bearing an item under conditions where the action of carrying objects was forbidden.

209. Samson b. Tzadok, *Sefer Tashbetz*, #68.

210. He is accredited with this response in one manuscript (MS Oxford Bodl. Opp. 77 [844], fol. 80d, #185), whereas this same response is attributed to his late thirteenth-century peer Judah Katz elsewhere (MS Hamburg 45, fol. 166c, #128). See *Responsa of R. Meir*, ed. Emanuel, #739, n. 1, and the text in #374.

211. South of Magdeburg.

212. *Responsa of R. Meir* ed. Emanuel, #739, n. 1, notes late medieval responsa that follow these directives.

213. Isaac b. Moses, *Sefer Or Zaru'a*, Hilkhot Erev Shabbat, #34.

214. Medieval Jews customarily lit more than two candles for the Sabbath; see Susan Nashman Fraiman's dissertation, "The Sabbath Light: Development of Vessels and Customs of Kindling Sabbath Lamps Among the Jews of Ashkenaz" (Hebrew University of Jerusalem, 2013). See also my "Tale of a Christian Matron," 83–99.

215. Jacob b. Moses Moellin, *Sefer Maharil: Minhagim*, Shabbat, #1.

216. Judah of London, *Sefer Etz Haim*, 2:277. The assignment of penance for adultery is raised frequently in medieval sources. Though examination of this material goes beyond the context of this discussion, one obvious question for such a study would be whether men and women's transgressions were treated in similar terms.

217. *Sefer haNiyar*, 166–67, hagahah.

218. According to one version, after a day of fasting, her evening meal should not include meat or wine. *Responsa of R. Meir*, ed. Emanuel, #742, n. 2.

219. Ibid., #376; see also Urbach, "Al Grimat Mavet," 322–23.

220. *Responsa of R. Meir*, ed. Emanuel, #108–9.

221. Ibid., 740–41, #375.

222. Ibid., 743, #377.

223. MS Oxford, Bodl. Opp. Add. 34 (641), fol. 57v in the margins. I thank Prof. Ivan Marcus for referring me to this manuscript.

224. Some writers objected to young women fasting this way lest it endanger their ability to become and remain pregnant; see Jacob Moellin's discussion of this penance, *Shut Maharil*, #45.

225. It is evident from early modern sources that women were accustomed to fasting; Hovav, *Maidens Love*, 256–60. This penance recurs in a number of early modern Polish sources that discuss women who consulted rabbis regarding penance, a practice that casts doubt on the abandonment of the role of the sage who counseled those wishing to atone for their sins. For example, Aharon haLevi of Barcelona, *Sefer Hidushei haRoeh*, 22–23, and "Teshuvot haBah" in *Asufat Ge'onim heHadash* (Jerusalem, 2010), 3. My thanks to Simcha Emanuel, who referred me to these sources.

226. See n. 223.

227. Num. 30: 3–16.

228. Ibid.

229. Mira Balberg, "Elu nedarim." I thank Balberg for sharing her thesis with me.

230. "Piskei Rabbenu Peretz," #65 and see also #40.

231. The broad topic of religious vows deserves further research, especially in the context of penance, as is evidenced in the Yom Kippur liturgy and related medieval commentaries.

232. The Hebrew is *ma'aseh*, "happening" or "event."

233. The previous evening was included in the fast day since the Jewish calendar marks the new day at sunset.

234. Tosafot, BT Avodah Zarah 34a, s.v. "mitanin leshaot." This concept has been debated in many of the Ashkenazic halakhic compendia; Henshke, "Conclusion of *Megillat Ta'anit*," 119–62.

235. See MS Paris héb. 380, fol. 26a, where the difference between the positions of Rabbenu Tam and Peretz is discussed. This matter is central in contemporary Christian thought as well; see Chapter 6, n. 85. See also Solomon b. Isaac, *Sefer haOrah*, #71, where it is stated that fasts must be declared.

236. As Haym Soloveitchik has remarked, in "Piety," 480–82, this practice of fasting remained current long after Judah's lifetime, even well after some of his other recommendations had been abandoned.

237. It is also worthwhile to inquire whether the role of confessor disappeared fully, as Marcus suggests. Medieval sources as well as early modern responsa refer to individuals who seek guidance to determine their penance; see the examples in the next sections.

238. Elizur, *Wherefore Have We Fasted?*, 1–12.

239. Ibid., 257–58.

240. Ibid. This position forms a central motif throughout this study.

241. Rafeld, "Ta'anit Esther," 4:204–20; Gartner, "Fasting on Rosh haShanah"; and Kanarfogel, *Peering*, 110–15, where he discusses the difficulties related to fasting on Rosh haShanah.

242. See Chapter 7.

243. Soloveitchik, "Three Themes"; idem, "Piety"; Marcus, *Piety and Society*, 7–10; idem, "Hierarchies," 7–26, where Marcus outlined his position more succinctly; and especially Schäfer, "Ideal of Piety," 9–23. Most recently, see Dan, "Note on the History," 221–28. I find Dan's argument difficult to accept as he is searching for a Christian source that is parallel to the writings of Hasidei Ashkenaz. Rather than seeking out textual comparison, I am examining practices and how they may resemble one another. For a different approach, see Baer, "Religious-Social Tendency," 1–50.

244. Grossman, "*He Shall Rule over You?*," 180–85, 216–19, has demonstrated the extent to which Jews living in southern Europe and under Islam were more open to the notion of celibacy, whereas for the Jews of northern Europe distancing themselves from celibacy was a defining feature of Jewish society.

245. Firey, "Blushing Before the Judge," 173–200.

246. Chiffoleau, "Sur la pratique," 351, discusses the high value placed on evidentiary proof in the thirteenth century; and see D. Elliott, *Proving Woman*.

247. Just as Bynum herself suggests a far broader foundation for cross-cultural comparison, I too understand radical fasting practices among ascetic Christian women as a useful comparison for contextualizing medieval Jewish fasting. Bynum, *Holy Feast*, 33–69.

248. P. 66.

249. This practice has been documented by Har-Shefi, "Women and Halakhah," 200–206. Also see the sources from the early twelfth through the fifteenth centuries from both Germany and northern France that discuss this as a distinctly Ashkenazic practice: Simha b. Samuel, *Mahzor Vitry*, Horowitz edition, #345; Solomon b. Isaac, *Sefer Likutei Pardes*, 50b; Eliezer b. Joel (Ra'aviah), *Sefer Ra'aviah*, ed. Deblytski, 2:Hilkhot Rosh haShanah, #529.

250. Simone Roux's study of medieval Paris illustrates the ongoing contact among neighbors in medieval cities: *Paris*, 29–37, 164–94.

251. De Jong describes this process and its publicity by concentrating on Louis the Pious, in *Penitential State*, 46–49. During his rule, Louis granted one of the earliest privileges to Jews. The existence of a community in Lyons has been documented from that time; *Gallia Judaica*, 306–10.

252. De Jong, *Penitential State*, 43–50; Mansfield, *Humiliation of Sinners*, 132, 155; Hamilton, *Practice of Penance*, 185.

253. Soloveitchik, "Three Themes," 320.

254. Berger, "Generation of Scholarship," 8.

255. A. Rubin, "Concept of Repentance," 161–76; Fishman, "Penitential System," 201–29.

256. A. Rubin, "Concept of Repentance," 168–75. This verbal link can be seen in passage 236 of *Sefer Nizzahon Vetus*, where *beicht* is the term for "confession," and see below, 265

257. Fishman, "Penitential System," esp. 214–18. Although Burchard lived significantly before the period under discussion, his work remained popular in the twelfth and thirteenth centuries. See Austin, "Jurisprudence," 931–33, 954–56.

258. Published recently in *Responsa of R. Meir*, ed. Emanuel, #394. I thank Simcha Emanuel for discussing this issue with me and for directing me to this source.

259. Ibid.

260. For example, when a Jew disclosed another Jew's actions to someone outside the community, as in this case involving a Christian authority. See Eleazar b. Judah, *Sefer Rokeah*, #27, and also #28 where a list of severe sins appears; however, no distinction is made between those that require private versus public confession.

261. *Responsa of R. Meir*, ed. Emanuel, #156.

262. I thank Rachel Furst for raising the consideration of this liturgical selection from Kol Nidrei and discussing it with me. See Hacohen, "Mihu Avaryan?" and Meir b. Barukh, *Teshuvot, Pesakim* (Cahana), 1: #552, p. 304; Samson b. Tzadok, *Sefer Tashbetz*, #131, and in its edition by Shmuel Menahem Shneorson (Jerusalem, 2005), #296. For a full list of parallels in late medieval Europe, see Hacohen, "Mihu Avaryan?" n. 8.

263. Mordekhai b. Hillel, Yoma, #725.

264. Berger notes the discussion in the Talmud where the question of public confession in the context of Yom Kippur appears: BT Yoma 86b. The medieval texts query how to mediate between two contradictory biblical statements: "He that covers sin shall not prosper" (Prov. 28:13) and "Blessed is he ... whose sin is covered" (Ps. 32:1). This question is unsurprising in light of the centrality of confession in Christian practice; D. Berger, *Jewish-Christian Debate*, 339.

265. D. Berger, *Jewish-Christian Debate*, 339. Simcha Emanuel brought my attention to Menahem haMeiri's book on atonement; see Mirsky, *Hibbur haTeshuva leRabbenu Menahem haMeiri*, where many ideas that are current in other northern European literature appear.

266. Buc, "David's Adultery," 101–3. Berger has also mentioned Meir of Narbonne's critique of confession in his *Milhemet Mitzvah* (MS Parma 2749, fol. 85a–b), where it is suggested that only older men and women confess; see D. Berger, *Jewish-Christian Debate*, 339.

267. D. Berger, *Jewish-Christian Debate*, #236, p. 223.

268. Schulenberg, *Forgetful*, 445n.116; Bynum, *Jesus as Mother*, 15–16. Innocent III's objection to women who perfom these actions: *cum igitur id absonum sit pariter et absurdum*. Innocentis III, *Nova quaedam nuper, Opera Omni*, PL 216: 356 A–B, 187, is comparable to Meir of Rothenburg's condemnation of women serving in an official capacity in a circumcision ritual as an "ugly deed": Samson b. Tzadok, *Sefer Tashbetz*, #397.

269. J. C. Scott, *Domination*.

270. *SHP*, #68.

271. People who feared becoming irritable are warned against fasting in the Talmud; see BT Ta'anit 10b.

272. This echoes the talmudic instruction that teachers of children should not fast, lest they be cross with their pupils. PT Demai, 7:3; *SHP*, #617; Mordekhai b. Hillel, Bava Mezi'a 76b.

273. *SHP*, #68, compare to de Pizan, *Les livre des trois vertus*, 2, XII, p. 219, and 3, IX, p. 208, who stated that farmer's wives and servants should not fast since their strength was required for their work. This suggests that everyone else was expected to fast.

274. *SHP*, #66, 1555.

275. The sixteenth-century author Rivkah Tiktiner discusses women who would fast to purify themselves during the day before they immersed in the mikveh and critiques this practice because of its weakening effect. See Rivkah bat Meir, *Meneket Rivkah*, 89.

276. There is explicit evidence of this in a medieval source from fourteenth-century Provence, Menahem haMeiri, *Perush haMeiri on Proverbs*, chap. 31. I have not found such evidence in German sources, but we do see that women were responsible for feeding their children. For example, Dulcia, the wife of Eleazar of Worms, is described in these terms; see *Sefer Gezerot Ashkenaz*, 166. Certainly women were responsible for feeding their children, a task that is reflected in medieval halakhic rulings that allow mothers to prepare food for their children in circumstances when cooking would normally not be permitted; see Baumgarten, *Mothers and Children*, 159–60.

277. Grossman, *Pious and Rebellious*, 192; Har-Shefi, "Women and Halakhah," 210–11; Hovav, *Maidens Love*, 260.

278. Bynum, *Holy Feast*, 219–44.

279. Thomas de Chobham, *Summa confessorum*, Article 4, q.VIIa, c. 11, p. 157; translated by Dyan Elliott in "Dress as Mediator," 288. See also Elliott's discussion of the subordinate nature of women in relation to their husbands in *Spiritual Marriage*, 208–10.

280. Biller, "The Common Woman," 134.

281. Caesarius, *Dialogus Miraculorum*, vol. 1, p. 165, III, 46: "De muliere in confessione se iustificante, cui prudens confessor ostendit plura mortalia peccata habere. Monachus: Hermannus Decanus Bonnensis, quando plebanus fuit apud sanctum Martinum in Colonia, venit ad eum mulier quaedam tempore quadragesimali peccata sua confiteri. Flectens coram eo genua, quicquid se boni meminerat commisse, coepit enumerare, et cum Pharisaeo evangelico iustificare se, dicens: Domine, tot sextis feriis soleo per annum in pane et aqua ieiunare, eleemosynas meas dare, ecclesiam frequentare, et multa in hunc modum." My translation is based on Biller, "Confession in the Middle Ages: Introduction," 1–33, at 4.

282. *Ménagier*, 55. I thank Shulamith Shahar for our ongoing discussions of this composition.

283. Ibid., 66.

284. Ibid., 84.

285. See n. 273.

286. Yassif, "Saint and the Bishop," 305–40; Baumgarten, "Shared Stories"; Oring, "Legendry," 27–66.

287. *SHP*, #1357. These stories were also discussed by Marcus, "Jewish-Christian Symbiosis," 489.

288. See below, p. 98.

289. For discussions of Jews entering churches to conduct business, see Shatzmiller, "Church Articles," 93–102; idem, *Cultural Exchange*, 42–44.

290. This story appeared in Meir b. Barukh, *Sefer Hilkhot Semahot*, #89, and see comments on it in Grossman, *Early Sages of France*, 503–4; also see Emanuel, *Fragments of the Tablets*, 309–10, and, more recently, Shoham-Steiner, "Vitam finivit infilecem," 71–90.

291. MS Paris héb.1408, fol. 140a.

292. This expression is based on the biblical Esther, who was depicted standing in the chamber of her husband, King Ahasuerus.

293. Judah b. Asher, *Teshuvot Zikhron Yehuda*, #92.

294. Kanarfogel, "Returning to the Jewish Community," 69–98.

295. Ibid., 71; Yerushalmi, "Inquisition," 363–67.

296. Jordan, *French Monarchy and the Jews*, 140–41.

297. Isaac b. Moses, *Sefer Or Zaru'a*, Part 1: She'elot uTeshuvot, #112.

298. Eleazar b. Judah, *Sefer Rokeah*, #31.

299. Herman's autobiography has been the subject of much discussion, including some doubts regarding its veracity. See Morrison in Herman-Judah, *A Short Account*, 39–75; Saltman, "Hermann's Opusculum," 31–56, has questioned its authenticity; and, for current discussions see Berger, "Mission to the Jews," 586–87; J. Cohen, *Living Letters*, 289–305; and, most recently, Schmitt, *Conversion*, 25–61.

300. Herman-Judah, *A Short Account*, 92, ll. 1128–29.

301. Clancy, "Fast and Abstinence," 848–49; LeClercq, "Jeunes," 2487.

302. Meir b. Yekutiel Cohen, *Hagahot Maimoniyot*, Hilkhot Shofar, #1; Jacob Moellin, *Sefer Maharil: Minhagim*, 262.

303. Ember Days were parallel to the *tekufah*—the solstices and equinoxes that were also observed by Jews; see Ta-Shma, "Danger of Drinking Water," 21–32; Baumgarten, "Remember That Glorious Girl," 180–209; Carlebach, *Palaces of Time*, 160–88. About the Ember Days, see Mershman, "Ember Days."

304. Sperber, *Minhagei Yisrael*, 2:41–42.

305. Though fasting "for hours" appears in the Talmud (BT Ta'anit 11b–12a), this practice is hardly mentioned in texts from the High Middle Ages. Rather, medieval authorities repeatedly emphasize that only complete fasts were considered valid; see n. 324.

306. Rafeld, "Ta'anit Esther," 4:204–20.

307. For discussions of fasts that fell on Fridays, see Solomon b. Isaac, *Teshuvot Rashi*, #128; Eleazar b. Judah, *Sefer Rokeah*, #36; Isaac b. Joseph, *Semak* #96 and Peretz's comments there.

308. Rafeld, "Ta'anit Esther," 4:206, 218–20.

309. This was a regular rule; see BT Ta'anit, 11b–13a.

310. Isaac of Corbeil, *Semak*, #96; Rosh, Ta'anit, chap. 1, #13–15.

311. P. 93.

312. Jacob b. Moses Moellin, *Maharil: Minhagim*, 262.

313. Ibid.

314. Ibid., n. 225.

315. Biller and Minnis, "Introduction," *Handling Sin*, 3–15.

316. Marcus, *Rituals of Childhood*, has emphasized the polemical elements in this process, as has Yuval, *Two Nations*. Must this mechanism be polemical in nature? I would argue that its nature depended on the circumstances involved, while acknowledging that such adaptations often contained polemical elements.

317. On the roles of Christians within Jewish homes, see Baumgarten, *Mothers and Children*, 134–44; on the need for servants in all medieval urban households, see Roux, *Paris*, 119–42.

318. Berger, *Jewish-Christian Debate*, 44; Carlebach, *Palaces of Time*, 141–59. For medieval Hebrew calendars and Jewish awareness of Christian holidays, see Ms British Library 11639, fol. 542b; Oxford Bodleian Ms Heb. D. 11 (2797), fols. 2b–3a; 372a–b; Jerusalem, MS 8° 3857, fols. 32b–33a; MS Cambridge Add. 3127, fols. 345a–351b.

319. It is interesting that despite his awareness of the calendar, he got this wrong.

320. Fagan, *Fish on Friday*.

321. For shared ovens, see Zimmer, "Baking Practices," 141–62. For markets, see Fagan, *Fish on Fridays*, 145–46.

322. *SHB*, #52.

323. This quotation comes from the narrative in Eleazar of Worms's treatise on penance. It was printed at the end of Meir b. Barukh's response, and see his *Shut Maharam* (Prague).

324. This fascinating topic in the history of halakhah deserves further scholarly attention. On the whole, Jews fasted until evening, although half-day fasts were recommended as well; see n. 305 above.

325. Bonfil, *History and Folklore*, 171.

326. Sperber, *Minhagei Yisrael*, 2:41–42, 3:80.

327. Bourdieu, *Logic*, 66–80.

328. Kashrut, wine, and laws pertaining to meat and bread are all examples of these restrictions. See Resnick, "Dietary Laws"; Schremer, "Realism," 97–143; Grayzel, *Church and the Jews*; Soloveitchik, *Wine in Ashkenaz*, 198–200, 370–71; and Baumgarten, *Mothers and Children*, 99–100, each outline different issues that have to do with food.

329. Admittedly, Jews and Christians in late antiquity also fasted, as did medieval Muslims and Jews living under Islam. Goitein noted private fasts as well, in *Mediterranean Society*, 2:301. He also made note of a pious proselyte who passed his days in fasting and prayer and only took food before daybreak, 2:307. Goitein remarked how unusually strict this behavior was in relation to normative Jewish practice. He includes other examples of fasting when traveling, 3:193; and as a tool used by women to exert pressure on their families, 3:196. In the latter case, he detailed that when a young couple experienced strife in their relationship, the woman vowed not to eat during the daytime until the issue was settled, and her husband responded, "If you do not break your fast, I shall come home neither on the Sabbath nor any other day." See also Talmon-Heller, *Islamic Piety*, 254–55, and Goitein, *Mediterranean Society*, 2:53, 97, 165, who discuss the practice of giving alms and fasting as paired actions.

330. Hamilton, *Practice of Penance*, 42; Bériou, Berlioz, and Longère, *Prier*, 164–91, esp. 180–83; Fishman, "Penitential System," 210n.34.

331. This idea was suggested in BT Berakhot 17a, which can be seen as a foundational text for considering piety at large, not just for fasting. It was further reinforced by the oft-quoted assertion that fasting was a greater deed than charity; see, for example, MS Paris héb. 646, 23b, where the practice of fasting is outlined; Moses b. Jacob, *Semag*, Aseh #3, who cites the Talmud about the importance of fasting; Asher b. Yehiel, *Ta'anit*, chap. 1, #15, 1, where Rosh first quoted a talmudic teaching that one

who fasted was effectively sacrificing himself and then remarked that he did not understand how giving charity could atone for sin or substitute for a promised fast.

332. Isolated incidents from other European Jewish centers provide evidence of a culture of repentance in those locales as well. For example, a Provençal source from the twelfth century tells of a murderer whose prescribed punishment featured repentance rituals that included flagellation and fasting; see *Sifran shel Rishonim*, #42.

333. Bynum, *Holy Feast*, 68–69.

CHAPTER 3

1. Though named Yehiel and called Rosh, this man is not related to Yehiel, the father of the famous medieval rabbi Asher b. Yehiel, known as Rosh, who was active in Spain after leaving Germany.

2. Grünwald, "Le cimetière de Worms."

3. Grünwald, ibid., published this epitaph in the feminine form. In our private correspondence on this text, Michael Brocke has recently suggested that these deeds are being attributed to Marat Yokheved's father. While this is feasible, I am unfamiliar with other gravestones that record deeds carried out by a parent of the deceased. The issue of whether Marat Yokheved or her father built the cemeteries and synagogue does not affect the content of this chapter.

4. The involvement of women in building projects was not unusual within Jewish communities. See Brooten, *Women Leaders*, 103–38; Safrai, "Women in the Ancient Synagogue," 39–50, esp. 41–42; and in medieval times see Salfeld, *Martyrologium*, 289.

5. See Gray, "Redemptive Almsgiving," 144–84.

6. Salfeld, *Martyrologium*, 87–90, quoted only a selection from the original manuscript that he had published in its entirety in a German transcription with Stern. See Salfeld and Stern, "Nürnberg im Mittelalter," 190–205; Barzen, "Nürnberger Memorbuch."

7. For a comment on the efficacy of charity, see *Tosafot haShalem*, Exod. 28:32, 194, where the exegete explains that each penny given to charity accrues to form a larger sum; he ends by saying of anyone who gives charity that "his righteousness stands forever."

8. Studies of charity in other locales draw on a more detailed surviving corpus than the sources transmitted from northern Europe. See S. D. Goitein, *Mediterranean Society*, 2:91–143; M. Cohen, *Poverty and Charity*, 243–52; idem, *Voice of the Poor*. In contrast to the Ashkenazic material, with its emphasis on donors, the texts from the Cairo Genizah convey far more information about the recipients of charity. For Spain, see Galinsky, "Commemoration"; idem, "Jewish Charitable Bequests"; Assis, *Golden Age of Aragonese Jewry*, 242–46. For Middle Eastern communities in the early modern period, see Ben-Naeh, "Poverty," 151–92.

9. For later examples, see Weinberg, *Memorbücher der jüdischen*; Greenblatt, "Community's Memory," 228–99. Whereas there are a variety of early modern examples, the Nürnberg Memorbuch is the sole medieval example and as a result it is impossible to determine if other records existed or what they consisted of.

10. The last entries are for 1346. We have no records of the period right before the Black Death.

11. For changes after the Black Death, see the introduction to this volume and Goldberg, *Crossing the Jabbok*.

12. Salfeld, *Martyrologium*, 85–87, transcribed them.

13. Salfeld and Stern, "Die israelitische Bevölkerung."

14. See n. 6; Lowe, *Memorbook of Nurnberg*; Neubauer, "Memorbuch de Mayence," 1–30; Lévi,

"Commémoration des âmes," 43–60; Freehof, "Hazkarath Neshamoth," 179–89; Yuval, "Donations," 182–97; Stow, "Jewish Family," 1085–110; Pomerance, "Bekannt in den Toren," 33–53.

15. As noted in the manuscript where Isaac b. Samuel is listed among the dead, see Salfeld, *Martyrologium*, 174n.3

16. Kressel, "Eliakim Carmoly," 5:189.

17. Twelve per year, down from the prior average of 27.51; see Yuval, "Donations," 186nn.24–25.

18. The last five years recorded before the Black Death were also noted individually.

19. Toch, "Numismatics."

20. Galinsky, "Public Charity"

21. Barzen, "Meaning of *Tzedakkah*," 7–17.

22. In the exceptional cases when a donor is mentioned more than once, the list usually indicates that the deceased was wealthy, as in the example of Kalonymus b. Abraham (discussed later in this chapter).

23. Pro anima charity seems to have been specifically defined as such, but significant additional charitable collections were also conducted within communities, whether on an obligatory or voluntary basis.

24. Despite the individual nature of each donation, as a whole they are indicative of a community norm. For a similar conclusion regarding Christian necrologies, see Neiske, "Ordnung der Memoria," 127–38.

25. Greenblatt, "Community's Memory," 232–54; Yuval, "Donations," 186; most recently Galinsky, "Public Charity."

26. Their appearance at the head of this list seems to indicate their status among the earliest members of the community, but see Salfeld, *Martyrologium*, 289n.2.

27. Ibid., 85.

28. Freehof, "Hazkarath Neshamoth."

29. This question is related to other memorial rituals; e.g., if relatives were saying kaddish on a yahrzeit, they might have wished to hear the name of the deceased read in synagogue.

30. Greenblatt, "Community's Memory," 232–40.

31. The word *tzedakah* may be translated as "charity" or "righteousness" here.

32. For understandings of this concept in the biblical period, see G. Anderson, "Almsgiving," 121–31.

33. Gray, "Redemptive Almsgiving," 144–84; Satlow, "Fruit."

34. Garrison, *Redemptive Almsgiving*, 10; Finn, *Almsgiving*.

35. Urbach, "Political and Social Tendencies," 1–27.

36. Gray, "Redemptive Almsgiving," 183–84. Compare to Brown, "Rise and Fall," 80–101; idem, *Poverty*, 45–73.

37. 2 Corinthians 9:5–12.

38. Satlow, "Fruit," 244–77. Satlow and Gray differ on their interpretations of the realities of late antiquity, but for my purposes they are equally helpful.

39. M. Rubin, *Charity*, 54–98, and see 237–88 for examples of the various forms of charity from that era.

40. Israel Lévi traced the development of this idea, "Commémoration," 54–60.

41. Gray, "Redemptive Almsgiving," 180–84; Satlow, "Fruit," 272–75.

42. Zimmer, "Minhag Matnat Yad"; Galinsky, "Public Charity," see n.87.

43. Charity was given in private as well, especially donations of food. Following the general course that I have taken throughout this book, I do not focus here on charity that was given in private

or in secret (*matan baseter*). For such charity see Maimonides, "Laws of Charity" (Matanot Aniyim), Mishneh Torah, chaps. 9–10. Texts from medieval Ashkenaz lack such discussions of matan baseter, even after Maimonidean codes reached northern Europe. For example, Jonah b. Abraham Gerondi's *Iggeret haTeshuvah,* #16; #59, #62–63, one of the most developed discussions of charity in medieval Europe, and Moses b. Isaac, *Sefer Or Zaru'a,* "Laws of Charity."

44. The formula from the Nürnberg Memorbuch was repeated in many other memorbücher; see Salfeld, *Martyrologium,* 85–86, as well as Weinberg, *Memorbücher.*

45. See above, pp. 106–7.

46. Some sources discuss charities that conflate voluntary support for the poor with communal decrees; see Galinsky, "Custom," 203–32.

47. As Steven Epstein has noted, charitable gifts at death are not necessarily indicators of lifelong patterns: generous lifelong donors may have been parsimonious at death and vice versa. S. Epstein, *Wills and Wealth,* 137.

48. MS Mainz IR Anon. 19 (73457 PH 2828), fol. 44b. The pagination of the manuscript is quite inconsistent. I have tried to the best of my ability to follow the numbers that appear on some pages of the manuscript and those suggested in Salfeld and Stern, *Die israelitische Bevölkerung.*

49. I thank Debra Kaplan for suggesting this formulation to me. The fact that some Jews donated to communities beyond their own can be seen as evidence of the affinity among medieval Jewish communities.

50. BT Bava Kama 119a.

51. S. Epstein, Wills and Wealth, 170, has commented that gifts for the soul were often decided on the deathbed and suggested that "social responsibility and guilt may have played a major part in the decision but so too did a variety of family ties, personal habit, the advice of others or sheer caprice." See also McLaughlin, "Consorting with Saints," 269–328.

52. Lauwers, *Mémoire des ancêtres,* 474–90; Loup-Lemaitre, "Un livre vivant."

53. McLaughlin, "Consorting with Saints," 559nn.129–43; Huyghebaert, *Documents nécrologiques,* 13–14; Anengendt, "*Donationes pro anima,*" 131–54; and also see Head, "Early Medieval Transformation," 155–60, where Head follows Rosenwein, *To Be the Neighbor,* 136–41, and refers to pro anima charity as a "countergift."

54. Lévi, "Commémoration," 58–60. In their transcription and discussion of the memorbuch, Stern and Salfeld, "Nürnberg," note: "In Anlage, Form und Ausführung den katholischen Nekrologien ähnlich sind" (96).

55. Originally published in 1925.

56. Algazi, "Doing Things," 9–28, has surveyed many of the discussions of Mauss as well as critiques of his theory.

57. Ibid.; Davis, *Gift,* esp. 100–123; Howell, *Commerce,* 151–59, 190–207; Geary, *Living with the Dead,* 77–92.

58. Pitt-Rivers, "The Anthropology of Honour," 1–17; Howell, *Commerce,* 191.

59. Anengendt, "*Donationes pro anima,*" 132–33.

60. Ibid., 141–45, 150–53; Chiffoleau, "Sur l'usage obsessional de la messe," 235–56.

61. Numerous books on this topic have been edited in Germany and France; these books were edited and described by Jean Loup-Lemaitre,"Un livre vivant," 92–94, and also Oexle, "Memoria"; and the other essays in that volume by Schmid and Wollasch, *Memoria.* For a recent discussion of them, see Greene, "Un cimetière," 208; Neiske, "Ordnung der Memoria," 127–38. See also Rosenthal, *Purchase of Paradise.* Uwe Ludwig used the necrologies from the cloister Novalese in Reichenau to figure out details concerning the place, in "Gedenklisten," 32–55, esp. 43–46; Algazi, "Doing Things"; Lauwers, *Mémoire des ancêtres,* 177–200.

62. For a description of these books, see Greene, "Un cimetière"; Magnani, "Almsgiving," 111–21.

63. McLaughlin, *Consorting with Saints*, 148–54, explains why rich patrons supported monasteries rather than local parish churches in the tenth and eleventh centuries. She also proposed that nuns were not considered as good an investment as monks.

64. McLaughlin, "Consorting with Saints," 161.

65. Ibid.; Oexle "Memoria und Memorialbild," 384–440.

66. Marcus, *Rituals*.

67. For the history of the Musaf service, see Elbogen, *Jewish Liturgy*, 97–99.

68. See above, pp. 104–5.

69. McLaughlin, *Consorting with Saints*, 173–76.

70. Bouchard, *Sword, Miter and Cloister*, 171–246; White, *Custom*, 87–97; Rosenwein, *To Be the Neighbor*; McLaughlin, *Consorting with Saints*, 136–66.

71. Brodman, *Charity and Religion*, 209.

72. Mollat, *Poor*, 41–42.

73. See Farmer, *Surviving Poverty*, 105–64. The importance of face-to-face relations and reciprocity is discussed by Parry, "Gift," 468–69, and Davis, *Gift*, 4–8.

74. Gold, *Lady and the Virgin*, 130; Lynch, *Individuals*, 93–95.

75. Lynch, *Individuals*, 95; Chiffoleau, *La comptabilité*, 277–78.

76. The obituaries began in the ninth century as described by McLaughlin, *Consorting with Saints*, 92–96.

77. For example, Judah b. Jacob haCohen heHasid; Salfeld and Stern, *Die israelitische Bevölkerung*, 101.

78. For example, Minna, the wife of Jacob b. the martyr Joseph, is also listed as the daughter of the martyr Moshe. In contrast, Yente is described as the wife of David b. Joseph, without any mention of her father. Salfeld, *Martyrologium*, 140 and 138, respectively.

79. McLaughlin, *Consorting with Saints*.

80. Magnani, "Almsgiving," 111–21; Avril, "Paroisse," 53–68. See also the essays in Schmid and Wollasch, *Memoria*, esp. Angenendt, "Theologie und Liturgie," 79–199; Oexle, "Memoria und Memorialbild," 384–440.

81. Chiffoleau, *La comptabilité*; 213–88, 323–55; McLaughlin, *Consorting with Saints*, 65–75.

82. BT Sukkah 49b.

83. Ibid., and Peretz b. Elijah, "Piskei Rabbenu Peretz," 12: "When one of his household members was sick or when he himself was very ill, Isaac would vow money according to the sin. For it says: 'A man may freely offer every day a guilt-offering' (BT Keritot 18a), he fell ill on account of that sin. And you should atone for a guilt-offering with silver coins, with a silver shekel equaling four dinars from Tournes or two Parisian coins."

84. *Sefer haMa'asim*, MS Oxford Bodl. Or. 135 (1466), fol. 251b.

85. *SHP*, #880.

86. Simhah b. Samuel, *Mahzor Vitry*, Horowitz edition, #190.

87. I thank Judah Galinsky for generously sharing his unpublished work on yizkor customs with me. The sources in this section are quoted in his work, and his discussion has guided my presentation.

88. Galinsky quotes several such responsa: see Isaac b. Moses, *Sefer Or Zaru'a* (Machon Yerushalayim), #20 and its parallels, Meir b. Barukh, *Responsa Meir of Rothenburg* (Prague), #474; Meir b. Yekutiel Cohen, *Hagahot Maimoniyot*, Sefer Kinyan, #19. According to *Sefer Or Zaru'a*, this woman had pledged this sum to charity, a portion of which had already been entrusted to Eliezer of Metz. See also *Responsa of R. Meir*, ed. Emanuel, #441, section 5.

89. As in a case reported in a responsa by Meir of Rothenburg where Lady Maimona pledges money for lighting the oil lamp in the synagogue as well as a kiddush cup; *Responsa of R. Meir*, ed. Emanuel, #998. An English summary can be found in Agus, *Rabbi Meir of Rothenburg*, #678.

90. Isaac b. Moses, *Sefer Or Zaru'a*, Hilkhot Tzedakah, #8: "So it would offer atonement for him, his charity would precede him."

91. Goldberg, *Crossing the Jabbok*, 106–10; Horowitz, "Jews of Europe," 271–81.

92. Another subject that merits greater elaboration relates to the periodization of Christian libri memoriales—which reached their apex as a genre in the thirteenth century—and how ties between liturgy and the dead were transformed into "commodities." In contrast, our knowledge of Jewish memorbuch start from the late thirteenth century, and no indication of commoditization emerges until the early modern period. See McLaughlin, "Consorting with Saints," 329–68.

93. Carmoly erroneously attributed this break in the list to 1283. See Salfeld and Stern's correction of this error, "Die israelitische Bevölkerung," 96, which demonstrates that martyrs appear on the 1298 list of the deceased and that entries after 1298 include individuals identified as children of those martyrs.

94. Salfeld, *Martyrologium*, 170–80nn.628

95. As Salfeld notes, ibid., 175, 298, these lists correspond with one another. Thus parents of children of martyrs are named on the list of martyrs; for example, Gutrat daughter of Chakim the martyr.

96. Ibid., 86.

97. This is hinted at in the benedictions as well, as the benediction for martyrs does not mention any donation whereas that for others does; MS Mainz IR Anon. 19, fol. 47a–b.

98. Such entries almost exclusively mention men.

99. See n. 6.

100. For these terms see Salfed, *Martyrologium*, XXIV–XXV.

101. Prior to 1298: Yehonatan (fol. 47b); Rabbah and his wife, Tziona (fol. 47b); Gershom b. Moses, who was noted as a martyr (fol. 48b); and Isaac b. Samuel (fol. 53b). None of these individuals appear on the list of the dead from 1298. After 1298: Pinhas b. Menahem the martyr (*hekadosh*); Joseph b. Isaac, who was tortured and died a martyr; Joseph b. Asher the martyr; Issaskhar b. Ovadyah; Bella daughter of Moses; Gutlin, daughter of Yehiel the Cohen; Rachel, whose father's name goes unmentioned; and Simhah b. Nathan. Pinhas and Joseph, described as the children of martyrs, were probably the offspring of men who were killed in 1298.

102. Nürnberg Memorbuch, 48a.

103. A similar phenomenon is seen in documentation from the building of the Chartres Cathedral; see Fassler, *Virgin of Chartres*, 179–208. I thank Prof. Fassler for discussing this matter with me.

104. This explanation has been suggested in research on Christian charity as well, where increasing specificity regarding the purposes of the charity appears during the thirteenth century. See Galinsky, "Jewish Charitable Bequests," 434–35 and the notes there.

105. For an explanation of this currency from Schwäbisch Hall, see pp. 124–25.

106. Nürnberg Memorbuch fol. 51a.

107. The number of Torah scrolls mentioned here is surprisingly high. Why would a community need so many Torah scrolls? A similar enigma is prompted by Eleazar b. Judah's eulogy of his wife, Dulcia, where he lauds her for having sewn (or overseen the sewing of) forty Torah scrolls; *Sefer Gezerot Ashkenaz, 167*

108. As I discuss later in this chapter, sixteen couples donated money alone; thus all material items donated by couples came from the other thirty.

109. Tykocinski, "Nürnberg," *Germania Judaica* 1:250. However, the earliest known Jewish

tombstone from Nürnberg is dated 1273; see Avneri, *Germania Judaica* II/2: 602, evidence that raises questions about the accuracy of Tykoncinski's proposed timeframe. I thank Rainer Barzen for pointing this out to me. Tykocinski also suggests a decline in the emphasis on giving to the synagogue and education, the sick and the poor at that time; however, the numbers do not support this. I have not found evidence to explain where interments took place before the dedication of the cemetery.

110. This idea exists in Maimonides, "Laws of Charity," and is repeated in thirteenth-century northern French compendia. See Maimonides, *Mishneh Torah,* Seder Zera'im, Hilkhot Matanot Aniyim, chap. 7; MS Montefiore 136, fols. 27b–d. This approach is also mentioned in a fourteenth-century manuscript of *Sefer Tashbetz,* where the copyist states that gabbaim are authorized to redirect the purpose of a donation; see MS Oxford Bodl. Opp. 642 (1106), fol. 351a, #155. The agency granted to church officials regarding the purposes of donations is included in medieval Christian records; see Greene, "Un cimetière," 327–30; Loup-Lemaitre, "Nécrologes et obituaries," 201–18. This trend is congruent with the increasing number of Christians who wrote wills starting in the late twelfth century; see Lorcin, "Testament," 143–56.

111. The gender disparity before 1298 in regard to lighting is very puzzling, as women often made candles.

112. For a comparative perspective, see le Belvec, "Role des femmes," 171–90; Cullum, "Gendering Charity," 135–51.

113. Toch, "Numismatics," 237–42.

114. As was common in Europe: 1 *litra* (pound) = 20 *dinarim* (solidi) = 240 *peshitin* (denarii); ibid.

115. A. Haverkamp, *Medieval Germany,* 298–300. "Hal" is a root for salt found in Celtic, and many medieval centers of salt production contained this root in their names, such as Hallstaat in today's central Austria or Halle in northern Germany.

116. This coin is the subject of Toch's article, "Numismatics."

117. Ibid., 238. Haverkamp, *Medieval Germany,* 298–300, has demonstrated how this coin became stronger over time.

118. Comparing the figures listed here to parallel medieval texts is one method for gauging their relative value. For example, the value of a medieval ketubbah was set according to a community-wide norm that Irving Agus and Avraham Freimann have demonstrated, with the standard ketubbah worth 100 pounds, dowries at 50 pounds. See Agus, "Development of the Money," 221–56; idem, "Standard Ketubah," 225–32; Freimann, "Amount of the Ketubbah," 371–85; Yuval, "HaHesderim haKaspiyim," 192–94. All these scholars have suggested that medieval ketubbot were set at exceptionally high sums.

119. Nürnberg Memorbuch, 44b.

120. For a history of the Rintfleisch attacks, see Müller, "*Erez gezerah,*" 251–54.

121. As remarked in Salfeld and Stern, "Die israelitische Bevölkerung," 96.

122. Lacking any indication as to whether those who gave small donations were considered impoverished, one can only wonder if the poor were expected to give. Perhaps future research will help clarify measures of medieval poverty.

123. This is evident in Christian discussions of similar donations. See Loup-Lemaitre, "Nécrologes et obituaries," 207–8; idem, "Un livre vivant," 92–94; Althoff, "Variability of Rituals," 71–88; Stoddard Tuten, "Fashion and Benefaction," 41–62, esp. 48–51; Rasmussen, "Monastic Benefactors," 77–90; Greene, "Un cimetière," 308–9, 327.

124. For a survey of naming practices, see L. Assaf, "Language of Names," 149–60.

125. Salfeld and Stern, "Die israelitische Bevölkerung," 104.

126. And see n. 128.

127. Salfeld and Stern, "Die israelitische Bevölkerung," 117.

128. No standard vocabulary for signifying age is evident in these entries. Girls are called *habetulah* (the virgin) or *hana'arah*, whereas boys are each referred to as *hana'ar*. Each of these terms indicates that they died in youth. See Salfeld and Stern, ibid., for the girls, by name and page number: Maimona and Guta, 106; Hannah, 110; Rivka, 122; Minna, 123; Lipheit, 124; Sprinza, 136; Zeruya, 142; Hannah, 145; Riza and Gutheil, 146; Sara, 154; Mija, 156. For the boys, designation as *hana'ar* appears on almost every page.

129. Yuval already commented on this feature in the entries after 1346: "Donations," 188n.34.

130. BT Bava Kama 119a.

131. For a discussion of the implications of this category, see Hauptman, *Rereading the Rabbis*, 77–102.

132. BT Bava Kama 119a.

133. Gray, "Married Women," 168–212. The following paragraphs outline recent research by Gray and other scholars, including Grossman and Baskin.

134. On marriage age, see Grossman, *Pious and Rebellious*, 33–48.

135. Children will also be discussed, but there is far less extant information on them.

136. This is also true outside the realm of charity, for example when discussing the assets that women brought into their marriages.

137. The question of women taking oaths underwent many changes in the Middle Ages as well; see Grossman, *Pious and Rebellious,* 117–22. We await Rachel Furst's study on this issue.

138. BT Bava Kama 119a.

139. MS Parma Palatina 2757, fol. 114b.

140. This idea has been confirmed by the well-documented life of Glückel of Hamel, who lived well after the period examined here. Living in seventeenth-century Germany, Glückel was an active partner alongside her husband in their business until, after his death, she took the lead role and supervised her sons and sons-in-law, who became her business partners: see Davis, *Women on the Margins*, 5–62; Turniyansky, *Glikl,* "Introduction," 39–44. While this early modern reality seems to continue medieval circumstances, the need to determine the extent to which this memoir characterizes the medieval Jewish family business remains.

141. See Toch, *Economic History,* 215–30, 248.

142. The extent of their ability to do business deserves further attention. For now see Agus, *Heroic Age*, 1:256–419; Jordan, "Jews on Top," 39–56; Grossman, *Pious and Rebellious*, 117–22; Gray, "Married Women"; and Baumgarten, "Charitable Like Abigail."

143. Grossman, *Pious and Rebellious*, 118–19.

144. Eliezer b. Nathan, *Sefer Ra'avan*, response #115, and idem, *Sefer Ra'avan*, Piskei Bava Kama 191a.

145. Eliezer b. Nathan, *Sefer Ra'avan*, Piskei Bava Kama 191a s.v. "velokhin." And see Gray's discussion of these texts, "Married Women," 188–96.

146. Jordan, "Women on Top"; Hoyle, "The Bonds That Bind," 119–29; Grossman, *Pious and Rebellious*, 114–22.

147. *Sefer Gezerot Ashkenaz,* 97; Ephraim b. Jacob of Bonn, *Sefer Zekhirah,* 30–34; and see Einbinder, "Pulcellina of Blois," 34–37.

148. Our earliest extant tax records—from the late thirteenth through fifteenth centuries—include a significant number of women. For these lists see Loeb, "Le role des juifs," 61–71; Toch, "Jüdische Frau in Erwerbsleben," 37–48; Keil, "Business Success," 103–23. As would be expected, only women from households without a male member appear in such records; therefore, tax lists lack any evidence of married women and their involvements in business. However, the frequent mention of

women in a large variety of businesses points to their active role. See the compelling analysis of non-Jewish women in the Paris tax lists in Roux, *Paris in the Middle Ages*, 148–55.

149. It was agreed that women could testify regarding financial matters, and see note 137.

150. This is a more general phenomenon relating to the role of the Talmud in thirteenth-century halakhic discourse. Fishman, *Becoming the People*, 121–54.

151. See, for example, MS Paris héb. 326 (23495), fol. 71b; Samson b. Tzadok, *Sefer Tashbetz*, #153; Asher b. Yehiel, *Shut haRosh*, #13, section 11.

152. Isaac b. Moses, *Sefer Or Zaru'a*, Piskei Bava Kama, 3: #468.

153. Ibid.; Moses b. Jacob, *Semag*, Aseh #162; Isaac b. Joseph, *Semak*, #247.

154. Samson b. Tzadok, *Sefer Tashbetz*, #153, and in many manuscripts: Ms Parma 1033, fol. 101b, MS Oxford Bodl. Opp. Add. Fol. 34 (641), fol. 84b; MS Oxford Bodl. Opp. 641 (1106), fol. 101b.; Asher b. Yehiel, *Shut haRosh*, Rule 13, #11.

155. See Baumgarten, "Charitable Like Abigail."

156. Cullum, "And Her Name Was Charite," 204.

157. See Table 4.

158. As Loup-Lemaitre has noted, this right had to be acquired: "Nécrologues et obituaries," 207.

159. Jordan, "Women on Top."

160. S. Epstein, *Wills and Wealth*, 141. Interesting statistics, though less relevant to the evidence from Nürnberg, were collected by Cullum, "And Her Name Was Charite."

161. An interesting comparison can be made to fourteenth-century wills written in Latin from Catalonia, as shown in Robert Burns's analysis of four Jewish women's wills from 1306. One was signed by the testator's husband, and in two others the testator had appointed her husband as the executor of her will. It is noteworthy that three of these four wills include pro anima donations; Burns, *Jews in the Notarial Culture*, 100–117. Alternatively, perhaps these wives did not need seek permission at all; Galinsky, "And It Is for the Glory," 113–31.

162. For example, Avraham b. Ephraim, *Compendium*, 103, where children contest their mother's gift.

163. Although a change may have occurred between the early and late thirteenth century, it is not indicated by this data.

164. One comment in a discussion on women's control of money in an early fourteenth-century manuscript from northern France provides additional evidence of attention to the subject of women's authority over financial assets, MS Cambridge Add. 3127, fol. 166b. Isaac of Corbeil is reported to have given women responsibility over a certain portion of their family assets. He is reputed to have advised: "Making women responsible for 100 dinars or pounds, according to her need for alimony." This citation further demonstrates that legal authorities in the late thirteenth and early fourteenth centuries were considering the parameters of women's financial agency.

165. See Hutton, "Women, Men and Markets," 409–31, esp. 416–21.

166. Bourdieu, "Rites," 81–88.

167. D. Elliott, *Spiritual Marriage*, 189–190; Farmer, "Persuasive Voices," 517–21.

168. As the manual written in Paris known as *le ménagier de Paris* instructed, wives should "cheerfully, rapidly, discreetly, devoutly and humbly give alms of your own lawful possessions without contempt for the needy in thought or in deed." *Ménagier*, 83.

169. Elliott, *Spiritual Marriage*, 190.

170. Ibid.

171. Caesarius , *Dialogus miraculorum*, VI 5, vol. 1:351.

172. Farmer, "Persuasive Voices," and see Baumgarten, "Charitable Like Abigail."

173. Cullum, "And Her Name Was Charite," 203.

174. M. Rubin, *Charity and Community,* 61.

175. Married women represent one cohort of those subjected to patriarchal authority, and children form another. Unfortunately, as explained above, the data in the memorbuch does not allow for a discussion of children's donations.

176. Howell's work provides a summary and analysis of these changes; see Howell, "Gender," 521–25.

177. Cullum, "Gendering Charity"; idem, "And Her Name Was Charite." More recently Jordan, "Gender Concerns," 62–84, has studied men's and women's donations to Cistercian nunneries, revisiting the idea that men donated at higher levels to men's than to women's communities. However, she only makes cursory mention of the sums of money given, 88. She contrasts her findings to those of Johnson, *Equal in Monastic Profession,* 136–38, who argued that women's houses received smaller contributions because they were not able to offer the pro anima services that men could provide.

178. Weinberg, *Memorbuch.*

179. The list from late fourteenth-century Nürnberg analyzed in Yuval, "Donations," includes more men than women, though not markedly so; however, roughly one-third more young boys than young girls are recorded. In later lists, the difference is much more marked, with a two-to-one ratio of men to women; Greenblatt, "Community's Memory," 252–53.

180. Geary, *Phantoms of Remembrance,* 65–69.

CHAPTER 4

1. For recent scholarship on the subject, see Grossman, *Pious and Rebellious,* 178–80; Har-Shefi, "Women and Halakhah," 214–66; Ta-Shma, "Ma'amad haNashim haMitnadvot," 262–79; and, most recently, Goldin, *Jewish Women,* 169–222, who summarizes Grossman and Har-Shefi. For nineteenth-century compositions, see Abrahams, *Jewish Life,* 170–72; Berliner, *Aus dem inneren Leben,* 15–19; and Güdemann, *Geschichte des Erziehungswesens,* 1:228–38.

2. Commandments (*mitzvot*) have historically been divided into "do's" and "do not's." The latter were seen as applying to all Jews (and certainly all adults), unless they were intended for a specific category such as those of priestly descent or first-borns.

3. Alexander, *Gender,* has addressed this topic in late antiquity. I thank her for sharing with me her recently published work.

4. These are only some of the deeds that were part of this group. To name a few examples, this category also includes counting the days between Passover and Pentecost (*Sefirat Haomer*), journeying to the Temple (when it was standing) on the three pilgrimage festivals, observing the Fast of the First-born on the eve day preceding Passover, etc. See Har-Shefi, "Women and Halakhah," who discusses many of these precepts in detail.

5. See BT Kiddushin 32b and parallels. Elizabeth Shanks Alexander discusses the difficulty of this definition in her work. She argues that these conceptual categories were conceived in the study hall, not as part of lived religion.

6. Har-Shefi, "Women and Halakhah," 267–68.

7. The four species would usually be shared by members of one or more communities, a practice that is well known from early modern Europe as well. See, for example, *Responsa of R. Meir,* ed. Emanuel, #191.

8. Kanarfogel, "Rabbinic Attitudes," 7–14. The Talmud indicates that the commandment of

tefillin was not strictly observed in the Land of Israel, in contrast to more stringent adherence in Babylon, PT Berakhot 2:3; *Pesikta Rabbati*, chap. 22, 111b. See also Habermann, "Al haTefillin," 175. For further discussion of this issue, see Chapter 6, pp. 196–97, 200–201.

9. *Newly Discovered Geonic Responsa*, ed. Emanuel, # 161, 234–35nn.16–18.

10. This is the picture that emerges from BT Rosh haShanah as well as ge'onic and medieval literature.

11. A history of such objects is still a desideratum. The example of the lulav is a case in point, since Christians paraded in the streets with palms as part of their ritual cycle as well, and a comparative study of these practices is still awaited.

12. Revel-Neher, *Image of the Jew*, 55–65.

13. BT Menahot 43b; see also *Midrash Tehillim*, ed. Buber, 2:13.

14. Goody, "Against 'Ritual,'" 25–35.

15. Grossman, *Pious and Rebellious*, 198–211; Noble, "Jewish Woman," 347–55; Marcus, "Mothers, Martyrs," 34–45; Gershenzon and Litman, "Bloody Hands," 73–91.

16. Kayserling, *Die jüdischen Frauen*, 134–40; see n. 1.

17. A strong interest in women's place and practice became a focal point in the late nineteenth century, as part of the apologetic tendency that prompted Jewish studies scholars to portray women's roles in Jewish life in a positive light. More recently, as feminist approaches have become more widespread, one can see this interest as a form of what Moshe Rosman has called "me-tooism." See Rosman, "History of Jewish Women," 29–30.

18. See, for example, the statement by Asher b. Yehiel to this effect, BT Kiddushin 31a, #49, describing this as a kind of piety (*hasidut*).

19. Kanarfogel, "Rabbinic Attitudes"; Malkiel, *Reconstructing Ashkenaz*, 161–68; 174–80.

20. See n. 1 above; see also Baskin, "Jewish Women," 94–114; Golinkin, *Status of Women*, 23–46; Fishman, "Kabbalistic Perspective."

21. As Ta-Shma outlined in "Ma'amad haNashim haMitnadvot," 266–73, women were forbidden to perform these commandments in all other diaspora communities.

22. Ibid. Within the halakhic system, one who is commanded is legally bound to observe the precept at hand, as distinct from choosing to perform a commandment voluntarily.

23. I am grateful to Mordechai Friedman for sharing his unpublished paper "Rabbinic Reactions to Women Performing Positive Time-bound Commandments" with me. I have benefitted tremendously from his close readings of these halakhic texts. While I have some reservations regarding his conclusions, they do not detract from all that I have learned from his textual analysis.

24. In cases where a single woman observed this commandment, she would often be mentioned by name; see n. 155.

25. As opposed to other chapters in the book, for the most part I have chosen not to present the primary sources since they have been discussed extensively in recent scholarship on this subject. Instead, I have tried to change the focus of the discussion by posing new questions in my analysis of these sources. In that vein, I have quoted only the primary sources necessary for my argument throughout this chapter.

26. The assumption of continuity stands out in Grossman, *Pious and Rebellious*, 273–80, and Ta-Shma, "Ma'amad haNashim haMitnadvot," 262–79, as well as Goldin, who follows in their footsteps, see n. 1. Friedman, "Rabbinic Reactions," emphasizes change over time. Friedman's work contains a different obstacle, as he seems bent on demonstrating that no elements of modern feminism are found in these halakhic discussions. While I agree that there is no "feminism" in these sources, his approach seems fairly radical and no less ideologically driven than feminist approaches that seek to demonstrate a feminist past.

27. Ta-Shma, "Ma'amad haNashim haMitnadvot," 262–63; Grossman, *Pious and Rebellious,* 178–80; Baumgarten, *Mothers and Children,* 87–89.

28. For thirteenth-century changes, see Kanarfogel, "Between the Tosafist," 85–108. We look forward to Judah Galinsky's work on Isaac of Corbeil.

29. See pp. 33, 67–68.

30. Grossman, *Early Sages of France,* 395–403, on the question of authorship.

31. *Mahzor Vitry* contains two similar positions that are related to this pair. For the differences between these positions, see Friedman, "Rabbinic Reactions," 19–27. These small emphases are less relevant to my argument.

32. Grossman and Japhet, *Rashi,* 23–28.

33. Simhah b. Samuel, *Mahzor Vitry,* ed. Goldschmidt, Hilkhot Sukkah, #34, 3:818–19.

34. Ibid., and see Grossman, *Pious and Rebellious,* 180–88; Har-Shefi, "Women and Halakhah," 172–74.

35. The identification of this position with Rashi in *Mahzor Vitry* is debatable. The text attributes this position to Rabbenu Shakh, but the validity of this ascription has been debated since the nineteenth century. If this were Rashi's position, why does it only appear in additions to the *Mahzor*? For a summary, see Golinkin, "Rabbenu Shakh." However, later thirteenth-century texts identify this position with Rashi, with the main objection being that for women to make blessings they are effectively adding commandments to the Bible (Deut. 13:1).

36. This opinion appears in Isaac b. Moses, *Sefer Or Zaru'a,* Hilkhot Rosh haShanah, 2: #266. This is only one part of his argument. He also offers a view that follows Rashi; see Friedman, "Rabbinic Reactions," 35–36. However, the formulation cited here conveys the comparison that I am suggesting.

37. BT Eruvin 96b.

38. Rabbenu Tam's position is summarized by Ta-Shma, "Ma'amad haNashim haMitnadvot," 266–69, as well as by Grossman, *Pious and Rebellious,* 178–80; Har-Shefi, "Women and Halakhah," 245–49. Also see Albeck, "Rabbenu Tam," 118; Friedman, "Rabbinic Reactions," 67–69.

39. Friedman, "Rabbinic Reactions," 33–62.

40. Eliezer b. Joel haLevi, *Sefer Ra'aviah,* ed. Deblytski, 2:#537, #640.

41. For a discussion of this responsum, see Roth, "Responsa from Heaven," 557.

42. For example, Moses b. Jacob, *Semag,* Aseh #26.

43. Friedman, "Rabbinic Reactions," 81–82.

44. Ibid., 80–90.

45. For example, Isaac b. Moses, *Sefer Or Zaru'a,* Hilkhot Rosh haShanah 2: #266. I am once again indebted to Mordechai Friedman for his lucid analysis of these sources.

46. Friedman, "Rabbinic Reactions," 96–97.

47. Ta-Shma, "Ma'amad haNashim haMitnadvot," 266–73. Moreover, Ta-Shma has argued that this position was attributed to Rabbenu Tam even though he wasn't the first to articulate it (268). See also Friedman, "Rabbinic Reactions," 68–69.

48. Almost every medieval book on halakhah included a section on the laws of various holidays, and each talmudic tractate had many commentaries. For this reason, it is impossible to provide a comprehensive listing of all pertinent sources. See, for example, the laws for Sukkot and Rosh haShanah in *Mahzor Vitry.*

49. In contrast to the case of tefillin (examined below), no adjectives accompany the mentions of these women.

50. For this idea, see the discussion later in this chapter.

51. Moses of Coucy, *Semag,* Aseh #44, based on BT Sukkah 41b. Although my discussion

examines positive time-bound commandments, it is noteworthy that this category was used in other contexts as well. See Simhah b. Samuel, *Mahzor Vitry*, ed. Goldschmidt, #105.

52. Moses b. Eleazar, *Sefer haMaskil*, Helek haMusar, 33, 35–36.

53. Ibid., 36. It should be noted that etrogim as well as lulavs were often purchased jointly by the entire community; see *Responsa of R. Meir*, ed. Emanuel, #154.

54. Jacob b. Asher, *Arba'ah Turim*, Orah Haim, siman a; Galinsky, "Four Turim," 34–39.

55. *Responsa of R. Meir*, ed. Emanuel, #431.

56. See n. 45.

57. See, for example, Jacob b. Moses Moellin, *Minhagim*, Hilkhot Rosh haShana, #14, where he suggests that only women who had recently given brith were absent from the synagogue on the High Holidays.

58. For a discussion of the blessing of each member of the community, see Baumgarten, "Gender," 69–75.

59. Eric Zimmer recently addressed elements of this issue at the Sixteenth World Congress for Jewish Studies (Jerusalem, 2013), and we await the publication of his findings. During his presentation, he examined when men started to wear a tallit gadol in prayer, concluding that, for the most part, this practice began during the late Middle Ages.

60. Simhah b. Samuel, *Mahzor Vitry*, ed. Horowitz, Hilkhot Tefillin, #638–46.

61. Kanarfogel, "Rabbinic Attitudes.."

62. BT Shabbat 49a. The danger of being perceived as arrogant begins in the Bible: Prov. 21:24, Hab. 2:5.

63. It is hard to determine whether he means that few Jews in the Land of Israel wrapped tefillin at all or that few wore them for the entire day.

64. *Newly Discovered Geonic Responsa*, ed. Emanuel, #161, 236–37.

65. See the responsum attributed to Hai Gaon in *Teshuvot haGe'onim*, #68. For further discussion see *Newly Discovered Geonic Responsa*, ed. Emanuel, #161, n. 38; MS Moscow 926 (Lisbon 1474), fol. 174a as well as *Responsa of R. Meir*, ed. Emanuel, #191.

66. Kanarfogel, "Rabbinic Attitudes"; see also Urbach, *Tosaphists*, 135; Zimmer, *Society*, 180–82, 287–90. This was true of Provence as well; see Jacob of Marvèges, *Shut Min haShamayim*, #26, 41.

67. Malkiel, *Reconstructing Ashkenaz*, 184–91.

68. For discussions of the term deviance and its usage, see Malkiel, *Reconstructing Ashkenaz*, 148–199, esp. 184–91; and specifically in the area of Jewish law and practice, see Schremer, *Brothers Estranged*, 69–71.

69. Eliezer b. Nathan, *Sefer Ra'avan*, #40.

70. Moses b. Jacob, *Semag*, Aseh #3. He ascribes this message to his preaching in Spain, but, as I describe below, his peers taught this message in Germany and northern France as well.

71. Ibid.

72. The terms translated here as "embarrassment, shame, and humiliation" (*boshet, khlimah,* and *halbanat panim*) are three forms of the English "humiliation"; without English equivalents, it is difficult to render a nuanced translation.

73. This last line is a quotation from BT Bava Mezi'a 59b.

74. *SHP*, #976.

75. See, for example, the Crusade chronicles: E. Haverkamp, *Hebräische Berichte*, 283, 339, 397, 435.

76. *SHP*, #439.

77. *SHP*, #1589, and see also #439, #552, #976.

78. See Soloveitchik, "Three Themes," 335–38, for a discussion of the shame that the pious were expected to endure.

79. *SHP*, #1670, #1719.

80. This idea appears in Joseph Bekhor Shor's commentary as well; see *Perushei R. Joseph Bekhor Shor*, Numbers, Shelah Lekha, #38.

81. Simhah b. Samuel, *Mahzor Vitry*, ed. Horowitz, 635, #509. This same idea is developed further in the closing section of a sermon by Moses b. Jacob, *Semag*, Aseh #26. Eleazar b. Judah stated in *Sefer Rokeah*, #361, that the children of those who do not wear tzitzit will die on account of their fathers' sins, a rather drastic statement.

82. For a discussion of this passage, see Galinsky, *Rabbenu Moshe*, 103–4.

83. Moshe b. Jacob, *Semag*, Aseh #3. See also both *Semak* and *Semag* on tzitzit.

84. Here Moses seems to be alluding to tzitzit rather than a tallit.

85. *Responsa of R. Meir*, ed. Emanuel, #174.

86. MS JTS Rab. 1077, fol. 19a.

87. This was already suggested in BT Shabbat 133b. See *Sefer haMaskil*, Helek haMusar, 32–33.

88. See, for example, in Moses of Evreux, "Sefer Al haKol," 110; Barukh b. Isaac of Paris, *Sefer haTerumah*, contains a lengthy discussion of tefillin.

89. Marcus, *Piety and Society*, 98–99.

90. Kogman-Appel, *Mahzor from Worms*, 68–76.

91. Eliezer b. Judah, *Sefer Rokeah*, #353; Jacob b. Moses Moellin, *Minhagim*, Hilkhot Hatuna, #10.

92. See, for example, in the thirteenth-century *sifrei mitzvot* (books of commandments), Moses b. Jacob, *Semag*, Aseh 3; Isaac b. Joseph, *Semak*, #31 and #32, where the discussion of mixed cloth immediately follows the section on tzitzit.

93. The authors debate whether silk clothing required tzitzit, for example. For a discussion of silk, see Chapter 5.

94. For discussions of this issue, see Simhah b. Samuel, *Mahzor Vitry*, ed. Horowitz, 246–47; *Kolbo*, #21; and see the famous story about Isaac b. Abraham (Rizba, d. 1199), who asked to be buried with his tzitzit. After his death his request was met with surprise until his students attested that this was indeed his desire; see Urbach, *Tosaphists*, 271. By the following century burial with tzitzit was no longer rare; see Schur, *Care for the Dead*, 125–28, where he notes that prominent community members were buried with tzitzit.

95. Joseph b. Moses, *Leket Yosher*, 10–11. Interestingly, he notes women producing tzitzit as well. My thanks to Rami Reiner for pointing me to this source.

96. The extent to which this practice became uniform cannot be judged; see a responsum that may be attributed to Isaac b. Samuel, stating that most people are not careful about observing this precept: *Responsa of R. Meir*, ed. Emanuel, #191.

97. Kanarfogel raises this as one of the reasons for not wearing tefillin, in "Rabbinic Attitudes," 7–14.

98. A. Berger, "Wrapped Attention"; Cayam, "Fringe Benefits." Har-Shefi sees these developments as one aspect of the tension between local custom and law, in "Women and Halakhah." While this may have been a factor, this study prioritizes gender as a category of analysis.

99. See, for example, Simhah b. Samuel, *Mahzor Vitry*, ed. Horowitz, Hilkhot Tzitzit and Hilkhot Tefillin; Eliezer b. Nathan, *Sefer Ra'avan*, Hilkhot Tzitzit; and Eleazar b. Judah, *Sefer Rokeah*.

100. Simhah b. Samuel, *Mahzor Vitry*, ed. Horowitz, 635, #509; Rashi, *Responsa*, #83. Her practice is credited to her brother. For a discussion of the pious customs performed by female relatives of rabbis, see Elias Bar Levav, "Our Women," 47–85; Urbach, *Tosaphists*, 61, 140.

101. Eleazar b. Judah, "Eshet Hayyil," in *Gezerot Ashkenaz veZarfat*, 165–66.

102. Moses b. Jacob, *Semag*, Aseh #26.

103. Herlihy, *Opera Muliebria*, 75–102, points to a division between men and women with men weaving and women spinning. However, I have not found this division in the Hebrew texts and this topic requires further study.

104. Tosafot, BT Gittin 45b, s.v. "kol sheyeshno."

105. Ibid. This position is often repeated; see MS Feinberg (formerly Montefiore 134), fol. 109b (*Sefer Asufot*); MS Oxford Add. Fol. 34 (641), fol. 118a in the margins; MS Oxford Mich. 84 (784), fol. 160a. Notably, Rabbenu Tam also extends this principle to the arranging of the four species for Sukkot.

106. Moses of Coucy, *Semag*, Aseh #26.

107. Jacob b. Moses Moellin, *Minhagim*, Hilkhot Tzitzit, #4. And see Moses b. Eleazar, *Sefer haMaskil*, 43. Maharil does not note whether a blessing should be said.

108. See Tosafot, BT Rosh haShanah 33a, s.v. "ha Rabi Yehudah"; Tosafot, BT Eruvin 96a, s.v. "Michal bat Kushi."

109. Golinkin presents many of the sources I discuss with different emphases.

110. A. Berger, "Wrapped Attention," 75. Berger suggests that this legend emerged because Rashi's daughters have been considered exceptional in other ways. For example, some scholars claimed they copied Rashi's notes. See Solomon b. Isaac, *Responsa Rashi*, #81, n. 3. For the arguments on how to interpret this source see I. Berger, "Folk Legends," 167–68.

111. Eliezer b. Samuel of Metz, *Sefer Yere'im*, b: #401.

112. Tosafot, BT Kiddushin 34b, s.v. "utefillin vetzitzit."

113. *Semag*, Aseh #26.

114. Ibid., and see Tosafot, BT Rosh haShanah 33a, s.v. "ha al shum."

115. Isaac b. Joseph, *Semak*, #32. This statement is repeated in the later manuscripts without having been erased. See MS Paris héb. 380, copied in 1342, fol. 13a, #31.

116. It is important to note that we have far fewer books from the twelfth century, and that asymmetry in transmission may skew this comparison between the twelfth and latter centuries. Yet within the limits of the literature that has reached us, this is the picture that emerges.

117. Isaac b. Moses, *Sefer Or Zaru'a*, Hilkhot Rosh haShanah, #266; Hilkhot Sukkah, #314.

118. Moses Parnas, *Sefer Parnas*, #421–22.

119. Golinkin makes this point as well.

120. Scholars have disagreed about where they were edited and formalized. Urbach, *Tosaphists*, 600–601, argued in Germany, mid-century; Epstein argued that Peretz b. Elijah was the editor,"Al haKol," 135.

121. At least one later commentator, Hagahot haBaH (Yoel Sirkes, 1561–1640), changed this phrase to lulav and *tekiot* (the shofar blasts): Hagahot haBaH, BT Berakhot 14a, s.v. "yamim." This is probably because, as we will see, by the seventeenth century women were forbidden to wrap tefillin.

122. *Hagahot Maimoniyot*, Hilkhot Tzitzit, chap. 3, #40. *Hagahot Maimoniyot*, Megillah #1, states that women were obligated to read the Book of Esther and could help others fulfil this obligation; *Hagahot Maimoniyot*, Megillah, chap. 3, #7, is an exact quotation of the Tosafot.

123. *Hagahot Maimoniyot*, Megillah, chap. 3, #7.

124. BT Berakhot 20b; BT Pesahim 43b, 50b; BT Beitzah 30a; BT Shabbat 148a.

125. Avigdor haTzarfati, *Perushim uPesakim*, Parashat Emor, #213, p. 172.

126. BT Shabbat 49a; BT Eruvin 96a.

127. Kanarfogel, "Rabbinic Attitudes," 8–9.

128. Tosafot, BT Eruvin 96a, s.v. "Michal bat Kushi."

129. Har-Shefi, "Women and Halakhah," 273–74.

130. Moses b. Jacob, *Semag*, Aseh #3. Also see Chapter 1, 29–31.

131. See also MS Cambridge Add. 3127, fol. 80a.

132. Barukh b. Isaac, *Sefer haTerumah*, #211, last lines of the section. See also the thirteenth-century book on the meanings of dreams, MS Paris héb 644, fol. 23b, where it is stated that anyone who dreams of himself wearing tefillin on his head can expect a long and successful life.

133. See A. Berger, "Wrapped Attention," 89–93, for her discussion of the complexity of distinguishing between cleanliness and purity.

134. Isaac b. Joseph, *Semak*, #150. Moses of Zurich quotes Meir of Rothenburg's ruling that women could not put on tefillin. However, unlike Maharil, who is cited later, Moses emphasizes that anyone who says the Shema should put on tefillin, even young men. In contrast, when discussing tzitzit, Isaac notes that women can make the blessing and Moses of Zurich also remarks that, despite Rabbenu Tam's effort to ban women from making tzitzit and the fact that Meir b. Barukh of Rothenburg (Maharam) followed suit, he sees no reason to ban women.

135. Eliezer b. Judah, *Sefer Rokeah*, 237.

136. The text says *kasher* (or *kosher*), meaning a good, God-fearing Jew.

137. Isaac b. Moses, *Sefer Or Zaru'a*, Hilkhot Tefillin, #531

138. Ibid.

139. One could argue that this had more to do with the nature of his book than with the precept itself, but since this reflects a broader trend, I consider it is noteworthy.

140. Isaac b. Moses mentions women and tefillin in a section on the laws of Rosh haShanah within a debate on women's obligations in relation to the shofar, *Sefer Or Zaru'a*, Dinei Rosh haShanah #266, but the point he is making does not relate to tefillin.

141. This comment only appears in some manuscripts and not in the earlier ones; see for example MS Paris héb. 643, fol. 21a.

142. Samson b. Tzadok, *Sefer Tashbetz*, #270.

143. This is a quotation from BT Mo'ed Katan 16b that does not appear in many manuscripts of *Sefer Tashbetz*. See, for example, MS Oxford opp. 642 (1106), fol. 348, #122, and compare with MS Paris héb. 380, fol. 177a, where these words do not appear.

144. Meir b. Yekutiel Cohen, *Hagahot Maimoniyot*, Hilkhot Tzitzit #3, and see MS Buda Kaufmann 77a, fol. 69r.

145. See above, n. 120.

146. Avigdor b. Elijah Katz, *Perushim uPesakim*, Parashat Emor, #213, p. 172.

147. Aaron b. Jacob haCohen of Lunelle, *Sefer Orhot Hayim*, Hilkhot Tefillin, #3. See A. Berger, "Wrapped Attention," 93–98.

148. Moses of Zurich, *Semak of Zurich*, #150, comment 42, 2:19.

149. Ibid., #24.

150. See R. Jacob b. Moses Moellin, *Minahgim*, Hilkhot Tefillin, #10.

151. Joseph Bekhor Shor (of Orléans) makes this argument, *Perushei*, 226–27, as does *SHP*, #252, and Benjamin of Regensburg; see MS Oxford Mich. 84 (784), fol. 147b. See also David Abudraham, *Sefer Abudraham*, Sha'ar 3:25; and Jacob Anatoly, *Melammed haTalmidim*, Lekh Lekha 16–17; Fishman, "Kabbalistic Perspective," 209; and Har-Shefi's summary of this reasoning in "Women and Halakhah," 295–96.

152. *SHP*, #1011.

153. See n. 151 as well as Hovav, *Maidens*, 74–77, 330–32, and esp. 382–84.

154. See, for example, Peretz on *Semak*, #31.

155. Jacob b. Moses Moellin, *Minahgim*, Hilkhot Tzitzit, #4.

156. Jacob b. Moses Moellin, *Shut Maharil haHadashot*, #7.

157. The issue being addressed here is whether the commandment of tzitzit pertains to the person performing the practice or to the specific object involved (*hovat gavra* or *hovat guf*), in this case an article of clothing with four corners that requires tzitzit.

158. BT Shabbat 72b.

159. Jacob b. Moses Moellin, *Shut Maharil haHadashot*, #7, n. 157.

160. Ibid.

161. *Shulkhan Arukh*, Orah Hayim, Hikhot Tzitzit 17:3.

162. BT Shabbat 72b.

163. BT Eruvin 96b. For a discussion of *nahat ruah*, see Grossman, *Pious and Rebellious*, 178–80; Ta-Shma, "Ma'amad haNashim haMitnadvot," 264–65; Har-Shefi, "Women and Halakhah," 222–54.

164. J. W. Scott, "Unanswered Questions," 1422–29.

165. Interestingly, it should be noted that men too were not obligated to make tzitzit; rather, they were obligated to wear them on four-cornered garments. But this remains the direction of Rabbenu Tam's argument.

166. Grossman, *Pious and Rebellious*, 273–81.

167. Kanarfogel, "Review," 850–51.

168. Isaac b. Joseph, *Semak*, #31.

169. Baumgarten, *Mothers and Children*, appendix to chap. 2 (90–91); and see, for example, Moses of Zurich, who also expressed reservations about Meir b. Barukh's instructions as they appear in *Sefer Tashbetz*, #273) regarding young men in the context of tefillin: Moses of Zurich, *Semak of Zurich*, #160. This hierarchy is also evident in later discussions of lulav. See Jousep (Juspa) Schammes, *Minhagim deKehilat Kodesh Wormeisa*, 1: #199, where he noted that women and children have fewer lulavim and etrogim than adult males.

170. Marx, "Rabbi Yosef of Arles," 294.

171. Hovav, *Maidens Love*, 382.

172. Ibid., 378–84.

173. Moses of Zurich, *Semak of Zurich*, #24.

174. BT Berakhot 18a.

175. Schur, *Care for the Dead*, 125–28.

176. MS Oxford Opp. 712 (2240), fol. 229a; Böhl, "Die hebräischen Handschriften," 127–38; Schur, *Care for the Dead*, 216–17.

177. BT Berakhot 18a; BT Sukkah 26b.

178. Moses Parnas, *Sefer Parnas*, #320; Eliezer b. Joel haLevi, *Sefer Ra'aviah*, new edition, 2: Sukkah, 640, and also see Sukkah 697; 1: Berakhot, 56.

179. Meir b. Barukh, *Shut Maharam* (Prague), #946. See Grossman, *Pious and Rebellious*, 443–45.

180. Moses of Zurich, *Semak of Zurich*, #24.

181. *Teshuvot Maimoniyot*, Hilkhot Ishut 7.

182. Asher b. Yehiel, *Shut haRosh*, #43, 8.

183. J. W. Scott, "Unanswered Questions."

184. Friedman offered this same argument in his claim that this was a halakhic issue rather than a social one. I believe the argument works in the opposite direction as well, that much like no single line of reasoning explains the halakhic change, so too there is not a single factor for the social transformations.

185. See introduction, 15.

186. D. Elliott, *Proving Woman*, 1–8.

187. Ibid., 47–84; Simons, *Cities of Ladies*, 118–37; Stabler-Miller, "What's in a Name," 60–86.

188. I thank Anne Lester for her help on these matters. See D. Elliott, *Proving Woman*; Bynum, *Holy Feast*, 26–27.

189. Innocent III, *Opera Omnia*, December 1210, *Nova quaedam nuper*, PL 216: 356 A–B, CLXXXVII.

CHAPTER 5

1. See Chapter 6 for tales that suggest one could "appear" pious and that those familiar with the social codes could read those cues as they were intended.

2. Rashi, BT Gittin 90b, s.v. "uferuma mishnei tzedadehah."

3. By way of comparison, see Graybill and Arthur, "Social Control," 9–29, who discuss why dress plays such a crucial role in expressions of piety.

4. These ideas are suggested in Bourdieu's discussion of habitus and in the writings of Michel Foucault. In the context of religious groups and systems, the work of Mary Douglas is invaluable in discussions of the relationship between individual bodies and the public body. For a concise and useful summary of this scholarship, see Bowie, *Anthropology of Religion*, 62–81. For a discussion of this specific issue in Christian society, see D. Elliott, "Dress as Mediator," 279–308.

5. D. Elliott, "Dress as Mediator," 279. See also E. Jane Burns, in the introduction to her *Medieval Fabrications*, 3: "Clothes in this sense are seen as social sites that stage gendered identities at the intersection of individual fantasies, social regulation and ethical concerns."

6. Constable, *Reformation*, 188–94. Constable was one of the first to discuss this matter of outward appearance in depth, and in many ways subsequent studies are based on him; see his introduction to *Burchardi,*, 47–130.

7. Klaniczay, "Fashionable Beards," 52.

8. M. Rubin, "Identities," 383–413.

9. D. Elliott, "Dress as Mediator," 279–308; Kowaleski, "Consumer Economy," 238–59.

10. Kowaleski, "Consumer Economy," 247–48.

11. Constable, *Reformation*, 188–92; Pipponier and Mane, *Se vêtir au moyen âge*, 153–64.

12. Constable, *Reformation*, 188–92 and see A. Haverkamp, *Medieval Germany*, 47, who mentions that they wore gray. See also Erler, "Margery Kempe's White Clothes," 78.

13. Lester, *Creating Cistercian Nuns*; de Miramon, *Les donnés*, noted how subtle differences in dress codes distinguished the so-called "semi-religious" groups of women from one another.

14. Klaniczay, "Fashionable Beards."

15. Lester, *Creating Cistercian Nuns*.

16. The question of which internal and external codes from the other community could be read by Jews and Christians is addressed below. See also *Sefer Tosafot haShalem*, Lev. 13:13, where the white clothes worn by Christians is discussed.

17. Toch, "Jüdisches Alltagsleben in Mittelalter," 19, points to fasts and feasts as primary means of identification.

18. Shalev-Eyni, *Jews Among Christians*, 85–87; Marcus, "Why Is the Knight Different," 140–44. One of the challenges encountered by modern scholars who wish to study medieval clothing is the absence of Hebrew vocabulary for many cloths, hats, and accessories, rendering them hard to identify. Medieval Jewish writers referred to these fabrics and garments in the vernacular; see Fudemann, "Old French Glosses," 160–65, where many sorts of hats and clothing are discussed. The numerous types of

head coverings referred to in one commentator's explanation in Isaiah are alone indicative of the richness of dress and the descriptive language that we lack.

19. Constable, *Reformation*, 188–92.

20. Berliner, *Aus dem inneren Leben*, 28–33, and Abrahams, *Jewish Life*, 273–306, both discuss this topic generally, as their evidence spans six centuries and many locales. Nevertheless, I view their two main points, that Jews wore distinctive clothing and they dressed like their neighbors (despite the apparent contradiction between them), as cogent, and I am following in their footsteps. Marcus has also briefly addressed the topic of what Hasidei Ashkenaz wore, as did Yassif, and see below, n. 80. Most recently see M. Epstein, *Medieval Haggadah*, 64–68.

21. See Tanner, *Ages of Faith*, 19–33, esp. 24–26.

22. See n. 21; for intra-Christian distinctions, see Constable, *Burchardi*, 85–130, who explains the preoccupation with this convention with regard to beards. His survey also demonstrates the complexity of this issue.

23. Tanner, *Ages of Faith*, 19–33.

24. Kisch, "Yellow Badge," 106–7; Abrahams, *Jewish Life*, 291–306; and, most recently, Cassen, "Identity or Control."

25. See, for example, Grayzel, *Church and the Jews*, 1:336–37 where the bulla (papal edicts) mention that Jews in Provence wore capes like those worn by Christian clergy and the Jews' concomitant need for an identifying ornament. Constable quotes the Cistercian abbot, Richalm of Schönthal, who said he was sometimes called a Jew because of his beard; *Burchardi*, 54n.25.

26. On the veracity of these depictions, see E. Schwartz, "Ultimate Other," 221–32. She notes that in Byzantium, Jews were depicted wearing tefillin.

27. Ibid., "Ultimate Other," 227; Melinkoff, "Round Cap-Shaped Hats," 155–66, and idem, *Antisemitic Hate Signs*, 31–34. The Fourth Lateran Council did not specifically mandate that hats be worn.

28. Zirlin, "Decoration of the Miscellany," 2:79–80.

29. See Klaniczay, "Fashionable Beards," 61, where such a hat is mentioned as typical of knights who strayed from the path of God. Pipponier and Mane discuss the progressive identification of certain garments as "Jewish" starting in the late thirteenth century and gaining momentum in the fourteenth century. *Se vêtir au moyen âge*, 164–70.

30. Strickland, *Saracens, Demons and Jews*, 105–6. See also Mellinkoff, *Anti-Semitic Hate Signs*, 31–34.

31. Zimmer, *Society*, 24n.35, where he quotes Ra'aviah and R. Meir b. Barukh of Rothenburg. See also Samson b. Tzadok, *Sefer Tashbetz*, #238. *Sefer haMaskil*, Helek hahalakhot, 33, #1, instructs men against sitting bareheaded. Zimmer points to the fifteenth century as the period when this changed. Marc Epstein also remarks on this in his recent book *Medieval Haggadah*, 64–75, esp. 69, where he talks about normative and pious customs.

32. *Sefer haKushiyot*, #290.

33. Zimmer, *Society*.

34. This is true in other cultures as well. For one of the studies on the anthropology of hair, see Hiltebeitel and Miller, *Hair*; Constable, *Burchardi*.

35. See n. 42 below.

36. E. Schwartz, "Ultimate Other," 221–32; M. Epstein, *Medieval Haggadah*, 64–75, has noted that adult men in the Bird's Head Haggadah (fourteenth century) are portrayed with beards.

37. Constable, *Burchardi*, 95.

38. Horowitz, "On the Significance of the Beard," 124–48.

39. Ibid.

40. Constable mentions a "Jewish beard," described as being under their chins "like goats," *Burchardi*, 54n.25. This may refer to Jews who did not shave closely enough for their jawlines to be visible; see also the discussion that follows also.

41. Avraham b. Ephraim, *Compendium*, Lavin #24, 148. I have not found this statement attributed to Jacob b. Meir (Rabbenu Tam) in any other source, and I thank Rami Reiner for discussing this issue with me. See also *Answers and Rulings* (Kupfer), #157.

42. Isaac b. Joseph, *Semak*, #70.

43. Meaning one who is highly delicate.

44. In Hebrew, "Pe'at roshkhem velo tashkhit."

45. For magical use of names, see Trachtenberg, *Jewish Magic*, 78–103. More recently, see Harari, "Jewish Magic," 13–85.

46. Yassif, "Shevarim Geluhei Zakan," 59–60. This story is quoted from *Sefer haGan* (Venice, 1596), 9b–10a.

47. See *KolBo*, #97, where Peretz is quoted as stating that Jews should not have similar hairstyles or shave like the gentiles, unless they have to go to court and will be scorned if they do not have similar hairstyles or shaves. I thank Eyal Levinson for this reference.

48. Constable, *Burchardi*, 119.

49. See n. 7.

50. Constable, *Burchardi*, 103–30; Klaniczay, "Fashionable Beards," 67.

51. Constable, *Burchardi*, 103–30; Klaniczay, "Fashionable Beards," 59–60.

52. Rashi notes Joseph's long, primped hair in his commentary on Gen. 37:2, s.v. "vehu na'ar," suggesting certain hairstyles that were popular among medieval youth.

53. Finkelstein, *Self-Government*, 225.

54. Van Engen, *Sisters and Brothers*, 2.

55. This phrase indicated customs that were not classified as idolatry but originated outside Jewish culture.

56. This restriction appears several times in the Talmud and is echoed in medieval literature. See BT Nazir 39a; BT Kiddushin 66b; BT Sotah 46b; BT Avodah Zarah 11b; and see *Answers and Rulings* (Kupfer), #157; Moses b. Jacob, *Semag*, Lo Ta'aseh, #57; Abraham b. Ephraim, *Compendium*, Lo Ta'aseh, #24; Isaac b. Joseph, *Semak*, #70–71. See also Jonah b. Abraham of Gerondi, *Iggeret haTeshuvah*, 36, who noted that French men shaved their beards. For German sources, see below.

57. Constable, *Reformation*, 194–95.

58. His comment refers to the past rather than to the present: Rashi, BT Me'ila 17a, s.v. "vesipper komi."

59. Judah b. Samuel, *Sefer haGematriyot*, #30. Judah includes any man who has his hair styled in a *blorit*, is shaven or has cut his beard, or is wearing "non-Jewish" clothing. See also *SHP*, #1664.

60. Moses b. Jacob, *Semag*, Lo Ta'aseh #57; Isaac b. Joseph of Corbeil, *Semak*, #71. Cutting the hair of priests and oblates was part of Christian ritual; see De Jonge, *In Samuel's Image*, 35–49, 61–62.

61. The Aragonese Jewish scholar Solomon Ibn Parhon mentioned that some Jewish men modeled their hairstyle after the knights of their generation; see his lexicon, *Salomonis b. Abrahami*, fol. 12b, "g.l.b."

62. See, for example, Tosafot, BT Avodah Zarah 29a, s.v. "hamistaper"; Isaac b. Moses, *Sefer Or Zaru'a*, 4: Piskei Avodah Zarah, #150–51; Samson b. Tzadok, *Sefer Tashbetz*, #542 old.

63. Zimmer, *Society*, 47–48.

64. Finkelstein, *Self-Government*, 59, 225. These statutes incorporate talmudic terminology.

65. This is in contrast to many contemporaneous sources that discuss the removal of pubic hair,

a subject that is beyond the scope of this inquiry. Women's head coverings are discussed in the context of the laws of the Sabbath, and see BT Shabbat 57a and the commentaries there as well as Simhah b. Samuel, *Mahzor Vitry*, ed. Horowitz, Hilkhot Shabbat, #31; Eliezer b. Nathan, *Sefer Ra'avan*, Shabbat, #354; Moses b. Jacob, *Semag*, Lo Ta'aseh, #65. It is evident from these passages that women covered their hair.

66. Much like in the purification processes examined in Chapter 1.

67. See the recent study by Zimmer, "Head Covering of Jewish Women," 1:404–14. This article has been the main source for my brief treatment of this topic.

68. *Sefer Tosafot haShalem*, Gen. 3:26. This is echoed in *Sefer haKushiyot*, as we saw above, n. 34.

69. Asher b. Yehiel (Rosh), BT *Ketubbot*, chap. 7, #9.

70. Many halakhic compendia discuss this issue, especially the popular genre of *sifrei mitzvot* (books of commandments). Moses b. Jacob, *Semag,* Lo Ta'aseh #283; Isaac b. Jacob, *Semak*, #32. See also Eliezer of Metz, *Sefer Yere'im*, #333.

71. I have been unable to find any extended scholarly discussion of this issue. One of the central medieval concerns was the status of kanbus (*cannabis*, hemp) and whether it could be woven with wool. Permissible uses of silk and scarlet were also at issue. For a brief discussion of this subject, see Urbach, *Tosaphists*, 200; Isaac b. Moses, *Sefer Or Zaru'a*, 1: #303. I thank Rami Reiner, who helped me investigate this matter.

72. See n. 109 below.

73. *SHP,* #1792; Eleazar b. Judah, *Sefer Rokeah*, MS Paris 363, fol. 8b, and see the next note.

74. Isaac b. Joseph, "Piskey Rabenu R"I MeCorbeil, ed. Sha'anan," 21, #41, where he debates the extent to which a Jew may wear clothes that were left in pawn by a non-Jew and where he also discusses the issue of sha'atnez. Isaac states that a gentile's clothing may surely be worn by a Jew whose life is endangered. See also Jacob of Marvèges, *Shut Min haShamayim*, #58–59, for a discussion of this matter in Provence.

75. See Shatzmiller, *Cultural Exchange.*

76. See Stuard, *Gilding the Markets;* Fleming, "Acquiring, Flaunting and Destroying Silk," 127–58; Heller, "Sumptuary Legislation," 121–36; idem, "Anxiety, Hierarchy, and Appearance," 311–48; Kinoshita, "Almería Silk," 165–76. E. Jane Burns's work also focuses on these issues; see her *Courtly Love Undressed*, esp. 181–210; Valerie R. Hotchkiss surveys some of the legislation restricting women's clothing between 1000 and 1400; see her *Clothes Make the Man,* 11–13; Howell, *Commerce,* 234–42.

77. For discussions of this matter, see *Otzar haGe'onim, Yom Tov,* 16, #28, which quotes the ge'onic responsum on this matter as recorded in Sefer haPardes, ed. Ehrenreich, 72b. This responsum reveals the extent to which these laws were ignored. Also see Rashi, BT Yevamot 4b s.v. "Ktiv hakanaf"; Mordekhai, *Halakhot Ketanot (Menahot),* Remez #930; Moses b. Jacob, *Semag*, Aseh #26; Isaac b. Joseph, *Semak*, #31; Samson b. Tzadok, *Sefer Tashbetz*, #267; Meir b. Yekutiel Cohen, *Hagahot Maimoniyot*, Hilkhot Tzitzit, chap. 3, halakhot 3–6.

78. Asher b. Yehiel, BT Kila'im, 9:2 (standard editions).

79. *SHP,* #1809.

80. For a discussion of the importance of cloth to the mendicants, see Constable, *Reformation*, 190–92.

81. E. Haverkamp, *Hebräische Berichte*, 473; Ephraim of Bonn, *Sefer Zekhirah.*

82. *SHP,* #60, #199, #1777; Isaac b. Moses, *Sefer Or Zaru'a*, 2: Hilkhot Erev Shabbat, #38. There is an unsavory undertone in this discussion that communicates that a Jew is not necessarily obligated to save a non-Jew on the Sabbath. See Kutner, "Night," 55–64, on fires. The Jewish community also had an interest in extinguishing fires so their Christian neighbors would not have reason to accuse them of hatred.

83. Isaiah 61:9.

84. *Wayyikrah Rabbah* (Vilna) 23; *Canticles Rabbah* (Vilna) 5, 6; *Tanhuma* (Buber), 4, 6; Menahem b. Shlomo, *Midrash Sekhel Tov*, ed. Buber, Gen. 17.

85. Menahem b. Shlomo , *Midrash Sekhel Tov*, ed. Buber, Gen. 17:11; Tosafot, BT Hagigah 3a, s.v. "tehila legerim"; Judah b. Samuel, *Sefer Gematriyot*, 146;

86. See *Midrash Wayyikra Rabbah*, 32, #5, where the Midrash recounts that the Jews in Egypt did not change their names, and an expanded version in *Midrash Lekah Tov*, ed. Buber, Exod. 6:6, where the midrash notes they did not change their style of clothing.

87. One example of distinctly Jewish signs of piety are ritual objects that played a role in externally displaying religious praxis. Ivan Marcus, *Piety and Society*, 99, has demonstrated that Hasidei Ashkenaz often wore tzizit to demonstrate their piety. Community members took note when members wore tefillin or tzizit, artifacts that were seen by all. Tzitzit and tefillin exemplify a range of manifestations of piety that were obvious to medieval Jews but remain elusive to most modern scholars.

88. SHP quotes this verse from Isaiah in a number of contexts; see, for example, *SHP,* #260, #554.

89. *SHP*, #554.

90. The special circumstances posed by travel merit further attention. For a discussion of alienation on the road, see Ladner, "Homo Viator," 233–59. I thank Ahuva Neuman for reminding me of this article. For discussions of other aspects of travel and pilgrimage, see Doležal and Kühne, *Wallfahrten*, and the amusing article in this collection by Hlaváček, "Pilgrimage Footwear," 139–46.

91. Lev. 18:3 states: "And you shall not walk in their paths," which was interpreted over time to indicate clothing and hairstyles that were elements of idol worship. See BT Avodah Zarah 11a. These definitions are repeated throughout the medieval literature.

92. In general, within Jewish practice and in other religions, different laws applied to traveling (e.g., regarding prayer). See Cuffel, "From Practice to Polemic," 401–19.

93. *SHP*, #199.

94. BT Avodah Zarah 16b. According to this passage, Eliezer was accused of heresy. When he was brought to the governor, he acknowledged his error to both God and the governor, and he was ultimately forgiven.

95. *SHP*, #259.

96. *SHP*, #202, #260, #1922. Another related issue discussed in *Sefer Hasidim* is what Jews are supposed to do when carrying a Jewish ritual object (such as a Hebrew book or tefillin) and coins that are inscribed with a cross; see *SHP,* #663.

97. *SHP*, #207.

98. The word *komeret* is difficult to translate in the late twelfth- and early thirteenth-century social context. Who was being identified with this word that literally means "priestesses"? Were they female members of mendicant orders, or were they women who were pursuing penitential life without officially belonging to an order? For the problem of defining these women, see Freed, "Urban Development," 311–27; Lester, *Creating Cistercian Nuns*.

99. *SHP*, #261.

100. BT Gittin 90b, Rashi, s.v. "uferumah mishnei tzedadehah."

101. The term used here for young girls is literally "young females" (*nekevot ketanot*), and this is the way young girls are referred to in medieval Hebrew texts; see Baumgarten, "Conceptions of Childhood," 56–74.

102. If these women tried to escape the convent, it seems that the young girls would be unable to flee.

103. Some especially pious laywomen wore black, as did beguines who lived with them in their

own homes. See Devlin, "Feminine Lay Piety," 183–96; Simons, *Cities of Ladies*; Lester, *Creating Cistercian Nuns*.

104. Here, too, it is difficult to know if this house belonged to an order or to a group of penitent women. Many such houses existed in medieval urban settings as described by Lester, *Creating Cistercian Nuns*, 93. For the purposes of this discussion, as I explain, I have interpreted this house as belonging to an order.

105. The Bologna edition views the option of wearing white and residing in a house as synonymous, which may reflect the period when the Bologna edition was printed (sixteenth century) and when the option of living a holy life without joining an order was far less prevalent.

106. MS New York (former) JTS Boesky 45, #115, reads *hakhamot* (wise women), in the feminine, and suggests that wise women formulated these solutions; see https://etc.princeton.edu/sefer_hasidim.

107. *SHP*, #262.

108. For an interesting analysis of this issue in Christian society, see Hotchkiss, *Clothes Make the Man*, 83–104.

109. Deut. 22:5; Spiegel, "Cross-Dressing," 329–52.

110. See n. 102 above. Moses b. Eleazar, *Sefer haMaskil*, 76, #40; MS Oxford Bodl. Mich. 84 (784), fol. 87a, where this issue is discussed and ultimately prohibited as well.

111. See Horowitz, "Cleanliness." Men were instructed against shaving their genital area, as women (and non-Jews) did.

112. To a large extent the medieval Jews here are illustrating an idea that had already been expressed in the Palestinian Talmud: "A woman is able to hide herself (among gentiles) and say: 'I am a gentile.' But a man is unable to hide himself (among gentiles) and say: 'I am a gentile.'" See a discussion of this passage in S. Cohen, *Beginnings of Jewishness*, 66.

113. *SHP*, #260.

114. *SHP*, #203.

115. *SHP*, #205, and see #204 as well.

116. *SHP*, #203, #205.

117. Urbach, *Tosaphists*, 308, and see Jacob of London, *Sefer Etz Hayim*, 2:119, and Elijah Menahem b. Moses of London, *Perushei R. Eliyahu meLondrish*, #1, p. 5 (Hebrew numbers). These authorities speak of the necessity to inspect how the cloth was woven according to locale. See also Samson b. Tzadok, *Sefer Tashbetz*, #371–73.

118. Among Christians these customs were considered mortifications, and in Jewish texts they are described as unusual practices. For example, *SHP*, #1566. See Baumgarten, "Seeking Signs?," 209–10.

119. Jacob b. Moses Moellin (Maharil), Sefer Maharil, Likutim, #24.

120. Samson b. Tzadok, *Sefer Tashbetz*, #10.

121. *Moshav Zekenim*, Lev. 13:47, p. 305, and see Kanarfogel, *Intellectual History*, 366n.220.

122. Jacob b. Moses Moellin (Maharil), *Sefer Maharil*, Likutim, #105.

123. See Chapter 1.

124. Interestingly, most Hebrew sources imply that individuals owned more than one set of clothing, an indicator of the socioeconomic standing among medieval Jews; for example, *SHP*, #529 and #1779, and see Pipponier and Mane, *Se vêtir au moyen âge*, 59–69.

125. Similarly, the white clothes worn on Yom Kippur are classified separately from the black clothes worn by most penitents. This theme in Leviticus Rabbah is expanded in medieval sources; see, for example, *Sefer haKushiyot*, #375.

126. Klaniczay, "Fashionable Beards," 61.

127. See n. 79 above.

128. These are common vows from antiquity; see BT Nedarim, chap. 4.

129. Compare Constable, *Reformation*, 188–92.

130. Baumgarten, *Mothers and Children*, 67.

131. *SHP,* #1, #529, #588, #945; Jaritz, "*Ira Die,*" 56.

132. For example, see Simhah b. Samuel, *Mahzor Vitry*, ed. Horowitz, #271.

133. *SHP,* #529, #588, #945 each suggest that ensuring the cleanliness of one's garments and dedicating them for exclusive use on the Sabbath or other special occasions was a measure of piety. *SHP,* #57, underlines the need for special garments for the Sabbath in emphatic terms.

134. Lipton, "Where Are the Gothic Jewish Women?," 142–44, 149–62.

135. D. Elliott, "Dress as Mediator."

136. "*Shehu nikkar,*" *Canticles Rabbah* on Cant. 6:2, and see Baron, "Problems of Jewish Identity," 33–67, 52n.23, and S. Cohen, *Beginnings of Jewishness*, 66. I thank Evyatar Marienberg for discussing this issue with me. Cohen does not discuss women in this context, although it would seem many of his conclusions would hold true for late antique women as well.

137. S. Cohen, *Beginnings of Jewishness*, 67.

138. Ibid., 67–68.

139. Cohen himself noted this difference, ibid., 167.

140. See Chapter 3.

141. Isaac b. Joseph, *Semak*, #32; Jonah b. Abraham, *Iggeret haTeshuvah*, 23.

142. Meir of Rothenburg refers to the distinctive cape-like tallitot that were worn by Hasidei Ashkenaz; *Shut Maharam* (Prague), #1608; *SHP*, #976, #986, #1036, #1344, #1589.

143. Owen-Hughes, "Distinguishing Signs," 3–59.

CHAPTER 6

1. The question of intentionality is expanded below, see pp. 207–11.

2. Compare this analysis to Talmon-Heller, *Islamic Piety,* 225–42, where impiety is coupled with antinomianism and religious dissent; see also Yefet-Refael, "Beware of Hypocrites," 13–53, for a comparison to medieval Spain.

3. Following the stories from their initial appearance in late antiquity through the Middle Ages, along with current scholars who have focused on these narratives to learn about the cultures where they were recounted, I am of the opinion that reworked tales reveal a great deal about the cultures in which they were revised. By focusing on these narratives, I would also like to underline the tremendous value that stories can have for historical research, as sources that are too often neglected by historians. Yassif, "Legends and History," 187–220; Kushelevsky, *Penalty and Temptation;* E. Reiner, "From Joshua to Jesus," 223–71; Baumgarten and Kushelevsky, "From 'The Mother and Her Sons,'" 273–300.

4. Alternatively, it has been suggested that this story became a cautionary tale against placing trust in someone who was otherwise a stranger on the basis of his wearing tefillin alone. See PT Berakhot 2:3, 178n.87.

5. Ibid., 2:3, 178.

6. *Midrash Pesikta Rabbati,* # 22, 111a.

7. In addition to the versions discussed here, see *Newly Discovered Geonic Responsa,* ed. Emanuel, #161. My thanks to Simcha Emanuel for this reference.

8. Nissim b. Jacob of Kirouan, *Hibbur haYafeh min haYeshu'ah,* 61.

9. Ibid.

10. The word *perushim* is of great import to understanding these comments on feigned piety. In texts that refer to the Second Temple period, this term is often translated as "Pharisees"; however, that meaning does not seem applicable to its usage in these stories of self-discipline from the Babylonian Talmud. Medieval Jews reading these stories saw them as discussing piety rather than Second Temple politics. Indeed, the Soncino translation of the Talmud has translated this to mean Pharisees, whereas the Blackman translation of the Mishnah translated *perishut* as "self-restraint" or "separation from evil," both of which seem to be more accurate.

11. Zimri was killed by Phineas in Num. 25:14, an act for which Phineas was rewarded.

12. These pretenders all appear in BT Sotah 22b. They each flaunt their piety in different ways that call attention to their actions. The rabbis dismiss some of these figures as charlatans while also debating whether some of these people and their piety earned a level of merit.

13. Yefet-Refael, "Beware of Hypocrites," 13–53, has demonstrated that this theme of pretenders or hypocrites was common in medieval Spanish literature—relying on the discussion of the paradigm of seven types of pretenders in Tractate Sotah—though it received little attention in medieval Ashkenaz. Three central features of the pretenders that emerge in the tales examined by Yefet-Refael are the beards on rabbinic figures and, even more so, the use of tallitot and especially of tefillin, all as signs of piety. Our story from the Palestinian Talmud received less attention, which is unsurprising given the preference toward Babylonian traditions in medieval Spain.

14. I thank Ryan Szpiech from the University of Michigan for pointing out this parallel to me.

15. Joseph b. Meir Ibn Zabara, *Sefer Sha'ashuim*, 62–64.

16. On *Disciplina Clericalis*, its popularity and audience, see Tolan, *Petrus Alfonsi*.

17. Tubach, *Index Exemplorum, # 3355*.

18. Schwarzbaum, "International Folklore Motifs," 286–87.

19. "Et ostenderunt ei antiquum hominem nominatum probitate fidelitatis." Translation based on *Disciplina Clericalis*, 128–30.

20. Schwarzbaum, "International Folklore Motifs"; Tolan, *Petrus Alfonsi*, 128–30.

21. MS Oxford Bodl. Or. 135 (1466), fol. 323b–324a. For a description of this collection of tales, see Yassif, "Sefer haMa'asim," 136–65.

22. A narrative that resembles this one from the Palestinian Talmud appears in the Tosafist commentary on BT Shabbat 49a, s.v. "Ke'Elisha ba'al kenafa'im." See also Isaac b. Moses, *Sefer Or Zaru'a*, Hilkhot Tefillin, #531; Yehiel b. Asher, BT Menahot, *Halakhot Ketanot*, #28; Samson b. Tzadok, *Sefer Tashbetz*, #272. These retellings each focus on the laws of tefillin. However, whenever the story is recounted in other contexts, it focuses on other practices related to prayer or synagogue.

23. The Hebrew here is not that clear. Literally translated, it means "would never change his place after finishing his prayers."

24. The original reads *lehayim uleshalom*; here I have translated *hayim* (lit., life) as "health."

25. MS Oxford Bodl. Or. 135 (1466), fol. 323a.

26. Ibid.

27. Ibid.

28. Ibid.

29. This is consistent with talmudic law concerning compensation for embarrassment (*boshet*); see BT Arakhin 14b; BT Kiddushin 3a.

30. This is an international motif. See Tubach, *Index Exemplorum*, # 3350, 4102, on penance.

31. This verse also concludes the next story in the manuscript (fol. 325a), depicting a poor boy.

32. The vocabulary of terms of embarrassment and humiliation in the writings of Hasidei Ashkenaz has been discussed by various scholars; see Marcus, *Piety and Society*, 124–25; Soloveitchik, "Three Themes."

33. For examples, see MS Hebrew National and University Library 8°3182, fols. 129b–130a, from sixteenth-century Germany; MS JTS Mic. 2374, fols. 121b–122b from fifteenth-century Italy. In contrast, the manuscript versions from the East follow the narrative of *Sefer haYafeh Min haYeshuah*, and see MS Oxford Bodl 4° 65, fols. 101b–102a from 1638 and MS Sasson 256, fols. 75–76, from eighteenth-century Yemen.

34. BT Berakhot 6b. I thank Rella Kushelevsky for bringing this source to my attention.

35. Tosafot, BT Berakhot 6a, s.v. "hamitpallel." This is based on the story told in this section of the tractate about Abba Benjamin who said: "When two people enter a synagogue to pray, but one finishes his prayer first and leaves without waiting for the other [to finish], his [the first one's] prayer is shredded before his face." BT Berakhot 5b.

36. This story tells of a pious but poor man whom Elijah the Prophet gave the option of receiving seven years of plenty, either immediately or in the future.

37. MS Oxford Bodl. Or. 135 (1466), fols. 317b–318a.

38. Ibid., 319a.

39. Ibid., 320a.

40. *SHP,* #403. *Sefer Hasidim* even suggests that seats take on the attributes of those who occupy them. Thus if a wicked man regularly used a specific seat, that seat could be expected to retain his evil qualities even after he had vacated it; *SHP,* #404.

41. The distinction between the "decent poor," implying less scrupulous persons in need who are presumably less deserving, is noteworthy.

42. This is another example of gifts pro anima, as in Chapter 3.

43. *SHP*, #1558.

44. This is in contrast to Byzantium, where tefillin remained a symbol of Jewish piety throughout the Middle Ages, as art historians have demonstrated; see 267n.12.

45. Rashi is interpreting "prushin ve'einan prushin" in BT Sotah 22b as those who wrap themselves in tallitot.

46. BT Berakhot 3b–4a.

47. *SHP*, #1589.

48. Ibid.

49. Based on BT Bava Batra 21b.

50. *SHP,* #1589.

51. This position is quite unusual, especially in the context of pretense, when avoidance of such behavior is typically emphasized.

52. Pp. 153–55.

53. See Chapter 1.

54. As discussed in the previous chapter, the nature of this pious appearance was evident to the medieval listeners of these tales.

55. PT Sotah 3:4, 98.

56. This story closely reflects the seven types of pretenders mentioned in BT Sotah 22a–b.

57. Mishnah Sotah 3:2.

58. See below.

59. BT Sotah 22a, trans. Soncino with slight changes.

60. Ibid.

61. See Baumgarten, *Mothers and Children*, 47–48.

62. Nissim of Kirouan, *Sefer haYafeh Min haYeshuah*, 35–37. See a discussion of this statement below, p. 207.

63. Baumgarten, *Mothers and Children*.

64. MS Oxford, Bodl. Opp. 540 (1567), published by Dan, "Sippurim Demonologim," 282, #13. Yohani bat Retavi is mentioned in other medieval sources as well: Nathan b. Yehiel, *Arukh haShalem*, 4:117, "Yohani."

65. Rashi, BT Sotah 22a, s.v. "harei elu mevalei olam."

66. The word comes from the Hebrew verb *lesovev*, root *s.v.v.*, which means "to turn around."

67. Nathan b. Yehiel, *Arukh haShalem*, 8, "shev" 9.

68. Tosafot, BT Sotah 22a., s.v. "kol she'eino."

69. See Chapter 2, pp. 55–56.

70. Another detail in the description of Miriam is that she was hanging by her nipples.

71. PT Hagigah 2:2, and see Chapter 2, pp. 55–56.

72. MS Parma 563 fol. 92b. For a discussion of this manuscript and story, see Kushelevsky, *Penalty and Temptation*, 60–63. Kushelevsky also provides a history of the story and its many extant versions.

73. The expressions "ishah hashuvah" or "ishah hagunah" are repeated throughout medieval literature and often appear on tombstones. For a discussion of these phrases, see Hacohen, "Nashim Atzlaniyot," 63–82, and the beginning of Chapter 7. On the word *hagunah* on tombstones, see, for example, Grünwald, "Cimetière de Worms," 107; Reiner et al., *Grabsteine*.

74. "Darkhei Teshuva" was published in *Shut Maharam* (Prague), #1023, p. 162v.

75. Nissim of Kirouan, *Sefer haYafeh Min haYeshuah*, 37, and see *Otzar haGe'onim leMassekhet Sotah*, Sotah 22b, 241–42. This presents an interesting difference between eastern and western traditions. In this case, Yohani is the only figure mentioned, albeit not by name.

76. Menahem haMeiri, *Beit haBehirah leMassekhet Sotah*, 46–47.

77. Ibid.

78. Men and women were portrayed as fasting as an expression of piety, as evident in the story of the female pretender and as seen in previous parts of this volume.

79. As is the case with numerous "classic" figures from late antiquity, for example, the story of Beruriah; see Grossman, *Pious and Rebellious*, 156–57.

80. For a discussion of hypocrisy, especially in connection to abstinence, see Bynum, *Holy Feast*, 46, 96.

81. Bynum, "Did the Twelfth Century," 101–2; Kramer, "We Speak to God," 22–23, 33–40; idem, "Priest in the House," 160–66.

82. Wagner, "Cum aliquis," 212–13.

83. Ibid.; Murray, "Piety and Impiety," 92–95.

84. See Chapter 7, p. 220.

85. Kramer, "We Speak to God," 20–23; Bynum, "Did the Twelfth Century," 101–2.

86. Mansfield, *Humiliation of Sinners*, 126.

87. Walter Simons has suggested that the term "beguines" is derived from the French verb "béguer," meaning "to stutter" or "to murmur." Simons, *Cities of Ladies*, 121; Stabler-Miller, "What's in a Name?" 62–63, 84–85.

88. Venarde, *Women's Monasticism*, 165–66.

89. Passenier, "Women on the Loose," 66; Blumenfeld-Kosinski, "Satires of the Beguines," 241; Stabler-Miller, "What's in a Name."

90. Rutebeuf, *Oeuvres complèts de Rutebeuf*, 1:334–35: "En riens que Beguine die, N'entendez tuit se bien non: Tot est de religion, Quanque hon treuve en sa vie. Sa parole est prophetie; S'ele rit, c'est compaignie; S'el pleure, devocion; S'ele dort, ele est ravie; S'el songe, c'est vision; S'ele ment, nou creeiz mie. Se Beguine se marie, C'est sa conversacion; Ses veulz, sa prophecion, N'est pas a toute sa vie. Cest an

pleure et cest an prie, Et cest an panrra baron; Or est Marthe, or est Marie, Or se garde, or se Marie; Mais n'en dites se bien non, Li roix no sofferoit mie." Translated by Simons, *Cities of Ladies*, 118–19.

91. For the history of the beguines, see McDonnell, *Beguines and Beghards*, 465–73; Simons, *City of Ladies*; Böhringer, "Kölner Beginen im Spätmittelalter," 7–34.

92. Lester, *Creating Cistercian Nuns*. I thank the author for generously sharing her work with me.

93. Stabler-Miller, "What's in a Name."

94. As described in many studies, see Bynum, *Holy Feast*, 21–24; Simons, *City of Ladies*, 118–37; Berman, *Women and Monasticism*; Wolbrink, "Women in the Premonstratensian Order," 387–408.

95. D. Elliott, *Spiritual Marriage*, 187.

96. Bynum, *Christian Materiality*, 269–73.

97. See, for example, D. Elliott, *Proving Woman*.

98. BT Sanhedrin 24a; BT Kiddushin 49b.

99. And see Rashi's explanation of the relationship between the stork (hasidah) and pretense, in BT Kiddushin 49b, s.v. "hakhamah."

100. See n. 67.

101. For a Jewish critique of Christian piety, see D. Berger, *The Jewish-Christian Debate*, 69–70, 205, 223.

102. See Chapter 1.

CHAPTER 7

1. Translated by Baskin, "Dolce of Worms," 436.
2. Steinheim database, #36.
3. Eliezer b. Joel, *Sefer Ra'aviah*, 1:#68.
4. Moses b. Yekutiel, *Sefer haTadir*, #38, p. 250.
5. Isaac b. Moses, *Sefer Or Zaru'a*, 2: #404.
6. Eleazar of Worms, "Darkhei Teshuva," in *Shut Maharam* (Prague), #1023, p. 162v.
7. The question of who qualified as a hasid was raised often in medieval Ashkenazic texts, as seen in the examples brought by Judah b. Asher in the Tur when discussing the practices of the distinctly pious in Ashkenaz. See Galinsky, *Four Turim*, 178n.172.
8. See Chapter 5.
9. See Steinheim database. A closer study of these tombstones is still necessary and I hope to undertake one in the future. See also A. Reiner, *Grabsteine*, 235–62, for an example of some of the possible analysis.
10. For a survey of these ideas, see Low and Lawrence-Zúñiga, *Anthropology*, following Bourdieu, *Logic*, 66–80; Mahmood, *Politics of Piety*, 24–34; Deeb, *Enchanted Modern*, 34–37.
11. Yuval, "Heilige Städte," 91–101.
12. Even within a given synagogue, some individuals were considered more pious than others. Nonetheless, collective pious practice could confer sacred status on the community as a whole.
13. An example of the inverse can be seen in Kanarfogel, *Peering*.
14. I have tried to tease apart the relationships between the highly articulated prescriptive texts that emerged as canonical and formative of traditions and the beliefs and behaviors that most Jews would have associated with those same traditions. I borrow this formulation from Satlow, "Fruit and the Fruit of Fruit," 276, based on Jacques Berlinerblau, who suggested that "popular religion must be studied with 'official religion'"; Berlinerblau, *Vow*, 13–45.

15. In *Reconstructing Ashkenaz*, Malkiel shares some of these goals but uses different methods to achieve them.

16. Despite the diverse approaches that scholars of Jewish history bring to their work, the notion that Jewish history is essentially an endeavor in intellectual history continues to have currency. See Wieseltier, "Jewish Bodies," 435–42, and responses to his essay in *JQR* 96 (2006).

17. Goodson, Lester, and Symes, "Introduction," in *Cities*, 1–19.

18. Even proponents of a more textual approach have debated whether the adaptation of these sources was done consciously. See D. Berger, "Generation of Scholarship," 483.

19. See the recently proposed by Prof. Haym Soloveitchik at the Sixteenth World Congress of Jewish Studies (Jerusalem, 2013), forthcoming in his *Collected Essays*, as well as David Berger's response and Soloveitchik's rejoinder. These papers have yet to be published. While these two scholars focus on the intellectual treatment of these themes, I examine them from a different angle.

20. See pp. 28–29, in the introduction.

21. See Chapter 2.

22. My argument follows the logic presented by Susan Sered in her study of traditional Kurdish customs, *Women as Ritual Experts*. I thank Moshe Rosman, who first introduced me to this perspective.

23. When discussing women and halakhah, Har-Shefi, "Women and Halakhah," frequently uses this line of reasoning, following her teacher Ta-Shma, *Early Franco-German Ritual*, 98–105. See also Woolf, "Medieval Models," 271–72; Zimmer, *Society and Its Customs*, 13–15. Other examples abound. For discussions of this complexity, see Soloveitchik, *Wine in Ashkenaz*, 321–26; and, for additional approaches, Grossman, *Early Sages of Ashkenaz*, 424–33; D. Berger, "Book Review: The Early Sages," 479–87, esp. 482–84.

24. Benin, "A Hen Crowing Like a Cock," 261–81, uses this case to argue that the division between the categories of "custom and law" among Jews in medieval Ashkenaz was fluid, claiming that Ashkenazic rabbis not only integrated common customs into their prescriptions but that they crafted a theoretical framework that would allow for such integration. For a recent discussion of this idea, see Fishman, *Becoming the People*, 177–78.

25. See Introduction.

26. Marcus, *Piety and Society*; and more recently Soloveitchik, "Piety," 466–83. Soloveitchik's argument focuses on sections of *Sefer Hasidim* that were or were not recopied. While they are related, these questions are beyond the parameters addressed here.

27. Baskin, "From Separation to Displacement," 1–18.

28. Soloveitchik, "Piety," 455–93.

29. For a similar conclusion having been drawn from different sources, see Kogman-Appel, *Mahzor from Worms*, 189–96.

30. Soloveitchik, "Piety," 477.

31. Ryan, "Some Reflections," 961–71.

32. For example, if one considers sources that reflect both German and northern French practices, such as the collection of moral dicta recently published by Haym Soloveitchik, "Piety," 492–93, from MS Cambridge Add. 3127, fols. 165b–166a, instructions concerning personal conduct (e.g., controlling anger, honoring one's fellows, etc.) appear alongside central issues in this study, namely charity, fasting, and time-bound commandments, such as tzitzit and tefillin. These dicta are presented between rulings (*pesakim*) attributed to Isaac of Corbeil of northern France and to *Sefer Tashbetz*, which was compiled by the German scholar Samson b. Tzadok.

33. Marcus, *Piety and Society*, 121–29; Kanarfogel, "German Pietism," 207–28; Elboim, *Repentance*, 12–17; and see Chapter 2.

34. Soloveitchik, "Piety," 468.
35. See Chapter 5.
36. Einbinder, *No Place of Rest*.
37. *SHP,* #975.
38. Eleazar b. Judah, *Perushey Siddur,* 2:513. This same comment appears in an explanation of *shoresh hahasidut,* the roots of pietism, MS Paris héb. 363, fol. 6b; *Sefer Rokeah* contains a variation on this theme, 10.
39. Albert Baumgarten discusses the roles of ridicule and the willingness to withstand it as features of religious fanaticism; see "Nature," 49–50.
40. J. W. Scott, *Gender,* 28–51.
41. Kelleher, *Measure of Woman,* 3
42. J. W. Scott, *Gender;* Davis, "Women's History," 83–103.
43. Here the defining feature is class rather than gender.
44. *Gezerot Ashkenaz,* 166.
45. See Chapter 3.
46. Rose, *Feminism and Geography,* 17.
47. Moses b. Eleazar, *Sefer haMaskil,* 56–57.
48. Bonfil, *History and Folklore,* 151–88, esp. 172–88.
49. See introduction.
50. See J. Z. Smith, *Drudgery Divine.*
51. J. W. Scott, "Unanswered Questions," 1428.
52. Kelleher, *Measure of Woman,* 10–11.
53. Jordan, *French Monarchy;* Einbinder, *Beautiful Death,* 115–16. See the overview provided by Abulafia-Sapir, *Christian-Jewish Relations.*
54. Krueger, "Christian Piety," 291–316; J. M. H. Smith, "Portable Christianity," 143–67.
55. See, n. 1 above.
56. Kamaludeen, Pereira, and Turner, *Muslims in Singapore,* 11–13.
57. Soloveitchik, *Pawnbroking.*
58. See Chapter 2.
59. Ibid.
60. Marcus, *Rituals of Childhood.*
61. For this term see Wiedl, "Jews and the City," 273–308, where she discusses the process of cultural translation. Also see Raingard, "Migrationsgeschichte," 69–82, esp. 73–74.
62. Yuval, *Two Nations.*
63. Shyovitz, "'He Has Created a Remembrance,'" 5–11, persuasively quotes Becker, "Comparative Study of 'Scholasticism,'" 99.
64. See http://bestiary.ca/beasts/beast244.htm for a comprehensive bibliography.
65. Ibid. See also Ferguson, *Signs and Symbols,* 23.
66. See Matt. 5:35. For a discussion of this idea in medieval times, see Ames, *Righteous Persecution,* 194–200.
67. *Midrash Tehillim,* Ps. 104:14.

BIBLIOGRAPHY

The transliteration of Hebrew follows that used by the authors, thus some words appear with varied spellings.

MANUSCRIPTS

The number in parentheses is the call number at the Institute of Microfilmed Hebrew Manuscript at the National Library of Israel (IMHM).

British Library
    Add. 11639, North French Miscellany, late thirteenth century
    The North French Hebrew Miscellany, British Library Add. MS 11639, ed. Jeremy Schonfield, 2 vols. London: Facsimile Editions, 2003.
Budapest Kaufmann
    A 77 (IMHM 2904), Mishneh Torah with Hagahot Maimoniyot, 1295. http://kaufmann.mtak.hu/img/ms77a-100pc/ms77a
Cambridge
    Add. 3127 (IMHM 17556), halakhic miscellany, 1414
Hamburg
    45 (IMHM 1041), Responsa of R. Meir b. Barukh of Rothenburg, fourteenth century
Jewish Theological Seminary
    2374 (IMHM 28627), ma'asiyot, fifteenth century
    Rab. 1077 (IMHM 43192), Piskei Isaac of Corbeil and Peretz
Leipzig, Universitätsbibliothek
    1102, Kennicott 665 (IMHM 20962), mahzor, fourteenth century
Mainz
    IR, Anon. 19 (IMHM 73457), Nürnberg Memorbuch, thirteenth–fourteenth century (currently privately owned)
Montefiore
    136 (IMHM 5138), halakhic miscellany, thirteenth-fourteenth century
Moscow
    Ginzburg 926 (IMHM 48272), 1474
New York (Feinberg)
    formerly Montefiore 134 (IMHM 7304), *Sefer Asufot*, fourteenth century
National and University Library, Jerusalem
    Heb. 4°681–82, siddur, fourteenth century
    Heb. 8°3182, miscellany, sixteenth century

http://dlib.nli.org.il/webclient/DeliveryManager?pid=1065985&custom_att_2=simple_viewer

Heb. 8°3857, folklore, 1500http://dlib.nli.org.il/webclient/DeliveryManager?pid=1336779&custom_att_2=simple_viewer

Heb. 34°1114, mahzor, 1419

http://dlib.nli.org.il/webclient/DeliveryManager?pid=239270&custom_att_2=simple_viewer

Oxford University, Bodleian Library

The first number in the parentheses represents the number in the Neubauer catalogue.

Heb. D. 11 (2797, IMHM 16716), miscellany, fourteenth century

Mich. 84 (784, IMHM 20321), halakhic miscellany, fifteenth century

Opp. 77 (844, IMHM 21605), Responsa of R. Meir b. Barukh of Rothenburg and others, 1375

Opp. 540 (684, IMHM 20599) halakhic miscellany, fifteenth century

Opp. 642 (1106, IMHM 17712), siddur, fourteenth century

Opp. 712 (2240, IMHM 20523), miscellany, 1547 Frankfurt

Opp. Add. Fol. 34 (641, IMHM 20557), Responsa of R. Meir b. Barukh of Rothenburg and others, fourteenth century

Or. 135 (1466, IMHM 16385), *Sefer haMa'asim*, thirteenth century, northern France

Or. 146 (782, IMHM 20319), *Sefer Parnas*, 1342

Paris

héb. 326 (IMHM 23495), halakhic miscellany, thirteenth-fourteenth century

héb. 363 (IMHM 20238), *Sefer Rokeah*, 1452

héb. 380 (IMHM 4359), *Sefer Tashbetz, Sha'arei Dura* and other compositions, 1342

héb. 407 (IMHM 27901), halakhic miscellany, 1418.

héb. 643 (IMHM 11539), *Semak, Tashbetz*, fourteenth century

http://gallica.bnf.fr/ark:/12148/btv1b53014817g.r=H%C3%A9breu.langEN

héb. 644 (IMHM 11540), siddur, thirteenth century

héb. 646 (IMHM 15708), mahzor

http://gallica.bnf.fr/ark:/12148/btv1b84701092/f12.image.r=H%C3%A9breu.langEN

héb. 1408 (IMHM 24886), *Sefer Rokeah, Kitzur Semag* and other compositions, fourteenth century

Parma, Biblioteca Palatina

2295 (de Rossi 563, IMHM 13202) miscellany, thirteenth century

2749 (de Rossi 155, IMHM 13599), polemics, ca. 1300

2757 (de Rossi 1305, IMHM 13606) Psakim, fifteenth century

3007 (de Rossi 407, IMHM 13726), mahzor, fourteenth century

3057 (de Rossi 1033 IMHM 13823), miscellany, 1310

PRIMARY SOURCES

Aaron b. Jacob haCohen of Lunelle. *Orhot Hayim*. Ed. Elyakim Schlesinger. Berlin: Zvi Hirsch Itzckowski, 1902.

———. *Sefer Orhot Hayim*. Ed. Moses Schlesinger, 3 vols. Repr. Jerusalem: haTehiya, 1955.

Abraham b. Azriel. *Sefer Arugat haBosem*. Ed. Ephraim Elimelekh Urbach. Jerusalem: Mekize Nirdamim, 1939.

Answers and Rulings by Scholars of Ashkenaz and France According to MS Bodleian 692, Along with an Introduction and Notes by Ephraim Kupfer. Jerusalem: Mekize Nirdamim, 1973 [Hebrew].
Asher b. Yehiel. *Shut haRosh.* Ed. Yitzhak Shlomo Yudelov. Jerusalem: Makhon Yerushalayim, 1994.
Augustinus Hipponensis Episcopi. *Sermones PL* 38, 40. Paris: J. P. Migne, 1841, 1857.
Avigdor b. Elijah Katz haTzarfati. *Perushim uPesakim al haTorah leRabbi Avigdor haTzarfati.* Jerusalem: Makhon Hararei Kedem, 1996.
Avraham b. Ephraim. *Compendium Libri Sefer Mitzvot Gadol.* Ed. Yehoshua Horowitz. Jerusalem: Mekize Nirdamim, 2005 [Hebrew].
Avraham Hildik. "Minhagei R. Avraham Hildik." Ed. Shlomoh Spitzer. *Kobez al Yad, Minora manuscripta hebraica* 9, 151–215. Jerusalem: Mekize Nirdamim, 1980.
———. "Minhagei R. Avraham Hildik." In *Sefer haMinhagim leRabbenu Avraham Klausner,* ed. Shlomoh Spitzer, 196–202. Jerusalem: Makhon Yerushalayim, 2005.
"Baraitah deMassekhet Niddah." In *Sefer Tosefta Atiktah,* ed. Haim M. Horowitz. Frankfurt: K. M. Horowitz, 1899.
Barukh b. Isaac. *Sefer haTerumah.* Warsaw: Wenterhendler, 1897.
Burchardus Wormatiensis, Episcopi. *Decretorum, PL* 140, 537–1096. Paris: J. P. Migne, 1853.
Caesarius Heisterbacensis. *Dialogus miraculorum.* Ed. Josephus Strange. Köln: H. Lempertz and Co., 1851.
———. *Dialogus miraculorum, The Dialogue on Miracles.* Trans. H. von E. Scott and C. C. Swinton Bland. With an introduction by G. G. Coulton. London: G. Routledge and Sons Ltd., 1929.
David Abudraham b. Joseph. *Sefer Abudraham.* Berlin: Zvi Hirsch Itzckowski, 1900; repr. Jerusalem: Machon Even Yisroel, 1995.
de Pizan, Christine. *Le livre des trois vertus. Edition critique.* Ed. Charity Cannon Willard and Eric Hicks. Paris: Libr. H. Champion, 1989.
de Rebus Alsaticis ineuntis saeculi XIII. Ed. P. Jaffé, *Monumenta Germaniae Historica* SS 17, Hanover 1861.
Durandus. Guilliame. *Rationale divinorum officiorum.* Louisville: Fons Vitae, 2007.
Eleazar b. Judah. *Oratio ad Pascum.* Ed. Simcha Emanuel Jerusalem: Mekize Nirdamim, 2006 [Hebrew].
———. *Perushey Siddur haTefilah laRokeah.* Ed. Moshe Hershler and Yehudah A. Hershler. Jerusalem: Makhon Harav Hershler, 1992.
———. *Sefer Rokeah.* Fano: Gershon Soncino, 1505.
———. *Sefer Rokeah haGadol.* Jerusalem: S. Weinfeld, 1960.
Eliezar b. Nathan. *Sefer Ra'avan, Hu Sefer Even haEzer.* Jerusalem: H. Vagshal, 1984.
Eliezer b. Joel haLevi. *Sefer Ra'aviah.* Ed. Victor Aptowizer. 4 vols. Berlin: Machon Harry Fischel, 1914; repr. Jerusalem: Mekize Nirdamim, 1983.
———. *Sefer Ra'aviah.* Ed. David Deblytski. 4 vols. Bnei Brak: David Deblytski, 2005.
Eliezer b. Samuel of Metz. *Sefer Yere'im.* Vilna, 1894, 1902; repr. Jerusalem: Makhon Torah shebeKhtav, 2002.
Elijah Menahem b. Moses of London. *Perushei R. Eliyahu meLondrish uPsakav.* Ed. Mordechai Yehuda Leib. Jerusalem: Mossad haRav Kook, 1956.
Ephraim b. Jacob of Bonn. *Sefer Zekhirah.* Ed. Avraham M. Habermann. Jerusalem: Bialik Institute, 1970.
Genesis Rabbah. Ed. Theodor Albeck. 3 vols. Jerusalem: Wahrman Books, 1965 [Hebrew].
Genesis Rabbah. Vilna, 1885, repr. Jerusalem: H. Vagshal, 1988.
Glikl, Memoires, 1691–1719. Ed. Chava Turniyansky. Jerusalem: Merkaz Zalman Shazar, 2006 [Hebrew].

Haim b. Isaac. *Drashot Maharah Or Zaru'a.* Ed. Yitzhak Shimshon Lange. Jerusalem: Daf Hen, 1972.
Herman-Judah. *A Short Account of His Own Conversion.* Trans. Karl F. Morrison. Charlottesville: University of Virginia Press, 1992.
Innocent III. *Opera Omnia, PL* 216. Paris: J. P. Migne, 1855.
Isaac b. Joseph of Corbeil. *Sefer Amudei Golah haNikra Sefer Mitzvot Katan.* Kapost: Israel Yafe, 1820; repr. Jerusalem, 1979.
———. *Piskey Rabenu R"I MeCorbeil.* Ed. Hayim Sha'anan. Bnei Brak: Sha'anan Family, 1988.
———. "Piskey R. Isaac of Corbeil." Ed. Isaac S. Lange. *HaMa'ayan* 16 (1976): 92–104.
Isaac b. Meir of Düren. *Sha'arei Dura.* Jerusalem: Or haSefer, 1974.
Isaac b. Moses. *Sefer Or Zaru'a.* 4 parts. 2 vols. Zhitomir: Hil, 1862.
———. *Sefer Or Zaru'a.* Ed. Shalom Klein et al. 2 vols. Jerusalem: Makhon Yerushalayim, 2001–2008.
Israel b. Petahyah Isserlein. *Terumat haDeshen.* Jerusalem: HaMossad le'Iddud Limmud Torah, 1992.
Jacob and Gershom the Circumcisers (haGozrim). *Sefer Zikhron Brit.* Ed. Jacob Glassberg. Berlin: Zvi Hirsch Itzckowski, 1892.
Jacob b. Abba Mari Anatoly. *Sefer Malmad haTalmidim.* Lyck: R. Siebert, 1866.
Jacob b. Judah of London. *Sefer Etz Hayim.* Ed. Israel Brodie. 3 vols. Jerusalem: Mossad haRav Kook, 1962–64.
Jacob b. Meir. *Sefer haYashar leRabbenu Tam. Heleq haHidushim.* Ed. Shimon Shlomo Schlesinger. Jerusalem: Kiryat Sefer, 1959.
Jacob b. Moses Moellin. *Shut Maharil* (Responsa of Rabbi Yaacov Moellin–Maharil). Ed. Yitzchok Satz. Jerusalem: Makhon Yerushalayim, 1979.
———. *Shut Maharil haHadashot* (New Responsa of Rabbi Yaacov Moellin–Maharil). Ed. Yitzchok Satz. Jerusalem: Makhon Yerushalayim, 1977.
———. *Sefer Maharil: Minhagim* (The Book of Maharil [Rabbi Yaacov Moellin]: Customs). Ed. Shlomoh J. Spitzer. Jerusalem: Makhon Yerushalayim, 1989.
Jacob Barukh b. Judah Landa. *Sefer haAgur haShalem.* Ed. Moshe Hershler. Jerusalem: Moznaim, 1960.
Jacob of Marvèges. *Shut Min haShamayim.* Ed. Reuven Margaliyot et al. Jerusalem: Mossad haRav Kook, 1957.
Jonah b. Abraham Gerondi. *Sefer Sod haTeshuvah, Iggeret haTeshuvah, Sefer Sha'arei Teshuvah.* Bnei Brak: Sifrei Chachamim, 1989; repr. 2011.
Jonas Aurelianensis Episcopus. "De institutione laicali." *PL* 106, 121–278. Paris: J. P. Migne, 1864.
Joseph b. Meir Ibn Zabara. *Sefer Sha'ashuim.* Ed. Judith Dishon. Jerusalem: R. Mass, 1985.
Joseph b. Moses, *Leket Yosher. Pesakim uMinhagim.* Ed. Jacob Freimann. Berlin: Zvi Hirsch Itzckowski, 1903, repr. Jerusalem, 1964.
Joseph Bekhor Shor. *Perushei R. Joseph Bekhor Shor al haTorah.* Ed. Yehoshafat Nevo. Jerusalem: Mossad haRav Kook, 1994.
Jousep (Juspa) Schammes. *Minhagim deKehilat Kodesh Wormeisa* (Wormser Minhagbuch). Ed. Benjamin Salomon Hamburger and Erich Zimmer. 2 vols. Jerusalem: Makhon Yerushalayim, 1988.
Judah b. Asher. *Teshuvot Zikhron Yehuda.* Ed. Yehuda Rosenberg. Jerusalem, 1972.
Judah b. Samuel. *Sefer haGematriyot.* Ed. Yaakov Israel Stahl. Jerusalem, 2005.
———. *Sefer Hasidim (Das Buch der Frommen).* Ed. Jehuda Wistinetzki. Frankfurt: M. A. Wahrmann, 1924.
———. *Sefer Hasidim according to MS Parma H3280.* Introduction by Ivan G. Marcus. Jerusalem: Merkaz Dinur, 1985.
———. *Sefer Hasidim.* Ed. Reuven Margaliot. Jerusalem: Mossad haRav Kook, 1957.
———. Princeton University Sefer Hasidim Database (PUSHD). https://etc.princeton.edu/sefer_hasidim.

Kol Bo. Jerusalem: Even Yisroel, 1997.
Le ménagier de Paris: A Medieval Household Book. Trans. Gina L. Greco and Christine M. Rose. Ithaca, N.Y.: Cornell University Press, 2009.
Mahzor leYamim Nora'im. Ed. Daniel Goldschmidt. 2 vols. Jerusalem: Koren, 1970.
Mahzor Pessah. Ed. Yonah Fraenkel. Jerusalem: Koren, 1993.
Mahzor Shavuot. Ed. Yonah Fraenkel. Jerusalem: Koren, 2000.
Mahzor Sukkot, Shmini Atzeret veSimhat Torah. Ed. Daniel Goldschmidt and Jonah Fraenkel. Jerusalem: Koren, 1981.
Massekhet Sofrim. Ed. Michael Higger. Newark: Bloch, 1931.
Megillat Ta'anit: Versions, Interpretation, History with a Critical Edition. Ed. Vered Noam. Jerusalem: Yad Yizhak Ben Zvi, 2003 [Hebrew].
Meir b. Barukh of Rothenburg. *Responsa of Meir of Rothenburg* (Prague). Ed. Moshe Blach. Budapest, 1895; repr. Tel Aviv and Bnei Brak: Yahadut, 1985.
———. *Responsa of R. Meir of Rothenburg and His Colleagues*. Ed. Simcha Emanuel. Jerusalem: World Union of Jewish Studies, 2012.
———. *Sefer haMinhagim deBei Maharam b. Barukh meRothenburg*. Ed. I. Elfenbein. New York: Beit haMidrash leRabbanim beAmerica, 1938.
———. *She'elot uTeshuvot*. Crimona edition. Repr. Bnei Brak: Yahadut, 1986.
———. *She'elot uTeshuvot*. Ed. R. N. Rabinowitz. Lvov: F. Galinski and S. L. Flecker, 1860; repr. Bnei Brak: Yahadut, 1985.
———. *She'elot uTeshuvot, Sha'arei Teshuvot*. Berlin: Zvi Hirsch Itzckowski, 1891; repr. Bnei Brak: Yahadut, 1985.
———. *Teshuvot, Pesakim uMinhagim* (Responsa, Rulings and Customs). Ed. Isaac Ze'ev Cahana, 3 vols. Jerusalem: Mossad haRav Kook, 1957–62.
Meir b. Yekutiel Cohen. *Hagahot Maimoniyot*. In Maimonides, *Mishneh Torah*, ed. Shabtai Frankel. 7 vols. Jerusalem: Frankel, 2005.
Menahem b. Shlomo. *Midrash Sekhel Tov*. Ed. Shlomo Buber. Berlin: Zvi Hirsch Itzckowski, 1900.
Menahem haMeiri. *Beit haBehirah leMassekhet Sotah*. Ed. Avraham Liss. Jerusalem: Hotza'at Makhon haTalmud haYisraeli haShalem, 1966.
———. *Hibbur haTeshuva leRabbenu Menahem haMeiri*. Ed. Samuel Mirsky. New York: Yeshiva University, 1950.
———. *Perush haMeiri on Proverbs*. Ed. Menahem Mendel Meshi Zahav. Jerusalem: Otzar haPoskim, 1969.
Midrash Rabbah. Ed. Moses Arye Mirkin. 11 vols. Tel Aviv: Yavneh, 1968.
Midrash Tanhuma. Ed. Shlomo Buber. 2 vols. Repr. New York: Hotza'at Sefer, 1946.
Midrash Tehillim haMekhune Shoher Tov. Ed. Shlomo Buber. Repr. New York: Om, 1947.
Midrash Wayyikra Rabbah. Ed. Mordecai Margulies. 2 vols. New York and Jerusalem: Beit haMidrash leRabbanim beAmerica, 1993.
Moses b. Eleazar. *Sefer haMaskil*. Ed. Shlomo Y. Yankowitz. Jerusalem: Yedei Khen, 2004.
Moses b. Jacob of Coucy. *Sefer Mitzvot Gadol (Semag)*. 2 vols. Venice, 1547; repr. Jerusalem: Defus S. Monzon, 1961.
Moses b. Menahem of Zurich. *Sefer haSemak miZurich*. Ed. Isaac Jacob Har-Shoshanim-Rosenberg. 3 vols. Jerusalem: Defus Alef-Bet, 1973–88.
Moses b. Yekutiel. *Sefer haTadir*. New York: M. Y. Blau, 1992.
Moses of Evreux. "Sefer Al HaKol." *HaGoren* 7 (1907).
Moses Parnas. *Sefer haParnas*. Vilna: Katzenelinbogen, 1891.

Moshav Zekenim al haTorah. Ed. Saliman Sassoon. London: Honig and Sons, 1959.
Nathan b. Yehiel. *Arukh haShalem.* Ed. Alexander Kohut. 8 vols. Vienna: Menorah, 1926.
Newly Discovered Geonic Responsa, edited from MS Guenzberg 566, Russian State Library, Moscow and Geniza Fragments. Ed. Simcha Emanuel. Jerusalem: Sifriyat Ofek-Friedberg Library, 1995.
Nissim b. Jacob of Kirouan. *Hibbur haYafe min haYeshu'ah.* Trans. and introduction by Hayim Z. Hirshberg. Jerusalem: Mossad haRav Kook, 1954.
Otzar haGe'onim, Massekhet Yom Tov. Ed. B. M. Levine. Jerusalem: H. Vagshal, 1984.
Peretz b. Elijah. "Piskei Rabbenu Peretz." Ed. Haim Sha'anan. *Moriah* 17, 9–10 (1991): 10–15.
Pesikta Rabbati. Ed. Meir Friedmann (Ish Shalom). Vienna, 1880; repr. Tel Aviv: Esther, 1923.
Petrus Alfonsi. *The Disciplina Clericalis of Petrus Alfonsi.* Trans. and ed. Eberhard Hermes. Berkeley: University of California Press, 1977.
Pirkei deRabbi Eliezer. Jerusalem: Eshkol, 1973.
Rivkah bat Meir. *Meneket Rivkah. A Manual of Wisdom and Piety for Jewish Women by Rivkah bat Meir.* Ed. Frauke von Rohden. Philadelphia: Jewish Publication Society, 2009.
Rutebeuf. *Oeuvres completes de Rutebeuf.* Ed. Edmond Faral and Julia Bastin. Paris: E. and J. Picard, 1959.
Samson b. Tzadok. *Sefer Tashbetz.* Warsaw: Yaakov Ze'ev Unterhanler, 1901.
Sefer Gezerot Ashkenaz veZarfat. Ed. Avraham M. Habermann. Jerusalem: Sifrei Tarshish, 1945.
Sefer haGan. Venice: Zaniato Zaniti, 1608.
Sefer haKushiyot. Ed. Yaakov Israel Stahl. Jerusalem: J. Stahl, 2007.
Sefer haMiktzo'ot. Ed. Simcha Assaf. Jerusalem: Mossad haRav Kook, 1947.
Sefer Makom sheNahagu. Minhag Bechhofen. Ed. Shlomo Katanka. London: Makhon Moreshet Ashkenaz, 2011.
Sefer haNiyar. Ed. Gershon Appel. New York: Sura, 1960.
Sefer Tosafot haShalem. Commentary on the Bible. Ed. Jacob Gellis et al. 12 vols. Jerusalem: Mif'al Tosafot haShalem, 1982–2009.
Shalom b. Isaac of Neustadt. *Decisions and Customs.* Ed. Shlomoh Spitzer. Jerusalem: Makhon Yerushalayim, 1977 [Hebrew].
Sifran shel Rishonim, Teshuvot uP'sakim uMinhagot, Yotzim Laor Pa'am Rishonah Mekitvey Yad. Ed. Simcha Assaf. Jerusalem: Mekize Nirdamim, 1935.
Simha b. Samuel of Vitry. *Mahzor Vitry.* Ed. Simon haLevi Horowitz. Nürnberg: Mekize Nirdamim, 1892.
———. *Mahzor Vitry.* Ed. Aryeh Goldschmidt. 3 vols. Jerusalem: Makhon Otzar haPoskim, 2004.
Solomon b. Abraham Parhon. *Salomonis b. Abrahami Parchon Aragonensis Lexicon Hebraicum.* Ed. Solomon Rapoport. Pressburg, 1844; repr. Jerusalem: Makor, 1970.
Solomon b. Isaac (Rashi). *Sefer Likutei haPardes.* Repr. Bnei Brak: HaSifriya haHaredit haOlamit, 1999.
———. *Sefer haPardes and Likutei haPardes (Liturgical and Ritual Work, attributed to Rashi).* Ed. Haym Judah Ehrenreich. Budapest: Defus haAhim Katsburg, 1924.
———. *Sefer haOrah. (Ritualwerk Raschi).* Ed. Salomon Buber. Lemberg: S. Buber, 1905.
———. *Responsa Rashi.* Ed. Israel Elfenbein. New York: Shulsinger Brothers Press, 1943.
———. *Siddur Rashi. (Ritualwerk, R. Salomo ben Isaak zugeschreiben).* Ed. Jacob Freimann and Shlomo Buber. Berlin: Mekize Nirdamim, 1911.
Steinheim database of epitaphs. http://www.steinheim-institut.de:50580/cgi-bin/epidat.
Teshuvot haGe'onim: Sha'arei Teshuvah. Livorno: A. Ben Amuzag, 1869.
Thomas de Chobham. *Summa confessorum.* Ed. F. Broomfield. Louvain: Editions Nauwelaerts; Paris: Beatrice Nauwelaerts, 1968.

Tuviah b. Eliezer. *Midrash Lekah Tov, haMekhune P'sikta Zutra al Hamisha Humshei Torah*. Ed. Shlomo Buber. Vilna: Re'em, 1884.
Tzidkiyah b. Abraham haRofeh. *Sefer Shibbolei haLeket*. Ed. Solomon Buber. Vilna: Re'em, 1887.
Yehiel b. Judah of Paris. *Vikuakh R. Yehiel miParis meBa'alei haTosafot*. Ed. Reuven Margaliyot. Jerusalem: Reuven Margaliyot, 1928.

SECONDARY SOURCES

Abrahams, Israel. *Jewish Life in the Middle Ages*. Philadelphia: Jewish Publication Society, 1896.
Abrams, Lesley. "Germanic Christianities 600–1100." In *Early Medieval Christianities, c. 600–c. 1100*. Vol. 3 of *The Cambridge History of Christianity*, ed. Thomas X. Noble and Julia H. M. Smith, 341–405. Cambridge: Cambridge University Press, 2008.
Abulafia-Sapir, Anna. *Christian-Jewish Relations, 1000–1300: Jews in the Service of Medieval Christendom*. Harlow, UK: Longman, 2010.
Agus, Irving A. "The Development of the Money Clause in the Ashkenazic Ketubah." *JQR* 30 (1939–40): 221–56.
———. *The Heroic Age of Franco-German Jewry: The Jews of Germany and France of the Tenth and Eleventh Centuries, the Pioneers and Builders of Town-Life, Town-Government, and Institutions*. 2 vols. New York: Yeshiva University Press, 1969.
———. *Rabbi Meir of Rothenburg: His Life and His Works as Sources for the Religious, Legal and Social History of the Jews of Germany in the Thirteenth Century*. Philadelphia: Dropsie College, 1947.
———. "The Standard Ketubah of the German Jews and Its Economic Implications." *JQR* 42 (1951–52): 225–32.
Albeck, Shalom. "Rabbenu Tam's Attitude to the Problems of His Time." *Zion* 19 (1954): 104–41 [Hebrew].
Alexander, Elizabeth Shanks. *Gender and Timebound Commandments in Judaism*. Cambridge: Cambridge University Press, 2013.
Algazi, Gadi. "Introduction: Doing Things with Gifts." In *Negotiating the Gift: Pre-modern Figurations of Exchange*, ed. Gadi Algazi, Valentin Gröbner, and Bernhard Jussen, 9–28. Göttingen: Vandenhoeck and Ruprecht, 2003.
Althoff, Gerd. "The Variability of Rituals in the Middle Ages." In *Medieval Concepts of the Past. Ritual, Memory, Historiography*, ed. Gerd Althoff, Johannes Fried, and Patrick J. Geary, 71–88. Washington, D.C.: German Historical Institute; Cambridge: Cambridge University Press, 2002.
Ames, Christina Caldwell. *Righteous Persecution: Inquisition, Dominicans, and Christianity in the Middle Ages*. Philadelphia: University of Pennsylvania Press, 2009.
Anderson, C. Colt. "Ritual Purity and Pastoral Reform in the Thirteenth Century." In *A Companion to Pastoral Care in the Late Middle Ages (1200–1500)*, ed. Ronald J. Stansbury, 73–94. Leiden: Brill, 2010.
Anderson, Gary A. "Almsgiving as an Expression of Faith." *Deuterocanonical and Cognate Literature Yearbook* (2011): 121–31.
Angenendt, Arnold. "*Donationes pro anima*: Gift and Countergift in the Early Medieval Liturgy." In *The Long Morning of Medieval Europe: New Directions in Early Medieval Studies*, ed. Jennifer R. Davis and Michael McCormick, 131–54. Aldershot: Ashgate, 2008.
———. "Theologie und Liturgie der mittelalterlichen Toten-Memoria." In *Memoria. Der Geschichtliche Zeugniswert des Liturgischen Gedenkens im Mittelalter*, ed. Karl Schmid and Joachim Wollasch, 79–199. Munich: W. Fink, 1984.

Aptowizer, Avigdor. *Mavo leSefer Ra'aviah*. Repr. Jerusalem: Sifrei Yahadut, 1984.
Arbesmann, Rudolph. "Fasting and Prophecy in Pagan and Christian Antiquity." *Traditio* 7 (1949): 1–71.
Ashley, Kathleen M. *Victor Turner and the Construction of Cultural Criticism*. Bloomington: Indiana University Press, 1990.
Assaf, David. "Meoravuta shel haKehila haYehudit beYemei haBenayim bePidyon Shvuyim." M.A. thesis, Hebrew University of Jerusalem, 1985.
Assaf, Lilach. "The Language of Names: Jewish Onomastics in Late Medieval Germany, Identity and Acculturation." In *Spätmittelalterliche Praktiken der Namengebung im europäischen Vergleich*, ed. Christof Rolker and Gabriela Signori, 149–60. Konstanz: UVK, 2011.
Assis, Yom Tov. *The Golden Age of Aragonese Jewry: Community and Society in the Crown of Aragon, 1213–1327*. London: Littman Library of Jewish Civilization, 1997.
Aston, Margaret. "Segregation in Church." In *Women in the Church*, ed. W. J. Shiels and Diana Wood. *Studies in Church History* 27 (1990): 237–94.
Austin, Greta. "Jurisprudence in the Service of Pastoral Care: The 'Decretum' of Burchard of Worms." *Speculum* 79 (2004): 929–59.
Avneri, Zvi, ed. *Germania Judaica II*. Tübingen: J. C. B. Mohr; Jerusalem: Leo Baeck Institute, 1968.
Avril, Israel Joseph. "La paroisse medieval et la prière pour les morts." In *L'église et la mémoire des mort dans la France medieval*, ed. Jean Loup-Lemaitre, 53–68. Paris: Etudes Augustiniennes, 1986.
Baer, Yitzhak. "Religious-Social Tendency of Sepher Hassidim." *Zion* 3 (1938): 1–50 [Hebrew].
Balberg, Mira. "Elu Nedarim sheHu Mefer. Iyyun beSheelat Hagdaratam veSivugam shel Nedarim Nitanim leHafara beSafrut haTanaim vehaAmoraim." M.A. thesis, Hebrew University of Jerusalem, 2005.
Baron, Salo Wittmayer. *The Jewish Community: Its History and Structure to the American Revolution*. Philadelphia: Jewish Publication Society, 1942.
———. "'Plenitude of Apostolic Powers' and Medieval 'Jewish Serfdom.'" In *Ancient and Medieval Jewish History: Essays*, 308–22. New Brunswick, N.J.: Rutgers University Press, 1972.
———. "Problems of Jewish Identity, from an Historical Perspective, A Survey." *Proceedings of the American Academy for Jewish Research* 46–47 (1979–1980): 33–67.
———. *A Social and Religious History of the Jews*. 18 vols. New York: Columbia University Press, 1952–1993.
Barzen, Rainer. "Das Nürnberger Memorbuch. Eine Einführung." In *Corpus der Quellen zur mittelalterlichen Geschichte der Juden im Reichsgebiet*, ed. Alfred Haverkamp and Jörg R. Müller. 2011. http://www.medieval-ashkenaz.org/quellen/nuernberger-memorbuch/einleitung.html.
———. "The Meaning of *Tzedakkah* for Jewish Self-Organisation Within a Non-Jewish Environment." *Iggud: Selected Essays in Jewish Studies* 2 (2009): 7–17.
Baskin, Judith R. "Dolce of Worms: The Lives and Deaths of an Exemplary Medieval Jewish Woman and Her Daughters." In *Judaism in Practice*, ed. Lawrence Fine, 429–37. Princeton, N.J.: Princeton University Press, 2001.
———. "From Separation to Displacement: The Problem of Women in Sefer Hasidim." *AJS Review* 19 (1994): 1–18.
———. "Jewish Women in the Middle Ages." In *Jewish Women in Historical Perspective*, ed. Judith R. Baskin, 101–27. Detroit: Wayne State University Press, 1998.
———. "Mabat Hadash al haIsha haYehudiya beAshkenaz Biyemey haBeinayim." In *"Lift up Your Voice": Women's Voices and Feminist Interpretation in Jewish Studies*, ed. Rina Levine Melammed, 72–84. Tel Aviv: Miskol, 2001.

———. "Male Piety, Female Bodies: Men, Women and Ritual Immersion in Medieval Ashkenaz." *Jewish Law Association Studies* 17 (2007): 11–30.
Baumgarten, Albert. "The Nature of Religious Extremism." In *Religious Extremism*, ed. Meir Litvak and Ora Limor, 43–56. Jerusalem: Merkaz Zalman Shazar, 2007 [Hebrew].
Baumgarten, Elisheva. "Charitable Like Abigail: The History of an Epitaph." *JQR* (2014) forthcoming.
———. "Conceptions of Childhood: Education of Young Children in Medieval Jewish Communities." In *Medieval Children and Childhood*, ed. Joel Rosenthal, 56–74. Sheffield: Shaun Tyas, 2007.
———. "Gender in der aschkenasischen Synagoge im Hochmittelalter." In *Die SchUM-Gemeinden Speyer–Worms–Mainz. Auf dem Weg zum Welterbe*, ed. Pia Haberer und Ursula Reuters, 63–75. Regensburg: Landesmuseum Mainz, 2013.
———. *Mothers and Children: Jewish Family Life in Medieval Europe*. Princeton, N.J.: Princeton University Press, 2004.
———. "'Remember That Glorious Girl': Jephthah's Daughter in Medieval Jewish Culture." *JQR* 97 (2007): 180–209.
———. "Seeking Signs? Jews, Christians, and Proof by Fire in Medieval Germany and Northern France." In *New Perspectives on Jewish-Christian Relations: Essays in Honor of David Berger*, ed. Elisheva Carlebach and Jacob J. Schacter, 205–25. Leiden: Brill, 2012.
———. "Shared Stories and Religious Rhetoric: R. Judah the Pious, Peter the Chanter and a Drought." *Medieval Encounters* 18 (2012): 36–54.
———. "A Tale of a Christian Matron and Sabbath Candles: Religious Difference, Material Culture and Gender in Thirteenth Century Germany." *JSQ* 20 (2013): 83–99.
———. "Two Tales of Pious Pretenders: Gender and Piety in Medieval Culture." In *Tov Elem: Memory, Community and Gender in Medieval and Early Modern Jewish Culture, Festschrift in Honor of Prof. Robert Bonfil*, ed. Elisheva Baumgarten, Roni Weinstein, and Amnon Raz-Krakotzkin, 68–90. Jerusalem: Mossad Bialik, 2011 [Hebrew].
Baumgarten, Elisheva, and Rella Kushelevsky. "From 'The Mother and Her Sons' to 'The Mother of the Sons' in Ashkenaz." *Zion* 71, (2006): 273–300 [Hebrew].
Becker, Adam H. "The Comparative Study of 'Scholasticism' in Late-Antique Mesopotamia: Rabbis and East Syrians." *AJS Review* 34 (2010): 91–113.
Beer, Moshe. "On Penances of Penitents in the Literature of Hazal." *Zion* 46 (1981): 159–81 [Hebrew].
Bell, Catherine M. *Ritual Theory, Ritual Practice*. New York: Oxford University Press, 1992.
Bell, Dean. *Sacred Communities: Jewish and Christian Identities in Fifteenth Century Germany*. Leiden: Brill, 2001.
Ben-Naeh, Yaron. "Poverty, Paupers and Poor Relief in Ottoman Jewish Society." *REJ* 163 (2004): 151–92.
Benin, Stephen D. "A Hen Crowing Like a Cock: 'Popular Religion' and Jewish Law." *Journal of Jewish Thought and Philosophy* 8 (1999): 261–81.
Bennett, Judith. "Forgetting the Past." *Gender and History* 20 (2008): 669–77.
Berger, Aliza. "Wrapped Attention: May Women Wear Tefillin?" In *Jewish Legal Writings by Women*, ed. Micah D. Halperin and Chana Safrai, 75–118. Efrat: Urim Publications, 1998.
Berger, David. "Book Review: The Early Sages of Ashkenaz." *Tarbiz* 53 (1981): 479–87 [Hebrew].
———. "A Generation of Scholarship on Jewish-Christian Interaction in the Medieval World." *Tradition* 38 (2004): 4–14.

———. "Jacob Katz on Jews and Christians in the Middle Ages." In *The Pride of Jacob: Essays on Jacob Katz and His Work*, ed. Jay M. Harris, 41–65. Cambridge, Mass.: Harvard University Center for Jewish Studies, 2002.

———. *The Jewish-Christian Debate in the High Middle Ages, Sefer Nizzahon Vetus*. Philadelphia: Jewish Publication Society, 1979.

———. "Mission to the Jews and Jewish-Christian Contacts in the Polemical Literature of the High Middle Ages." *American Historical Review* 91 (1986): 586–87.

Berger, Isaiah. "Folk Legends on Rashi." In *Rashi: His Teachings and Personality*, ed. Simon Federbush, 147–79. New York: Torah Culture Department of the Jewish Agency, 1958 [Hebrew].

Bériou, Nicole. "La confession dans les écrits théologiques." In *L'aveu: Antiquité et moyen âge*, ed. Jean-Claude Maire Vigueur, 261–82. Rome: Ecole française de Rome, 1986.

Bériou, Nicole, Jacques Berlioz, and Jean Longère, eds. *Prier au moyen age. Pratiques et experiences (Ve-XVe siecles)*. Turnhout: Brepols 1991.

Berkey, Jonathan. "Popular Culture Under the Mamluks: A Historiographical Survey." *Mamluk Studies Review* 9 (2005): 133–46.

Berliner, Adolf. *Aus dem inneren Leben der deutschen Juden im Mittelalter: Nach gedruckten und ungedruckten Quellen. Zugleich ein Beitrag für deutsche Culturgeschichte*. Berlin: Julius Benzian, 1871.

Berlinerblau, Jacques. *The Vow and the "Popular Religious Groups" of Ancient Israel: A Philological and Sociological Inquiry*. Sheffield: Sheffield Academic Press, 1996.

Berman, Constance H. *Women and Monasticism in Medieval Europe: Sisters and Patrons of the Cistercian Reforms*. Kalamazoo, Mich.: Medieval Institute Publications 2002.

Biale, David, ed. *Blood and Belief: The Circulation of a Symbol Between Jews and Christians*. Berkeley: University of California Press, 2007.

———. *Cultures of the Jews: A New History*. New York: Schocken Books, 2002.

Biller, Peter. "The Common Woman in the Western Church in the Thirteenth and Early Fourteenth Centuries." *Studies in Church History* 27 (1990): 127–57.

———. "Popular Religion in the Middle Ages." In *Companion to Historiography*, ed. Michael Bentley, 221–46. New York: Routledge, 1997.

Biller, Peter, and Alastair J. Minnis, eds. *Handling Sin: Confession in the Middle Ages*. Woodbridge: York Medieval Press, 1998.

———. "Confession in the Middle Ages: Introduction." In *Handling Sin: Confession in the Middle Ages*, ed. Peter Biller and Alastair J. Minnis, 1–33. Woodbridge: York Medieval Press, 1998.

Blumenfeld-Kosinski, Renate. "Satires of the Beguines in Northern French Literature." In *New Trends in Feminine Spirituality: The Holy Women of Liège and Their Impact*, ed. Juliette Dor, Lesley Johnson, and Jocelyn Wogan-Browne, 233–46. Turnhout: Brepols, 1999.

Bock, Gisela. "Challenging Dichotomies: Perspectives on Women's History." In *Writing Women's History: International Perspectives*, ed. Karen Offen, Ruth Roach Pierson, and Jane Rendall, 1–24. Bloomington: Indiana University Press, 1991.

Böhl, Felix. "Die hebräischen Handschriften zur Verfolgung der Juden Nordhausens und ihrem Tanz zum Tode im Jahre 1349." In *Tanz und Tod in Kunst und Literatur*, ed. Franz H. Link, 127–38. Berlin: Duncker und Humblot, 1993.

Böhringer, Letha. "Kölner Beginen im Spätmittelalter Kloster und Welt." *Geschichte in Köln* 53 (2006): 7–34.

Bonfil, Robert. "Cultural and Religious Traditions of French Jewry in the Ninth Century as Reflected in the Writings of Agobard of Lyons." In *Studies in Jewish Mysticism, Philosophy and Ethical*

Literature: Presented to Isaiah Tishby on His Seventy-fifth Birthday, ed. Joseph Dan and Joseph R. Hacker, 327–48. Jerusalem: Magnes Press, 1986 [Hebrew].

———. *History and Folklore in a Medieval Jewish Chronicle: The Family Chronicle of Ahima'az ben Paltiel*. Leiden: Brill, 2009.

———. *Jewish Life in Renaissance Italy*. Trans. Anthony Oldcorn. Berkeley: University of California Press, 1994.

———. "The Right to Cry Aloud." In *From Sages to Savants: Studies Presented to Avraham Grossman*, ed. Joseph R. Hacker, Yosef Kaplan, and B. Z. Kedar, 145–56. Jerusalem: Merkaz Zalman Shazar, 2010.

Bouchard, Constance Brittain. *Sword, Miter and Cloister: Nobility and the Church in Burgundy, 980–1198*. Ithaca, N.Y.: Cornell University Press, 1987.

Bourdieu, Pierre. *The Logic of Practice*. Trans. Richard Nice. Stanford, Calif.: Stanford University Press, 1990.

———. *Outline of a Theory of Practice*. Trans. Richard Nice. Cambridge: Cambridge University Press, 1977.

———. "Rites as Acts of Institution." In *Honor and Grace in Anthropology*, ed. John G. Peristiany and Julian Pitt-Rivers, 81–88. New York: Cambridge University Press, 1992.

Bowie, Fiona. *The Anthropology of Religion: An Introduction*. Oxford: Blackwell Publishers, 2000.

Brakke, David. "The Problematization of Nocturnal Emissions in Early Christian Syria, Egypt, and Gaul." *Journal of Early Christian Studies* 3 (1995): 416–60.

Breuer, Mordechai. "The 'Black Death' and Antisemitism." In *Antisemitism Through the Ages: A Collection of Essays*, ed. Shmuel Almog, 139–52. Jerusalem: Merkaz Zalman Shazar, 1980.

Brodman, James William. *Charity and Religion in Medieval Europe*. Washington, D.C.: Catholic University of America Press, 2009.

Brongers, Henrik Antonie. "Fasting in Israel in Biblical and Post-Biblical Times." *Oudtestamentische Studiën* 20 (1977): 1–21.

Brooke, Rosalind, and Christopher Brooke. *Popular Religion in the Middle Ages: Western Europe, 1000–1300*. London: Thames and Hudson, 1984.

Brooten, Bernadette. *Women Leaders in Ancient Synagogues*. Chicago: Scholars Press, 1982.

Browe, Peter. *Beiträge zur Sexualethik des Mittelalters*. Breslau: Müller und Seiffert, 1932.

Brown, Peter L. *The Cult of the Saints: Its Rise and Function in Latin Christianity*. Chicago: University of Chicago Press, 1981.

———. *Poverty and Leadership in the Later Roman Empire*. Hanover, N.H.: University Press of New England, 2002.

———. "The Rise and Fall of the Holy Man in Late Antiquity." *Journal of Roman Studies* 61 (1971): 80–101.

Brühl, Carlrichard. *Deutschland-Frankreich: Die Geburt zweier Völker*. Cologne and Vienna: Böhlau, 1990.

Buc, Philippe. "David's Adultery with Bathsheba and the Healing of Capetian Kings." *Viator* 24 (1993): 101–20.

Büchler, Adolf. *Types of Jewish-Palestinian Piety from 70 BCE to 70 CE: The Ancient Pious Men*. London: Jews College, 1922.

Buckley, Thomas, and Alma Gottlieb, eds. *Blood Magic: The Anthropology of Menstruation*. Berkeley: University of California Press, 1988.

Burke, Peter. *History and Social Theory*. Cambridge: Polity, 1992.

———. *Popular Culture in Early Modern Europe*. Aldershot: Ashgate, 1994.

———. *What Is Cultural History?* Cambridge: Polity, 2008.
Burns, E. Jane. *Courtly Love Undressed: Reading Through Clothes in Medieval French Culture.* Philadelphia: University of Pennsylvania Press, 2002.
———. "Introduction: Why Textiles Make a Difference." In *Medieval Fabrications: Dress, Textile, Clothwork and Other Cultural Imaginings,* ed. E. Jane Burns, 1–19. New York: Palgrave Macmillan, 2004.
Burns, Robert I. *Jews in the Notarial Culture: Latinate Wills in Mediterranean Spain, 1250–1350.* Berkeley: University of California Press, 1996.
Bynum, Caroline Walker. *Christian Materiality: An Essay on Religion in Late Medieval Europe.* New York: Zone Books, 2011.
———. "Did the Twelfth Century Discover the Individual?" In *Jesus as Mother: Studies in the Spirituality of the High Middle Ages,* 85–109. Berkeley: University of California Press, 1982.
———. *Holy Feast and Holy Fast: The Religious Significance of Food to Medieval Women.* Berkeley: University of California Press, 1987.
———. *Jesus as Mother: Studies in the Spirituality of the High Middle Ages.* Berkeley: University of Claifornia Press, 1982.
———. "Perspectives, Connections and Objects: What Is Happening in History Now?" *Daedalus* 138 (2009): 71–86.
———. *Wonderful Blood: Theology and Practice in Late Medieval Northern Germany and Beyond.* Philadelphia: University of Pennsylvania Press, 2007.
Carlebach, Elisheva. "Early Modern Ashkenaz in the Writings of Jacob Katz." In *The Pride of Jacob: Essays on Jacob Katz and His Work,* ed. Jay M. Harris, 65–85. Cambridge, Mass.: Harvard University Center for Jewish Studies, 2002.
———. *Palaces of Time: Jewish Calendar and Culture in Early Modern Europe.* Cambridge: Belknap Press of Harvard University Press, 2011.
Cassen, Flora. "Identity or Control: The Jewish Badge in Renaissance Italy." Ph.D. diss., New York University, 2008.
Cayam, Aviva. "Fringe Benefits: Women and Tzitzit." In *Jewish Legal Writings by Women,* ed. Micah D. Halperin and Chana Safrai, 119–42. Efrat: Urim Publications, 1998.
Chamberlain, Michael. *Knowledge and Social Practice in Medieval Damascus, 1190–1350.* Cambridge: Cambridge University Press, 1994.
Chartier, Roger. *Cultural History: Between Practices and Representations.* Ithaca, N.Y.: Cornell University Press, 1988.
———. "Culture as Appropriation: Popular Cultural Uses in Early Modern France." In *Understanding Popular Culture: Europe from the Middle Ages to the Nineteenth Century,* ed. Steven L. Kaplan, 229–53. Berlin: Mouton, 1984.
Chazan, Robert. *The Jews of Medieval Western Christendom, 1000–1500.* Cambridge: Cambridge University Press, 2006.
———. *Reassessing Jewish Life in Medieval Europe.* Cambridge: Cambridge University Press, 2010.
Chiffoleau, Jacques. *La comptabilité de l'Au-Delà: Les hommes, la mort et la religion dans la région d'Avignon à la fin du Moyen Age (vers 1320–vers 1480).* Rome: École française de Rome, 1980.
———. "Sur la pratique et conjoncture de l'aveu judiciaire en France et en Italie du XIIIè au XVè siècle." In *L'Aveu. Antiquité et Moyen Age. Actes de la table-ronde de Rome (Mars 1984),* ed. Jean-Claude Marie Viguer, 341–80. Rome: Ecole française de Rome, 1986.
———. "Sur l'usage obsessional de la messe pour les morts à la fin du Moyen Âge." In *Faire croire:*

Modalités de la diffusion et de la reception des messages religieux du XII au XV siècle, ed. André Vauchez, 235–56. Rome: École française de Rome, 1981.

Clancy, P. M. J. "Fast and Abstinence." *New Catholic Encyclopedia* 5:847–50. New York: McGraw-Hill, 1967.

Classen, Albrecht, ed. *Urban Space in the Middle Ages and the Early Modern Age*. Berlin: Walter de Gruyter, 2010.

Cohen, Daniel. "He'arot uMilu'im leMehkaro shel A. Ya'ari al Tefillat Mi sheBerakh." *Kiryat Sefer* 40 (1964–1965): 542.

Cohen, Jeremy. *Living Letters of the Law: Ideas of the Jew in Medieval Christianity*. Berkeley: University of California Press, 1999.

———. *Sanctifying the Name of God: Jewish Martyrs and Jewish Memories of the First Crusade*. Philadelphia: University of Pennsylvania Press, 2004.

Cohen, Mark R. *Poverty and Charity in the Jewish Community of Medieval Egypt*. Princeton, N.J.: Princeton University Press, 2005.

———. *Under Crescent and Cross: The Jews in the Middle Ages*. Princeton, N.J.: Princeton University Press, 1994.

———. *The Voice of the Poor in the Middle Ages: An Anthology of Documents from the Cairo Geniza*. Princeton, N.J.: Princeton University Press, 2005.

Cohen, Shaye J. D. *The Beginnings of Jewishness: Boundaries, Varieties, Uncertainties*. Berkeley: University of California Press, 1999.

———. "Purity and Piety: The Separation of Menstruants from the Sancta." In *Daughters of the King: Women and the Synagogue*, ed. Susan Grossman and Rivka Haut, 103–15. Philadelphia: Jewish Publication Society, 1992.

———. "Purity, Piety, and Polemic, Medieval Rabbinic Denunciations of 'Incorrect' Purification Practices." In *Women and Water: Menstruation in Jewish Life and Law*, ed. Rahel R. Wasserfall, 82–100. Hanover, N.H.: University Press of New England for Brandeis University Press, 1999.

———. *Why Aren't Jewish Women Circumcised? Gender and Covenant in Judaism*. Berkeley: University of California Press, 2005.

Colgrave, B., and R. A. B. Mynors. *Bede's Ecclesiastical History of the English People*. Oxford: Clarendon, 1969.

Constable, Giles. "Introduction." In *Burchardi, ut videtur, abbatis Bellevallis, Apologia de barbis*. CCCM 62, 47–130. Turnhout: Brepols, 1985.

———. *The Reformation of the Twelfth Century*. Cambridge: Cambridge University Press, 1996.

Counihan, Carol, and Penny van Esterik, eds. *Food and Culture: A Reader*. New York: Routledge, 1997.

Cuffel, Alexandra. "From Practice to Polemic: Shared Saints and Festivals as 'Women's Religion' in the Medieval Mediterranean." *Bulletin of School of Oriental and African Studies* 68 (2005): 401–19.

Cullum, Patricia. "'And Her Name Was Charite': Charitable Giving by and for Women in Late Medieval Yorkshire." In *Women in Medieval English Society*, ed. P. J. P. Goldberg, 182–210. Stroud: Sutton Publishing, 1997.

———. "Gendering Charity in Medieval Hagiography." In *Gender and Holiness: Men, Women and Saints in Late Medieval Europe*, ed. Sarah Salih and Sam Riches, 135–51. London: Routledge, 2002.

Cullum, Patricia H., and Katherine J. Lewis, eds. *Holiness and Masculinity in the Middle Ages*. Cardiff: University of Wales Press, 2005.

Dan, Joseph. "A Note on the History of 'Teshuvah' Among Ashkenaz Chasidim." In *The World of*

Rav Kook's Thought, Yovel Orot, ed. Benjamin Ish-Shalom, 221–28. Jerusalem: Sifriat Eliner, 1998 [Hebrew].
———. *Safrut haMusar vehaDrush*. Jerusalem: Keter, 1975.
———. "Sippurim Demonologim miKitvei R. Judah heHasid." In *The Religious and Social Ideas of the Jewish Pietists in Medieval Germany: Collected Essays*, ed. Ivan G. Marcus, 165–82. Jerusalem: Merkaz Zalman Shazar, 1987.
Davis, Natalie Zemon. "From Popular Religion to Religious Cultures." In *Reformation Europe: A Guide to Research*, ed. Steven Ozment, 321–42. St. Louis: Center for Reformation Research, 1982.
———. *The Gift in Sixteenth Century France*. Madison: University of Wisconsin Press, 2000.
———. *Women on the Margins: Three Seventeenth-Century Lives*. Cambridge, Mass.: Harvard University Press, 1995.
———. "Women's History in Transition: The European Case." *Feminist Studies* 3 (1976): 83–103.
De Certeau, Michel. *Practice of Everyday Life*. Trans. Steven Rendall. Berkeley: University of California Press, 1984.
De Jong, Mayke. *In Samuel's Image: Child Oblation in the Early Medieval West*. Leiden: Brill, 1996.
———. *The Penitential State: Authority and Atonement in the Age of Louis the Pious, 814–840*. Cambridge: Cambridge University Press, 2009.
———. "What Was Public About Public Penance, Paenitentia Publica and Justice in the Carolingian World." In *La Guistizia nel'alto medioevo* (secolo ix–xi), 863–902. Rome: Centro italiano di studi sull'alto Medioevo, 1996.
Deeb, Lara. *An Enchanted Modern: Gender and Public Piety in Shi'i Lebanon*. Princeton, N.J.: Princeton University Press, 2006.
Delaruelle, Etienne. *La piété populaire au moyen age*. Torino: Bottega d'Erasmo, 1975.
Delumeau, Jean. *L'aveu et le pardon. Les difficulties de la confession XIII–XVIII siècle*. Paris: Fayard, 1990.
Deutsch, Yaacov. *Judaism in Christian Eyes: Ethnographic Descriptions of Jews and Judaism in Early Modern Europe*. New York: Oxford University Press, 2012.
Devlin, Dennis. "Feminine Lay Piety in the High Middle Ages: The Beguines." In *Distant Echoes: Medieval Religious Women*, ed. John A. Nichols and Lillian Thomas Shank, 183–96. Kalamazoo, Mich.: Cistercian Publications, 1984.
Diamond, Eliezer. *Holy Men and Hunger Artists: Fasting and Asceticism in Rabbinic Culture*. New York: Oxford University Press, 2004.
Diem, Albrecht. *Das monastische Experiment. Die Rolle der Keuschheit bei der Entstehung des westlichen Klosterwesens*. Münster: LIT Verlag Münster, 2005.
Dinari, Yedidya. "The Impurity Customs of the Menstruant Woman: Sources and Developments." *Tarbiz* 49 (1989): 302–24 [Hebrew].
———. "The Profanation of the Holy by the Menstruant Woman and 'Takanat Ezra.'" *Te'uda* 3 (1983): 17–37 [Hebrew].
Diner, Hasia R. *Hungering for America: Italian, Irish and Jewish Foodways in the Age of Immigration*. Cambridge, Mass.: Harvard University Press, 2001.
Dinzelbacher, Peter. *Das fremde Mittelalter: Gottesurteil und Tierprozess*. Essen: Magnus, 2006.
Doležal, Daniel, and Hartmut Kühne, ed. *Wallfahrten in der europäischen Kultur*. Frankfurt: P. Lang, 2006.
Douglas, Mary. "Deciphering a Meal." In *Food and Culture: A Reader*, ed. Carol Counihan and Penny van Esterik, 36–54. New York: Routledge, 1997.
———. *Purity and Danger: An Analysis of Concepts of Pollution and Taboo*. New York: Praeger, 1966.

Downey, Sarah. " 'Too Much of Too Little': Guthlac and the Temptation of Excessive Fasting." *Traditio* 63 (2008): 89–127.
Einbinder, Susan L. *Beautiful Death: Jewish Poetry and Martyrdom in Medieval France*. Princeton, N.J.: Princeton University Press, 2002.
———. "Jewish Women Martyrs: Changing Modes of Representation." *Exemplaria* 12 (2000): 105–27.
———. *No Place of Rest: Jewish Literature, Expulsion, and the Memory of Medieval France*. Philadelphia: University of Pennsylvania Press, 2008.
———. "Pulcellina of Blois, Romantic Myths and Narrative Conventions." *Jewish History* 12 (1998): 29–46.
Elbogen, Ismar. *Jewish Liturgy: A Comprehensive History*. Trans. Raymond P. Scheindlin. New York: Jewish Theological Seminary of America, 1993.
Elbogen, Ismar, Aaron Freimann, and Chaim Tykocinski, eds. *Germania Judaica I*. Tübingen: J. C. B. Mohr, 1963.
Elboim, Jacob. *Repentance and Self-Flagellation in the Writings of the Sages of Germany and Poland*. Jerusalem: Magnes Press, 1992.
Elias Bar Levav, Leora. "Our Women Have a Lovely Custom: Halakhic Decisions in Accordance with Women's Practices in the Middle Ages." *Massekhet* 6 (2007): 47–85 [Hebrew].
Elizur, Shulamit. *Wherefore Have We Fasted? Megilat Ta'anit Batra and Similar Lists of Fasts*. Jerusalem: World Union of Jewish Studies, 2007 [Hebrew].
Elliott, Dyan. "Dress as Mediator Between Inner and Outer Self: The Pious Matron of the High and Later Middle Ages." *Medieval Studies* 53 (1991): 279–308.
———. *Fallen Bodies: Pollution, Sexuality, and Demonology in the Middle Ages*. Philadelphia: University of Pennsylvania Press, 1998.
———. *Proving Woman: Female Spirituality and Inquisitional Culture in the Later Middle Ages*. Princeton, N.J.: Princeton University Press, 2004.
———. *Spiritual Marriage: Sexual Abstinence in Medieval Wedlock*. Princeton, N.J.: Princeton University Press, 1993.
Elliott, Lynne. *Food and Feasts in the Middle Ages*. New York: Crabtree, 2004.
Elukin, Jonathan. *Living Together, Living Apart: Rethinking Jewish-Christian Relations in the Middle Ages*. Princeton, N.J.: Princeton University Press, 2007.
Emanuel, Simcha. *Fragments of the Tablets: Lost Books of the Tosaphists*. Jerusalem: Magnes Press, 2006 [Hebrew].
———. "Introduction." In R. Eleazar b. Judah, *Oratio ad Pascam*, ed. Simcha Emanuel, 1–66. Jerusalem: Mekize Nirdamim, 2006 [Hebrew].
———. "Niddah in the Synagogue: New Sources." In *Festschrift in Honor of Professor Daniel Sperber*, ed. Adam Ferziger and David Sperber (forthcoming) [Hebrew].
Epstein, Marc Michael. *The Medieval Haggadah: Art, Narrative and Religious Imagination*. New Haven, Conn.: Yale University Press, 2011.
Epstein, Steven. *Wills and Wealth in Medieval Genoa, 1150–1250*. Cambridge, Mass.: Harvard University Press, 1984.
Epstein, Yaacov Nahum. "Al haKol." *Sinai* 94 (1984): 123–36.
Erikson, Kai T. *Wayward Puritans: A Study in the Sociology of Deviance*. New York: Wiley, 1966.
Erler, Mary C. "Margery Kempe's White Clothes." *Medium Aevum* 62 (1993): 78–85.
Evergates, Theodore, ed. *Aristocratic Women in Medieval France*. Philadelphia: University of Pennsylvania Press, 1999.

Fagan, Brian M. *Fish on Friday: Feasting, Fasting, and the Discovery of the New World.* New York: Basic Books, 2007.

Falk, Nancy Auer, and Rita Gross, eds. *Unspoken Worlds: Women's Religious Worlds.* Belmont: Wadsworth, 1989.

Farmer, Sharon. "Persuasive Voices: Clerical Images of Medieval Wives." *Speculum* 61 (1986): 517–43.

———. *Surviving Poverty in Medieval Paris: Gender, Ideology and the Daily Lives of the Poor.* Ithaca, N.Y.: Cornell University Press, 2002.

Fassler, Margot Elsbeth. *The Virgin of Chartres: Making History Through Liturgy and the Arts.* New Haven, Conn.: Yale University Press, 2010.

Ferguson, George. *Signs and Symbols in Christian Art.* Oxford: Oxford University Press, 1954.

Fine, Lawrence, ed. *Judaism in Practice: From the Middle Ages Through the Early Modern Period.* Princeton, N.J.: Princeton University Press, 2001.

Finkelstein, Louis. *Jewish Self-Government in the Middle Ages.* Repr. New York: Feldheim, 1964.

Finn, Richard B. *Almsgiving in the Later Roman Empire: Christian Promotion and Practice 313–450.* Oxford: Oxford University Press, 2006.

Firey, Abigail. "Blushing Before the Judge, and Physician: Moral Arbitration in the Carolingian Empire." In *A New History of Penance*, ed. Abigail Firey, 173–200. Leiden: Brill, 2008.

———. *A Contrite Heart: Prosecution and Redemption in the Carolingian Empire.* Leiden: Brill, 2009.

———, ed. *A New History of Penance.* Leiden: Brill, 2008.

Fishman, Talya. *Becoming the People of the Talmud: Oral Torah as Written Tradition in Medieval Jewish Cultures.* Philadelphia: University of Pennsylvania Press, 2011.

———. "A Kabbalistic Perspective on Gender-Specific Commandments: On the Interplay of Symbols and Society." *AJS Review* 17 (1992): 199–245.

———. "The Penitential System of Hasidei Ashkenaz and the Problem of Cultural Boundaries." *Journal of Jewish Thought and Philosophy* 8 (1999): 201–29.

———. "Rhineland Pietist Approaches to Prayer and the Textualization of Rabbinic Culture in Medieval Northern Europe." *JSQ* 11 (2004): 313–31.

Fleming, Robin. "Acquiring, Flaunting and Destroying Silk in Late Anglo-Saxon England." *Early Medieval Europe* 15 (2007): 127–58.

Flint, Valerie I. *The Rise of Magic in Early Medieval Europe.* Princeton, N.J.: Princeton University Press, 1991.

Flood, Finbarr B. *Objects of Translation: Material Culture and Medieval "Hindu-Muslim" Encounter.* Princeton, N.J.: Princeton University Press, 2009.

Fram, Edward. *Ideals Face Reality: Jewish Life and Law in Poland, 1550–1655.* Cincinnati: Hebrew Union College Press, 1997.

———. *My Dear Daughter: Rabbi Benjamin Slonik and the Education of Jewish Women in Sixteenth-Century Poland.* Cincinnati: Hebrew Union College Press, 2007.

Fredriksen, Paula. "Just Like Everyone Else, Only More So." *JQR* 95 (2005): 119–30.

Freed, John B. "Urban Development and the 'Cura Monalium' in Thirteenth Century Germany." *Viator* 3 (1972): 311–27.

Freehof, Solomon H. "Hazkarath Neshamoth." *Hebrew Union College Annual* 36 (1965): 179–89.

Freimann, Avraham H. "The Amount of the Kethubah in Medieval Germany and France." In *Alexander Marx Jubilee Volume* (Hebrew Section), ed. Saul Lieberman, 371–85. New York: Jewish Theological Seminary of America, 1950 [Hebrew].

French, Katherine L. *The Good Women of the Parish: Gender and Religion After the Black Death.* Philadelphia: University of Pennsylvania Press, 2008.

Freud, Sigmund. *Civilization and Its Discontents*. Trans. James Strachey. New York: W. W. Norton, 1961.

Friedenreich, David. *Foreigners and Their Food: Constructing Otherness in Jewish, Christian and Islamic Law*. Berkeley: University of California Press, 2011.

Friedman, Mordechai. "Rabbinic Reactions to Women Performing Positive Time-bound Commandments in the Eleventh Through the Fourteenth Century: German and French Tosafists." Unpublished paper, Revel Graduate School, Yeshiva University.

Frishman, Asher. *The Early Ashkenazi Jews: Since Their Settlement in North-West Europe to the First Crusade*. Tel Aviv: HaKibbutz haMe'uhad, 2008 [Hebrew].

Fudemann, Kirsten A. "The Old French Glosses in Joseph Kara's Isaiah Commentary." *REJ* 165 (2006): 147–77.

———. *Vernacular Voices: Language and Identity in Medieval French Jewish Communities*. Philadelphia: University of Pennsylvania Press, 2010.

Funkenstein, Amos. *Perceptions of Jewish History*. Berkeley: University of California Press, 1993.

Furst, Rachel. "Conversion and Communal Identity: Sexual Angst and Religious Crisis in Frankfurt, 1241." *Jewish History* 22 (2008): 179–201.

Galinsky, Judah D. "'And It Is for the Glory of the Great That Their Name Be Remembered': Commemorating the Dead and the Practice of Establishing a *Hekdesh* in Christian Spain." *Masechet* 2 (2004): 113–31 [Hebrew].

———. "'And to Be a Loyal Servant All of the Days': A Chapter in R. Moshe of Coucy's Religious Thought." *Da'at* 42 (1999): 13–31 [Hebrew].

———. "Commemoration and Heqdesh in the Jewish Communities of Germany and Spain in the 13th Century." In *Stiftungen in Christentum, Judentum und Islam vor der Moderne*, ed. Michael Borgolte, 191–204. Berlin: Akademie, 2005.

———. "Custom, Ordinance or Commandment? Evolution of the Medieval Tithe in Ashkenaz." *Journal of Jewish Studies* 62 (2011): 203–32.

———. "The Different Hebrew Versions of the 'Talmud Trial' of 1240 in Paris." In *New Perspectives on Jewish-Christian Relations: Essays in Honor of David Berger*, ed. Elisheva Carlebach and J. J. Schacter, 109–40. Leiden: Brill, 2011.

———. "The Four Turim and the Halakhic Literature of Fourteenth Century Spain." Ph.D. diss., Bar Ilan University, 1999 [Hebrew].

———. "Jewish Charitable Bequests and the Hekdesh Trust in Thirteenth-Century Spain." *Journal of Interdisciplinary History* 33 (2004): 423–40.

———. "On Popular Halakhic Literature and the Emergence of a Reading Audience in Fourteenth-Century Spain." *JQR* 98 (2008): 305–27.

———. "Public Charity in Medieval Germany: A Preliminary Investigation." In *Toward a Renewed Ethic of Jewish Philanthropy*, ed. Yossi Prager, 79–92. New York: Michael Scharf Publication Trust of Yeshiva University Press, 2010.

———. "Rabbenu Moshe meCoucy: A Pious Preacher and a Polemicist, Aspects from His World of Thought and His Public Activities." Master's thesis, Yeshiva University, 1993 [Hebrew].

Garrison, Roman. *Redemptive Almsgiving in Early Christianity*. Sheffield: JSOT Press, 1993.

Gartner, Yaakov. "Fasting on Rosh haShanah." *Hadarom* 36 (1972): 125–62; *Hadarom* 38 (1974): 69–77 [Hebrew].

Gauvain, Richard. "Ritual Rewards: A Consideration of Three Recent Approaches to Sunni Purity Law." *Islamic Law and Society* 12 (2005): 333–93.

Geary, Patrick J. *Living with the Dead in the Middle Ages*. Ithaca, N.Y.: Cornell University Press, 1994.

———. *Phantoms of Remembrance: Memory and Oblivion at the End of the First Millennium*. Princeton, N.J.: Princeton University Press, 1994.
Gershenzon, Shoshanna, and Jane Rachel Litman. "The Bloody Hands of Compassionate Women: Portrayals of Heroic Women in the Hebrew Crusade Chronicles." *Studies in Jewish Civilization* 6 (1995): 73–91.
Gilat, Yitzhak D. "Two Bakashot of Moses of Coucy." *Tarbiz* 28 (1959): 54–58 [Hebrew].
Gilat, Yitzhak D., and Yaakov Gartner. "Fasting on the Sabbath." *Tarbiz* 52 (1983): 1–15 [Hebrew].
Ginzburg, Carlo. *Night Battles: Witch Craft and Agrarian Cults in the Sixteenth and Seventeenth Centuries*. Baltimore: Johns Hopkins University Press, 1983.
Goering, Joseph. "The Scholastic Turn (1100–1500): Penitential Theology and the Law in the Schools." In *A New History of Penance*, ed. Abigail Firey, 219–37. Leiden: Brill, 2008.
———. *William de Montibus c. 1140–1213. The Schools and the Literature of Pastoral Care*. Toronto: Pontifical Institute of Mediaeval Studies, 1992.
Goitein, Shlomo Dov. *A Mediterranean Society: The Jewish Communities of the Arab World as Portrayed in the Documents of the Cairo Geniza*. 6 vols. Berkeley: University of California Press, 1967–1993.
———. "Ramadan, the Muslim Month of Fasting." In *The Development of Islamic Ritual*, ed. Gerald Hawting, 151–71. Aldershot: Ashgate Variorum, 2006.
Gold, Penny Schine. *The Lady and the Virgin: Image, Attitude, and Experience in Twelfth-Century France*. Chicago: University of Chicago Press, 1985.
Goldberg, Sylvie Anne. *Crossing the Jabbok: Illness and Death in Ashkenazi Judaism in Sixteenth-Through Nineteenth-Century Prague*. Berkeley: University of California Press, 1996.
Goldin, Simha. *Jewish Women in Europe in the Middle Ages: A Quiet Revolution*. Manchester: Manchester University Press, 2011.
———. *Uniqueness and Togetherness: The Enigma of the Survival of the Jews in the Middle Ages*. Tel Aviv: HaMakhon leHeker haTefutzot, 1997 [Hebrew].
Golinkin, David. "Rabbenu Shakh." *Sinai* 98 (1986): 201–10 [Hebrew].
———. *The Status of Women in Jewish Law*. Jerusalem: Schechter Institute, 2001.
Goodson, Caroline, Anne E. Lester, and Carol Symes, eds. *Cities, Texts and Social Networks, 400–1500: Experiences and Perceptions of Medieval Urban Space*. Farnham and Burlington: Ashgate, 2010.
Goody, Jack. "Against 'Ritual': Loosely Structured Thoughts on a Loosely Defined Topic." In *Secular Ritual*, ed. Sally F. Moore and Barabara G. Myerhoff. Assen: Van Gorcum, 1977.
Graetz, Heinrich. *History of the Jews*. Philadelphia: Jewish Publication Society of America, 1956.
Gray, Alyssa. "Married Women and Tsedaqah in Jewish Law: Gender and the Discourse of Legal Obligation." *Jewish Law Association Studies* 17 (2007): 168–212.
———. "Redemptive Almsgiving and the Rabbis of Late Antiquity." *JSQ* 18 (2011): 144–84.
Graybill, B., and Linda B. Arthur. "The Social Control of Women's Bodies in Two Menonite Communities." In *Religion, Dress and Body*, ed. Linda B. Arthur, 9–29. Oxford: Berg, 1999.
Grayzel, Solomon. *The Church and the Jews in the XIIIth Century: A Study of Their Relations During the Years 1198–1254, Based on the Papal Letters and the Conciliar Decrees of the Period*. New York: Hermon Press, 1966.
Green, Niles. "Ostrich Eggs and Peacock Feathers: Sacred Objects as Cultural Exchange Between Christianity and Islam." *Al-Masaq: Islam and the Medieval Mediterranean* 18 (2006): 27–66.
Greenberg, Joseph C. *Foreign Words in the Bible Commentary of Rashi*. Jerusalem: J. Greenberg, 1991.
Greenblatt, Rachel L. "A Community's Memory: Jewish Views of Past and Present in Early Modern Prague." Ph.D. diss., Hebrew University of Jerusalem, 2006.
Greene, Virginie. "Un cimetière livresque: la liste nécrologie médiévale." *Le Moyen Age: Revue d'histoire et de philologie* 105 (1999): 307–30.

Greenup, Albert William. "Fast and Fasting." In *Essays in Honor of J. H. Hertz on the Occasion of His Seventieth Birthday*, ed. I. Epstein, E. Levine, and C. Roth, 203–14. London: Edward Goldston, 1942.
Grimm, Veronika E. "Fasting Women in Judaism and Christianity in Late Antiquity." In *Food in Antiquity*, ed. John Wilkins, David Harvey, and Mike Dobson, 225–40. Exeter: University of Exeter Press, 1995.
———. *From Feasting to Fasting, the Evolution of a Sin: Attitudes to Food in Late Antiquity*. London: Routledge, 1996.
Gross, Henri. *Gallia Judaica, Dictionnaire géographique de la France d'après les sources rabbiniques*. Ed. Simon Schwarzfuchs. Paris: Peeters, 2011.
Grossman, Avraham. *The Early Sages of Ashkenaz: Their Lives, Leadership and Works, 900–1096*. Jerusalem: Magnes Press, 1981 [Hebrew].
———. *The Early Sages of France: Their Lives, Leadership and Works*. Jerusalem: Magnes Press, 1995 [Hebrew].
———. "He Shall Rule over You?" *Medieval Jewish Sages on Women*. Jerusalem: Merkaz Zalman Shazar, 2011 [Hebrew].
———. "The Origins and Essence of the Custom of Stopping the Service." *Milet* 1 (1983): 199–221 [Hebrew].
———. *Pious and Rebellious: Jewish Women in Europe in the Middle Ages*. Jerusalem: Merkaz Zalman Shazar, 2001 [Hebrew].
———. *Pious and Rebellious: Jewish Women in the Middle Ages*. Waltham, Mass.: Brandeis University Press, 2004.
Grossman, Avraham, and Sara Japhet, eds. *Rashi: The Man and His Work*. Jerusalem: Merkaz Zalman Shazar, 2008 [Hebrew].
Grün, Anselm. "Fasting." In *The Encyclopedia of Christianity*, 2:295–96. Leiden: Brill, 2001.
Grünwald, Max. "Le cimetière de Worms." *REJ* 104 (1938): 71–111.
Güdemann, Moritz. *Geschichte des Erziehungswesens und der Cultur der abendländischen Juden während des Mittelalters und der neueren Zeit*. 3 vols. Vienna: Hölder, 1880–88.
Gurevitch, Aaron. *Historical Anthropology of the Middle Ages*. Chicago: University of Chicago Press, 1992.
Gy, Pierre-Marie. "Les définitions de la confession." In *L'aveu: Antiquité et moyen âge*, ed. Jean-Claude Maire Vigueur, 283–96. Rome: Ecole française de Rome, 1986.
Habermann, Abraham M. "Al haTefillin beYemei Kedem." *Eretz Israel* 3 (1954): 174–77.
Hacham, Noah. "Ta'aniyot Tzibur beTekufat haBayit haSheni." Master's thesis, Hebrew University of Jerusalem, 1996 [Hebrew].
Hacohen, Aviad. "Mihu Avaryan? Al Hadarat haAcher veTiyugo." *Daat* 300 (1988). http://www.daat.ac.il/mishpat-ivri/skirot/300-2.htm.
———. "Nashim Atzlaniyot Hen?! Nashim Hashuvot Hen! leToldot Shtayim meHilchot Pesach." *Alon Shvut leBogrei Yeshivat Har Etzion* 11 (1998): 63–82 [Hebrew].
Hamilton, Sarah. *The Practice of Penance 900–1050*. Woodbridge and Rochester: Boydell Press, 2001.
Har-Shefi, Bitha. "Al Tevilat Niddah beYemei haBenayim: Ma'aseh veHalakhah." In *Lihiyot Ishah Yehudiyah*, ed. Tova Cohen, 4:65–76. Jerusalem: Kolech, 2007 [Hebrew].
———. "Women and Halakhah in the Years 1050–1350 C.E.: Between Law and Custom." Ph.D. diss., Hebrew University of Jerusalem, 2002 [Hebrew].
Harari, Yuval. "Jewish Magic: An Annotated Overview." In *El Presente 5, Studies in Sephardic Culture, Magic and Folk Medicine*, ed. Tamar Alexander, Yaakov Bentolila, and Eliezer Papo, 13–85. Beer Sheva: Moshe David Gaon Center for Ladino Culture, Ben Gurion University, 2011 [Hebrew].

Haverkamp, Alfred. "Concivilitas von Christen und Juden in Aschkenas im Mittelalter." In *Jüdische Gemeinden und Organisationsformen*, ed. Robert Jütte, 103–36. Vienna: Böhlau Verlag, 1996.

———, ed. *Geschichte der Juden im Mittelalter von der Nordsee biz zu den Südalpen*. Hannover: Hahn, 2002.

———. "Jews and Urban Life: Bonds and Relationships." In *The Jews of Europe in the Middle Ages (Tenth to Fifteenth Centuries)*, ed. Christoph Cluse, 55–70. Brepols: Turnhout, 2004.

———. *Medieval Germany, 1056–1273*. Trans. Helga Braun and Richard Mortimer. Oxford: Oxford University Press, 1988.

Haverkamp, Eva. *Hebräische Berichte über die Judenverfolgungen während des Ersten Kreuzzugs*. Hannover: Hahnsche Buchhandlung, 2005.

Head, Thomas. "The Cult of Relics in the Eleventh Century." In *Medieval Hagiography: An Anthology*, ed. Thomas Head, 273–95. New York: Garland Publishing, 2001.

———. "The Early Medieval Transformation of Piety." In *The Long Morning of Medieval Europe: New Directions in Early Medieval Studies*, ed. Jennifer R. Davis and Michael McCormick, 155–62. Aldershot: Ashgate, 2008.

———. "The Genesis of the Ordeal of Relics by Fire in Ottonian Germany: An Alternative Form of Canonization." In *Medieval Canonization Processes: Legal and Religious Aspects*, ed. Gabor Klaniczay, 19–31. Rome: Ecole française de Rome, 2004.

———. "Saints, Heretics and Fire: Finding Meaning Through the Ordeal." In *Monks and Nuns, Saints and Outcasts: Religion in Medieval Society: Essays in Honor of Lester K. Little*, ed. Sharon A. Farmer and Barbara H. Rosenwein, 220–38. Ithaca, N.Y.: Cornell University Press, 2000.

Hecker, Joel. *Mystical Bodies, Mystical Meals: Eating and Embodiment in Medieval Kabbalah*. Detroit: Wayne State University Press, 2006.

Heller, Sarah Grace. "Anxiety, Hierarchy, and Appearance in Thirteenth-Century Sumptuary Laws and the Roman de la Rose." *French Historical Studies* 27 (2004): 311–48.

———. "Sumptuary Legislation in Thirteenth Century France, Languedoc and Italy." In *Medieval Fabrications: Dress, Textile, Clothwork and Other Cultural Imaginings*, ed. E. Jane Burns, 121–36. New York: Palgrave Macmillan, 2004.

Henshke, David. "On the Conclusion of *Megillat Ta'anit* and the Metamorphosis of Its Interpretations in the Two Talmudim." *Bar-Ilan* 30–31 (2006): 119–62 [Hebrew].

Herlihy, David. *Opera Muliebria: Women and Work in Medieval Europe*. Philadelphia: Temple University Press, 1990.

Heschel, Susannah. "Jewish Studies as Counterhistory." In *Insider/Outsider: American Jews and Multiculturalism*, ed. David Biale, Michael Galchinsky, and Susannah Heschel, 101–13. Berkeley: University of California Press, 1998.

Hiltebeitel, Alf, and Barbara D. Miller, eds. *Hair: Its Power and Meaning in Asian Cultures*. Albany: State University of New York Press, 1998.

Hlaváček, Petr. "Pilgrimage Footwear: Luxury, Necessity or Needless?" In *Wallfahrten in der europäischen Kultur*, ed. Daniel Doležal and Hartmut Kühne, 139–46. Frankfurt: P. Lang, 2006.

Hoffman, Lawrence A. *The Canonization of the Synagogue Service*. Notre Dame, Ind.: University of Notre Dame Press, 1979.

Hollender, Elisabeth. *Clavis Commentariorum of Hebrew Liturgical Poetry in Manuscript*. Leiden: Brill, 2005.

Honig, Mordechai. "Al Mahadurato haHadashah shel Sefer haMaskil leRabbi Moshe Ben Rabbi Elazar haCohen." *Yerushatenu* 1 (2007): 196–240.

Horowitz, Elliott S. "Between Cleanliness and Godliness: Aspects of Jewish Bathing in Medieval and

Early Modern Times." In *Tov Elem: Memory, Community and Gender in Medieval and Early Modern Jewish Societies; Essays in Honor of Robert Bonfil*, ed. Elisheva Baumgarten, Roni Weinstein, and Amnon Raz-Krakotzkin, *29–*54. Jerusalem: Mossad Bialik, 2011.

———. "The Jews of Europe and the Moment of Death in Medieval and Modern Times." *Judaism* 44 (1995): 271–81.

———. "On the Significance of the Beard in Jewish Communities in the East and in Europe in the Middle Ages and Early Modern Times." *Pe'amim* 59 (1994): 124–48 [Hebrew].

Hotchkiss, Valerie R. *Clothes Make the Man: Female Crossdressing in Medieval Europe*. New York: Garland Publishers, 1996.

Hovav, Yemima. *Maidens Love Thee: The Religious and Spiritual Life of Jewish Ashkenazic Women in the Early Modern Period*. Jerusalem: Merkaz Dinur leHeker Toldot Yisrael, 2009 [Hebrew].

Howell, Martha C. *Commerce Before Captialism in Europe, 1300–1600*. Cambridge: Cambridge University Press, 2010.

———. "The Gender of Europe's Commercial Economy, 1200–1700." *Gender and History* 20 (2008): 519–38.

———. *The Marriage Exchange: Property, Social Place and Gender in the Cities of the Low Countries, 1300–1550*. Chicago: University of Chicago Press, 1998.

———. "The Properties of Marriage in Late Medieval Europe." In *Love, Marriage and Family Ties in the Later Middle Ages*, ed. Isabel Davis, Miriam Müller, and Sarah Rees Jones, 17–62. Turnhout: Brepols, 2003.

———. *Women, Production, and Patriarchy in Late Medieval Cities*. Chicago: University of Chicago Press, 1986.

Hoyle, Victoria. "The Bonds That Bind: Money Lending Between Anglo-Jewish and Christian Women in the Plea Rolls of the Exchequer of the Jews, 1218–1280." *Journal of Medieval History* 34 (2008): 119–29.

Hundsbichler, Helmut. "Die Fastenpraxis und ihre soziokulturellen Aspekte." *Lexikon des Mittelalters* 4 (1989): 306.

Hundsbichler, Hemult, et al. "Fasten." *Lexikon des Mittelalters* 4 (1989): 304–12.

Hutton, Shannon. "Women, Men and Markets: The Gendering of Market Space in Late Medieval Ghent." In *Urban Space in the Middle Ages and the Early Modern Age*, ed. Albrecht Classen, 409–31. Berlin: Walter deGruyter, 2009.

Huyghebaert, Nicolas. *Les documents nécrologiques*. Turnhout: Brepols, 1972.

Isaacs, Alick. "An Anthropological and Historical Study of the Role of the Synagogue in Ashkenazi Jewish Life in the Middle Ages." Ph.D. diss., Hebrew University of Jerusalem, 2002 [Hebrew].

———. "'Kevod haTzibbur': Towards a Contextualist History of Women's Role in Torah Reading." *Nashim* 12 (2006): 261–88.

Jaritz, Gerhard. "*Ira Die*: Material Culture, and Behavior in the Late Middle Ages: The Evidence from German-Speaking Regions." *Essays in Medieval Studies* 18 (2001): 53–66.

———. *Zwischen Augenblick und Ewigkeit. Einführung in die Alltagsgeschichte des Mittelalters*. Vienna: Böhlau, 1989.

Johnson, Penelope. *Equal in Monastic Profession: Religious Women in Medieval France*. Chicago: University of Chicago Press, 1991.

Jordan, Erin. "Gender Concerns: Monks, Nuns and Patronage." *Speculum* 87 (2012): 62–84.

Jordan, William Chester. *The French Monarchy and the Jews: From Philip Augustus to the Last Capetians*. Philadelphia: University of Pennsylvania Press, 1989.

———. "Jews on Top: Women and the Availability of Consumption Loans in Northern France in the Mid-Thirteenth Century." *Journal of Jewish Studies* 29 (1978): 39 57.

Judic, Bruno. "Confessio chex Grégoire le Grand." In *L'aveu: Antiquité et moyen âge*, ed. Jean-Claude Maire Vigueur, 147–68. Rome: Ecole française de Rome, 1986.

Kamaludeen, Mohamed Nasir, Alexius A. Pereira, and Bryan S. Turner. *Muslims in Singapore: Piety, Politics and Policies*. London: Routledge, 2010.

Kanarfogel, Ephraim. "Between the Tosafist Academies and the Academic Milieu in France in the Twelfth and Thirteenth Centuries: Parallels Which Do Not Meet." In *Yeshivot and Battei Midrash*, ed. Immanuel Etkes, 85–108. Jerusalem: Merkaz Zalman Shazar, 2006 [Hebrew].

———. "German Pietism in Northern France." In *Hazon Nahum: Studies in Jewish Law, Thought, and History Presented to Dr. Norman Lamm*, ed. Yaakov Elman and Jeffrey S. Gurock, 207–27. New York: Michael Scharf Publication Trust of Yeshiva University Press, 1997.

———. *The Intellectual History and Rabbinic Culture of Medieval Ashkenaz*. Detroit: Wayne State University Press, 2012.

———. *Jewish Education and Society in the High Middle Ages*. Detroit: Wayne State University Press, 1992.

———. *"Peering Through the Lattices": Mystical, Magical and Pietistic Dimensions in the Tosafist Period*. Detroit: Wayne State University Press, 2000.

———. "Prayer, Literacy, and Literary Memory in the Jewish Communities of Medieval Europe." In *Jewish Studies at the Crossroads of Anthropology and History: Authority, Diaspora, Tradition*, ed. Ra'anan S. Boustan, Oren Kosansky, and Marina Rustow, 250–70. Philadelphia: University of Pennsylvania Press, 2010.

———. "Rabbinic Attitudes Toward Nonobservance in the Medieval Period." In *Jewish Tradition and the Non-Traditional Jew*, ed. Jacob J. Schacter, 3–35. Northvale, N.J.: Aronson, 1992.

———. "Returning to the Community in Ashkenaz." In *Turim: Studies in Jewish History and Literature Presented to Dr. Bernard Lander*, ed. Michael A. Shmidman, 1:69–98. New York: Touro College Press, 2007.

———. "Review of *Mothers and Children*." *American Historical Review* 111 (2005): 850–51.

Kandiyoti, Deniz. "Bargaining with Patriarchy." *Gender and Society* 2 (1988): 274–90.

Kaplan, Debra. *Beyond Expulsion: Jews, Christians, and Reformation Strasbourg*. Stanford, Calif.: Stanford University Press, 2011.

Katz, Jacob. *Exclusiveness and Tolerance: Studies in Jewish-Gentile Relations in Medieval and Modern Times*. New York: Schocken Books, 1961.

———. "Law, Spirituality and Society." *Jewish Social Studies* 2 (1996): 87–98, 105–8.

———. *Out of the Ghetto: The Social Background of Jewish Emancipation 1770–1870*. Cambridge, Mass.: Harvard University Press, 1973.

———. *Tradition and Crisis: Jewish Society at the End of the Middle Ages*. New York: New York University Press, 1993.

Katz, Marion Holmes. *Body of Text: The Emergence of the Sunni Law of Ritual Purity*. Binghamton: State University of New York Press, 2002.

Kayserling, Meyer. *Die jüdischen Frauen in der Geschichte, Literatur und Kunst*. Leipzig: Brockhaus, 1879.

Keil, Martha. "Business Success and Tax Debts: Jewish Women in Late Medieval Austrian Towns." *Jewish Studies at Central European University* 2 (2002): 103–23.

Kelleher, Marie. *The Measure of Woman: Law and Female Identity in the Crown of Aragon*. Philadelphia: University of Pennsylvania Press, 2011.

Kerber, Linda. "Separate Spheres, Female Worlds, Women's Place: The Rhetoric of Women's History." *Journal of American History* 75 (1988): 9–39.
Kieckhefer, Richard. *Unquiet Souls: Fourteenth Century Saints and Their Religious Milieu*. Chicago: University of Chicago Press, 1984.
Kiel, Yishai. "The Moral and Religious Instruction of Ashkenazi Pietism Between Asceticism and Sensuality." *Da'at* 73 (2012): 85–101 [Hebrew].
King, Karen. *What Is Gnosticism?* Cambridge, Mass.: Belknap Press of Harvard University Press, 2003.
Kinoshita, Sharon. "Almería Silk and the French Feudal Imaginary." In *Medieval Fabrications, Dress, Textiles, Clothwork, and Other Cultural Imaginings*, ed. E. Jane Burns, 165–76. New York: Palgrave Macmillan, 2004.
Kisch, Guido. "The Yellow Badge in History." *Historia Judaica* 4 (1942): 106–7.
Klaniczay, Gabor. "Fashionable Beards and Heretic Rags." In *The Uses of Supernatural Power: The Transformation of Popular Religion in Medieval and Early Modern Europe*, ed. Gabor Klaniczay, 51–78. Princeton, N.J.: Princeton University Press, 1990.
Kogman-Appel, Katrin. *A Mahzor from Worms: Art and Religion in a Medieval Jewish Community*. Cambridge, Mass.: Harvard University Press, 2012.
Koren, Sharon F. *Forsaken: The Menstruant in Medieval Jewish Mysticism*. Waltham, Mass.: Brandeis University Press, 2011.
Kowaleski, Maryanne. "A Consumer Economy." In *A Social History of England, 1200–1500*, ed. Rosemary Horrox and W. Mark Ormrod, 238–59. Cambridge: Cambridge University Press, 2006.
———. *Medieval Towns: A Reader*. Peterborough: Broadview Press, 2006.
Kramer, Susan R. "The Priest in the House of Conscience: Sins of Thought and the Twelfth-Century Schoolmen?" *Viator* 37 (2006): 149–66.
———. "We Speak to God with Our Thoughts: Abelard and the Implications of Private Communication with God." *Church History* 69 (2000): 18–40.
Kressel, Getzel. "Eliakim Carmoly (1802–1875)." *Encyclopedia Judaica* 5:189. Jerusalem: Encyclopedia Judaica, 1973.
Krinsky, Carole H. *Synagogues of Europe: Architecture, History and Meaning*. Mineola, N.Y.: Dover, 1996.
Krueger, Derek. "Christian Piety and Practice in the Sixth Century." In *The Cambridge Companion to the Age of Justinian*, ed. Michael Mass, 291–315. Cambridge: Cambridge University Press, 2005.
Kushelevsky, Rella. *Penalty and Temptation: Hebrew Tales in Ashkenaz: Ms. Parma 2295 (de-Rossi 563)*. Jerusalem, 2010 [Hebrew].
Kutner, Anat. "The Night in the Late Middle Ages in Ashkenaz." Ph.D. diss., Bar Ilan Univeristy, 2008 [Hebrew].
Laderman, Shulamit. "What Do Jewish Artistic Findings Teach Us About Head Covering for Men?" In *Studies on the History of the Jews of Ashkenaz Presented to Eric Zimmer*, ed. Gershon Bacon, Daniel Sperber, and Aharon Gaimani, 135–56. Ramat Gan: Bar-Ilan University, 2008.
Ladner, Gerhart B. "Homo Viator: Medieval Ideas on Alienation and Order." *Speculum* 42 (1967): 233–59.
Lambert, David. "Fasting as a Penitential Rite: A Biblical Phenomenon?" *Harvard Theological Review* 96 (2003): 477–512.
Landes, Joan B., ed. *Feminism: The Public and the Private*. Oxford: Oxford University Press, 1998.
Latour, Bruno. *Reassembling the Social: An Introduction to Actor-Network-Theory*. Oxford: Oxford University Press, 2005.

Lauwers, Michel. *La mémoire des ancêtres, le souci des morts: Morts, rites, et société au Moyen Âge: Diocèse de Liège, XIe–XIIIe siècles.* Paris: Beauchesne, 1997.

le Belvec, Daniel. "Le role des femmes dans l'assistance et le charité." In *Cahiers de Fanjeux 23: La femme dans la vie religieuse du Languedoc (XIIe–XIVe s.)*, ed. Paul Amargier et al., 171–90. Toulouse: E. Privat, 1988.

Lea, Henry Charles. *A History of Auricular Confession and Indulgences in the Latin Church.* Philadelphia: Lea Brothers, 1896; repr. New York: Greenwood Press, 1968.

LeClercq, Henri. "Jeunes." *Dictionnaire d'archéologie chrétienne et de liturgie*, 2483–2502. Paris: Letouzey and Ané, 1927.

Leiman, Sid Z. "The Scroll of Fasts." *JQR* 74 (1983): 174–95.

Lerner, Gerda. *The Creation of Patriarchy.* New York: Oxford University Press, 1986.

Lester, Anne E. *Creating Cistercian Nuns: The Women's Religious Movement and Its Reform in Thirteenth-Century Champagne.* Ithaca, N.Y.: Cornell University Press, 2011.

Lévi-Strauss, Claude. "The Culinary Triangle." In *Food and Culture: A Reader*, ed. Carol Counihan and Penny van Esterik, 28–35. New York: Routledge, 1997.

Lévi, Israel. "La commémoration des âmes dans le judaïsme." *REJ* 29 (1894): 43–60.

Levine, David. *Communal Fasts and Rabbinic Sermons: Theory and Practice in the Talmudic Period.* Bnei Brak: HaKibbutz haMeuhad, 2001 [Hebrew].

Levinson, Eyal. "The Conceptualization of the Yetzer and the Male Body in the Masculine Sexual Discourse in Sefer Hasidim." Master's thesis, Bar Ilan University, 2011 [Hebrew].

Leyser, Catherine. "Masculinity in Flux: Nocturnal Emission and the Limits of Celibacy in the Early Middle Ages." In *Masculinity in Medieval Europe*, ed. David Hadley, 103–20. London: Longman, 1999.

Liebschutz. H. "Relations Between Jews and Christians in the Middle Ages." *Journal of Jewish Studies* 16 (1965): 35–46.

Lipton, Sara. "Where Are the Gothic Jewish Women? On the Non-Iconography of the Jewess in the *Cantigas de Santa Maria*." *Jewish History* 22 (2008): 139–77.

Loeb, Isidore. "La controverse de 1240 sur le Talmud." *REJ* 2–3 (1881): 247–61, 39–57.

———. "Le role des juifs de Paris." *REJ* 1 (1880): 61–71.

Loewe, Raphael. *The Position of Women in Judaism.* London: SPCK in conjunction with the Hillel Foundation, 1966.

Lorcin, Marie Thérèse. "Le Testament." In *A réveiller les morts. La mort au quotidien dans l'occident médiéval*, ed. Danièle Alexandre-Bidon and Cécile Treffort, 143–56. Lyon: Presses universitaires de Lyon, 1993.

Loup-Lemaitre, Jean. "Nécrologes et obituaries. Une source privilégiée pour l'histoire des institutions ecclésiastiques et de la société au Moyen Age?" In *Memoria. Erinnern und Vergessen in der Kultur des Mittelalters*, ed. Michael Borgolte, Cosimo Damiano Fonesca, and Herbert Houben, 201–18. Bologna and Berlin: Duncker and Humbolt Erinnern, 2005.

———. "Un livre vivant, l'obituaire." In *Le livre au moyen âge*, ed. Jean Glenisson, 92–94. Paris: Press du CNRS, 1988.

Low, Setha M., and Denise Lawrence-Zúñiga, eds. *The Anthropology of Space and Place: Locating Culture.* Malden, Mass.: Blackwell, 2003.

Lowe, W. H., ed. *The Memorbook of Nurnberg Containing the Names of the Jews Martyred in that City in the Year 5109, 1349 A.D.: From the Unique Manuscript Preserved in the University Library, Cambridge, and Marked "Add. 1506."* London: Jewish Chronicle Office, 1881.

Ludwig, Uwe. "Die Gedenklisten des Klosters Novalese." In *Memoria in der Gesellschaft des Mittelalters*,

ed. Dieter Geunich and Otto Gerhard Oexle, 32–55. Göttingen: Vandenhoeck and Ruprecht, 1994.
Lynch, Katherine. *Individuals, Families and Communities in Europe, 1200–1800: The Urban Foundations of Western Society*. Cambridge: Cambridge University Press, 2003.
Magnani, Eliana. "Almsgiving, Donatio pro Anima and Eucharistic Offering in the Early Middle Ages of Western Europe (4th–9th Centuries)." In *Charity and Giving in Monotheistic Religions*, ed. Miriam Frankel and Yaacov Lev, 111–21. Berlin: W. de Gruyter, 2009.
Mahmood, Saba. *Politics of Piety: The Islamic Revival and the Feminist Subject*. Princeton, N.J.: Princeton University Press, 2005.
Malkiel, David. *Reconstructing Ashkenaz. The Human Face of Franco-German Jewry, 1000–1250*. Stanford, Calif.: Stanford University Press, 2009.
———. "The Vision and Realization." *JQR* 95 (2005): 131–41.
Mansfield, Mary C. *Humiliation of Sinners: Public Penance in Thirteenth-Century France*. Ithaca, N.Y.: Cornell University Press, 1995.
Marcus, Ivan G. "Hasidei Ashkenaz Private Penitentials: An Introduction and Descriptive Catalogue of Their Manuscripts and Early Editions." In *Studies in Jewish Mysticism*, ed. Joseph Dan and Frank Talmadge, 57–83. Cambridge: Association for Jewish Studies, 1982.
———. "Hierarchies, Religious Boundaries and Jewish Spirituality in Medieval Germany." *Jewish History* 1 (1986): 7–26.
———. "A Jewish-Christian Symbiosis: The Culture of Early Ashkenaz." In *Cultures of the Jews: A New History*, ed. David Biale, 449–516. New York: Schocken Books, 2002.
———. "Kiddush Hashem beAshkenaz veSipur Rabbi Amnon miMagentza." In *Sanctity of Life and Martyrdom: Studies in Memory of Amir Yekutiel*, ed. Isaiah M. Gafni and Aviezer Ravitsky, 131–48. Jerusalem: Merkaz Zalman Shazar, 1992.
———. "Medieval Jewish Studies: Toward an Anthropological History of the Jews." In *The State of Jewish Studies*, ed. Shaye J. D. Cohen and Edward Greenstein, 113–42. Detroit: Wayne State University Press, 1990.
———. "Mothers, Martyrs, and Moneymakers: Some Jewish Women in Medieval Europe." *Conservative Judaism* 38 (1986): 34–45.
———. *Piety and Society: The Jewish Pietists of Medieval Germany*. Leiden: Brill, 1981.
———, ed. *The Religious and Social Ideas of the Jewish Pietists in Medieval Germany: Collected Essays*. Jerusalem: Merkaz Zalman Shazar, 1986 [Hebrew].
———. *Rituals of Childhood: Jewish Acculturation in Medieval Europe*. New Haven, Conn.: Yale University Press, 1996.
———. "Why Is This Knight Different? A Jewish Self-Representation in Medieval Europe." In *Tov Elem: Memory, Community and Gender in Medieval and Early Modern Jewish Societies. Essays in Honor of Robert Bonfil*, ed. Elisheva Baumgarten, Roni Weinstein, and Amnon Raz-Krakotzkin, *139–*52. Jerusalem: Mossad Bialik, 2011.
Marienberg, Evyatar. "Menstruation in Sacred Spaces: Medieval and Early Modern Jewish Women in the Synagogue." *Nordisk Judaistik* 25 (2004): 17–27.
———. *Niddah. Lorsque les juifs conceptualisent la menstruation*. Paris: Les Belles Lettres, 2003.
Marx, Alexander. "Rabbi Yosef of Arles as a Teacher and Head of a Yeshiva in Siena." In *The Jubilee Book in Honor of Levi Ginzburg on His 70th Year*, ed. Shaul Lieberman et al., 271–304. New York: HaAkedemia haAmerikanit leMad'ei haYahadut, 1946 [Hebrew].
Mauss, Marcel. *The Gift: The Form and Reason for Exchange in Archaic Societies*. Trans. W. D. Hall. London: Routledge, 1990.

McDonnell, Ernest W. *Beguines and Beghards in Medieval Culture: With Special Emphasis on the Belgian Scene.* New Brunswick, N.J.: Rutgers University Press, 1954.

McDowell, Linda. *Gender, Identity and Place: Understanding Feminist Geographies.* Minneapolis: University of Minesota Press, 1999.

McLaughlin, Megan M. *Consorting with Saints: Prayer for the Dead in Early Medieval France.* Ithaca, N.Y.: Cornell University Press, 1995.

———. "Consorting with Saints: Prayer for the Dead in Early Medieval French Society." Ph.D. diss., Stanford University, 1985.

———. "Women and Men." In *Christianity in Western Europe, 1100–1500*, ed. Miri Rubin and Walter Simons, 187–99. Cambridge: Cambridge University Press, 2009.

McNeill, John T., and Helena M. Gamer. *The Medieval Handbooks of Penance: A Translation of the Principal Libri Poenitentiales and Selections from Related Documents.* 1938; repr. New York: Columbia University Press, 1990.

Meens, Rob. "The Frequency and Nature of Early Medieval Penance." In *Handling Sin: Confession in the Middle Ages,* ed. Peter Biller and Alastair J. Minnis, 35–62. Woodbridge: York Medieval Press, 1998.

———. "The Historiography of Early Medieval Penance." In *A New History of Penance,* ed. Abigail Firey, 73–96. Leiden: Brill, 2008.

———. "Pollution in the Early Middle Ages: The Case of Food Regulations in Penitentials." *Early Medieval Europe* 4 (1995): 3–19.

———. "A Relic of Superstition, Bodily Impurity and the Church from Gregory the Great to the Twelfth Century Decretists." In *Purity and Holiness: The Heritage of Leviticus,* ed. M. J. H. M. Poorthuis and J. Schwartz, 281–93. Leiden: Brill, 2000.

———. "Ritual Purity and the Influence of Gregory the Great in the Early Middle Ages." *Unity and Diversity in the Church,* ed. R. N. Swanson, Studies in Church History 32 (1996): 31–43.

Mellinkoff, Ruth. *Antisemitic Hate Signs in Hebrew Illuminated Manuscripts from Medieval Germany.* Jerusalem: Center for Jewish Art, Hebrew University of Jerusalem, 1999.

———. "The Round Cap-Shaped Hats on Jews in BM Cotton Claudius B. IV." *Anglo-Saxon England* 2 (1973): 155–66.

Mentgen, Gerd. *Die Juden des Mittelrhein-Mosel-Gebietes im Hochmittelalter unter besonderer Berücksichtigung der Kreuzzugsverfolgungen.* Bonn: Rheinland Verlag, 1995.

———. *Studien zur Geschichte der Juden im mittelalterlichen Elsass.* Hannover: Hahn, 1995.

Merchavia, Chen. *The Church versus Talmudic and Midrashic Literature 500–1248.* Jerusalem: Mossad Bialik, 1970 [Hebrew].

Mershman, Francis. "Ember Days." *Catholic Encyclopedia.* Vol. 5. New York: Robert Appleton Company, 1909.

Minty, Mary. "Judengasse to Christian Quarters: The Phenomenon of Converted Synagogues in the Late Medieval and Early Modern Holy Roman Empire." In *Popular Religion in Germany and Central Europe,* ed. Robert Scribner, 58–68. Basingstoke: Macmillan, 1996.

Mintz, Sidney. "Food and Eating: Some Persisting Questions." In *Food Nations: Selling Taste in Consumer Societies,* ed. Warren Belasco and Phillip Scranton, 37–48. New York: Routledge, 2002.

Miramon, Charles de. "Déconstruction et reconstruction du tabou de la femme menstruée (XII–XIII siècle)." In *Kontinuitäten und Zäsuren in der Europäischen Rechtsgeschichte,* ed. A. Their, G. Pfeifer, and P. Grzimek, 79–107. Frankfurt: Peter Lang, 1999.

———. "La fin d'un tabou? L'interdiction de communier pour la femme menstruée au moyen âge. Le cas du XII siècle." In *Le sang au moyen âge. Actes du quatrième colloque international de Montpellier,* ed. Marcel Faure, 163–81. Montpellier: Association C.R.I.S.I.M.A., Universite Paul-Valery, 1999.

———. *Les "donnés" au Moyen Âge: Une forme de vie religieuse laïque v.1180–v.1500*. Paris: Cerf, 1999.

Mollat, Michel. *The Poor in the Middle Ages: An Essay in Social History*. Trans. Arthur Goldhammer. New Haven, Conn.: Yale University Press, 1986.

Monlash, Otto. *Epitaphs from the Ancient Jewish Cemetery of Prague*. Jerusalem: HaAkademiah haLeumit haYisraelit leMadaim, 1988.

Moore, Robert I. *The Formation of a Persecuting Society: Power and Deviance in Western Europe, 950–1250*. Oxford: Blackwell, 1987.

Müller, Jörg R. "*Erez gezerah*—'Land of Persecution': Pogroms Against the Jews in the *Regnum Teutonicum* from c. 1280–1350." In *The Jews of Europe in the Middle Ages (Tenth to Fifteenth Centuries)*, ed. Christoph Cluse, 245–60. Brepols: Turnhout, 2004.

Mundy, John Hine. "The Medieval Scarlet and the Economics of Sartorial Splendor." In *Cloth and Clothing in Medieval Europe: Essays in Memory of Professor E. M. Carus-Wilson*, ed. N. B. Harte and K. G. Ponting, 13–70. London: Heinemann Educational Books, 1983.

———. *Men and Women at Toulouse in the Age of the Cathars*. Toronto: Pontifical Institute of Mediaeval Studies, 1990.

Murray, Alexander. "Confession as a Historical Source in the Thirteenth Century." In *The Writing of History in the Middle Ages, Essays Presented to Richard William Southern*, ed. R. H. C. Davis and J. M. Wallace-Hadrill, 275–322. Oxford: Clarendon 1981.

———. "Confession Before 1215." In *Transactions of the Royal Historical Society*, 6th ser., 3 (1993): 51–81

———. "Piety and Impiety in Thirteenth Century Italy." *Studies in Church History* 8 (1972): 92–95.

Murray, Jacqueline. "Gendered Souls in Sexed Bodies: The Male Construction of Female Sexuality in Some Medieval Confessors." In *Handling Sin: Confession in the Middle Ages*, ed. Peter Biller and Alistair J. Minnis, 79–93. Rochester: York Medieval Press, 1998.

———. "Masculinizing Religious Life: Sexual Prowess, the Battle for Chastity and Monastic Identity." In *Holiness and Masculinity in the Middle Ages*, ed. P. H. Cullum and Katherine J. Lewis, 24–42. Cardiff: University of Wales Press, 2004.

Musurillo, Herbert. "The Problem of Ascetical Fasting in the Greek Patristic Writers." *Traditio* 12 (1956): 1–64.

Neiske, Franz. "Die Ordnung der Memoria. Formen necrologischer Tradition im mittelalterlichen Klosterverband." In *Institution und Charisma, Festschrift für Gert Melville zum 65 Geburtstag*, ed. Franz J. Felten, Annette Kehnel, and Stefan Weinfurter, 127–38. Cologne: Böhlau, 2009.

Neubauer, Adolf. "Le Memorbuch de Mayence." *REJ* 4 (1882): 1–30.

Newman, Louise M. "Critical Theory and the History of Women: What's at Stake in Deconstructing Women's History." *Journal of Women's History* 2 (2010): 58–68.

Nicholas, David. *The Growth of the Medieval City: From Late Antiquity to the Early Fourteenth Century*. London: Longman, 1997.

———. *The Later Medieval City, 1300–1500*. London: Longman, 1997.

Nirenberg, David. *Communities of Violence: Persecution of Minorities in the Middle Ages*. Princeton, N.J.: Princeton University Press, 1996.

Noam, Vered. *From Qumran to the Rabbinic Revolution: Conceptions of Impurity*. Jerusalem: Yad Yizhak Ben Zvi, 2010 [Hebrew].

Noble, Shlomo. "The Jewish Woman in Medieval Martyrology." In *Studies in Jewish Bibliography, History and Literature, in Honor of I. Edward Kiev*, ed. Charles Berlin, 347–55. New York: Ktav Publishing House, 1971.

Oexle, Otto Gerhard. "Die Gegenwart der Toten." In *Death in the Middle Ages*, ed. Herman Braet and Werner Verbeke, 19–77. Leuven: Leuven University Press, 1983.

———. "Memoria und Memorialbild." In *Memoria. Der geschichtliche Zeugniswert des liturgischen Gedenkens im Mittelalter*, ed. Karl Schmid and Joachim Wollasch, 384–440. Munich: W. Fink, 1984.

Oring, Elliott. "Legendry and the Rhetoric of Truth." *Journal of American Folklore* 121 (2008): 27–66.

Ortner, Sherry. *Making Gender: The Politics and Erotics of Culture*. Boston: Beacon Press, 1996.

Owen-Hughes, Diane. "Distinguishing Signs: Ear-rings, Jews and Franciscan Rhetoric in the Italian Renaissance City." *Past and Present* 112 (1986): 3–59.

Parry, Jonathan. "The Gift, the Indian Gift, and the 'Indian Gift.'" *Man* 21 (1986): 453–73.

Passenier, Anneke. "Women on the Loose: Stereotypes of Women in the Story of the Medieval Beguines." In *Female Stereotypes in Religious Traditions*, ed. Rita Kloppenborg and W. J. Hanegraff, 61–88. Leiden: Brill, 1995.

Payer, Pierre J. "Early Medieval Regulations Concerning Marital Sexual Relations." *Journal of Medieval History* 6 (1980): 364–70.

Pelikan, Jaroslav J. *Jesus Through the Centuries: His Place in the History of Culture*. New Haven, Conn.: Yale University Press, 1999.

Perry, Micha. "Female Slaughterers: Halakhic Traditions and Late Medieval Realities." In *Tov Elem: Memory, Community and Gender in Medieval and Early Modern Jewish Societies. Essays in Honor of Robert Bonfil*, ed. Elisheva Baumgarten, Roni Weinstein, and Amnon Raz-Krakotzkin, 127–46. Jerusalem: Mossad Bialik, 2011 [Hebrew].

———. *Tradition and Transformation: Knowledge Transmission Among Jews in in the Middle Ages*. Tel Aviv: HaKibbutz haMeuhad, 2010 [Hebrew].

Pipponier, Françoise, and Perine Mane. *Se vêtir au moyen âge*. Paris: A. Biro, 1995.

Pitt-Rivers, Julian. "The Anthropology of Honour." In *The Fate of Shechem*, ed. Julian Pitt-Rivers, 81–88. Cambridge: Cambridge University Press, 1977.

Pollack, Herman. *Jewish Folkways in Germanic Lands (1648–1806): Studies in Aspects of Daily Life*. Cambridge, Mass.: MIT Press, 1971.

Pomerance, Aubrey. "'Bekannt in den Toren.' Name und Nachruf in Memorbüchern." In *Erinnerung als Gegenwart. Jüdische Gedenkkulturen*, ed. Sabine Hödl and Elenore Lappin, 35–53. Berlin: Philo, 2000.

Porter, Roy. "History of the Body." In *New Perspectives on Historical Writings*, ed. Peter Burke, 206–32. 1991; repr. Cambridge: Polity Press, 1994.

Pullan, Brian. *Poverty and Charity: Europe, Italy, Venice, 1400–1700*. Aldershot and Brookfield: Variorum, 1994.

Rafeld, Meir. "Ta'anit Esther." In *Minhagei Yisrael*, ed. Daniel Sperber, 4:204–20. Jerusalem: Mossad haRav Kook, 1995.

Rasmussen, Linda. "Monastic Benefactors in England and Denmark: Their Social Background and Gender Distribution." In *Religious and Laity in Western Europe, 1000–1400: Interaction, Negotiation, and Power*, ed. Emilia Jamroziak and Janet Burton, 77–90. Turnhout: Brepols, 2006.

Raspe, Lucia. "Jewish Saints in Medieval Ashkenaz: A Contradiction of Terms?" *Frankfurter Judaistische Beiträge* 31 (2004): 75–90.

———. *Jüdische Hagiographie im mittelalterlichen Aschkenas*. Tübingen: Mohr Siebeck, 2006.

Reif, Stefan C. *Judaism and Hebrew Prayer: New Perspectives on Jewish Liturgical History*. Cambridge: Cambridge University Press, 1993.

Reiner, Avraham. *Die Grabsteine vom jüdischen Friedhof in Würzburg aus der Zeit vor dem Schwarzen*

Tod (1147–1346). Ed. Karlheinz Müller, Simon Schwarzfuchs, and Abraham (Rami) Reiner. Würzburg: Gesellschaft für Fränkische Geschichte, 2011.

Reiner, Elchanan. "From Joshua to Jesus: The Transformation of a Biblical Story to a Local Myth. A Chapter in the Religious Life of the Galilean Jew." In *Sharing the Sacred: Religious Contacts and Conflicts in the Holy Land, First–Fifteenth Centuries CE,* ed. Arieh Kofsky and Guy G. Stroumsa, 223–71. Jerusalem: Yad Yizhak Ben Zvi, 1998.

Resnick, Irven. "Dietary Laws in Medieval Christian-Jewish Polemics: A Survey." *Studies in Christian-Jewish Relations* 6 (2011): 1–15.

Revel-Naher, Elisabeth. *The Image of the Jew in Byzantine Art.* Trans. David Maizel. Oxford: Pergamon Press, 1992.

Rieder, Paula M. *On the Purification of Women: Churching in Northern France, 1100–1500.* New York: Palgrave, 2006.

Röckelein, Hedwig. "Marienverehrung und Judenfeindlichkeit im Mittelalter und früher Neuzeit." In *Maria in der Welt: Marienverehrung im Kontext der Sozialgeschichte 10.–18. Jahrhundert,* ed. C. Opitz et al., 279–307. Zurich: Chronos, 1993.

Rokéa, Zefira Entin. "The State, the Church and the Jews in Medieval England." In *Antisemitism Through the Ages: A Collection of Essays,* ed. Shmuel Almog, 99–126. Jerusalem: Merkaz Zalman Shazar, 1980 [Hebrew].

Rose, Gillian. *Feminism and Geography: The Limits of Geographical Knowledge.* Minneapolis: University of Minnesota Press, 1993.

Rosenthal, Joel. *The Purchase of Paradise: Gift Giving and the Aristocracy, 1307–1485.* London: Routledge and Kegan Paul, 1972.

Rosenwein, Barbara. *To Be the Neighbor of St. Peter: The Social Meaning of Cluny's Property, 909–1049.* Ithaca, N.Y.: Cornell University Press, 1989.

Rosman, Moshe. "The History of Jewish Women in Early Modern Poland: An Assessment." *Polin* 18 (2005): 25–56.

———. *How Jewish Is Jewish History.* Oxford: Littman Library of Jewish Civilization, 2007.

Roth, Pinchas. "Responsa from Heaven: Fragments of a New Manuscript of 'She'elot u-Teshuvot min Ha-Shamayim' from Gerona." *Materia Guidaica* 15–16 (2010–2011): 555–64.

———. "Sefer haPardes, leDarkhei Hivazrutu shel Sefer Hilkhati Yemei Benaymi." Master's thesis, Hebrew University of Jerusalem, 2008 [Hebrew].

Roux, Simone. *Paris in the Middle Ages.* Trans. Jo Ann McNamara. Philadelphia: University of Pennsylvania Press, 2009.

Rubin, Asher. "The Concept of Repentance Among Hasidey Ashkenaz." *Journal of Jewish Studies* 16 (1965): 161–76.

Rubin, Miri. *Charity and Community in Medieval Cambridge.* Cambridge: Cambridge University Press, 1987.

———. *Gentile Tales: The Narrative Assault on Late Medieval Jews.* New Haven, Conn.: Yale University Press, 1999.

———. "Identities." In *A Social History of England, 1200–1500,* ed. Rosemary Horrox and W. Mark Ormrod, 383–413. Cambridge: Cambridge University Press, 2006.

———, ed. *Medieval Christianity in Practice.* Princeton, N.J.: Princeton University Press, 2009.

Rubin, Miri, and Walter Simons, eds. *Christianity in Western Europe c. 1100–c. 1500.* Cambridge: Cambridge University Press, 2009.

Ruderman, David B. *Early Modern Jewry: A New Cultural History.* Princeton, N.J.: Princeton University Press, 2010.

———, ed. *Preachers of the Italian Ghetto*. Berkeley: University of California Press, 1992.

Rustow, Marina. *Heresy and the Politics of Community: The Jews of the Fatimid Caliphate*. Ithaca, N.Y.: Cornell University Press, 2008.

Ryan, Salvador. "Some Reflections on Theology and Popular Piety: A Fruitful or Fraught Relationship." *Heythrop Journal* 53 (2012): 961–71.

Sabar, Shalom. "Childbirth and Magic: Jewish Folklore and Material Culture." In *Cultures of the Jews*, ed. David Biale, 671–722. New York: Schocken Books, 2002.

Safrai, Chana. "Women in the Ancient Synagogue." In *Daughters of the King: Women and the Synagogue: A Survey of History, Halakhah, and Contemporary Realities*, ed. Susan Grossman and Rivka Haut, 39–50. Philadelphia: Jewish Publication Society, 1992.

Salfeld, Siegmund, ed. *Das Martyrologium des Nürnberger Memorbuches*. Berlin: Simion, 1898.

Salfeld, Siegmund, and Moritz Stern. "Nürnberg im Mittelalter." In *Die israelitische Bevölkerung der deutschen Städte*, 190–205. Kiel: H. Fiencke, 1894–1896.

Saltman, Avrom. "Hermann's *Opusculum de conversione sua:* Truth or Fiction." *REJ* 147 (1988): 31–56.

Satlow, Michael. "Fruit and the Fruit of Fruit: Charity and Piety Among Jews in Late Antique Palestine." *JQR* 100 (2010): 244–77.

Schäfer, Peter. "The Ideal of Piety of the Ashkenazi Hasidim and Its Roots in Jewish Tradition." *Jewish History* 4 (1990): 9–23.

———. "Jews and Christians in the High Middle Ages: The Book of the Pious." In *The Jews of Europe in the Middle Ages (Tenth to Fifteenth Centuries)*, ed. Christoph Cluse, 45–59. Turnhout: Brepols, 2004.

———. *Rivalität zwischen Engeln und Menschen, Untersuchungen z. rabbin. Engelvorstellung*. Berlin: de Gruyter, 1975.

Schmelzer, Menachem H. "Penitence, Prayer and (Charity?)." In *Minhah leNahum: Biblical and Other Studies Presented to Nahum M. Sarna in Honour of His 70th Birthday* (JSOT Supplement 154), ed. Marc Brettler and Michael Fishbane, 291–99. Sheffield: JSOT Press, 1993.

Schmid, Karl, and Joachim Wollasch, eds. *Memoria. Der geschichtliche Zeugniswert des liturgischen Gedenkens im Mittelalter*. Munich: W. Fink, 1984.

Schmitt, Jean-Claude. *La conversion d'Hermann le Juif. Autobigraphie, histoire et fiction*. Paris: Seuil, 2003.

———. "Religion populaire et culture folklorique." *Annales ESC* 31 (1976): 941–53.

Schremer, Adiel. *Brothers Estranged: Heresy, Christianity, and Jewish Identity in Late Antiquity*. Oxford: Oxford University Press, 2010.

———. "Realism in Halakhic Decision-Making: The Medieval Controversy Concerning Examination of Lungs (*Pelugat haRe'a*) as a Test Case." *Diné Israel* 28 (2011): 97–143 [Hebrew].

Schulenberg, Jane Tibbets. *Forgetful of Their Sex: Female Sanctity and Society ca. 500–1000*. Chicago: University of Chicago Press, 1998.

Schur, Yechiel Y. *The Care for the Dead in Medieval Ashkenaz, 1000–1500*. New York: ProQuest, 2008.

Schwartz, Ellen C. "The Ultimate Other: Jews and the Construction of Images in Later Medieval Art." In *Pictorial Languages and Their Meanings: Liber Amicorum in Honor of Nurith Kenaan-Kedar*, ed. Christine B. Verzar and Gil Fishhof, 221–32. Tel Aviv: Tel Aviv University Press, 2006.

Schwartz, Seth. *Imperialism and Jewish Society, 200 BCE to 640 CE*. Princeton, N.J.: Princeton University Press, 2001.

Schwarzbaum, Haim. "International Folklore Motifs in Petrus Alfonsi's *Disciplina Clericalis*." In *Jewish Folklore Between East and West: Collected Papers*, ed. Eli Yassif. Beersheva: Ben Gurion University Press, 1989.

Schwarzfuchs, Simon. "Mekomam shel Masaei haZlav beDivrey Yemey Israel." In *Tarbut veHevra*

beToldot Israel, Kovetz Ma'amarim leZichro shel Chaim Hillel Ben-Sasson, ed. Reuven Bonfil, Menahem Ben-Sasson, and Joseph R. Hacker, 251–67. Jerusalem: Magnes Press, 1989 [Hebrew].
Scott, James C. *Domination and the Arts of Resistance: Hidden Transcripts.* New Haven, Conn.: Yale University Press, 1990.
Scott, Joan Wallach. *Gender and the Politics of History.* New York: Columbia University Press, 1988.
———. "Unanswered Questions." *American Historical Review* 113 (2008): 1422–30.
Scribner, Robert. *For the Sake of the Simple Folk.* Oxford: Oxford University Press, 1994.
Sered, Susan Starr. *What Makes Women Sick: Maternity, Modesty, and Militarism in Israeli Society.* Hanover, N.H.: New England University Press, 2000.
———. *Women as Ritual Experts: The Religious Lives of Elderly Jewish Women in Jerusalem.* Oxford: Oxford University Press, 1992.
Shalev-Eyni, Sarit. *Jews Among Christians: Hebrew Book Illumination from Lake Constance.* London: H. Miller, 2010.
Shatzmiller, Joseph. "Church Articles: Pawns in the Hands of Jewish Money Lenders." In *Wirtschaftsgeschichte der mittelalterlichen Juden,* ed. Michael Toch, 93–102. Munich: R. Oldenbourg, 2008.
———. *Cultural Exchange: Jews, Christians, and Art in the Medieval Marketplace.* Princeton, N.J.: Princeton University Press, 2013.
Shaw, Teresa M. *The Burden of Flesh: Fasting and Sexuality in Early Christianity.* Minneapolis: Augsburg Fortress, 1998.
Shinners, John, ed. *Medieval Popular Religion: A Reader, 1000–1500.* Toronto: University of Toronto Press, 2002.
Shoham-Steiner, Ephraim. *Involuntary Marginals.* Jerusalem: Merkaz Zalman Shazar, 2007 [Hebrew].
———. "Vitam finivit infelicem": Madness, Conversion, and Adolescent Suicide Among Jews in Late Twelfth-Century England." In *Jews in Medieval Christendom: "Slay Them Not,"* ed. Kristine T. Utterback and Merrall Llewelyn Price, 71–90. Leiden: Brill, 2013.
Shyovitz, David I. "'He Has Created a Remembrance of His Wonders': Nature and Embodiment in the Thought of the Hasidei Ashkenaz." Ph.D. diss., University of Pennsylvania, 2011.
Signer, Michael A., and John Van Engen, eds. *Jews and Christians in Twelfth-Century Europe.* Notre Dame, Ind.: University of Notre Dame Press, 2001.
Simons, Walter. *Cities of Ladies: Beguine Communities in the Medieval Low Countries, 1200–1565.* Philadelphia: University of Pennsylvania Press, 2001.
Skinner, Patricia, ed. *The Jews in Medieval Britain: Historical, Literary, and Archeological Perspectives.* Woodbridge: Boydell Press, 2003.
Smith, Jonathan Z. *Drudgery Divine: On the Comparisons of Early Christianities and the Religions of Late Antiquities.* Chicago: University of Chicago Press, 1990.
Smith, Julia M. H. "Portable Christianity: Relics in the Medieval West (c. 700–1200)." *Proceedings of the British Academy* 181 (2012): 143–67.
Soloveitchik, Haym. "Bein Hevel Arav leHevel Edom." In *Sanctity of Life and Martyrdom: Studies in Memory of Amir Yekutiel,* ed. Isaiah M. Gafni and Aviezer Ravitsky, 149–52. Jerusalem: Merkaz Zalman Shazar, 1992.
———. *Pawnbroking: A Study in the Interrelationship Between Halakhah, Economic Activity, and Communal Self-Image.* Jerusalem: Magnes Press, 1985 [Hebrew].
———."Piety, Pietism and German Pietism. 'Sefer Hasidim I' and the Influence of 'Hasidei Ashkenaz.'" *JQR* 92 (2002): 455–93.
———. "Religious Law and Change: The Medieval Ashkenazic Example." *AJS Review* 12 (1987): 205–21.

———. "Review Essay of *Olam keMinhago Noheg*." *AJS Review* 23 (1998): 223–25.
———. "Three Themes in the Sefer Hasidim." *AJS Review* 1 (1976): 311–58.
———. *Wine in Ashkenaz in the Middle Ages, Yeyn Nesekh: A Study in the History of Halakhah*. Jerusalem: Merkaz Zalman Shazar, 2008 [Hebrew].
Sperber, Daniel, ed. *Minhagei Yisrael*. 8 vols. Jerusalem: Mossad haRav Kook, 1989–2007 [Hebrew].
Spiegel, Yaacov Shmuel. "Berur beDivrei haPaytan 'uTeshuvah uTefillah uTzedaka Ma'avirin et Ro'a haGezerah' ve'al Kefifut haPaytanim laHalakhah." In *Pithei Tefillah uMo'ed*, 271–90. Elkanah: Mikhlelet Orot Yisrael, 2010.
———. "Cross-Dressing for Special Occasions." In *From Sages to Savants: Studies Presented to Avraham Grossman*, ed. Joseph R. Hacker, Yosef Kaplan, and B. Z. Kedar, 329–52. Jerusalem: Merkaz Zalman Shazar, 2010 [Hebrew].
Sponsler, Claire. "In Transit: Theorizing Cultural Appropriation in Medieval Europe." *Journal of Medieval and Early Modern Studies* 32 (2002): 17–39.
Stabler-Miller, Tanya. "What's in a Name? Clerical Representations of Parisian Beguines, 1200–1327." *Journal of Medieval History* 33 (2007): 60–86.
Stahl, Yaakov I. "Inyanei Nissuin mitokh Sefer haKushiyot." *Jeshurun* 18 (2007): 57–70.
———. "Inyanei Tefilla miSefer haMaskil leR. Simha meTroyes." *Jeshurun* 26 (2012): 40–61.
———. "Tefillat Neshamot haNiftarim beBeit haKnesset." *Yerushatenu* 3 (2009): 177–236.
Stoddard, Belle Tuten. "Fashion and Benefaction in Twelfth-Century Western France." In *Religious and Laity in Western Europe, 1000–1400: Interaction, Negotiation, and Power*, ed. Emilia Jamroziak and Janet Burton, 41–62. Turnhout: Brepols, 2006.
Stökl ben Ezra, Daniel. *The Impact of Yom Kippur on Early Christianity: The Day of Atonement from Second Temple Judaism to the Fifth Century*. Tübingen: Mohr Siebeck, 2003.
Stow, Kenneth R. *Alienated Minority: The Jews of Medieval Latin Europe*. Cambridge, Mass.: Harvard University Press, 1992.
———. "The Jewish Family in the Rhineland: Form and Function." *American Historical Review* 92 (1987): 1085–110.
Strickland, Debra Higgs. *Saracens, Demons and Jews: Making Monsters in Medieval Art*. Princeton, N.J.: Princeton University Press, 2003.
Stuard, Susan Mosher. *Gilding the Markets: Luxury and Fashion in Fourteenth-Century Italy*. Philadelphia: University of Pennsylvania Press, 2006.
Subrahmanyam, Sanjay. "Connected Histories: Notes Towards a Reconfiguration of Early Modern Eurasia." *Modern Asian Studies* 31 (1997): 735–62.
———. "Holding the World in Balance: The Connected Histories of the Iberian Overseas Empires, 1500–1640." *American Historical Review* 112 (2007): 1359–85.
Swanson, R. N. "Angels Incarnate: Clergy and Masculinity from Gregorian Reform to Reformation." In *Masculinity in Medieval Europe*, ed. D. M. Hadley, 160–77. New York: Longman, 1999.
———. *Religion and Devotion in Europe, 1215–1515*. Cambridge: Cambridge University Press, 1995.
Symes, Carol. "Out in the Open in Arras: Sightlines, Soundscapes and the Shaping of a Medieval Public Sphere." In *Cities, Texts and Social Networks, 400–1500: Experiences and Perceptions of Medieval Urban Space*, ed. Caroline Goodson, Anne E. Lester, and Carol Symes, 279–302. Burlington: Ashgate, 2010.
Ta-Shma, Israel M. "The Danger of Drinking Water During the Tequfa: The History of an Idea." *Jerusalem Studies in Jewish Folklore* 17 (1995): 21–32 [Hebrew].
———. *Early Franco-German Ritual and Custom*. Jerusalem: Magnes Press, 1992 [Hebrew].
———. "Hasidut Ashkenaz beSefarad." In *Galut Ahar Golah*, ed. Aaron Mirsky et al., 165–73. Jerusalem: Makhon Ben Zvi, 1988.

———. "Ma'amad haNashim haMitnadvot leKayem Mitzvot shehaZman Graman." In *Ritual, Custom and Reality in Franco-Germany, 1000–1350*, ed. Israel M. Ta-Shma, 262–79. Jerusalem: Magnes Press, 1996.

———. "Minhagei Harhakat haNiddah beAshkenaz haKedumah: heHayim vehaSifrut." In *Ritual, Custom and Reality in Franco-Germany, 1000–1350*, ed. Israel M. Ta-Shma, 280–88. Jerusalem: Magnes Press, 1996.

———. "Mitzvat Talmud Torah, keBa'aya Hevratit-Datit beSefer Hasidim: Lebikoret Shitat haTosafot beAshkenaz baMe'a haYud-Gimel." In *Ritual, Custom and Reality in Franco-Germany, 1000–1350*, ed. Israel M. Ta-Shma, 112–29. Jerusalem: Magnes Press, 1996.

———. *Ritual, Custom and Reality in Franco-Germany, 1000–1350*. Jerusalem: Magnes Press, 1996 [Hebrew].

———. *Studies in Medieval Rabbinic Literature*. 4 vols. Jerusalem: Mossad Bialik, 2004 [Hebrew].

———. "Synagogal Sanctity: Symbolism and Reality." In *Knesset Ezra: Literature and Life in the Synagogue, presented to Ezra Fleischer*, ed. Shulamith Elizur et al., 351–64. Jerusalem: Makhon Ben Zvi, 1994 [Hebrew].

Taitz, Emily. "Women's Voices, Women's Prayers: Women in the European Synagogues of the Middle Ages." In *Daughters of the King: Women and the Synagogue: A Survey of History, Halakhah, and Contemporary Realities*, ed. Susan Grossman and Rivka Haut, 59–79. Philadelphia: Jewish Publication Society, 1992.

Talmon-Heller, Daniella. *Islamic Piety in Medieval Syria: Mosques, Cemeteries and Sermons Under the Zangids and Ayyūbids (1146–1260)*. Leiden: Brill, 2007.

Tanner, Norman. *The Ages of Faith: Popular Religion in Late Medieval England and Western Europe*. London: I. B. Tauris, 2009.

———. "Least of the Laity." *Journal of Medieval History* 32 (2006): 395–423.

Toch, Michael. *Die Juden im mittelalterlichen Reich (Enzyklopädie deutscher Geschichte 44)*. Munich: R. Oldenbourg, 1998.

———. "Die jüdische Frau im Erwerbsleben des Spätmittelalters." In *Zur Geschichte der jüdischen Frau in Deutschland*, ed. Julius Carlebach, 37–48. Berlin: Metropol-Verlag, 1993.

———. "Economic Activities of German Jews in the Middle Ages." In *Wirtschaftsgeschichte der mittelalterlichen Juden*, ed. Michael Toch, 181–210. Munich: Oldenbourg, 2008.

———. *The Economic History of European Jews: Late Antiquity and Early Middle Ages*. Leiden: Brill, 2013.

———. "The Formation of a Diaspora: The Settlement of the Jews in the Medieval German Reich." *Aschkenas* 7 (1997): 55–78.

———. "Jüdisches Alltagsleben im Mittelalter: Fragen an die Archäologie." In *Synagogen, Mikwen, Siedlungen. Jüdisches Alltagsleben im Lichte neuer archäologischer Funde*, ed. Egon Wamers and Fritz Backhaus, 11–24. Frankfurt: Archäologisches Museum Frankfurt, 2004.

———. "Numismatics and History: The Hebrew 'Mancus.'" *Zion* 46 (1981): 237–42 [Hebrew].

Tolan, John V. *Petrus Alfonsi and His Medieval Readers*. Gainesville: University Press of Florida, 1993.

Trachtenberg, Joshua. *Jewish Magic and Superstition*. Philadelphia: Jewish Publication Society, 1939.

Tropper, Amram. "Motivations for Fasting in Second Temple Period." Master's thesis, Hebrew University of Jerusalem, 1999 [Hebrew].

Tubach, Frederic C. *Index Exemplorum: A Handbook of Medieval Religious Tales*. Helsinki: Suomalainen Tiedeakatemia, 1969.

Turner, Victor Witter. *Dramas, Fields, and Metaphors: Symbolic Action in Human Society*. Ithaca, N.Y.: Cornell University Press, 1974.

Uhalde, Kevin. "The Church and Pastoral Care in Late Antiquity." In *A New History of Penance*, ed. Abigail Firey, 97–120. Leiden: Brill, 2008.
Urbach, Ephraim E. "Al Grimat Mavet beShogeg uMavet ba'Arisa." *Asufot, Jewish Studies Yearbook* 1 (1987): 319–32.
———. "Political and Social Tendencies in Talmudic Concepts of Charity." *Zion* 16 (1951): 1–27 [Hebrew].
———. *The Tosaphists: Their History, Writings and Methods*. Jerusalem: Mossad Bialik, 1980 [Hebrew].
Vajda, Georges. "Fasting in Islam and Judaism." In *The Development of Islamic Ritual*, ed. Gerald Hawting, 133–49. Aldershot: Ashgate Variorum, 2006.
van Boxel, Piet. "The Virgin and the Unicorn." In *Crossing Borders: Hebrew Manuscripts as a Meeting Place of Cultures*, ed. Piet van Boxel and Sabine Arndt, 57–68. Oxford: Bodleian Library, 2007.
Van Engen, John. *Sisters and Brothers of the Common Life: The Devotio Moderna and the World of the Later Middle Ages*. Philadelphia: University of Pennsylvania Press, 2008.
———. "Practice Beyond the Confines of the Medieval Parish." In *Educating People of Faith. Exploring the History of Jewish and Christian Communities*, ed. John Van Engen, 150–77. Grand Rapids, Mich.: William B. Eerdmans Publishing, 2004.
Vauchez, André. "Conclusion." In *La réligion populaire en Languedoc*, 429–44. Toulouse: E. Privat, 1976.
———, ed. *The Laity in the Middle Ages: Religious Beliefs and Devotional Practices*. Trans. Margery J. Schneider. Notre Dame, Ind.: University of Notre Dame Press, 1993.
———. "Religion populaire dans la France méridionale au XIVe siècle d'après les procès de canonisation." In *La réligion populaire en Languedoc*, 91–107. Toulouse: E. Privat, 1976.
———. *Sainthood in the Later Middle Ages*. Trans. Jean Birrell. Cambridge: Cambridge University Press, 1997.
Venarde, Bruce. *Women's Monasticism and Medieval Society: Nunneries in France and England, 890–1215*. Ithaca, N.Y.: Cornell University Press, 1996.
Vogel, Cyrille. *Le pecheur et la peniténce au moyen âge*. Paris: Editions du Cerf, 2007.
Wagner, Karen. "Cum aliquis venerit ad sacerdotem: Penitential Experience in the Central Middle Ages." In *A New History of Penance*, ed. Abigail Firey, 201–18. Leiden: Brill, 2008.
Wamers, Egon, and Fritz Backhaus, eds. *Synagogen, Mikwen, Siedlungen. Jüdisches Alltagsleben im Lichte Neuer Archäologischer Funde*. Frankfurt: Archäologisches Museum Frankfurt, 2004.
Weinberg, Magnus. *Das Memorbuch von Hagenbach*. Frankfurt: D. Droller, 1927.
———. *Die Memorbücher der jüdischen Gemeinden in Bayern*. Frankfurt: S. Neuman, 1937.
Weinstein, Donald, and Rudolph M. Bell. *Saints and Society: The Two Worlds of Western Christendom, 1000–1700*. Chicago: University of Chicago Press, 1982.
Weinstein, Sara Epstein. *Piety and Fanaticism: Rabbinic Criticism of Religious Stringency*. Northvale, N.J.: Jason Aronson, 1997.
Weisner-Hanks, Merry. "Do Women Need the Renaissance." *Gender and History* 20 (2008): 539–57.
Weissler, Chava. "The Missing Half and the Other Half: A Feminist and Anthropological Response." *Jewish Social Studies* 2 (1996): 99–105, 108–15.
———. *Voices of the Matriarchs: Listening to the Prayers of Early Modern Jewish Women*. Boston: Beacon Press, 1998.
West, Cadence, and Don H. Zimmerman. "Doing Gender." *Gender and Society* 1 (1987): 121–51.
White, Stephen D. *Custom, Kinship and Gifts to Saints, The Laudatio Parentum in Western France, 1050–1150*. Chapel Hill: University of North Carolina Press, 1988.
Wiedl, Birgit. "Jews and the City: Parameters of Jewish Urban Life in Late Medieval Austria." In *Urban Space in the Middle Ages and the Early Modern Age*, ed. Albrecht Classen, 237–308. Berlin: Walter de Gruyter, 2010.

Wieseltier, Leon. "Jewish Bodies, Jewish Minds." *JQR* 95 (2005): 435–42.
Williams, Margaret H. "Being a Jew in Rome: Sabbath Fasting as an Expression of Romano-Jewish Identity." In *Negotiating Diaspora: Jewish Strategies in the Roman Empire*, ed. John M. G. Barclay, 8–18. London: T. and T. Clark, 2004.
Wolbrink, Shelley Amiste. "Women in the Premonstratensian Order of Northwestern Germany, 1120–1250." *Catholic Historical Review* 89 (2003): 387–408.
Wolf, Lepenies, ed. *Entangled Histories and Negotiated Universals*. Frankfurt: Campus, 2003.
Wolfson, Elliot R. "The Mystical Significance of Torah Study in German Pietism." *JQR* 84 (1993): 34–77.
Woolf, Jeffrey R. "Medieval Models of Purity and Sanctity: Ashkenazic Women in the Synagogue." In *Purity and Holiness: The Heritage of Leviticus*, ed. M. J. H. M. Poorthuis and Joshua J. Schwartz, 263–80. Leiden: Brill, 2000.
Ya'ari, Avraham. "The Mi Sheberakh Prayers: History and Texts." *Kiryat Sefer* 33 (1955): 118–30, 233–35.
———. "Tefilot Mi Sheberakh." *Kiryat Sefer* 33 (1957–1958): 118–30, 230–50; *Kiryat Sefer* 36 (1960–1961): 103–18.
Yassif, Eli. "Legends and History: Historians Read Hebrew Legends of the Middle Ages." *Zion* 64 (1999): 187–220 [Hebrew].
———. "The Saint and the Bishop: Diaspora Tales in Ms Jerusalem 3182." *Zion* 76 (2011): 305–40 [Hebrew].
———. "Sefer haMa'asim." In *The Hebrew Collection of Tales in the Middle Ages*, 42–79. Tel Aviv: HaKibbutz haMeuhad, 2004.
———. "Shevarim Geluhei Zakan, haMa'avak Al haMitus shel Tzfat baYamim haHem baZman haZeh." *Mikan* 4 (2005): 42–79.
Yefet-Refael, Revital. "Beware of Hypocrites: Religious Hypocrisy in Medieval Spanich Hebrew Prose." *Hispania Judaica* 6 (1999): 9–51 [Hebrew].
Yerushalmi, Yosef Hayim. "The Inquisition and the Jews of France in the Time of Bernard Gui." *Harvard Theological Review* 63 (1970): 363–67.
———. «Un champ à Anathoth: Vers une histoire de l'espoir juif.» In *Mémoire et histoire: Données et débats: Actes du XXVe Colloque des intellectuels juifs de langue francaise*, ed. Jean Halperin and Georges Lévitte, 91–108. Paris: Denoel, 1986.
Yuval, Israel J. "Donations from Nürnberg to Jerusalem (1375–1392)." *Zion* 46 (1981): 182–97 [Hebrew].
———. "Heilige Städte, heilige Gemeinden: Mainz als das Jerusalem Deutschlands, Aschkenaz." In *Jüdische Gemeinden und Organisationsformen von der Antike bis zur Gegenwart*, ed. Jütte Robert and Kustermann Abraham, 91–101. Cologne: Böhlau Verlag, 1996.
———. "Monetary Arrangements and Marriage in Medieval Ashkenaz." In *Religion and Economy: Connections and Interactions*, ed. Menahem Ben-Sasson, 191–208. Jerusalem: Merkaz Zalman Shazar, 1995 [Hebrew].
———. *Scholars in Their Time: The Religious Leadership of German Jewry in the Late Middle Ages*. Jerusalem: Magnes Press, 1988 [Hebrew].
———. *Two Nations in Your Womb, Perceptions of Jews and Christians in Late Antiquity and the Middle Ages*. Trans. Barbara Harshav and Jonathan Chipman. Berkeley: University of California Press, 2006.
Zahavy, Tzvee. "Politics of Piety: Social Conflict and the Emergence of Rabbinic Liturgy." In *The Making of Jewish and Christian Worship*, ed. Lawrence Hoffman and Paul Bradshaw, 42–68. Notre Dame, Ind.: University of Notre Dame Press, 1991.
Zilberstein, Roly. "The Role of Jews in Greek-Latin Polemics: Beards and a Comment About Fasting

on the Sabbath." In *Tov Elem: Memory, Community and Gender in Medieval and Early Modern Jewish Societies. Essays in Honor of Robert Bonfil*, ed. Elisheva Baumgarten, Roni Weinstein, and Amnon Raz-Krakotzkin, 23–39. Jerusalem: Mossad Bialik, 2011.

Zimmels, H. J. "Nach-Talmudische Fasttage." In *Jewish Studies in Memory of George A. Kohut*, ed. Salo Baron and Alexander Marx, 599–614. New York: Alexander Kohut Memorial Foundation, 1935.

Zimmer, Eric (Yitzhak). "Baking Practices and Baking in Medieval Ashkenaz." *Zion* 65 (2000): 141–62 [Hebrew].

———. "Head Covering of Jewish Women: Characteristics and Historical Development." In *Ta-Shma: Studies in Judaica in Memory of Israel M. Ta-Shma*, ed. Rami Reiner et al., 1:404–14. Alon Shvut: Tevunot, Mikhlelet Herzog, 2011 [Hebrew].

———. "Minhag Matnat Yad baRegalim." *Yerushatenu* 3 (2009): 145–55 [Hebrew].

———. "Minhag 'Matnat Yad' and 'Hazkarat Neshamot.'" In *The Scepter Shall Not Depart from Judah: Leadership, Rabbinate and Community in Jewish History. Studies Presented to Professor Simon Schwarzfuchs*, ed. Joseph R. Hacker and Yaron Harel, 71–88. Jerusalem: Mossad Bialik, 2011 [Hebrew].

———. *Society and Its Customs: Studies in the History and Metamorphosis of Jewish Customs*. Jerusalem: Merkaz Zalman Shazar, 1996 [Hebrew].

Zimmerman, Benedicté, and Michael Werner. "Beyond Comparison: Histoire Croisée and the Challenge of Reflexivity." *History and Theory* 45 (2006): 30–50.

Zirlin, Yael. "The Decoration of the Miscellany, Its Iconography and Style." *The North French Hebrew Miscellany, British Library Add. MS 11639*, ed. Jeremy Schonfield, 2:74–161. London: Facsimile Editions, 2003.

Ziwes, Franz-Josef. *Studien zur Geschichte der Juden im mittleren Rheingebiet während des hohen und späten Mittelalters*. Hannover: Hahnsche Buchhandlung, 1995.

Zunz, Leopold. *Der Ritus des synagogalen Gottesdienstes, geschichtlich entwickelt*. Berlin: Louis Lamm, 1919.

INDEX

Aaron (biblical), 61
Abraham (biblical), 146
Abraham b. Azriel, 246 n.71
Abraham b. Ephraim, 178–79
Abraham Hildik, 246 n.71
Abrahams, Israel, 9, 23, 243 n.12, 275 n.20
Absolution, 72
Acculturation. *See* appropriation
Adam (biblical), 70, 75
Adler, Nathan, 168
Adultery, 74–75, 81, 88, 252 n.216
Amnon of Mainz, 76
Anderson, C. Colt, 41
Angels, 35–39, 42, 45, 220, 239 n.92
Angenendt, Arnold, 111
Animals, 36–37
Appropriation, 7, 88, 110–15, 179, 181, 222–23, 230 n.39, 257 n.316
Aristocracy, 175
Arrogance, 150, 165–67, 168–70, 182, 202
Asceticism, 2, 54–55, 57, 61, 87, 183, 190
Asher b. Yehiel, 96, 148, 169, 183, 258 n.1
Atonement. *See* Repentance
Augustine, 76, 135
Austria, 4
Avigdor b. Elijah Katz, haTzarfati, 159, 162

Babylon, 60, 107, 196, 198, 200–201, 215; in contrast to Palestine 56–57, 63, 107–8, 150, 267 n.8
Babylonian Talmud. *See* Talmud
Bad dreams. *See* Fasting for bad dreams
Baer, Yitzhak (Fritz), 72–73
Baptism, 6
Baraita de Niddah, 28–29, 39, 215
Barbers. *See* Hair
Barby, 80
Baron, Salo, 9, 229 n.29, 231 n.55
Barzen, Rainer, 105

Baskin, Judith, 13–14, 43, 142–43, 243 n.170
Beards, 96, 173, 178–79, 276 n.40. *See also* Hair
Bede, 40
Beer, Moshe, 56
Beguines, 170, 174–75, 208–9, 278–79 n. 103
Belle (Bellette), 156, 270 n.100
Benedictines, 174
Benjamin, Selnik, 168
Berger, Aliza, 155–56
Berger, David, 88, 285 n.19
Berliner, Adolf (Abraham), 9, 275 n.20
Bernard Gui, 96
Berthold of Regensburg, 15
Beruriah, 283 n.79
Biale, David, 43
Bible, 6, 26, 34, 44, 51, 54–56, 61, 79, 83, 85, 170, 181, 214, 222, 224 n.18, 246 n.57, 266 n.35, 269 n.62
Birth and pregnancy, 41, 55, 69, 82, 204, 253 n.224
Black Death, 4–5, 7, 65, 104, 116, 128, 135, 247 n.93
Blind men, 145–46, 158, 165
Blois, 64–65, 130, 183, 247 n.93
Blood. *See Niddah*
Bohemia, 4
Bonfil, Robert, 9, 23
Books, 120, 127
Bruna (rabbanit), 164–65, 167
Burchard of Worms, 41, 88, 254 n.257
Burning of Talmud. *See* Talmud Trial
Bynum, Caroline Walker, 57–58, 92–93, 254 n.247
Byzantium, 282 n.44

Caesarius of Heisterbach, 94, 135
Cairo Genizah, 8, 258 n.8

Calendar, 52, 54, 58, 61, 79, 243 n.12, 257 n.318
Candles, 80–81, 112, 122, 124, 252 n.214, 263 n.111
Carmoly, Eliakim, 105
Cayam, Aviva, 155–56
Celibacy, 6, 14, 16, 58, 86, 208, 249 n.133, 253 n.244
Cemetery, 103, 120–23, 262 n.109
Charity, 16–18, 45, 55, 120–28, 195, 218, 219, 258 n.8, 285 n.2; for education 121–25; and gender 116–28, 266 n.177; as a gift 111, 260 n.53; given by couples 113, 116, 117, 123, 126–27, 262 n.108; to Land of Israel 105; *matnat yad* 105, 108–10; as penance 79, 133; for poor 113, 122–24, 282 n.41, 263 nn. 109, 122; private 259 n.43; pro anima 18, 103–28; as redemptive 103, 107–15, 136, 258 n.7; for sick 261 n.83, 263 n.109; women's 132–33. See also Fasting, and prayer and charity (as trio)
Chartres, 262 n.103
Children, 13, 67, 74, 81–82, 128, 129, 167–68, 250 n.170, 264 n.128
Christian knowledge of Jewish practice, 45, 58–59, 100. See also Jewish knowledge of Christian practice
Church (as a structure), 95, 108, 219, 256 n.289
Circumcision, 24, 184, 191
Cistercians, 174, 175
Cloth, 173–74, 182–84, 189, 277 n.71; silk 183, 191, 270 n.93, 277 n.71. See also Mixed cloths
Clothing, 18, 83, 172–73, 175–76, 182–90, 218–19, 274 n.18; black 73, 95, 186–87; 191, 250 n.164; cross-dressing 173, 185–89; dress codes 274 n.13; for fasting 58, 190–91; for menstruation 27, 190; monastic 174, 186–87; for mourning 191; as pawns 182; and penance 71, 191; regulation of 192–93; ritual garments 210–11; for Sabbath 280 n. 133; sackcloth 56, 79, 99, 191, 245 n.36; and social status 173–74; for synagogue 183, 190–91; white 27, 31, 47, 66, 71, 186–87, 191, 237 n.43; women's 172–73, 192; wool 156. See also Mixed cloths
Cohen, Shaye, 43–44, 192–93
Cologne, 4, 48, 94, 125, 209
Commandments (*mitzvot*), 266 n.2; positive time-bound 18, 138, 142, 144–55, 172, 221

Community and individual. See Individual and community
Confession, 6, 15, 42, 46, 75, 77, 81, 87, 88–91, 208, 218, 221; Christian 70–72, 255 n.268; confessor in Christianity 46, 70–72, 93–94, 134–35, 308, 241n.148, 250 n.169; confessor in Judaism 74, 77, 253 n.237; and liturgy 63, 66, 70–71, 73
Constable, Giles, 174, 180, 274 n.6, 275 n.25
Conversion, 67, 91, 95–98, 187, 193, 197, 222, 230 n.43, 249 n.118; of women 96; return to Judaism 95–96
Corbeil, 78
Corporal punishment, 74–75
Count Emicho, 168
Courts, 130–31
Creation of the world, 36
Cross, 95, 186, 188, 197
Crusades, 4, 5, 6, 63–64, 77, 142, 168
Cuffel, Alexandra, 43
Cullum, Patricia, 136
Currency, 124–28

Daniel (biblical), 67, 96
David (biblical), 90, 141, 171, 201, 217
Day of Atonement. See Yom Kippur
De Jong, Mayke, 72
de Miramon, Charles, 39–41
Death, 66, 74, 78, 81–82, 259 n.29; burial with tzitzit 154–55, 168, 270 n.94; pledges 115, 260 n.51
Demons, 245 n.44
Deviance, 11, 151
Diamond, Eliezer, 54–55
Dinari, Yedidyah, 237 n.35, 238 n.54
Disciplina Clericalis. See Petrus Alfonsi
Divorce, 48, 129, 131
Dominicans, 174
Donin, Nicholas, 85
Donors, 103, 110–28, 131–37. See also Charity
Dulcia of Worms, 49, 156, 218–19, 222, 262 n.107, 255 n. 276

Easter, 99
Eclipse, 74
Education, 115, 122–24, 263 n.109
Eleazar b. Judah of Worms (*Rokeah*), 12, 29–31, 35, 43, 45, 49, 61, 72–79, 81, 96, 154, 160, 190, 193, 205, 216–18, 247 n.93, 270 n.81. See also *Hilkhot Teshuvah*; *Sefer Rokeah*

Index 325

Eleazar b. Pedat, 55
Eleazar b. Samuel of Metz, 69, 157–58
Elhanan b. Samuel, 82
Eliezer b. Nathan (Ra'avan), 130–31, 135, 151
Eliezer b. Joel haLevi (Ra'aviah), 28–29, 61, 146, 168–69
Elijah (biblical), 197, 198, 282 n.36
Elijah b. Judah of Paris, 66
Elite and lay, 6, 8, 9–11, 42, 45, 56, 103–4, 113, 147, 155, 167, 170, 215, 218, 227 n.5, 232 n.69. *See also* Laity
Elizur, Shulamit, 60–61, 85–86
Elliott, Dyan, 41–42, 134, 170, 173–74, 209
Emanuel, Simcha, 31, 81
Ember Days, 58, 97
England, 4, 189
Epitaphs, 49, 103, 212, 248 n.105, 258 n.3, 283 n.73, 284 n.9
Epstein, Steven, 132
Erfurt, 49
Esther (Book of), 199
Etrog and lulav, 139, 143–49, 170, 215, 269 n.53, 273 n.169
Eucharist, 6, 72, 87, 94, 111, 114
Evreux, 78, 251 n. 194
Excommunication (*herem*), 23, 24
Exodus (from Egypt), 184
Expulsion of Jews, 7, 217, 239 n.74
Ezra the Scribe, 26

Farmer, Sharon, 113, 135
Fasting, 17–18, 35, 45, 172, 191, 195, 204; and age 83; and agency 82–85; and anger 81; announcing fasts 84, 205, 208, 212, 215, 217, 222; for bad dreams (*ta'anit halom*) 54, 66, 69, 74, 244 n.21; after birth 249 n.118; and charity 55, 63–64, 109–10, 257 n. 331; and children 67, 248 nn.107–12; commemorating events 64–65, 67; communal 54, 58, 63–66; and conversion 95–98; and death 74, 92; critique of 54, 244 n.18; and demons 245n.44; and drought 63; duration of 81–82, 95, 99, 250 n. 164; of Esther 67; and prayer and charity (as trio) 57–58, 72, 76–78, 94, 243 n.11, 246 n.67; and food eaten 66, 81–82, 98, 246 n.78, 251 n.175; on Fridays 98; of Gedaliah 65, 67; and immersion 248 n.105; individual fasts 54–55, 58, 66–70; in Islam 53, 244 n.13; in late antiquity 54–58; limitations 91–92; Mondays and Thursdays 61, 63, 66, 68–69, 75, 78–79, 82–83, 247 n.80; motivations 54, 55–56, 72–74; and mourning 78; and nursing 82; and penance 70–85, 99; postponing fasts 68; and prayers 56, 84, 252 n.201; and Rosh haShanah 57, 60, 61–63, 97, 246 n.69; on Sabbath 57, 60, 66, 69; and sacrifice 55, 61, 70, 101, 250 n.154; for sick children 68, 74, 250 n.170; and travel 68; and virgins 203–7; visibility 55–56, 84, 85, 94, 99, 100; on wedding day 66, 67, 248 n.100; and women 55–56, 67–68, 80, 81, 82–84, 91, 92, 244 n.30, 253 n.225. *See also* Yom Kippur
Feminism, 13, 267 nn.17, 26
Finn, Richard, 107
Fires, 79, 89, 184, 207, 252 n.205, 277 n.82
Fishman, Talya, 88
Flagellation, 73, 75, 76, 85, 95
Food, 1, 51–52, 81–82, 93, 101, 184, 197, 257 n.328, 259 n.43. *See also* Fasting
Four species. *See* Etrog and lulav
France, 1, 3, 4, 12, 19, 61, 77, 78, 102, 172, 177, 189, 198–200, 202, 206–7, 217. *See also* Germany vs. northern France
Franciscans, 174
Frankfurt, 4
Frauenschul, 48–49
Freehof, Solomon, 106
Freidman, Mordechai, 143, 146–48
Fund (communal), 115, 122–24

Galilee, 198
Galinsky, Judah, 105, 108, 114–15
Garrison, Roman, 107
Gartner, Yaacov, 86
Ge'onim, 32, 56, 60, 81, 150, 238 n.68, 277 n.77
Genesis, 79
Genoa, 132
German pietism. *See Hasidei Ashkenaz*
Germany, 1, 3, 4, 7, 19, 61, 101–2, 177, 202, 206–7, 217; Germany vs. northern France 31–32, 78, 101–2, 151–52, 158, 200, 202, 217, 228 n.16
Gershom b. Judah (Light of Exile, *Me'or haGolah*), 106
Glückel, 248 n.105, 264 n.140
Goitein, Shlomo Dov, 8, 53
Goldin, Simha, 23, 142–43
Golinkin, David, 157
Gossip, 73, 203, 205

Gratian, 41
Gray, Alyssa, 107, 129
Greenblatt, Rachel, 106
Gregorian Reform, 41
Gregory IX (pope), 58–59
Gregory the Great, 39–41, 241 n.125
Grossman, Avraham, 14, 86, 92, 142–43, 228 n.16, 248 n.113, 253 n.244
Güdemann, Moritz, 9

Hai Ga'on, 60
Haim b. Isaac, 30–31
Haim Barukh, 69, 82
Hair, 18, 73, 96, 162, 173, 180, 181, 184, 187; tonsure 180, 188. *See also* Beards
Hamilton, Sarah, 71–72
Hannukah, 81, 82, 146
Har-Shefi, Bitha, 14, 86, 92, 142–43, 155–56, 160, 248 n.113
Hasid/ah (as designation), 1, 13, 16, 17, 70, 142, 212, 224, 284 n.7
Hasidei Ashkenaz (German Pietists), 3, 12–13, 72–76, 154, 163, 178–80, 185–89, 200, 216–17, 223–24, 232 n.76, 233 nn.78–90, 250 n.167, 280 n.142
Head coverings, 176–78, 181–82
Heaven and hell, 55, 103, 113, 179, 205, 219
Hekhalot literature, 73, 237 n.49, 250 n.160
Hell. *See* Heaven and hell
Herman-Judah, 51, 96–97, 222
Hermit, 198
Hibbuv mitzvah, 148–49, 153–54, 202
High Holidays, 32, 54, 77, 108–9. *See also* Rosh haShanah; Yom Kippur
Hilkhot Teshuvah, 77, 98, 251 n.190. *See also* Eleazar b. Judah
Holidays, 13, 167. *See also* Hannukah; High Holidays; Passover; Purim; Rosh haShanah; Yom Kippur
Honorius (pope), 242 n.154
Horowitz, Elliott, 178
Hovav, Yemima, 49, 92, 168, 253 n.225
Howell, Martha, 111
Humiliation (*bushah*), 32, 151–53, 199, 202, 217, 224, 269 n.78, 281 n.29
Huna b. Pappa, 224
Hypocrisy, 54, 200, 202, 207–11, 245 n.33, 280 n.2

Identity (religious), 2, 7–8, 16, 17, 43–44, 47, 52, 160, 172–73, 213, 216, 221–22, 230 n.43

Immersion, 29, 35–39, 47, 96, 239 n.96, 240 nn.97–103. *See also* Mikveh
Impurity, 24–50, 41, 141, 150, 195, 219, 182–83. *See also* Menstruation; Purity
Individual and community, 11–12, 17, 22, 46–50, 51, 52, 63, 66, 70, 138, 213
Innocent III (pope), 255 n.268
Interrupting services, 49
Isaac b. Abraham (Ritzba), 49, 270 n.94
Isaac b. Asher (Riva), 145, 159, 166
Isaac b. Eliezer haLevi, 61, 144
Isaac b. Joseph of Corbeil, 31, 61, 77–78, 79, 131, 157–58, 160, 162, 179, 193, 242 n.162, 264 n.164, 277 n.74, 285 n.32
Isaac b. Judah, 144
Isaac b. Meir haLevi of Düren, 30–31
Isaac b. Menahem of Le Mans, 156
Isaac b. Mordekhai, 88–89
Isaac b. Moses, 30, 79, 80–81, 115, 131, 160–61
Isaac b. Samuel Meiningen, 104, 106
Isaac of Dampierre (R"I), 61, 84, 146–47, 159–60, 161, 165–66, 200
Isaacs, Alick, 23
Islam, 10, 14, 18, 60, 177, 178, 203–4, 234 n.109, 241 n.146, 253 n.244, 257 n.329
Israel Isserlein, 31–32
Italy, 4

Jacob b. Asher, 78–79
Jacob b. Judah Hazan of London, 81
Jacob b. Judah Landau, 31
Jacob b. Meir (Rabbenu Tam), 65, 66, 67, 84, 145–47, 156–59, 166, 178–79
Jacob b. Moses Moellin (Maharil), 36, 76, 81, 97, 157, 164–66, 170, 189, 190
Jacob of Languedoc, 146
Jerome, 59
Jerusalem, 198
Jewish knowledge of Christian practice, 14–16, 45, 59–60, 88–89, 99, 219, 220–24. *See also* Christian knowledge of Jewish practice
Jonah of Gerondi, 251 n.194
Jonah of Orleans, 41
Jonathan (biblical), 247 n.97
Jordan, William Chester, 96, 132
Joseph (biblical), 79, 276 n.52
Joseph b. Meir ibn Zabara, 197, 201
Joseph Bekhor Shor, 163, 241 n.140, 270 n.80, 273 n.151
Joshua (biblical), 61
Juda'i Ga'on, 60

Judah b. Asher, 284 n.7
Judah b. Barukh, 61
Judah b. Samuel (the Pious), 12–13, 26, 37, 48, 61, 72, 77, 79, 85, 91–92, 99, 151–55, 180, 185–89, 193, 194, 200–202, 204, 216–18. See also *Sefer Hasidim*
Judah Sirleon, 157
Judel b. Shalom of Neustadt, 35–39
Juspa Schammes, 273 n.169

Kaddish, 200, 259 n.29
Kalonymous family (Nürnberg), 127–28
Kanarfogel, Ephraim, 10, 24, 66, 78, 86, 96, 139, 150–51
Katz Jacob, 9, 23
Ketubbah, 81, 263 n.118
Kirouan, 207
Klaniczay, Gabor, 174
Knights, 175, 190, 274 n.18, 276 n.61
Kogman-Appel, Katrin, 154
Kol Nidrei, 89–90
Koren, Sharon, 33, 237 n.35

Laity, 2, 6, 8, 10, 15, 58, 70–72, 113, 213, 227 n.5, 232 n.69. See also Elite and lay
Land of Israel, 86, 105, 107, 214–15, 269 n.63
Lateran Council (IV), 6, 70, 170, 194, 221, 250 n.151, 275 n.27
Lent, 58, 71
Leprosy, 45
Lester, Anne E., 175
Literacy, 24, 49
Liturgy. See Confession; Prayer
London, 81
Louis the Pious, 254 n.251
Lulav. See Etrog and lulav

Ma'aseh haGeonim, 29
Magdeburg, 82
Magnani, Eliana, 114
Mahzor Vitry, 144–45, 150, 153, 156, 268 n.30
Maimonides, 77, 260 n.43
Mainz, 4, 168, 246 n.70
Malkiel, David, 151
Mansfield, Mary, 72
Marcus, Ivan, 9, 12–13, 72–76, 154, 222–23, 230 n.38, 243 n.170, 253 n.237, 275 n.20
Marriage, 6, 14, 66, 67, 74, 81, 154, 167, 169, 184, 187, 248 n.100
Martyrs and martyrdom, 5, 105, 112, 113, 116, 142, 152, 262 nn.93, 97, 101

Mass, 39–42, 46, 72, 110–14
Matnat yad. See Charity
Mauss, Marcel, 111
Meat, 61, 75, 81–82, 95, 96, 98, 99, 100, 101, 252 n.218, 257 n.328
Medicine, 44
Meens, Rob, 39, 71
Megillat Ta'anit, 54
Megillat Ta'anit Batra, 60–61, 85
Meir b. Barukh of Rothenburg, 24, 68–69, 80, 81–82, 90, 98, 106, 131, 159, 160–62, 166, 169, 280 n.142
Meir b. Kalonymous, 204
Meir b. Yekutiel, 97, 159, 161–62
Memorbuch (of Nürnberg), 18, 103, 104–6, 108–10, 111, 116–28, 131–35
Menagier de Paris, 94
Menahem haMeiri, 206–7
Mendicants, 175, 183
Menstruation, 21–37, 39–47, 145, 181–82, 190, 215, 237 n.37; and covenant 42–45, 47–48; visibility of 46–50. See also Impurity; Purity
Merchavia, Chen, 59
Mezuzah, 138
Mi sheBerakh prayer, 247 n.85
Michal (biblical), 145, 147, 156, 161, 168
Mikveh, 48, 96, 126, 248 n. 105. See also Immersion
Minyan, 22, 33, 242 n.153
de Miramon, Charles, 274 n.13
Miriam (biblical), 55, 56, 61, 205
Mishnah, 54, 83, 129, 203, 237 n.46, 238 n.55, 281 n.10
Mixed cloths (*sha'atnez*), 182, 189, 193, 270 n.92
Modesty, 169, 205, 212
Mollat, Michel, 113
Monastic orders, 6, 15, 41, 108, 112, 174, 185, 190, 209, 261 n.63
Mordekhai b. Hillel, 69, 90
Moses (biblical), 61
Moses b. Judah of Coucy, 31, 36, 151–53, 155, 157–58, 160
Moses Isserlein, 32
Moses of Zurich, 131, 162
Moses Parnas, 158, 168–69
Mourning, 65, 78, 191. See also Death
Murray, Alexander, 71
Murray, Jacqueline, 42

Nathan of Rome, 204, 210
Necrologies, 105, 110–15

Netane Tokef. See Yom Kippur liturgy
New Moon (*Rosh Hodesh*), 81, 82
Nicholas Donin, 58–59
Nicholas of Bibera, 209
Niddah. See Menstruation
Nissim of Kirouan, 197, 201, 204, 206–7
North Africa, 197, 200
Northern France. See France
Numerology, 77
Nuns. See Monastic orders
Nürnberg, 4, 18, 103–37; cemetery 103, 120–23, 262 n.109; construction of synagogue 117–20
Nursing, 82. See also Birth and pregnancy 82

Oaths, 198–99
Obituaries, 113
Outhouses, 190
Owen–Hughes, Diane, 194

Palestine. See Land of Israel
Parades, 88, 199, 207
Paris, 3, 58–59, 85, 88, 156
Passover, 54, 197
Patriarchy, 14, 129, 133, 135, 166, 219, 220, 266 n.175
Pawns, 182, 277 n.74
Payer, Pierre, 40
Pelican, 223–24
Penance. See Repentance
Peretz b. Elijah, 47, 68, 78, 83–84, 131, 153, 162, 242 n.162, 276 n.47
Persecution, 186–87
Peter of Poitiers, 45
Petrus Alfonsus, 197–98
Picardy, 132
Pietism. See *Hasidei Ashkenaz*
Pilgrimage, 145
Piponnier, Françoise, 174
Pitt-Rivers, Julian, 111
Poland, 7, 228 n.20
Poor. See Charity
Prague, 48, 106, 247 n.91
Prayer, 17, 23, 52, 104, 112, 154, 183, 204, 207, 208, 211, 222, 235 n.4, 236 n.12; private 235 n.4; for Sabbath 104–5, 106; for Yom Kippur 76–77, 89–90, 244 n.17. See also Fasting, and prayer and charity (as trio)
Preachers manuals, 5, 15
Pregnancy. See Birth and pregnancy

Pretenders and pretense, 18, 184, 195–211, 281 n.13. See also Hypocrisy
Private and public. See Public
Property, 112
Prostitution, 204, 208–9
Provence, 146, 206–7, 251 n.181, 258 n.332, 275 n.25
Public and private, 12, 46–50, 71–72, 75, 89, 141–42, 201–12, 234 n.104, 254 n.264, 255 n.268
Purim, 81, 82, 146, 187
Purity, 16, 17, 18, 21–46, 165–66, 173, 191, 196, 235 n.7, 239 n.86, 277 n. 66. See also Impurity; Menstruation

Quantitative analysis, 105–6
Quorum. See *Minyan*

Rabbenu Tam. See Jacob b. Meir
Rafeld, Meir. 86
Rape, 186–87
Rashi, 1, 19, 21, 27, 28, 32, 38, 40, 49, 61, 67, 144, 172–73, 186, 201, 204, 210, 217, 234 n.1, 268 n.35, 276 n.52, 282 n.45, 284 n.99
Rashi's daughters, 157, 271 n.110
Raymond de Penafort, 134
Regensburg, 4, 12, 49, 252 n.207
Relics, 16
repentance (teshuvah), 35, 52, 56, 58, 70–85, 87, 95–96, 99, 111, 114–15, 189, 191, 195, 199–200, 239 n.92, 244n.18, 250 n.166, 251n.81; and murder 73, 75, 88, 251 n.181
Rhine River, 4
R"I. See Isaac of Dampierre
Rintfleisch (1298), 5, 105, 116–17, 127
Ritual garments. See Clothing
Ritual objects, 120, 123, 133, 141, 172, 190, 210, 267 n.11
Rivkah b. Meir, 248 n. 105
Rivkah Tiktiner, 255 n.275
Rogation Days, 58
Rosaries, 16
Rosh haShanah, 57, 60, 61–63, 97, 138, 146, 246 n.69
Rosman, Moshe, 267 n.17
Rotboeuf of Paris, 209
Roth, Pinchas, 238 n.50
Roux, Simone, 87–88
Rubin, Asher, 88
Rubin, Miri, 135
Reuben (biblical), 79, 252 n.203

Sabbath, 69, 79–81, 104–5, 106 109, 153, 280 n. 133. *See also* Fasting on Sabbath
Sachenspiegel, 176–77
Sackcloth. *See* Clothing
Sacrifice. *See* Fasting as sacrifice
Saints and sainthood, 58, 87, 174, 249 n.132
Salfeld, Siegmund, 105, 115, 116
Salt, 263 n.115
Samson b. Samson of Coucy, 159, 162
Samson b. Tzadok, 61–63, 80, 157–58, 189, 285 n.32
Samuel b. Isaac, 80
Samuel b. Judah, 12, 72, 73
Samuel b. Barukh of Bamberg, 69
Sarah (biblical), 146
Satlow, Michael, 107–8
Saul (biblical), 247 n. 97
Schmelzer, Menachem, 76–77
Schwäbisch Hall, 125–28
Sefer Arukh haShalem. See Nathan of Rome
Sefer ha'Agur. See Jacob b. Judah Landau
Sefer haGematriyot, 72, 180. *See* Judah b. Samuel
Sefer Halakhot Gedolot, 60–61
Sefer haKushiyot, 177
Sefer haMa'asim, 114, 198–201, 202
Sefer haMaskil, 148, 154, 219; French *Sefer haMaskil* 162–63
Sefer Hasidim, 24, 27, 29, 49, 72, 74, 77, 86, 95–96, 114, 151–53, 183, 185–89, 190, 193, 200–202, 217. *See also* Judah b. Samuel
Sefer haYafeh min haYeshu'ah. See Nissim of Kirouan
Sefer Likutei haPardes, 30, 32
Sefer Nizzahon Vetus, 44, 99
Sefer Or Zaru'a. See Isaac b. Moses
Sefer Rokeah, 72, 77, 79, 86, 160. *See also* Eleazar b. Judah of Worms
Sefer Sha'ashu'im. See Joseph b. Meir ibn Zabara
Sefer Tashbetz. See Samson b. Tzadok
Semag. See Moses b. Judah of Coucy
Semak. See Isaac b. Joseph of Corbeil
Semen, 21, 26–29, 34–36, 41–42, 70, 167, 239 n.88
Servants in Jewish homes, 49, 99, 241 n.143
Sexual relations, 29, 41–42, 45, 70, 72, 73, 76, 83–84, 233 n.94, 241 n.148
Sha'arei Dura. See Isaac b. Meir haLevi of Düren

Shame. *See* Humiliation
Shaw, Teresa, 57
Sherira Ge'on, 150
Sheshet, 55
Shofar, 139, 141, 143–49, 170
Shulkhan Arukh, 32, 165
Shut min haShamayim. See Jacob of Languedoc
Siena, 168
Silk. *See* Cloth
Silver, 120, 124–28
Simhah of Speyer, 96, 153, 239 n.96
Simons, Walter, 170
Slaughterers, women, 240 n.114
Slaves, 157
Solomon Ibn Parhon, 276 n.61
Soloveitchik, Haym, 12–13, 72–73, 81, 88, 228 n.16, 230 n.39, 233 n.79, 242 n.145, 253 n.236
Spain, 7, 79, 148, 151, 177, 197, 200, 207, 230 n.43, 253 n.244
Sperber, Daniel, 86, 97
Speyer, 4, 12, 48, 179
Stabler-Miller, Tanya, 209
Stern, Moritz, 105, 116
Stork, 1, 19, 210, 217–18, 223–24, 227 n.3, 284 n.99
Sukkah, 16–19, 138, 139, 171
Sumptuary laws, 183
Swanson R. N., 42
Synagogue, 21–26, 29, 47, 66, 75, 103, 117–21, 145, 149, 183, 197–201, 213, 218, 219, 235 n.10. See also *Frauenschul;* Women in synagogue

Tallit, 154, 201, 202, 211, 269 n.59, 280 n.142, 281 n.13. *See also* Tzitzit
Tally stick, 82
Talmud, 5, 54–56, 58–59, 69, 70, 83, 114, 129–31, 138, 141, 145–47, 150, 156–68, 172, 180, 184, 186–87, 196, 203; Babylonian Talmud 31, 56, 59, 60, 63, 107, 129, 158, 203; Palestinian Talmud 39, 55, 76, 196, 203, 204; Talmud Trial 58–59, 65, 247 n.93
Ta-Shma, Israel, 142–43, 228 n.16
Taxes, 264 n.148
Tefillin, 13, 16, 138, 139–41, 145, 147, 149–66, 167–71, 184–85, 193, 196, 201, 202, 211, 213, 217, 218, 268 n.49, 281 n.13, 282 n.44, 285 n.32; and Rashi's daughters 157
Temple, 24–26, 55, 70, 112, 114, 237 n.38

Ten Days of Repentance, 61, 63. *See also* High Holidays
Terumat haDeshen. *See* Israel Isserlein
Tetragrammaton, 66
Theft, 72
Thomas of Chobham, 93–94, 134
Tish'ah be'Av, 54
Tobias, book of, 107
Toch, Michael, 105, 124–25
Torah, 30, 105, 109, 180, 201; Torah reading 23, 63, 109, 112, 144, 247 n.83; scrolls 16, 120, 121, 123, 126, 127, 128, 262 n.107
Trade, 3, 4, 247 n.80
Travel, 80, 83, 185–89, 196–202, 207
Trier, 63, 183
Tropper, Amram, 55
Troyes, 156
Tykocinski, Hayim, 121
Tzaddik/ah (as designation), 17, 142
Tzitzit 13, 18, 138, 139, 149–71, 183, 184–85, 193, 213, 285n.32. *See also* Death, burial with tzitzit; Tallit

Urbach, Ephraim Elimelech, 107, 231 n.65
Urban culture, 7, 19, 88, 111–13, 133, 143, 172–94, 214, 223–24

Vauchez, André, 10, 57–58
Venarde, Bruce, 208–9
Virgin Mary, 191
Virginity, 36, 57, 202–7, 210
Visibility, 46–50, 88, 195, 196–202, 205, 208, 211, 217–18, 222
Vows, 83–84, 253 n.231

Wagner, Karen, 71
Weaving, 156. *See also* Cloth
Widows, 48, 129, 131, 163, 203, 210
Wife of Jonah, 145
Wife of Judah Sirleon, 156–57
Wills, 136, 265 n.161
Wine, 67, 81–82, 96, 96, 98, 99, 100, 101, 252 n.218
Winter, 183
Women, 13–15, 36, 126, 128–33, 169–71, 220–22; and agency 83, 133–37; and angels 35–39; and divorce 48, 129,131; and donations 123–28, 131–32; and charity 108, 128–33; and children 266 n.175; and commandments 18, 154–66, 270 n.95; and conversion 96; and finances 129–33, 264 n.148, 265 n.164; and food 255 n.276; and head covering 177–78, 181–82, 277 n.65; as heads of families 149; and literacy 14; and mass 39–41; and *nahat ruah* 32, 239 n.75, 273 n.163; and pretense 202–7; and synagogue 28–29, 30–32, 49, 126. *See also* Fasting, and women
Worms, 4, 12, 48, 61, 103, 154, 212, 243 n.171, 247 n.93
Würzburg, 4

Yassif, Eli, 179
Yizkor, 105, 108–10, 114–15
Yohanan (amora), 203
Yohani bat Retivi, 203–4, 206, 283 nn.64, 75
Yoharah. *See* Arrogance
Yokheved b. Yehiel, 103
Yom Kippur (Day of Atonement), 29, 34–36, 49, 54, 55, 60, 61, 65, 67, 70, 76–77, 89–90, 99, 191, 197, 244 n. 17
Yom Tov of England, 95
Yom Tov of Joigny, 246 n.72
Yorkshire, 136
Yuval, Israel Jacob, 105

Zalman b. Judah, 179
Zerbst, 80
Zimmer, Eric, 108, 177, 181, 269 n.59

ACKNOWLEDGMENTS

This book began with an idea a decade ago, and its making has been a multi-stage process. The debts of gratitude that I have acquired over these years are many, and it is with appreciation that I wish to acknowledge the institutions and individuals that have supported me. While this text has been reviewed and improved along the way, any and all mistakes within this volume are mine alone.

My thanks go to the Memorial Foundation for Jewish Culture, which granted me the Ephraim E. Urbach Fellowship on the basis of a preliminary proposal that evolved into this book. The Fanya Gottesfeld Heller Center at Bar Ilan University, the Hadassah Brandeis Institute, and the Israel Science Foundation (grant 328/06) provided generous research funds along the way. Finally, this book was published with the support of the Israel Science Foundation thanks to a grant from its Humanities Publishing Program in 2014. One of the benefits provided by these grants was research assistance from students and friends: Anat Kutner, Rena Bannett, Sara Tova Brody, Naomi Simansky Avraham, and, above all, Orit Kandel. Orit soon became a close friend as well as a valued colleague, and I thank her for our continued friendship, especially at times when our office served as a haven from outside storms. I am also grateful to my editor, Susan Oren, who skillfully accompanied the final stages of this project and helped me revise and edit this manuscript, constantly pushing me to figure out what it was I wanted to say. I thank her for her friendship, enthusiasm, and continuous guidance.

During my years working on the manuscript, I made a transition from seeking women in the sources to posing gendered questions, changing this project from a study of women to an investigation of men and women. My academic home throughout those years was Bar Ilan University, where the full-time demands of teaching and administration often distanced me from my research but where my colleagues were a source of engagement and intellectual stimulation. I thank the faculty in the Gender Studies Program, with special gratitude to Tova Cohen and Heli Hillel, as well as Gershon Bacon,

Shmuel Feiner, Yaron Harel, David Malkiel, Dan Michman, Adi Schremer, and, above all, Kimmy Caplan and Moshe Rosman in the Department of Jewish History for their interest in my work and their collegiality and friendship. Rella Kushelevsky introduced me to the wealth of medieval Hebrew stories, and I am grateful for our professional and personal connection. My greatest thanks go to my students, for our interactions always drew me to assess and further clarify my thoughts and arguments.

The bulk of my research and writing for this book was done in my favorite work environment, the National Library of Israel (NLI). I would like to highlight the role of the librarians in the Judaica Reading Room and in the Institute for Microfilmed Hebrew Manuscripts for making them such wonderful places for scholarly pursuits. During my days at the NLI, local colleagues and friends were regularly available to help decipher sources and to introduce concepts that spurred me to new insights, whether in the reading room, in hallway conversations, or over coffee. Colleagues from other parts of Israel and from abroad were ever available for consultation by email and, when possible, in person. My thanks to Rainer Barzen, David Berger, Elisheva Carlebach, Jeremy Cohen, Naama Cohen-Hanegbi, Yaacob Dweck, Susan Einbinder, Simcha Emanuel, Rachel Furst, Tova Ganzel, Eva Haverkamp, Elisabeth Hollender, Ephraim Kanarfogel, Sharon Koren, Sheila Kurtzer, Anne Lester, Sara Lipton, Evyatar Marienberg, Dena Ordan, Micha Perry, Lucia Raspe, Rami Reiner, Pinchas Roth, Michael Satlow, Elisabeth Shanks Alexander, Haym Soloveitchik, Daniella Talmon-Heller, Amram Tropper, and Eli Yassif for their friendship and scholarship.

Two colleagues deserve special mention. Debra Kaplan has shown unflagging enthusiasm for this project and has generously read drafts of many chapters, helping me to further hone my message. Above all, Judah Galinsky has brought consistent interest and energy to this project. Over these years, he has referred me to dozens of sources and read multiple drafts, suggesting the term "competitive piety" that became central to my analysis. I am indebted to both of them for their friendship and boundless wisdom.

A Gladys Krieble Delmas Foundation Fellowship for a year-long membership at the School of Historical Studies at the Institute for Advanced Study in Princeton (2008–2009) allowed me the time needed to draft the manuscript, and a Rose and Henry Zifkin Teaching Fellowship at the Katz Center for Advanced Judaic Studies (University of Pennsylvania, fall 2012) provided time to complete it. I am grateful to the libraries of both these institutions for their unstinting support during my stay. I also thank all of the scholars who participated in the research groups from those two periods for their contributions as conversation partners. Each of these fellowships brought opportunities to deepen existing ties with colleagues and to form new friendships. At IAS Princeton, conversations with Giles Constable, Margo Fassler, Lynn Staley, and, especially, Julia Smith influenced my thinking with lasting effects on my work. At Penn, I enjoyed daily conversations with numerous colleagues, and I thank all the members of the "Thirteenth Century" group. I extend special thanks to Sharon Koren and Matthew Cohen for providing a home away from home during my months in Philadelphia.

At the invitation of Sylvie Anne Goldberg, I presented major portions of this study at the Ecole des hautes études en sciences sociales in Paris (spring 2012); I thank her for this exceptional opportunity. Sections of the book were also presented in papers and at conferences in Ann Arbor, Hamilton (N.Y.), Jerusalem, Mainz, Munich, New York, Philadelphia, Princeton, Providence, Tel Aviv, and Toronto. I am grateful to my hosts and audiences for their comments and critique.

Mentors who accompanied the early stages of my academic career have continued the pursuit of the pious with me. Robert Bonfil and Shulamith Shahar have remained invaluable advisors, often serving as initial sounding boards for new ideas and first drafts. Ivan Marcus made himself available at many stages of this project, always offering useful feedback and, after reading an advanced draft of the manuscript, suggesting critical revisions. A correspondence with Emanuel Sivan toward the final phase of this study helped me refine my purpose in new and useful ways. I am grateful to have such teachers. Special thanks go to Caroline Walker Bynum. Since our first encounter in spring 2000, I have been fortunate to learn from her as a scholar and as a person. Conversations with her at IAS in Princeton and over the years have been an ongoing source of inspiration. Her comments on this manuscript led me to revise and reconsider significant points, and I am grateful for her continuous encouragement and her shining example.

David Ruderman not only hosted me at the Katz Center and took a strong interest in this project, but he also invited me to submit this book to the Jewish Culture and Contexts series. He has been a model of scholarship and mentorship for me since we met over a decade ago. I thank Jerry Singerman, who shepherded this book through the acceptance and publication process. I also am grateful to Caroline Hayes, Erica Ginsburg, and Eric Schramm, who guided me through the preparation of the manuscript for publication. The readers for the University of Pennsylvania Press, Ruth Mazo Karras and

Ephraim Kanarfogel, reviewed the manuscript with great care, and their critical comments were catalysts for important revisions. I feel fortunate to have had two such insightful readers.

Last but not least, this book came into being with the help and support of my family: my parents, Al and Rita Baumgarten, my sisters, Shoshana, Margalit, and Na'ama, and their families. My parents each read and heard parts of the book, and my whole family provided encouragement along the way. My husband, Yaacov Deutsch, a scholar in his own right, was a partner in conversation throughout this process, reading drafts and hearing ideas well beyond his interest in this topic. Without his dedication, confidence, and love, this book would not have been written. What is mine over these past two decades of our lives together is truly his. Our children, Yonatan, Ayelet, Nitzan, and Amir, provide the balance and love that make work worthwhile, and I thank them for being who they are.

As this book evolved and I realized that praxis interested me over the written word, it became apparent that this work is intrinsically bound to the legacies of four women, our family's grandmothers. Their recipes, handiwork, and customs shape the continuation of our traditions and identities. I dedicate this book to their memories. I didn't have the opportunity to know two of them well, Frances Feder Karp (1906–1970) and Ella Fischer Deutsch Williams (1909–1994), and we still constantly miss Sabina Baumgarten Berkowitz (1909–2004) and Margot Darmstädter Seeligmann (1916–2010). May their memories and traditions continue to be a blessing.

www.ingramcontent.com/pod-product-compliance
Lightning Source LLC
Chambersburg PA
CBHW020330240426
43665CB00043B/202